MAN RAY

AMERICAN ARTIST

MAN
AMERICAN ARTIST
RAY

BY NEIL BALDWIN

Clarkson N. Potter, Inc., Publishers
DISTRIBUTED BY CROWN PUBLISHERS, INC., NEW YORK

Frontispiece: MAN RAY AND MARCEL DUCHAMP ENJOYING A PRIVATE JOKE AT LA RUE FÉROU STUDIO. Photograph by Ira Nowinski.

A LIST OF ACKNOWLEDG-MENTS BEGINS ON PAGE 382.

GRATEFUL ACKNOWLEDG-MENT IS GIVEN TO THE MAN RAY TRUST FOR PERMISSION TO REPRINT FROM PREVIOUSLY PUBLISHED WORKS BY MAN RAY; TO PUBLISH EXCERPTS FROM PREVIOUSLY UNPUB-LISHED WRITINGS BY MAN RAY; AND TO PUBLISH PHOTO-GRAPHS BY MAN RAY AND OF HIS WORKS OF ART.

Published by Clarkson N. Potter, Inc., 225 Park Avenue South, New York, New York 10003, and represented in Canada by the Canadian M A N D A Group

CLARKSON N. POTTER, POTTER, and colophon are trade-marks of Clarkson N. Potter, Inc.

Manufactured in the United States of America

Book design by Gael Towey

LIBRARY OF CONGRESS CATALOGING-IN-PUBLI-CATION DATA
Baldwin, Neil, 1947—
   Man Ray, American artist.
   Bibliography.
   Includes index.
   1. Ray, Man, 1890—1976. 2. Artists—United States—Biography. I. Title.
N6537.R3B3 1988 709'.2'4 [B]
87-29181
ISBN 0-517-56001-1
10 9 8 7 6 5 4 3 2 1
FIRST EDITION

For **ROBERTA**

CONTENTS

INTRODUCTION

I WAS MOVED to write this book after the pleasant yet tantalizingly incomplete experience of reading Man Ray's memoir of his life and times, *Self Portrait* (1963), an immensely entertaining saga about the making of a modernist from most unlikely circumstances.

In Man Ray's movie-script-like rendition, it seemed as if even the down-and-out stretches when he could not find a dealer and his art was not taken seriously were occasions for light-heartedness. Only a single date is mentioned in the entire autobiography, undermining its dependability, not as an impressionistic, lively, atmospheric account (which it certainly is) but, rather, as a document. Many questions emanating from my need to establish an historical basis for Man Ray's life and times led me first to research and set down my own record of the facts. And even now, dramatic issues still remain, for history (to borrow Stephen Dedalus's haunting phrase) was a nightmare from which Man Ray was trying to awake.

The "problem" of Man Ray begins with the matter that he cannot be classified as an artist in one genre. Painter, photographer, filmmaker, printmaker, object-maker, poet, essayist, philosopher —his eclecticism flaunts the ground rules of art history. Man Ray is a chain of enigmas. Paradoxes characterize each phase of his long and complex career and combine to make him the quintessential modernist personality.

Why, to begin with, did he believe that family ties and roots existed to be severed? Information about Man Ray's childhood and formative years was exceptionally difficult to obtain because Man Ray did not want people to know about his youth. He did not want his family in America to grant interviews about his past. The special tension of Man Ray's early life emerges like a photographic print slowly developing in the tray.

He insisted that dates were meaningless and bore that out within the stream-of-consciousness, out-of-sync narrative of his memoirs; yet at the same time, he compulsively catalogued all his works over nearly three-quarters of a century, to the extent that he always knew at any time the status, ownership, and location of everything he had ever produced.

Man Ray participated centrally in Dada—a loosely formed movement motivated by the urge to subvert the entire range of artistic endeavor preceding it—yet at the same time he maintained a reverence for the Old Masters, and for the value of tradition as it shaped individual talent.

Even with disappointments and embitterment about his position as an artist, he insisted upon making his way as a painter, to the point where visitors to his studio who sought to bring up the subject of photography were brusquely turned away.

Was the fabrication of a persona called Man Ray ultimately more significant to him than the reputation of the artist Man Ray? If the impression his paintings made was important to Man Ray, why did he pride himself on being such *un type rapide* (quick study), able to knock off a portrait in a headlong rush? Why did he insist upon the inherent passivity of the artist as the most harmless member of society—when his passion and commitment were boundless and electrically apparent to anyone in his presence?

Man Ray's greatest conflict was his lifelong struggle with the one form of expression in which he had no peer: photography. His unerring eye could pick out a constellation of details and frame them so that they appeared to have arranged themselves. In the studio on the rue Férou, among thousands of outtakes from portrait sessions and *en plein air* ramblings never revealed to public view, it is nearly impossible to find a bad picture.

Man Ray's photography is great because it embraces variety. It represents a virtual new order of reality; it is its own world. It is restless and omnivorous, taking on all the possibilities of perception as its territory.

The supreme present, another modernist obsession, was all that mattered, and the photograph, as a "certificate of presence," in Roland Barthes's definition, embodied that instant in time. In 1966 Man Ray told Jules Langsner, the curator of the Man Ray retrospective at the Los Angeles County Museum of Art, that "A camera alone does not make a picture. To make a picture, you need a camera, a photographer, and above all a subject. It is the subject alone," he insisted "that determines the interest of the photograph."

Talking to journalist Colette Roberts, Man Ray alighted upon another metaphor for photography's place in his life, calling it a "second violin for me, just as necessary in the orchestra as the first violin."

Man Ray was blessed with lifelong curiosity verging upon voyeurism; he was naturally intrigued by the way people looked and lived. The camera was "his passport, permitting safe passage across otherwise perilous boundaries"—however, he did not inhabit these new and exotic countries for very long. The camera was also a shield defending him while serving as a key to the secrets of others, and therefore a perfect vehicle for Man Ray's reflective personality.

To his detractors, Man Ray's solarizations, rayographs, and distortion studies were *trucages,* the ultimate technical tricks produced by a magician who was not to be taken seriously. However, his admirers were—and continue to be—those who recognized his capacity to pierce the protective veil of what seemed real. The eyes in Man Ray's portrait photographs always appear liquid, softened just enough for us to think they might indeed open upon the soul. His outdoor shots force us to rethink nature as something less than natural and closer to imaginary. His fashion photography is so dynamic it wants to leap from the page. His nudes manage to be sensual and untouchable simultaneously.

Like its creator, a Man Ray photograph is singularly self-contained.

"It has never been my object to record my dreams," Man Ray admitted, "just the determination to realize them." After years spent observing the successes of others in his generation, how would the artist have felt if he had lived to attend the monumental auction of his friend William Copley's vast Surrealist collection at Sotheby

Parke Bernet on November 5, 1979? How would he have felt to see what was arguably his greatest painting, one of the landmark Surrealist canvases of this century, *A l'heure de l'observatoire—Les amoureux* (Observatory Time—The Lovers), sell for a staggering $750,000? Would it have been the realization of a dream for Man Ray to watch this massive painting of glowing red lips hovering disembodied in a gray sky go off the auction block after a prolonged and fierce telephone bidding session, and into an important European private collection? Or would ultimate recognition before a standing-room-only audience—the highest price ever paid at auction for a Surrealist painting, far outstripping the fine examples also offered that evening by Ernst, Magritte, de Chirico, Balthus, Brauner, Arp, Duchamp, Cornell, Schwitters, and Bellmer—have seemed to Man Ray the ultimate irony?

PERHAPS THE FINAL GOAL DESIRED
BY THE ARTIST IS A CONFUSION OR MERGING OF ALL
THE ARTS, AS THINGS MERGE IN REAL LIFE.

MAN RAY
INTERVIEW, 1951

EMMANUEL RADNITSKY, HIS MOTHER, FATHER,
AND SISTER DORA, 1896.
Collection Naomi Savage.

EMMANUEL
IN
BROOKLYN

A L L   D U R I N G the spring and summer of 1890, Manya Radnitsky labored, cross-stitch by cross-stitch, on a baby carriage coverlet for her first child; so that when Emmanuel was born, on August 27, the tapestry was ready. When the whole multicolored work was unfurled, it looked like a crazy-quilt from some unknown country. It was fashioned of silk fragments Manya had collected from the workroom floor in her modest frame house at 418 Carpenter Street on Philadelphia's South Side, where her husband, Melach, worked extra hours to make ends meet as a tailor after his shift at the factory nearby. Each bright scrap was attached by meticulously networked black thread to a soft cotton backing.

Manya sewed with natural inventiveness. She never used a pattern. As a little girl growing up in a suburb of Minsk, she had often hidden under the house and crocheted silken threads into decorative collars. The white borders were especially appealing against her pale skin and deep black hair piled high on her head; her eyes were unexpectedly blue.

Manya was raised by a young pharmacist and his mother. After her parents had died, she and her five sisters had scattered to live with different families in the town of Babreusk. Enthralled by her natural beauty, the pharmacist asked Manya to marry him. He gave her an ornately engraved silver bracelet. He brought her

1

aromatic mixtures of glycerine and rose water to keep her delicate hands fresh while she sewed. He refused to allow her to do any heavy housework or cleaning, for fear this would damage her hands, and then the calluses might pull on the silk. But she rebuffed his affectionate advances.

Manya was barely eighteen when a peddler named Radnitsky stopped in at the pharmacy on his way to Minsk and was also struck by her beauty. He reported back to his son, Melach, in Kiev about her. Wasn't it time he thought about settling down? That same year, 1886, the dark-complexioned young man with deep-set eyes and curly black hair turned twenty-one and received notice to report for military service in Kiev. He decided to escape the draft and his family by running away to America. His mother had died when he was still a child, and his stepmother had been abusive to him and his four older sisters. She had beaten the children often and locked them in the closet as punishment. Impulsive, given to daydreaming, Melach had once let his temper get the better of him and pulled a knife on the woman, threatening to kill her.

In 1886, Melach left for New York on the *Bremen,* working his way across in steerage class. Fined one hundred rubles for his son's draft evasion and imprisoned for six months, the peddler managed to keep in touch with Melach by letter—and, once again, to raise the subject of "Manya who lives at the pharmacy," passing along her address. But the stint in prison had irreparably damaged the elder Radnitsky's health. News of his father's passing reached Melach in New York several months later, and he never forgave himself for the sad consequence of having followed his desire to be free.

Melach and Manya exchanged pictures through the mails. He was working at a cap factory, saving money for the sixty-dollar boat ticket to bring her over. Living alone and sparsely, he bought a violin; evenings were spent re-creating the folk songs he'd grown up with, singing to himself amid the silence.

In the spring of 1888, Manya Louria (or it could have been Lourie; her family, generations back, had originated in the Loire Valley in France) arrived in New York City. Melach awaited his betrothed on the pier and was shocked to see a heavyset, slouched figure stumbling down the gangplank, encumbered by a bulky wicker basket in one hand, a carpetbag in the other. He had expected a slender, raven-haired beauty. Scornfully, he told her to carry her own bags.

They were married by a rabbi that same day. At Melach's flat after the ceremony, she began to shed her garments. In a practice common to the day, Manya had worn most of her clothes on the overseas passage, and she finally emerged as the exquisite figure her husband expected.

Their marriage was not consummated that night. She slept on the bed and he curled up on the floor. The following day, Manya left to stay with one of her older sisters, Hannah, who lived in the city. The newlyweds remained apart for several weeks.

Emmanuel was conceived in the fall of 1889. A couple of months later, Melach received word of a good job in a Philadelphia garment factory and the couple left New York. One of Melach's older sisters, Jenny, had also married and moved to Philadelphia; the two were very close, and this may have attracted Melach to the city.

By all accounts, Manya Radnitsky was a sharp-tongued, strict, and frequently overbearing woman with a theatrical streak. She could be protective and kind, but for the most part her manner was undemonstrative and dignified. She would, for instance, pretend to pinch her children's cheeks in affection, and pinch the air instead. Manya made it no secret that she resented housework. Satisfying handiwork, for her, was to sit down with a bundle of threads and some rags, relying upon her resourceful imagination to create something of beauty. She made all her children's clothes. Melach, on the other hand, was the conciliator of the family. Aside from rare eruptions of temper, he was soft-spoken (when he spoke at all), soulful, and a hard worker.

Three more children followed Emmanuel. Samuel was born in 1893; Devorah, or Dora, named in memory of Melach's mother, in 1895; and Elka, or Elsie, named after Manya's mother, in 1897.

Virtually nothing is known about the first seven years of Emmanuel's life, until the Radnitskys moved back to New York City shortly before Elsie's birth and settled into a three-room flat on De Bevoise Street in Brooklyn's Williamsburg section. Through a friend, Melach—who now called himself Max—got a job at a local garment factory, which paid better than the work in Philadelphia. And money was even more important with a growing family.

Over the next decade, following a common immigrant practice, the Radnitskys moved several times to avoid paying a month's rent, but always within the same general neighborhood—to Ellery Street, Park Street, and Beaver Street, all just south of De Bevoise, between Flushing Avenue and Broadway; then to Throop Avenue; and to Broadway itself—where they had a double apartment with an extra room that eventually became Emmanuel's studio. They never lived in the mainstream Jewish sections of town. The parents were traditional but not religious or intensely observant—although, of course, Emmanuel (whose name in Hebrew meant "God with us") was bar mitzvahed.

The earliest known artistic effort by Emmanuel Radnitsky—the first foreshadowing of his metamorphosis into "Man Ray"—was created on February 15, 1898, when the USS *Maine* was blown up in Havana harbor. A graphic drawing of the event appeared in all the papers, and Emmanuel was moved to copy it.

Like his parents, he was handy, adept at building, fixing, and even inventing. He constructed a locomotive out of a wagon, stealing the wheels from another child's toy to get just the right type. When Manya discovered her son had come by the materials dishonestly, she destroyed what must have been one of the first objects of his affection, his unique, idiosyncratic creations. She explained her other reasons to Dora: "Daughter, have you ever seen a runaway horse go by, pulling a milk wagon or a fire engine down the street? Well, suppose it were to run into Emmanuel while he was driving that contraption—he could be killed!" Man Ray never forgave his mother for interfering so forcefully with his work, even if it was a plaything. He referred to the incident throughout his life as the earliest root of his eventual estrangement from her.

Emmanuel was also developing into something of a dreamer, like his father, fantasizing about "strange people that were geometric forms walking in the street, or pushing a cart." He later recalled that as a child he was "fascinated by color and in [his] dreams these personages were very colorful."

Aside from one major ear infection, an abscess that had to be lanced when he was ten or eleven years old, Emmanuel was a healthy, active child, who loved to play with guns and swords. Like most boys of his time, his imagination was fueled by Dick Carter adventure stories and "the Liberty Boys of Seventy-Six" pulp picture books. He belonged to a neighborhood gang but was picked on inordinately because of his small size and took some beatings. After one such skirmish, Emmanuel ran home, grabbed an old Civil War saber his father had picked up from a pushcart peddler, and went running out into the street, ready to cut the boys' heads off.

At fourteen, Emmanuel entered Boys' High School. A rambling brick building dating from the Civil War era, it was just half a mile down Marcy Avenue from his home. He began a training program in draftsmanship, architecture, engineering, and lettering but soon became consumed by a passion for art—its history was as important to him as his own artistic efforts.

The very first term at Boys' High, fall 1904, Emmanuel constructed a piece in woodworking shop that vividly illustrated his emerging talents. It was an ingenious combination shelf-bookend, all in one unit. Each end of the foot-long rack rotated upward from a flat, flush position to reveal curved flaps secured by carefully inserted screws, so well executed that, even today, more than eighty years later, it functions effortlessly.

By January 1908, Emmanuel had seen Rodin's drawings and watercolors at Alfred Stieglitz's 291 Gallery, the first exhibition of a modern artist in America. He was impressed by their ebullience and freedom from restrictive form. Then, midway through his senior year, "The Eight"—Maurice Prendergast, George Luks, Everett Shinn, Ernest Lawson, John Sloan, Arthur B. Davies, William Glackens, and Robert Henri—mounted their notorious exhibition at the Macbeth Gallery at 450 Fifth Avenue. When the show—a protest against the restrictive rules of the conservative National Academy of Design—opened in the first week of February 1908, at least three hundred people an hour came through. A wide-eyed Emmanuel Radnitsky, who had already begun weekend forays to the city's museums, especially the Metropolitan Museum of Art and the Brooklyn Institute of Arts and Sciences, was at the Macbeth, stunned by the audaciousness of the "Ashcan School" (more vilifyingly known in the local press as "the Revolutionary Black Gang," or the "outlaw salon").

The Macbeth show was the talk of New York, an unusual outburst of realism in American painting. Emmanuel saw shadowy cityscapes and portraits; dark, ruminative canvases in which the glow of light fell casually across a woman's face, not as if she were a goddess, but as if she were a real person. And he was particularly drawn to the works of Robert Henri, the outspoken pedagogue of the group, whose paintings were characteristically quick and unromantic. Henri sought the vital note in his subject, the element that gave it life as it was lived. No matter how common your theme, how close to the miserable and seamy side of life, the Ashcan group said, the object was to get it down; to look first at what is closest to home, almost journalistically, catch it, and make it part of the painting; to focus directly upon the model's expression and the communication of feelings. At the Macbeth Gallery, Emmanuel saw a "world of saloons, tenements, urchins . . . an old woman with a goose . . . people dining in a restaurant."

His illustrations for the Boys' High yearbook, produced at this period, show a steady hand. Swirls and curlicues serve as borders, baroque elaboration as section dividers, and tiny thematic sketches depict school activities. Emmanuel was training to be an architect—a career for which a young man needed a strong sense of discipline and a capacity for previsualization (the ability to imagine how something would appear on completion). To be an architect, one had to be both artisan and engineer, to have an instinct about the way a well-constructed building would look and function. Naturally inquiring and active—some might even have said jumpy—Emmanuel had an inclination to seek solutions before inventing problems.

The Radnitskys were justifiably proud of their firstborn son. He was performing well in his studies, heading for the top of his class, and he still found time after school to help his father and mother with their tailoring work. Everyone crowded into the custom vest-making shop situated in the front room: little Elsie was old enough now to pull out the bastings, Dora hand-sewed linings, Sam went out on simple errands around the immediate neighborhood—the buttonhole maker was his favorite side trip. And Emmanuel, as the oldest, was privileged to make long-distance deliveries by trolley car, which suited his wanderlust. The Radnitskys worked hard. Max, more often than not, fell asleep over his sewing machine at 2 A.M. In a good week, allowing for the dollar-per-child salary he doled out, Max might still end up with $32.50 clear.

But life was not exclusively sewing, basting, cutting, and stitching. Brother Sam was developing into a serious poet. He wrote songs and accompanied himself on the zither. Emmanuel was capable of picking a tune on the guitar. Max pulled out his old fiddle from time to time. The family rented a piano and bought a Victrola. When Father declared they had done enough work for one day, the Radnitskys would retire to the parlor, gaily decorated by Minnie, as Manya had come to be known, with an "Oriental" rug she'd scrounged from some pushcart on the Lower East Side and green velvet cushions fitted to mahogany furniture. Curled up at their feet, the baby collie dog, Pinny, named after the hat pin he'd swallowed, would listen to the Radnitskys make music.

The problem was that such cultural activities were viewed by everyone as peripheral to the true, ongoing process of making a living and getting by in the world. To Emmanuel's parents, his current interest in art was acceptable only insofar as it was a sideline, not to be taken too seriously. What would they have done had they known that, as graduation neared, their son's interest in painting had deepened to the point where he viewed it as one of the greatest possible human endeavors?

All the other boys at the high-school graduation ceremony in June 1908 were dressed in white shirts and gray trousers. Emmanuel, habitually different, cut a dashing figure in the bright red shirt his mother had made for him, and when he stepped up onto the stage to accept a leather-bound volume of Walt Whitman's poetry— the prize for graduating with the best grades in English—his mind was already made up. He was going to turn down the architecture scholarship he'd been offered at New York University and devote himself to painting and earning a living through means of *his* choosing.

"I celebrate myself," indeed—Whitman was right; his songs in praise of individualism, paeans to striking out on your own, attracted Emmanuel and gave him hope. The artist's first duty was to himself.

More relatives, on both sides, had settled in America by now, and Emmanuel alone of the new generation was on the threshold of making a career in the new land. His decision precipitated a family crisis. Max and Minnie were astounded; his mother's surprise gave way to anger, and the friction between her and Emmanuel intensified. Minnie had also lived life as a free spirit and was now shackled to home, work, and family. Her bitterness took on a new edge as the son she adored moved toward independence. She viewed Emmanuel's decision as nothing short of self-indulgent, and she let him know it. Yet, at the same time, much to the amazement of the younger children, Father Max rearranged the living space in their apartment so that Emmanuel could have a studio until he made enough money to find his own place to work. They scraped together whatever funds they could to buy him painting supplies when he was short of cash. It was a theme that would be repeated over and over again in the years to come: Emmanuel's parents were deeply proud of him. They did not understand him, but they did not want to lose him and were desperate to accommodate him. For his part, he honored and appreciated their love, but—and this was an ever larger "but"—he did not want his life to follow the respectable direction they had in mind. Emmanuel remained discontented with other people's vision of his future. The summer following graduation, ripe for liberation, he plunged into painting with unprecedented fervor.

Most mornings, Emmanuel was up by five o'clock to catch the Reid Avenue trolley, a forty-five minute, five-cent ride out to Coney Island, the end of the line. Arriving by dawn, he set up his easel on the beach and daubed out oils onto composition board or thick cardboard, whatever was at hand, sometimes painting with a palette knife. They were quick, sketchy, immediate "takes," muddy browns and blues predominating, expressing Emmanuel's desperate need to make contact with the landscape, in solitude. "I thought of myself as a Thoreau," he wrote, "breaking free of all ties and duties to society." Other days, the Broadway and Myrtle lines of the Brooklyn and Union El took him on field trips to Ridgewood Reservoir and Forest Park, closer to home, where he painted pastoral scenes by the water—lush trees overhanging a lake, shadowy figures promenading. He loved to be *en plein air*. Always, these efforts were signed with his little monogram, "ER."

Emmanuel's skills as a draftsman are evident in one of the representational exercises made at this time. Echoing the post-Impressionist affinity for Oriental pictorial art, he sectioned off into squares a postcard-size image of a Japanese woman in a kimono, then replicated it as a large-scale oil painting, transferring the image square-by-square to the canvas.

Sister Dora—or Dorothy, as Emmanuel was now fond of calling her when he introduced her to his friends—had developed into a dark-haired beauty of thirteen and was a favorite model. An asthmatic young woman, she was confined often, missed many days of school, and fell into exceptionally frail spells when she was forced to sit in bed with her head and back propped up. Emmanuel liked to sketch her with her hair piled high. For one portrait, she wore the silver bracelet the pharmacist in Minsk had given her mother all those years ago. It had been passed along to Dora during one drastically serious asthma attack, when her breathing became so labored that her father had bundled her up and taken her for a midnight trolley ride across the Williamsburg Bridge, to get some cool, fresh air into her lungs. As Max was leading his coughing, gasping daughter out of the house, Minnie slipped the bracelet onto her wrist, for good luck, quietly assuring Dora she would "outlive all of us in the end." While sketching a portrait of Dora around 1909, Emmanuel instructed her to hide her hands in the folds of her dress—"I can't draw hands," he confessed, "but be sure to leave the bracelet showing."

He was a devoted, protective brother who took his sister to Broadway musicals, such as *The Chocolate Soldier,* and then to Child's for a meal, carefully observing her table manners, warning Dora not to slurp her soup, arranging her jacket properly on the back of her chair where she'd slung it casually. He told her from the time she was thirteen or fourteen and he was all of eighteen—that first summer of freedom—he was "going to Paris—I'm dreaming of it all the time." "Why, Emmanuel?" she asked, plaintively, fearful he'd follow through, knowing all too well that once he set his mind to something, there was no stopping him. He replied, simply, "Because of the *art.*"

For her birthdays, he gave her specially inscribed books— Balzac was one of Emmanuel's favorite authors—and he told Dora to read the novels carefully; they would give her a sense of what Parisian life was once like. She loved his attention, and she feared his critical opinions.

Emmanuel was developing an interest in another art, too— jazz and new music at the Hammerstein Opera House, where the most modern compositions were played. He later remembered thinking at the time, "It would be wonderful to do paintings like music, that are abstract, that would be immediately accepted, understood by all nations."

The desire was there, to find a way to *say more* through the work, to stretch the formal limits of art or even invent new forms. And Emmanuel was indeed on the brink of such a breakthrough, but, for the time being, he was gaining increased facility in depicting reality. A 1909 portrait shows a young man gazing off to the left, calmness and self-confidence glowing in his pale gray eyes, a white ascot or scarf tied loosely around his open jacket collar. The gracefully curved fingers of the subject's right hand are vaguely

9

executed at the bottom of the picture. The face seems to leap forward out of obscurity, much like the candor, immediacy, and directness of The Eight portraits Emmanuel so much admired.

The works of the masters—Rembrandt, Goya, Whistler, and Ingres—entered Emmanuel's visual vocabulary while he was still in his teens. With Sister Dora in tow, his excursions to the Brooklyn Institute of Arts and Sciences were becoming more and more frequent. The massive, colonnaded building at the corner of Eastern Parkway and Washington Avenue was a treasure trove. Brother and sister would immediately dash up to the third floor, passing the huge collection in the "Square Room," 250 watercolors and 161 sketches from J. J. Tissot's *Illustrations of the Life of Our Lord Jesus Christ.* Telling Sister Dora he didn't want her exposed to "all that bloody and violent imagery," he guided her to the adjacent Oils and Portraits rooms, the main galleries, where luminous works by John Singer Sargent, J. Alden Weir, Hamilton Field, Rembrandt Peale, and Fantin-Latour were on display. Emmanuel was voracious in his appetite for portraits. More than anything else, he wanted to understand the play of light and color upon the contours of the human face. An impressionable young man, receptive, open-minded, ready and willing to be influenced, he was learning by imitation. His was a self-taught program so far, but he was beginning to feel the need for a mentor other than art books or pictures on the wall. He had reached the point where he could turn out charcoal studies of his two sisters knitting that echoed Renoir in their sedate composition and domestic warmth. He could gaze out his bedroom window and, when the spirit moved him, capture light against trees and geometrically arranged fire escapes at dusk.

During the several years following high school, Emmanuel held a hodgepodge of jobs, working as a newsstand attendant, an engraver of umbrella and cane handles in a small factory (justifiably proud of his ability to produce more than twenty pieces per hour), and doing layout, lettering, and design in an advertising office on Fourteenth Street. He did not enjoy working for other people, and his positions were short-lived—they were a way to make money, which then allowed him to pursue his artistic goals.

But the work ethic had been deeply ingrained during all those nights in his father's tailor shop. He was always driven to produce, even if, in the spirit of one of his quintessentially American heroes,

Thoreau, Emmanuel marched to the beat of a different drummer that became increasingly different as time passed. He was intoxicated by paint.

In 1910, two years after high school, he began to take commissions for portraiture in his studio room at home. His first client was a Mrs. Medvedev, who came by only once or twice to pose. This canvas, now lost, was evidently a magisterial, full-length work, reminiscent of the Sargents he'd seen, all maroons and grays to offset the woman's fair skin. He began to dream of becoming a society painter who would do only beautiful ladies. For practice, there were always his sisters and brother, but he never painted or drew the likenesses of his parents.

In the spring of 1910, the rebellious, democratic Robert Henri organized the "Exhibition of Independent Artists," the first non-juried show in America. All works were hung in alphabetical order by artist. As with The Eight show two years earlier, crowds and riots were the order of the day. Sloan, Glackens, Prendergast, Rockwell Kent, and more than two hundred other artists were ridiculed by the press as vulgar. Emmanuel was moved, after seeing the show, to imitation in his own way.

He imagined a scene out of medieval times, a castle perched upon a distant hill, and segmented it into almost "paint by numbers" forms, filling in sharp, black outlines with vivid coloration, delicately shaded, to mimic a stained-glass window. At first glance, clouds overhead, clustered treetops, and rolling waves all seem derived from the same rounded template, repeated over and over. He was casting about for a style that would meld realism with fantasy.

MAN RAY. *DEPARTURE OF SUMMER*, 1914. OIL.
Courtesy Middendorf Gallery, Washington, D.C.

FIRST

MENTORS

THE ART gallery had been founded in November 1905 by photogra
phers Alfred Stieglitz and Edward Steichen, in Steichen's former
studio on Fifth Avenue and Thirtieth Street. Its name had changed
from The Little Galleries of the Photo-Secession to 291 three years
later, when Stieglitz was expelled from the Camera Club. Visitors to
291 took an elevator to the brownstone's top floor and then crossed
over to what was actually 293 Fifth, through an archway where there
had once been a dividing wall. A mere fifteen feet by fifteen feet,
"the largest small room of its kind in the world," as Marsden
Hartley was fond of calling it, the gallery fronted the avenue, and
the sounds of traffic drifted up.

The walls were gray. A ledgelike shelf running at waist level
around the room held small sculptures and framed photographs,
paintings, and watercolors. Below the ledge hung a dark green,
burlap curtain. Natural light, favored by Stieglitz, glanced off a
large, decorative brass bowl displayed upon a central platform.

Stieglitz, the proprietor, or, more appropriately, the guiding
spirit, was invariably present, dressed in a sober business suit and
engrossed in talk, one elbow against the shelving, his mane of iron-
gray hair always in motion. "The eyebrows were bushed, the eyes
deep-set and assumed a certain uncertainty," Djuna Barnes observed of him. "Stieglitz had a manner of speaking at once quick
and hesitating."

13

He was dedicated to endorsing the new. His relentless crusade to introduce the American public to European modernism—photographs by Alvin Langdon Coburn, drawings by Rodin, Matisse's etchings, lithographs by Toulouse-Lautrec—was well known by the time Emmanuel began to frequent the gallery.

Stieglitz thought nothing of deflecting queries about the meaning of pictures. Zen-master–like, he turned viewers back to the works themselves, insisting they stand and stare until meaning was made manifest. He denied that the function of his gallery was as a showcase for art; he preferred to see it as "a place of contact," where people's ideas naturally and spontaneously mixed. Occasionally he even made prospective buyers fill out a detailed questionnaire, asking them, "How much is the picture worth in emotions?" and "With what other pictures would you place it?" before he allowed any money to change hands. At the same time that he gave advice on art, he seemed to be giving advice on life.

Combining isolation on the one hand ("secession" from outworn tradition) with a belief in an elite aesthetic community on the other, Stieglitz's attitude struck a nerve in young Emmanuel. At 291, he first heard a doctrine that espoused the benign significance of art—and a resounding rejection of all trends in favor of the aliveness of the moment. This vitality came through in Stieglitz's photographs of the time, teams of horses mired in the mud of an excavation site; dark brownstones huddled before the skeleton of a rising skyscraper; a dirigible soaring in flight above sun-lined clouds; the Staten Island ferry pulling away from the quay, passengers' white straw hats echoed in the bleached dock stanchions.

The photographer in his midforties took a warm and paternal interest in Emmanuel, this curious, younger artist, who began to frequent the gallery during the pivotal Cézanne watercolors show in the spring of 1911. He admired the economical touches of color and the white spaces that made the landscapes look unfinished and quite abstract—so different from any watercolors he had seen before. Emmanuel was driven in two clear directions. Like Stieglitz, he was quite naturally interested in making documentary works, capturing his native environment—the local park, Coney Island at dawn, the view from his fire escape—in paintings and watercolors made on site. At the same time, he was impatient to break into an idiom that was more uniquely his own. The abstract qualities of Cézanne's work, the attentiveness to light that lay behind or around the colors, attracted him. He liked the artist's use of white paper as part of the composition.

The following month, April 1911, Emmanuel returned to 291 to see the Picasso exhibition, which included the artist's recent Cubist work.

Over lunches at the nearby Holland House, or at Mouquin's Restaurant on Twenty-eighth Street and Sixth Avenue, where he habitually picked up the bill, Stieglitz held forth at what came to be known as his "Round Table" for an audience that included photographer Paul Haviland, painters John Marin, Max Weber, Marsden Hartley, and Arthur Dove, critic and caricaturist Marius de Zayas, and the quiet, shy, and modest Emmanuel Radnitsky. Stieglitz told the group he had been skeptical of Cézanne's works when he first viewed them several years earlier in Paris. But he had suspended his disbelief in deference to partner Steichen's enthusiasm. The Picasso show—the artist's first one-man exhibition in America—he admitted, was quite a risk to take in the critical climate of the day. The Academy still exercised a strong influence on the arbiters of taste who wrote for the daily papers, even as the new, Paris-trained, color-intoxicated school of young American artists was liberating painting from its allegiance to verisimilitude.

Stieglitz remained undaunted by dismissals of Picasso's work in the press as resembling "a glorified fire-escape, a wire fence . . . Its owner, Mr. Stieglitz," wrote one indignant critic, "declares in all sincerity that when he has had a tiring day at the gallery or elsewhere he goes home at night, stands before this drawing in black and white, which hangs over his fireplace, and gains from it genuine stimulus."

"Picasso . . . is the man that will count," Stieglitz insisted with prophetic enthusiasm to Sadakichi Hartmann, one of the few art critics sympathetic to his cause. "His show at 291 . . . was possibly the most interesting yet held there. . . . We have certainly shown the quintessence of many big men's work. . . ."

Stieglitz's dogged endorsement of Rodin, Cézanne, Renoir, van Gogh, and Picasso, and his fearlessness in displaying such visions within his miniature space impressed Emmanuel. His method, or nonmethod, of instruction—letting the viewer grope toward his own interpretation—also captured Emmanuel's imagination. Just as he had been jumping around lately from job to job,

Emmanuel Radnitsky was moving, disgruntled, from art class to art class, unable to persist in environments where the rigid didacticism of Academy-trained teachers held sway. When Stieglitz, however, simply and continuously talked to anyone willing to listen to him, Emmanuel, the free spirit, relaxed and learned: "There is no such thing as the impossible if you really want to do a thing badly enough," Stieglitz said. "If you have to do a thing with all your being, then you will find a way, even if you have to die for it."

With the construction of one unusual work, Emmanuel demonstrated his willingness to draw upon resources no farther away than his father's cutting-room floor. His *Tapestry* of 110 fabric sample swatches, assembled in checkerboard rows to form a wall-hanging a full five feet by three and a half feet, is a masterpiece of improvisation. In its subtle gradations of color areas, moving from dark to light and back again, it represents abstraction united with function. It is both an exercise in cubist form and a quilt, at the same moment. The materials of *Tapestry* reflect the domestic environment Emmanuel was forced by constraints to inhabit. Instead of resenting the need to share space with his family when he yearned for emancipation, he made good use of what was at hand, placing his stamp of individuality onto otherwise mundane squares of wool—pinstripe, tattersall, plaid, charcoal-gray flannels—oddments of current fashion. This signal effort was pinned to a sheet of canvas, as if to say, "Like the tapestries of antiquity it works as display art as well." And the canvas was signed, "Man Ray, 1911."

Emmanuel had passed his twenty-first birthday and both he and his brother Sam were having difficulty finding steady work. He still harbored bitter memories of having been teased at school because of his foreign name—and now the brothers felt their name was making it hard for them to get by without experiencing discrimination. For Mother Manya, who had constantly strived to assimilate, shunning ghettoized Jewish residential areas, shedding the family's ethnic-sounding last name would not have been a problem. Many people called Emmanuel "Manny" for short, and he had been toying with his signature initials on recent work, changing them to "MR" occasionally.

The two brothers came up with "Ray" as a direct shortening, an abbreviation for Radnitsky. Despite Sister Dora's protestations when she found out, too late, that it sounded "too Irish"—she would have preferred something like "Radin"—the whole family, not just Emmanuel, took the new name, although Max never had it legally altered. Countless immigrant families with multisyllabic, ethnic last names made the shift for practical reasons. For others, the transformation had been effected by impatient customs officers on Ellis Island.

Armed with his exotic new persona, Man Ray broke from the cocoon of his early life. One day at Stieglitz's he heard about an ongoing series of art classes and lectures sponsored by the Ferrer Modern School, which had just moved to a brownstone building at 63 East 107th Street from downtown headquarters, first at St. Mark's Place, then on East Twelfth Street. Thursday and Friday evening art classes ("with living model") were twenty cents per session. And on Wednesday nights, the popular critic John Weichsel spoke on cultural and aesthetic topics.

The Ferrer School had been founded by Emma Goldman, in commemoration of Francisco Ferrer y Guardia, the libertarian Spanish educator shot in Barcelona on October 13, 1909. Goldman traveled tirelessly across the country, addressing audiences of anarchists, freethinkers, and progressives in the aftermath of Ferrer's death, raising funds to start an association in his honor and spirit, predicated upon her shared belief that "dogmatism is the worst enemy of education."

"What is the Modern School?" asked sculptor and poet Adolf Wolff in the pages of the school's magazine. "It is a sort of alchemist's laboratory where the philosopher's stone of education is being evolved. It is the great pedagogic experimental station of the new society. . . . It invites investigation and criticism. . . ." Open every day for the instruction of children, and evenings and weekends as well for adult classes, the Ferrer School "seethed with animation and debate of vital issues . . . and no cause was too poor nor too radical or delicate to be denied a hearing," as scholar Paul Avrich has noted. The art class was one of many activities. There were new plays constantly being staged, concerts and dance classes, poetry workshops—and the day school was under the direction of the great philosopher and teacher Will Durant.

Man Ray began making the trek uptown to the Ferrer School in the early fall of 1912, attracted by its reputation for expansive, unrestricting, and liberating instruction. The trip was made even more tolerable by the fact that Robert Henri was the art teacher. It was four years since the Macbeth Gallery exhibition where Emmanuel had first seen the vibrant, pulsating portraits by this founding member of the Ashcan School.

It is a reflection of Man Ray's open sensibility at this early point in his career that he was inspired by both Stieglitz and Robert Henri, who each encouraged young artists to break from the Academy, but who had, indeed, feuded with each other in the past. Stieglitz was the proponent of high modernist art. Henri celebrated democratic vistas and gritty, impoverished urban landscapes in the spirit of his hero, Walt Whitman. He was a partisan of paint applied with gusto and energy. Both men satisfied Man Ray's thirst for theory, his intellectual affinity for ideology, and his need to pursue pleasure in the act of making art.

Robert Henri was a tall, thin, quietly intense man, who donated his services to the Ferrer School. An anarchist since his student days in Paris, he had followed Emma Goldman's philosophy closely in her magazine, *Mother Earth,* and after attending one of her lectures, he described her in his diary as "a woman of remarkable address and convincing presence. . . . This is a very great woman." Emma Goldman invited Henri to join the Ferrer School faculty in late 1911—by then he had painted her portrait and shared his admiration of Walt Whitman with her—and he stayed on for seven years.

Robert Henri believed in devoting attention to real subjects in real settings. Glamorizing and prettifying were of no interest to him. His love for Whitman was a strong point of convergence with Man Ray, who had been finding solace in his well-worn copy of *Leaves of Grass* for some time. Its endorsement of essential independence, no matter how fearful, taught Man Ray that courage was the artist's credo. Like Henri, who once chided his colleague John Sloan for working too laboriously at his painting, Man Ray had become a devotee of speed in composition. Man Ray took pride in his ability to paint from memory, a skill he cultivated his whole life. He spoke and dressed in a down-to-earth, straightforward fashion, free from pretense. Man Ray was striving to develop an inner conviction that the path he had chosen to follow was the correct one.

In his warm and informal classes at the Ferrer School, Robert Henri made a point of circulating among the students—again, reminiscent of Whitman, rubbing shoulders with everyone. He

MAN RAY. *AD MCMXIV*, 1914. OIL.
Philadelphia Museum of Art, A. E. Gallatin Collection.

MAN RAY. *JAZZ*, 1919. AEROGRAPH.
Columbus Museum of Art, Ohio, gift of Ferdinand Howald.

"never. . . criticized adversely," Man Ray noted with pleasure, always managing to base his observations on a positive point in the work, to improvise pronouncements: "If a man has the soul of an artist he needs a mastery of all the means of expression so that he may command them," he said. "Art appears in many forms. To some degree, every human being is an artist, dependent on the quality of his growth." Henri cautioned his students against succumbing to the temptation of the group mentality; large societies are the death of creativity; "schools" of art never confine the truly great artist. Henri urged them to reassess the notion of completion—the artist should understand his work in progress well enough to know when it was done to his own satisfaction; polish was not a prerequisite for a good painting. Henri warned his students against the pitfalls of excessive competitiveness: it would damage their integrity. "Art is art," he said, "whether on a canvas, on stone, on a book cover, an advertisement, or a piece of furniture." The *idea* for the work had greater value than any refinement of technique.

"The one great thing in the Ferrer Center art class," Henri wrote, "is to establish the idea that each student is his own teacher . . . that students can learn from each other as well as from the instructor, or by natural accident. . . . The student should inquire. Let nothing that has a suspicion of value pass."

Heady stuff for the young Man Ray in search of a role model; and still more exciting when one night George Bellows, Henri's student, friend, fellow Ashcan realist painter, and shortstop of the artists' softball team at the Ferrer School, came by for a visit and singled out Man Ray's charcoal drawing, holding it in front of the rest of the class as a model of initiative and imagination.

The broader school community had an opportunity to view the fruits of Man Ray's labor when an exhibition of student work was mounted at the center in late December 1912, the first such show ever held at the school. Man Ray's contribution, *A Study in Nudes,* foreshadows a concept that he was still three years away from entitling in another painting, "an arrangement of forms." Seven odalisquelike figures are arrayed in a variety of poses, as if to prove that the artist has triumphed over the challenge to portray the female shape. Like a dancer, the central, dominant figure stands boldly facing us, her feet pointed outward, pelvis thrust slightly to the side, arms raised behind her head. It is one of Man Ray's earliest efforts at updating traditional imagery into more free-flowing form.

Ingres's *baigneuse* comes to mind—and not surprisingly, considering Henri's admiration for that artist as an exponent of realism and the frequency with which he directed his students to study the master's works. There is a preoccupation in Man Ray's painting with the idea of movement set against stasis. The dignity of the woman at the center is heightened by the restlessness of the figures surrounding her.

In the school basement, a kitchen opened into a dining room where the day-school children had lunch and where, in the evening, adult students and faculty members lingered over coffee and tea. During one such social hour—perhaps Man Ray arrived early and had some spare time before class began—he met Samuel Halpert. Born in Bialystok, Russia, and six years Man Ray's senior, Halpert had just returned to New York City after a decade in Paris. He had studied at the Ecole des Beaux Arts under Léon Bonnat, shown in the Paris Salons of 1903–05, met Le Douanier Rousseau, been a member of the Salon d'Automne, and painted side by side with Albert Marquet. A post-Impressionist turned Fauvist, Halpert encouraged Man Ray in his struggle for expressiveness in painting. He believed in giving freedom to broad color. The artist should mix techniques within his work, Halpert said, should use the brush as if he were drawing with a pencil. He should have no fear in confrontation with the blank canvas. The Ferrer Center was founded upon anarchist principles, and the wildness of Fauvism came close to a kind of anarchy in its "anything goes" spirit. Fauvist theory dictated that it was acceptable to apply pigment liberally, in heavy brilliant strokes and bands; the artist could absorb and break apart realistic images and, as Matisse himself put it, thereby "construct [a painting] by colored surfaces."

Over the course of several weeks, the two young artists enjoyed heated, enthusiastic discussions on these painterly issues and cemented their friendship. When Man Ray invited Halpert out to Brooklyn for a good meal as only Minnie could prepare, the wordly European traveler was instantly attracted to Dora, who dutifully helped set the table, her eyes demurely downcast, her thick, black hair falling in wisps over her white brow. Continuing his mission of culturally enriching his younger sister, Man Ray invited her to a performance of a new play, *The Yellow Jacket,* by George Hazelton and J. Harry Ben Rimo, at the Fulton Theater on West Forty-sixth

Street. He asked Halpert, footloose and lonely in the city, if he'd like to accompany them. Dora sat between her brother and Samuel Halpert. Halfway through the drama, she sensed Halpert's gaze upon her in the darkness. "Why aren't you watching the play?" she asked him in a low whisper, fearful of what brother Man might do if he noticed anything untoward. The smitten Halpert replied, "When I was at the Louvre, I saw a portrait of a woman there, a woman I have dreamed of ever since—like you, slender, fine-boned, with gleaming eyes. I resolved to myself that if I ever saw that woman in the flesh, I would marry her."

Desperately in love, Halpert began sending missives to Dora through Man Ray; his jealous friend systematically destroyed them without passing the letters on. Halpert came to the house. He pleaded with Dora to run away to Paris with him. And she would have flown, was quite ready and willing, if Mother had not put her foot down. Minnie had already written to Rose Levinson—Max's sister Jenny's daughter in Philadelphia—crying out for advice: "Save my daughter from Samuel Halpert!" Protective older brother Man was against the match, too, sharing his mother's fear that yet another artist would confuse and fragment the family, and even compete with him. If only he hadn't asked Halpert over in the first place, he thought, this never would have happened.

Although Dora did see Halpert on a few occasions in the new year, the flirtation was virtually over by the end of 1912, when she was just past her seventeenth birthday. To commemorate the breakup, Man Ray decided to present his sister with a leather-bound copy of *Crime and Punishment*.

The last straw in Man Ray's domestic relations with his family came when he began to abuse his at-home studio privileges. The family had scrimped and saved to move into a five-room flat so that he could have a sunny, front-room studio all to himself—and now he was bringing women in to pose nude before a private painting class he arranged for himself and a few select colleagues. Although Man Ray made certain to close and lock the door to his atelier, his three younger siblings peeked through the keyhole. When Minnie found out about the models, she was furious.

Obviously, the time had now come to leave home. Man Ray achieved the transition in stages over the course of several months during the winter and spring of 1913, thanks to the help of another Ferrer School ally, Adolf Wolff, a Belgian-born sculptor. Wolff taught the children's art class at Ferrer during the day and studied with Robert Henri at night, while his eight-year-old daughter, Esther, posed as a model. In addition to being a revolutionary, an artist, a profligate spender, and a neglectful husband, divorced from his blond, gray-eyed wife, Adon, Adolf Wolff had another dubious feather in his cap. He was a well-meaning but rather bombastic poet. He, too, had fallen under Whitman's spell.

"He discards rhyme," read the introduction to a selection of Wolff's verse published in the school magazine, "and takes quite naturally to the free chants that Walt Whitman pioneered. . . . Yet ever he sees beyond the turmoil of our capitalistic era into the freer age that is to be." Wolff's ode to the Good Gray Poet attests,

> An exaltation to the lowly,
> A vindication of the truth,
> A glorification of the human body,
> A declaration of the right of all
> To live, to love, to dare and to do,
> A hymn to life, a rhapsody of joy!

Adolf Wolff's poems express his belief in the importance of individual freedom and the exercise of free will. He was naturally sympathetic to the plight of Man Ray, a young artist trying to make his own way. Wolff offered his friend the key to his West Thirty-fifth Street studio—until he had the wherewithal to find a place of his own, he was welcome to pay a fraction of the rent. Man Ray accepted and, soon after, landed a job nearby at the McGraw Book Company on Thirty-ninth Street between Seventh and Eighth avenues. He worked there for the next six years, designing maps and atlases, a talent he'd nurtured from the time he was a little boy curled up on the parlor floor creating intricate plans of imaginary landscapes with fanciful rivers and mountains.

It was even easier now to stop in at 291 Gallery, just a few short blocks away on Thirtieth and Fifth, and view exhibitions of works by the generation of American artists that was taking the city by storm: Abraham Walkowitz's naïve, fresh, and energetic paintings and drawings; John Marin's airy, light oils and watercolors, (he was one of Stieglitz's favorite artists); and photographs by A.S. himself. Stieglitz's show of his work at 291 that winter was his first retrospective, displaying examples culled from twenty-one years of taking pictures.

It was clear he was entering a new phase, by this time convinced that photography should be more deeply engaged with the world at large, rather than being so purely art for art's sake, as it had been for the Photo-Secessionists. Gone were the soft images of a decade past. Stieglitz's subject matter was less romantic, more focused upon what he called New York City's "obscure geometry." He was using the camera to record planes and surfaces, seeing the world more cubistically.

Man Ray was still a year away from embarking upon his own relationship with the camera, although, since 1909, he had been recording his paintings with a simple Brownie. ("You press the button, we do the rest," promised the early advertisements.) But constant exposure to Stieglitz's philosophy and work was beginning to impress upon him a particularly appealing use for the instrument that critic Paul Rosenfeld called "a machine in perfect obedience to the human spirit." The danger—which Stieglitz assiduously avoided—the subversive pitfall of photography, and what made it so seductive, was the temptation to let the camera determine one's artistic style and manner. Stieglitz's view, reiterated constantly, was that the photographer had to remember to make his camera subservient to himself, the person behind it.

Photographs could only be as fulfilled as the sensibility that inspired them. Furthermore, Rosenfeld wrote, the photographer had to be brave, willing, and ready "to shove the nozzle of his camera into hells where man's hand has rested cruellest, to catch filthy smoke and grimy skies, iron and cinders and strung steely wires . . . backyards hung with laundry and cut by fire escapes." Realism, representationalism, even hard-edged documentation were all becoming the rightful domain of the camera, a simple extension of the eye. The photographer's job was to know *what* to transform and *how* to transform it in the service of his imagination.

The same issue of Stieglitz's quarterly, *Camera Work,* that contained his 1911 snapshots of Paris, also on view at 291 as part of his show, provided the forum for a provocative essay by Marius de Zayas, "Photography Is Not Art," which piqued Man Ray's interest. "Photography is the plastic verification of fact," the critic stated. "Art presents to us what we may call the emotional or intellectual truth; photography the material truth." De Zayas, a Mexican-born critic and caricaturist on staff at the *New York Evening World,* served as a talent scout for his friend Stieglitz. While on extended trips to Paris, de Zayas

reported back about new currents in Cubism; later on he discovered
Apollinaire's Simultanism in poetry. De Zayas was one of the most
articulate theorists in New York during those crucible years. His
carefully thought-through monographs and prefaces to exhibition
catalogues provided uninitiated audiences with a clearer vocabulary
for modern art and helped them toward new ways of seeing.

The debate about the functions of photography and painting had
been going on since long before the days of 291, and it continued long
after. But for Man Ray the dialectic had particular pertinence. He was
in the process of developing an attitude toward the "quick medium" of
photography, shifting from the critical stance to that of activist. He
would eventually come to believe, or at least declare, that "there is no
progress in art." But, even so, incessantly working his way through
different modes of expression was crucial to the development of his
craft.

The timing of the Alfred Stieglitz retrospective at 291 was no
accident. The International Exhibition of Modern Art, more popu-
larly known as the Armory Show, was due to open in New York the
following month. Stieglitz urged everyone who came by 291 to make
certain to attend the forthcoming exhibition, for it "was bound to help
put life into the dead corpse of painting. Put yourself in an
unprejudiced mental attitude, in a receptive mood," he advised all
comers, "and chances are that you will see a great light."

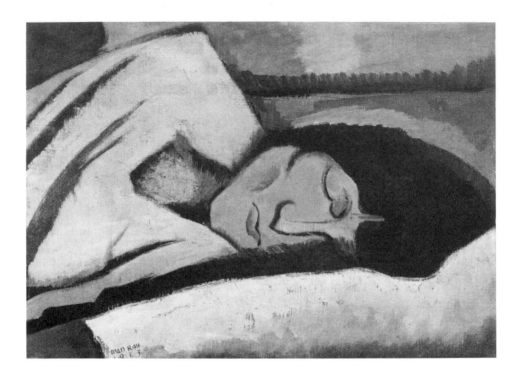

MAN RAY. WOMAN ASLEEP, 1913. OIL.
Collection Whitney Museum of American Art. Purchase 33.30.

B R E A K I N G
A W A Y

FOR MAN RAY, who had been invited to exhibit but felt he had
nothing he cared to show, the Armory Show was an opportunity to
learn as much as possible about the movements that had gone
before. This was the only way an artist could break into new
territory. The show's organizers—a committee of artists including
Walt Kuhn, Jerome Myers, Walter Pach, Arthur B. Davies, and
other members of the newly formed Association of American
Painters and Sculptors—had precisely this goal in mind. The idea
for a large exhibition tracing the roots and inspirations of American
painting grew out of the Independent Exhibition of 1910, which had
been designed to compete with the Academy. The big new show
would illustrate trends from both sides of the Atlantic. It was not
meant to be threatening or revolutionary but, rather, progress
oriented and evolutionary.

    The Armory Show opened on February 17, 1913, for invited
guests. The huge, open space, which usually served as an artillery
drill floor, was divided by burlap-lined panels and tall potted plants.
Bolts of cloth filtered the glare of floodlights overhead. Of the more
than thirteen hundred works of art on display, two-thirds were by
American artists, reflecting the priorities of the American committee that had assembled the exhibition. The average viewer, whose
awareness went back no further than twenty-five years to the

beginnings of American Impressionism, here saw European works—chiaroscuro Delacroix and precise Ingres from the mid-nineteenth century—presented as starting points for the art of the present day. The show was a vivid reaffirmation of Man Ray's conviction that anything new had its wellsprings deep in previous generations.

The work of The Eight—already known to Man Ray from the pivotal Macbeth Gallery exhibition and from his classes with Henri—was also on view. The play of light was juxtaposed against areas of darkness in such John Sloan scenes of the hustle and bustle of "real" New York as his *6th Avenue at 30th Street* during rush hour; in Jerome Myers's *The Glow* and *End of the Walk,* with their distinctively down-and-out mood; in George Bellows's predominantly gray and black washes on bleached-out white paper; and in Everett Shinn's women in nonchalant poses. Man Ray's teacher, Robert Henri, was represented by his portrait *The Gypsy,* in which one could practically hear the woman thinking—so intensely pensive was her expression, so abstracted her gaze. Henri captured a moment, arrested a thought, by concentrating most of his deliberate brushwork on the face, then rapidly and deftly working the suggestion of a body in afterward.

Against the coal-dust–lined, twilight-hued Ashcan works, the Fauves were wild, hot, jazzed-up. Derain's vivid, inappropriate colors gave his figures an illusion of movement; Braque's landscapes glowed. Francis Picabia laid the paint on as if with a trowel, and there was something intentionally infantile in his technique; he seemed to be daring viewers to join his speculations about seriousness in "high art" and become more self-conscious as they viewed the work. With a similar goal but entirely different technique, Cézanne permitted patches of canvas to show, bare and bone-white, applying paint so thinly in places one could not avoid seeing the nubby surface of the cloth—a reminder that this was an artificial thing, not a true replication of reality. Cézanne's work occupied a large center section of the room.

The Cubists caused the biggest furor, far out of proportion to their modest representation in the show, because their experiments with the fracturing of the pictorial plane underscored the narrowness of American modernism. Conservative critics like Kenyon Cox and Royal Cortissoz saw the anarchist strain in Cubism as posing nothing short of the total destruction of the art of painting. Picasso and Braque were viewed as self-indulgent, following mere personal whims that led them far away from the traditional mission of the creative person, which was to glorify reality, to show the world as it was *seen*.

Buried within the critical commentary was a fear of foreign invasion—an attempt in the daily papers to put up beachheads against the European forces—and a deeper fear that realism would die; that there would henceforth be no more "holding a mirror up to nature in American art." The critics wanted more than anything else to believe that these latest uprisings, disruptions in the painter's traditionally mimetic role, were but a passing phase, and that once there had been a venture into modern art, the return to academic style would follow.

The general public was slow in responding to the exhibition. Despite the immediate response of the press, the man in the street hadn't quite got around to making up his mind. Then, suddenly, midway through its four-week run, "the storm broke," remembered Walt Kuhn, one of the exhibition's key organizers. "Students, teachers, brain specialists, the exquisite, the vulgar, from all walks of life they came." You could not get close enough to the Cézanne canvases to hear the instant experts explain him "nine ways or more." Brancusi's smooth, luminous, organic sculptures caused a stir: "Actors, musicians, butlers, and shopgirls all joined in the pandemonium."

Upwards of fifty-seven thousand New Yorkers passed through the Armory gates that month, despite having been cautioned against visiting this "pathological museum" (as Kenyon Cox described it) by none other than instant art critic Theodore Roosevelt. To him, "Cubists, Octagonists, Parallelopidonists," and all the rest were simply "fatuous." The crowds pressing into the Sixty-ninth Regiment Armory on Lexington Avenue and Twenty-fifth Street were possessed by such hysteria—guards had to be posted around the Cubist section to restrain the pressing throng—that it seemed as if a palace revolt was in progress.

At the center of the disturbance was the painting listed in the catalogue as no. 241, Marcel Duchamp's *Nude Descending a Staircase*. More than any Picasso "wire fence" or Brancusi egglike "affectation," more than Cézanne's *Blue Mountain* or Picabia's machinelike primitive canvases, this slanted succession of planes, derisively dubbed "Slats Falling Down Stairs," "the explosion in a shingle factory" (or "lumberyard," depending upon which newspaper one read), this "collection of saddlebags," was derided, abused, and scorned as the most vivid example of the insane extremes to which modern art had pushed itself.

Duchamp had shown the notorious work the previous year at the Salon des Indépendants in Paris for one day, before removing it at the request of his artist-brothers, Jacques Villon and Raymond Duchamp-Villon. The painting had actually begun as a sketch for a poem—indeed, one of its most unusual features was the title written directly on the canvas. Duchamp tried to explain what he was after in a carefully worded statement: the work was "an organization of kinetic elements, an expression of time and space through the abstract presentation of motion. . . . When the vision of the Nude flashed upon me, I knew that it would break forever the enslaving chains of naturalism."

After the sensory explosion of the Armory Show, Man Ray found his "mind in a turmoil, the turmoil of a seed that has been planted in fertile ground, ready to break through." Sam Halpert, ever attentive, asked his friend if he would like to take an excursion just across the river to New Jersey. At the Ferrer School he had heard about a small isolated community there, and he thought it might be a good place to work. Halpert's timing could not have been better. Man Ray was eager to move out of the way station that was Adolf Wolff's studio; he dreamed of a proper homestead.

One day in early spring, the two set out. The journey began with a bus ride up Riverside Drive to the Fort Lee ferry crossing and continued with a spray-drenched ride across the Hudson, then a slow, clacking journey on an open trolley for several more miles. The end of the line still left the pair with a two-mile trudge uphill to the top of the Palisades, just north of the famed amusement park.

Ridgefield was a quiet town, its silence accentuated by thick woods and a steady, damp breeze off the river. The hilly terrain was so steep that the little white frame houses seemed to be set virtually into the mountain, surrounded by dense greenery. Below, in the village proper, was a two-hundred-year-old stone church, with a grassy graveyard where old headstones tilted every which way.

The tiny white cottage Man Ray and Samuel Halpert rented for nine dollars a month had a view of the Jersey meadows with the Passaic and Hackensack rivers lazily rolling away to the horizon.

Halpert, not much of a cook, specialized in pasta dishes. Man Ray was responsible for making coffee and tea and for postprandial dishwashing and cleanup.

"My dear Sam," Man Ray wrote to his younger brother, after he had been settled in for a few weeks, "I feel so much at cross purposes, both wishing to return and to remain here awhile yet. It isn't exactly concern for the future, it is the happy-go-lucky existence without any goal." Man Ray had taken a Thoreau-like giant step, "cut [himself] off from the rest of the world" and gone back to the land—but he was not free and clear. The ambivalence expressed in this confidential letter was an emotion that would resurface time and again in his restless relocations. He was trying to adopt, at least with some part of his being, a withdrawn posture free of entangling alliances, to live the life of an artist in the modern mode. But the ties would not sever cleanly. Man Ray was still working downtown at McGraw, still, it turned out, paying visits to his family in Brooklyn, while he spent long weekends painting and long, dark evenings listening to the rush of wind in the evergreens. He wasn't yet a pastoral convert, nor was he quite the urban boulevardier.

Man Ray's early Ridgefield canvases exemplify classic Cubist technique, forms flattened and interlocking, the roofs of village houses overlapping with rounded treetops and jagged bushes. In his painting, *The Village* (1913), Man Ray broke up familiar hillside houses into a study of planes, arranged and rearranged to show their relativity to one another. He stripped down and flattened trees into two-toned shapes—the whole landscape existing remarkably in two dimensions. The given world at Man Ray's doorstep was no longer simply transposed. Now, it was *translated* into a new idiom. Like the scraps of cloth on his father's workroom floor, the scraps of color and detail from the village were appropriated and acknowledged as legitimate for art simply because they were at hand and meant to be used.

The lessons of the Armory Show had been learned: Cubist doctrine held that the visible world as known by the artist became real only after *thought*. Scenes and objects had multiple significances and possibilities for portrayal. Braque put it succinctly, "There is no certainty except in what the mind conceives." Man Ray's Cubist landscapes in the Armory Show aftermath reveal—as the painters Albert Gleizes and Jean Metzinger stated in their definitive essay about the movement, "On Cubism"—the capability of "discerning a form . . . in an external world, which is, to most people, amorphous." Man Ray was beginning to divide the surface of the canvas and "[invest] each part with a quality. . ." representative of the whole. Most important, he was showing a wholly subjective "intensity" of design, which Cubist theorists believed was the fundamental distinction between what they did and the Impressionists' "snatching imagery from the sensate world."

Man Ray was also moving into other areas of expression. An avid reader of poetry since his teen years, he would freely critique the manuscripts brother Sam sent his way. "While there is great improvement," he wrote in the course of one reply, "there is also, as you say, room for more." He took the same gentle and encouraging approach with regard to his younger brother's work as he did with the canvases of other artists: all artistic expression was inherently good, simply by virtue of the positive energy that brought it into being. There was no need to be destructive in critical discourse.

Samuel Halpert—who, by this time, was focusing his painterly efforts on dark, thickly etched interiors, even as housemate Man Ray was setting up his easel out of doors—invited his friend Alfred Kreymborg, a New York–based journalist, chess enthusiast, and mandolin player, out to Ridgefield for the summer. His arrival marked the beginning of an intense encounter with poetry for Man Ray and a rush of new verse.

The modern mode in painting was infiltrating America's literary world as well. The "Imagist" ethos—tightly crafted poems resonating with themes from antiquity—was most clear in *Poetry,* the new Chicago journal edited by Harriet Monroe. Through Ezra Pound's forceful editorial influence from London, work by Hilda Doolittle (H.D.) appeared in the pages of *Poetry,* the hard edges of her verse offset by their lyric quality. William Carlos Williams, the doctor-poet living in nearby Rutherford, New Jersey, also debuted in the new magazine, as did Marianne Moore, Richard Aldington, and Amy Lowell. However, Miss Monroe did not seem to appreciate the "peculiarities" in Alfred Kreymborg's poems.

In the evening, after a simple meal, Halpert, Kreymborg, and Man Ray would gather on the front porch and concoct schemes for the publication of a more homegrown magazine, one that would welcome their work and be completely under their control. It would grow out of the spirit of the earth, Nature's very soil. The magazine would be feisty, gutsy, and Whitmanesque in its passions but intentionally without sophistication and political consciousness.

It was fitting, then, that *The Glebe*'s inaugural issue spotlighted Adolf Wolff's poetry, "Songs, Sighs, and Curses." Ridgefield was becoming a magnet for the Ferrer School crowd. Manuel Komroff, Bill Shatoff, Hippolyte Havel, Max Eastman—who was to become editor of his own magazine, *The Masses*—thronged to the hideaway community for undisturbed debates and exhilarating tramps through the forests.

When Alfred Kreymborg, with trembling hands, unwrapped a thick manuscript parcel freshly arrived from London, Man Ray was looking over his coeditor's shoulder in his quiet, pensive manner, his deep dark eyes absorbing all, under a cascade of curly brown hair. A florid cover letter warned that "unless you're another American ass, you'll set this up just as it stands!—Ezra Pound." Pound tirelessly impressed his credo on receptive minds. Anyone who agreed with his taste, his predilection for "the new," became his friend. Anyone who disagreed could still be Pound's ally, if he had the boldness to come back at "Ol' Ez" with an aesthetic position that held water. Kreymborg was further advised that any issue of *The Glebe* would be incomplete without Williams's work: "Get in touch with old Bull," as Pound called him—"he lives in a hole called Rutherford, New Jersey."

Despite the trials and tribulations of a broken printing press, which had been delivered safely all the way from downtown Manhattan to Man Ray's cabin door, whereupon it was unceremoniously dropped by careless workmen, *The Glebe* appeared, short-lived but unique. Editing and publishing a magazine side by side with such a dedicated, principled writer as Kreymborg, Man Ray read some of the most forward-looking verse of his generation, verse that opened up new vistas for the poem in much the same way that Cubism had widened the province of painting. Taking Whitman as their standard-bearer, American poets were breaking the chains of iambic pentameter, choosing introspection and subjectivity as governing principles. Like Cubist painters, poets were looking at words for their textural, image-inspiring, plastic qualities, moving them here and there upon the page the way pigments were used to fill out flattened shapes. Language's imitative properties were redefined by the poet's imagination.

Just as Cubist painters made their pictures primarily authentic to feelings that conditioned how the thing *seen* became the thing *depicted,* the poets used this emotional state as the foundation upon which the poem was built. "Travail," a Man Ray lyric composed during that summer of 1913 and published in the autumn issue of *Modern School Magazine,* is a good example of a young man's attempt to map his emotional landscape.

> The days are dead for me,
> And the nights live
> Thru the day I dream
> At night I wake
> And when I wake I die.
>
> I do not count the hours
> Nor watch the sun
> But thru a monotone of time I drift
> My senses numbed.
>
> From afar
> Dim music rocks my restless soul to sleep—
> Death's lullaby
> I sleep—I wake—I die.
>
> Give me a draught of life ere I depart,
> Red sparkling life—not over-sweet
> Then let me sleep
> Fatigued.

Aside from a few lapses into archaic diction, the poem is notable for its tricky rhyme scheme, carefully modulated syllabic count, and consistent back-and-forth, metronomelike, contrasting momentum. Because it reads so smoothly, so deceptively simply, we are caught in the reader's trap Yeats spoke of when he articulated the poet's curse, "We must labor to make it natural."

This is the writing of a romantic, a dreamer who welcomes, yet dreads, his dream. Man Ray wants to tightrope-walk the boundary line between sleep and waking, to inhabit the twilight world from which art springs. Yet with his insistently practical side—the side disciplined enough to get him up during predawn hours to commute to a midtown office—he knows that a misstep on the tightrope means death of the spirit.

Adolf Wolff's ex-wife, the tall, blond poet Adon Lacroix, accompanied him on weekend excursions to Ridgefield. Although no longer together, they took turns caring for their nine-year-old daughter, Esther, and remained casual friends.

Man Ray had noticed Adon here and there at the Ferrer Center. She was Belgian-born, French-speaking, and possessed an exotic allure with her poised, cool gaze, aquiline nose, and fair hair pinned up by a single brooch or secured by a headband. It was as if Europe, the place Man Ray dreamed of visiting, had descended upon him in the form of a woman.

The two drifted off from the talkative crowd huddled on the front steps of the compound and took a private stroll in the woods. Adon confided in Man Ray that she was lonely in the city and yearned "to get away." She was certainly quite a departure from the neighborhood girls he'd known—several years older than he, and with a child, too. Conquering his fears, he invited Adon to stay in Ridgefield.

A snapshot of the couple on the porch, taken in evening light, shows a pensive woman with high cheekbones, a string of beads hanging around her neck, her hands cupped loosely in her lap, long fingers intertwined. Her mouth is set in the faintest intimation of a smile; she does not look into the camera, but peers off inquisitively to the right. Next to her, as close as possible, sits an equally calm and serious Man Ray; shirt collar open, he leans against the doorjamb, holding a corncob pipe, most likely about to enjoy his after-dinner smoke. There is an equality, a "coupleness" about them.

"Oh talk about the whole world and tell it in your own way," he pleaded with Adon in the leaves of his journal, "I am very quiet and interested when you talk that way. . . I unbind your strange pale hair which falls down about your strange pale face and rests on your pale shoulders. My hands tremble then as they tremble when I hold the pencil to draw from you." The days of having to bring home models to copy were past. She was with him all the time; he wanted to possess her in his work. An early watercolor sketch of Adon, seen seated and nude from the back, reveals rosy, Odalisquelike expanses of flesh. "I should like to draw from you very much if you were my wife," Man Ray imagined himself telling Adon—again, in his secret diary—"When you are my wife and I sit down to draw from you I shall not think about drawing. When you are my wife and I start to draw from you I shall think about you . . . then, when your hair was down I would stroke you. And while I stroked you, you would purr, purr, purr."

It is not known to what extent Man Ray revealed these ardent wishes to Adon. They would not be wed until the following spring. Perhaps in the wake of her unsuccessful marriage, she was hesitant to make another commitment. But Adon did stay with Man Ray, and he painted her portraits, always angular, eyes downcast, long legs crossed under the sharply defined drapery of a striped floor-length dress that emphasized her willowy shape. He painted her by lamplight, sleeping, only to discover the next morning that the tube of pigment he'd been using—which he thought in the half darkness was white—was lemon-yellow, lending an unintentional distortion and grotesqueness to his lover's face. He did not change the color, respecting the accidental as natural.

Adon and Man Ray moved into a house of their own. It had four rooms and a garret upstairs that he turned into an art gallery for impromptu showings of new work when visitors came. The view was spectacular to the north, west, and south. On a clear day, he could see beyond the Hackensack River and Orange Mountains clear to Paterson. And the rent was cheaper than the place Man Ray had shared with Kreymborg and Halpert, a mere eight dollars a month.

Chagrined and a touch jealous of Man Ray's good fortune, Samuel Halpert returned to the city, and the two lost contact. But Kreymborg's admiration for Man Ray continued. He wrote a laudatory piece for the *Morning Telegraph* in homage to "these two youthful economist-dreamers," marveling at their ability to derive such pleasure from their simple life, and at such little cost: "They live on twenty-five dollars a month and enjoy it," Kreymborg raved to the New York public in the full-page, illustrated spread.

"He owes much to Cézanne, the Byzantine, and Egyptian," observed erstwhile art critic Kreymborg, thinking perhaps of Man Ray's affinity for primitive, flat, angular portrayals of the human form, "but most particularly to Picasso and some of the Futurists." At this stage in Man Ray's career as a painter, one could include almost any art trend in the recipe, for he had tasted all of them. His goal was always the same: to paint his way into a style as a method for understanding it empirically, not merely theoretically.

Man Ray and Adon sometimes whiled away the evening hours by playing the guitar—which they both did well—and singing together in front of the fire. More likely, they would keep working. It is no accident that in many photographs and paintings of Adon, including the picture running with Kreymborg's article, she is seen before a backdrop of crowded bookshelves.

She was a serious poet. Man Ray realized the depth of her involvement with literature when Adon's household goods and books arrived in Ridgefield after her legal separation from Wolff in early 1914: "She began removing her books carefully one by one," he wrote, "stopping now and then to turn the pages of one, reading some lines to herself, then translating into English a poem by Mallarmé, another by Rimbaud, and a paragraph from Lautréamont's *Chants de Maldoror*. . . . Then there was Apollinaire . . . and Baudelaire."

A cache of riches—Man Ray's first and most intimate sampling of French poetry—filled the little house that spring. There was Charles Baudelaire's decadent, sensual *Les fleurs du mal,* a romantic hymn to the poet's mission to find *correspondances* for his emotions in the phenomenal world, which marked the beginning of modern French verse. Obsessed with tracing the roots of modern language in antiquity, Stéphane Mallarmé took the opposite approach, however, transforming objects into ideas. By evoking rather than describing, his verses took poetry itself as their single goal. To Arthur Rimbaud, the poet was a seer, a man who lived in dreams and fantasies. By the age of twenty-one, with the completion of *Une saison en enfer,* he'd abandoned writing poems completely, to become a restless wanderer flirting with danger in exotic places; his recklessness finally killed him. Guillaume Apollinaire straddled the realms of the romantic and the surreal. In *Alcools,* published in 1913, he eliminated punctuation from his verse and invited his readers to become caught up in an incessant stream of language and "to be drunken—on the spiritual air of Nietzschean high places." Man Ray was introduced by Adon to the work of these literary adventurers, who led him ever deeper into his own imaginative voyages at an important time in his artistic growth.

But of all the writers whose work Adon read to Man Ray, the Comte de Lautréamont (pseudonym for Isidore Lucien Ducasse, 1846–1870) had the most profound impact. Almost nothing is known about the circumstances of Isidore Ducasse's childhood and youth—simply that his mother committed suicide shortly after his birth in Montevideo, Uruguay, and that by the time he was twenty-one, he was living shabbily in an *appartement meublé* on the rue Faubourg-Montmartre, in Paris. *Les chants de Maldoror,* his most well known work, was published in Belgium in 1869 (it is possible Adon may have picked up her copy there), one year before the author's death at age twenty-four.

Les chants is a surreal, violent, brutally erotic *bildungsroman* with heavy debts to de Sade and Dante. Its main theme, appropriate to Man Ray's own situation at the time he first read it, is the child's obsessive struggle to separate from his parents, to achieve freedom through escape. Mervyn, the ultimate symbol of purity and good, is brutally pursued by Maldoror, the dark, demonic representative of evil. Mervyn's beauty is so unparalleled that mortal language cannot do it justice. The shock his beauty creates is described in the text as being comparable to *"la rencontre fortuite sur une table de dissection d'une machine à coudre et d'un parapluie"* (the meeting on a dissecting table of a sewing machine and an umbrella).

This notorious phrase would be seized upon by nascent surrealists André Breton and Philippe Soupault in Paris during the early 1920s as a metaphor for the movement's primary aesthetic raison d'être, to manufacture jarring juxtapositions in which disparate elements illuminated each other through their extreme inappropriateness. Man Ray penetrated Maldoror's collagelike world while still in Ridgefield. And before he left New York in 1921, he made a haunting photograph, *L'énigme d'Isidore Ducasse*, replicating the imagery in Lautréamont's bizarre language.

Like Mervyn, the young Man Ray was in rebellion against his ancestors, preserving himself from following in their footsteps. Like Mervyn, Man Ray was holding on to his personal freedom in the midst of an emotional cyclone. Like Mervyn, Man Ray insisted upon autonomy in each act he performed.

After their May 1914 wedding, Man Ray took Adon to Brooklyn to meet his family. "I'm a married man now," he announced proudly. His mother was cordial but noncommittal. Her son had found a woman who was not only several years older than he, but with a daughter, too; it was decided that Esther, now enrolled in the older class at the Modern School, would live with the couple in Ridgefield.

Later that night, after her son and new daughter-in-law had left, Minnie confessed to Dora that she was willing to accept the match — the ceremony had been performed by a minister, not even a rabbi— because "If I say no, I will lose my son. I don't want to lose Man." The Rays knew their oldest child was slowly slipping away, and they were

concerned about alienating him to the point where he might decide not
to come back at all.

Man Ray wrote in a poem dedicated to his new wife,

> O love bruised hands
> O winged face,
> O rooted body
> In naked dress encased
> With silent girdle round the waist
> And full toned trinkets round the throat
>
> O bodied soul
> By love set free—
> The sun embraces the desert
> And the desert its oasis
> While a whole life
> That varies from beginning to end
> Contains itself.

The self-printed, self-published booklet was called *Adonisms, Some
Poems by Man Ray*. A testimony to his abiding love, the verses were also
remarkable for their distance from the conventions of formally
structured verse. Adon was inspiration of the finest kind, because she
did not stand in the way of Man Ray's compulsion to live the varied
life.

Aware that her realm was language, Adon attempted to express
what it was in her husband's spirit that moved her, reciprocating thus:

> Were I a painter I should not seek to paint minutely
> the collarette which fits so snugly around your neck—but
> what I'd seek would be the spirit which dominates your
> entire poise. Lyrical art-inspiring Pierot—appearing
> in my remotest dreams, I'll put that expression into
> your face alone and in one gesture.
> > Pierot—I love you!

Their *Book of Divers Writings* (written in the summer of 1914,
published February 1915), with pen-and-ink drawings by Man Ray,
included portraits of Adon (her gaze penetrating, her brow furrowed)

and her husband (earnest and determined). The book "concreted," as they phrased it in an explanatory note enclosed for friends and purchasers, "an epitome of their work since their partnership." The folio, they emphasized, was "made up of elements from the animal, vegetable, and mineral kingdoms—leather, paper, and paint. Its spiritual elements are equivalents for fire, earth, and water. They are in terms of love, life, and art."

Printed on the finest English Whatman drawing paper in an edition of twenty copies, the *Book* was a homegrown product. It was distributed and sold around the city, and the couple actually made some money from it. Man Ray was an energetic self-promoter and a natural publisher who enjoyed getting the work out to the public just as much as he enjoyed its creation.

Domestic rhythms were proving to Man Ray's liking. But he was restless and still dreamed of Paris. Adon, too, hoped to return to Belgium to see her family after a long and agonizing silence. The advent of war ended their plans. By the turbulent summer of 1914, Man Ray was at work on a nameless canvas that assumed prophetic dimensions as the international crisis developed: a procession of men and horses seemed to move majestically, ominously from left to right, part of a martial ceremony depicted in grays and blues and ochres. Adon told him to call it *MCMXIV*.

The canvas, a special Irish linen, was prepared laboriously "with fish glue and plaster dissolved in water. Then," the artist explained, "I worked on it with palette-knives like a mason building a house with bricks." And, most unusual of all, Man Ray worked on it for a year. His exceptional degree of attention shows in the detail work, the subtle shadings, and the finely honed edges of figures resonating into the distance. *MCMXIV* was Man Ray's first monumental work, an indication of what he might have been able to achieve if he had kept seriously at painting. The intentional contradiction between perspective and flatness makes the painting into an artful optical illusion, Man Ray's exploration of the dimensions of a plane.

At the same time, the artist was responding to the war overseas as a political cartoonist. Man Ray's ties to the Ferrer School were still strong and he was asked to design the August and September 1914 covers of their *Mother Earth News*. On one, a dragon with two heads named "Capitalism" and "Government" devours the struggling, helpless figure of "Humanity." On the other, two despairing prisoners, in starkly striped garb, gaze helplessly at a bloody battle scene affixed, flaglikc, to a crucifix. Look how conflict still victimizes mankind, the image seems to say—have we learned nothing since Christ's martyrdom?

Man Ray's response to the issues of the day was versatile, inspired by the affinity with the oppressed classes he keenly felt, the same spirit that had drawn him to Robert Henri's teachings. This consciousness, a natural outgrowth of Man Ray's humble upbringing as the son of a Jewish vest maker, coexisted in the same vibrant imagination with Stieglitz's ideal of the contemporary artist who was supposed to be one step removed from the hurly-burly of everyday life.

MAN RAY. *BELLE HALEINE, EAU DE VOILETTE*, 1920.
MARCEL DUCHAMP AS RROSE SÉLAVY, PUBLISHED IN *NEW
YORK DADA*, APRIL 1921.
Collection Robert Shapazian.

E N T E R

M A R C E L

D U C H A M P

"THE OLD expressions are with us always, and there are always others," declared the self-confident and mysterious slogan for yet another new literary magazine, invented by Alfred Kreymborg and his newfound friend, the poet, art patron, and collector Walter Conrad Arensberg.

The two met through the good graces of Allan Norton, who was the editor, with his wife, Louise, of a lively Greenwich Village paper called *The Rogue*. In addition to sharing a love for the game of chess, Arensberg and Kreymborg were equally fanatic in their desire to see American poetry pull itself up by its bootstraps and forge ahead into more experimental territory; besides, Kreymborg was still smarting from his failure to keep *The Glebe* afloat.

The idea for *Others* magazine was hatched during a brainstorming session that began one evening in Arensberg's apartment on West Sixty-seventh Street just off Central Park, continued during several hours of walking after dinner, broke for five hours of sleep, and picked up again after breakfast the next day.

Walter Arensberg had moved to New York the previous year, 1914, with his wife, Lou, heiress to a fortune left by her father, a textile manufacturer. The Arensbergs had lived in Cambridge and Boston for several years, where, thanks to their lack of financial worries, Walter was able to pursue his love of composing and translating poetry in the French Symbolist mode. Two visits to the Armory Show—first on a trip down to New York City when it was at the end of its run there, next when nearing the conclusion of its stay in Boston—had turned Arensberg into an impassioned collector. Powered by his wife's resources and encouraged and guided by his friend Walter Pach, one of the show's original organizers, Walter Arensberg developed into an unerring connoisseur of modernism. Within a few years, the high walls of his apartment were lined with the works of Braque, Duchamp, Sheeler, Matisse, Cézanne, Picasso, Joseph Stella, Derain, and a host of others.

Caught up in the swirl of the New York art scene, Arensberg nevertheless maintained his enthusiasm for Imagist writing. In the same spirit that moved him to purchase modernist paintings he liked—ones he felt made statements destined to endure—he told Kreymborg he wanted to do something for poets. *Others* would be similarly on the cutting edge in tone and conception. The small magazine—sixteen pages and five hundred copies per issue—would sell for fifteen cents a copy and a dollar and a half a year, and it would print simply the work of men and women who were trying themselves in the new forms. Contributors would not be paid; the privilege of being taken on at a time when it was tough to gain acceptance elsewhere was remuneration enough.

By the summer of 1915, *Others* was sufficiently developed in editorial concept that the Arensbergs could leave for their country home in Pomfret Center, Connecticut. Kreymborg was manuscript handler and general manager. He rented a shack out at Ridgefield again for himself and his new wife, Gertrude. Life on the western slope of the Palisades was as lively as ever during busy weekends, when the pioneering poets who wrote for "the little yellow dog," as the magazine was now affectionately dubbed, mingled with anarchists, self-styled nature lovers, and artists taking a break from the city. Wallace Stevens, Arensberg's Harvard classmate and an early and much-revered contributor to *Others,* never made the trip across—the surroundings might have proved a touch too rustic for him. But others did: Orrick Johns, who rented a cabin up the hill from the Kreymborgs; Mina Loy, appearing the next year when she arrived in New York from Europe; Mary Carolyn Davies, working during the week at a Lower West Side settlement house; the red-haired, astonishingly articulate Marianne Moore; Skipwith Cannell and his dancer-wife Kathleen; William Carlos Williams, dismounting from his rickety Model T after the bumpy ride from nearby Rutherford—and, of course, Man Ray and Adon Lacroix were there.

On Sundays, the "*Others* group," which they called themselves despite the founders' staunch avowal that they'd not be beholden to any unifying principle or special interest, would bring along picnic lunches and lie about on the grass, read freshly minted manuscripts to one another, discourse on what the moody Williams called "the present state of American poetry," perform in one another's one-act plays, and even indulge in a ragtag game of—what else but that quintessentially American pastime—baseball, one of Miss Moore's obsessions.

In the sixth issue, Man Ray published his one and only contribution to *Others,* a spare, quiet, and subtle poem, which reflected the enduring concern he was grappling with in his painting: how to portray multiple dimensions seen and experienced in the phenomenal world within the confines of two-dimensional art.

"Three Dimensions" was equally a poem about limits and a declaration of the artist's saving grace, inquisitiveness.

Several small houses
Discreetly separated by foliage
And the night—
Maintaining their several identities
By light

Which fills the inside of each—
Not as masses they stand
But as walls
Enclosing and excluding
Like shawls

About little old women—
What mystery hides within
What curiosity lurks without
One the other
Knows nothing about.

Poems by Marianne Moore ("If external action is effete/And rhyme outmoded . . .") and Adon Lacroix ("Room sing low/The day is done/Shadows press hard . . .") were also included, on facing pages.

Women writers were represented by quite a number of works. The general "feel" of the issue was both pastoral and iconoclastic, reflecting Kreymborg's acceptance of a wide range of styles.

The summer of *Others* was also the summer of the momentous arrival of Marcel Duchamp in New York. The *Nude* had been a *succès de scandale* at the Armory Show, and Walter Pach again acted as mediator, by convincing Duchamp in Paris that—as he was exempt from military service—there was nothing to prevent him from reaping the benefits of celebrity in star-hungry America.

When the SS *Rochambeau* docked in New York harbor on June 15, 1915, Pach was there to greet his friend, and the two went immediately to the Arensbergs' place, where Duchamp was welcomed with warmth and enthusiasm. Arensberg lent Duchamp his apartment for the summer, returning periodically from Pomfret Center to make sure that the artist was adjusting to his new life.

One day in early fall, Arensberg drove Duchamp out to Ridgefield to mingle with the *Others* crowd. It was there he met Man Ray. Duchamp's English was only a few steps beyond rudimentary and Man Ray's French not much more advanced, but Adon Lacroix served as interpreter. Their first encounter was marked by a tennis match played in front of the cottage without a net. Man Ray recalled that he "called the strokes to make conversation: fifteen, thirty, forty, love, to which Duchamp replied each time with the same word: yes."

They must have made quite a sight. Duchamp was a man who possessed, as his friend André Breton described it, "elegance in its most fatal quality, that went beyond elegance, a truly supreme ease," along with "laughing eyes" and admirable beauty. Tall, graceful in bearing, polite, Duchamp was unfailingly reserved in behavior and conversation, with the self-effacing mannerism of coughing drily into his hand before speaking.

Man Ray, by contrast, stood just a shade over five feet and was compactly built. His manner was perpetually intense, his movements adept and dartlike. His voice at times was gruff and faintly sarcastic; vowels were bitten off, and there was a hint of the gangster in his inflection. Man Ray could be aggressively warm and engaging. Where Duchamp was subtle to the verge of understatement, Man Ray was witty and tricky. Where Duchamp seemed to invite people to approach him, Man Ray radiated coarse irony.

These two artists—who would become fast friends without a

trace of rivalry between them for the next fifty years—had developed along remarkably similar lines. As a student at the Académie Julian in Paris, where Robert Henri had studied, Duchamp had experimented with Renaissance and Impressionist techniques in portraiture and landscapes. A likeness of a friend painted when Duchamp was a mere eighteen years old reveals him as a skilled imitator of styles. Like Man Ray, he dipped into political cartooning, for two newspapers, *Le Courrier Français* and *Le Rire*.

Duchamp experimented with Fauvist coloration and Cubism "for its intellectual aspect," in 1910, but by the following year he was speaking of "getting away from isms" as fast as possible. Studies for *The Nude* and exercises in the problems of motion soon followed, and his *Chess Players* painting—the sketch for it had also been at the Armory Show—demonstrated Duchamp's use of subdued tones as a conscious reaction against the vividness of his earlier work. By 1913, in yet another turnaround, he was well on the way to giving up *all* conventional painting and sketching. Family members and friends—who had populated Man Ray's earlier work as well and were now absent— would be a subject of the past for Duchamp. Even the portraits of his brothers playing chess, their wives drinking tea nearby, show hunched-over forms with averted, shadowy faces.

Duchamp's path over the ten years prior to meeting Man Ray had been a similarly rapid dance, in and out of media and movements. Like Man Ray, he had encountered styles with energy and virtuosity, exhausting each one then breaking away. The important point was to remain free and vital. Duchamp did not feel the need to paint a subject to make it worthy of being called a work of art. He was becoming engaged in the process of selecting simple objects—a bottle rack picked up in a bazaar in Paris; a snow shovel and a ventilator—with no particular aesthetic value and, through an act of impartial discrimination made legitimate by his sensibility, inventing an entirely new genre, the "readymade." Like Man Ray in 1915, Duchamp was fascinated by the *idea* behind the work of art. But while Man Ray was at heart an activist, a doer, and a producer, Marcel Duchamp produced only as one step further toward "not creating," exploring ways in which the dynamic of "not making" could sustain him, arranging his objects in lonely and ever so slightly manipulated poses. Duchamp would soon devote himself to "not caring" about fame so strongly that his very disclaimers attracted attention.

For Duchamp, who was *pulling away* from "art," the life of an artist was a refined succession of artifices extending even to the way he spoke and dressed, never asked for favors, and never said "thank you." For his friend Man Ray, who was *diving into* work of all shapes and kinds, drowning in it, an artist's life was a succession of assignments and rapidly thrown-together labors. The body of Duchamp's work, the artist later insisted, was *one* work. The body of Man Ray's work was a multitude of things, a jostling crowd of entertainment.

Octavio Paz has observed that "Art, for Duchamp, was a secret . . . to be passed on like a message between conspirators." Marcel Duchamp and Man Ray continued for the next five decades to play their tennis match with no obstructing net, disavowing rules and rituals and conventions and extending the score as they went along.

In Ridgefield, where more of Man Ray's friends were writers than painters, or so it seemed, another member of the group was Alanson Hartpence, a publicity-shy poet who labored hard at his craft but did not have the hunger to publish. Hartpence often visited from his country place in the Adirondacks to help with *Others*. He admired Man Ray's painting and, as manager and partner in the Daniel

Others magazine, January 1919.
*The Poetry/Rare Books Collection, University Libraries,
SUNY, Buffalo, New York.*

Gallery at 2 West Forty-seventh Street in New York City, was in a position to help him. The gallery, pet project of Charles Daniel, had opened in the fall of 1913 following the Armory Show, along with Knoedler, Keppel & Co. and Durand-Ruel nearby. Daniel was a saloon proprietor who had grown up in a family of restaurateurs and had always had an interest in art; he purchased his first picture at age fourteen—as he described it, "a little watercolor which cost $1.50 and hung over my bed."

Not a connoisseur by any means, Charles Daniel had ignored his brother's warning that association with artists "would give him a bad name in business," and allowed his "passion for pictures" to move him to leave his former occupation and "become a collector-dealer." The Daniel Gallery was to be decidedly different in tone and emphasis from the carpeted, plush sanctuaries the owner had explored as a young man. Daniel was determined to feature the new modernist breed— John Marin, Ernest Lawson, Marsden Hartley, Max Weber, Jules Pascin, Charles Demuth, Samuel and Edith Gregor Halpert. The younger artists were struggling, and he enjoyed being with them.

Hartpence engineered a meeting to have his friend Man Ray admitted to this pantheon. Mr. Daniel was easily convinced. He was attracted to Man Ray's unique brand of Cubism, remarking years later that his work had "strength and rich color...he always understood what he was doing. Man Ray had a marvelous analytical mind." In addition, capitalizing on Man Ray's draftmanship and expert lettering, Daniel commissioned him to execute catalogue covers for several seasons.

Man Ray's first one-man show ran at the Daniel Gallery during October 1915. Thirty canvases were on display, a mixture of semirepresentational landscapes of the artist's pastoral home and the flattened, abstract "arrangements of forms" characterizing his newer, more cerebral efforts. The exhibition also marked another first for Man Ray, his initial use of the camera to photograph his paintings for documentary purposes. Now that he had more work available in his studio than ever before, it was no longer possible to keep track of them merely by listings alone. Man Ray had tried hiring professional photographers, but the results had not been up to his standards. In a method that would not change for the next half century, he set up his paintings outdoors, in sunlight, and photographed them naturally, without depending upon elaborate equipment or intricate lighting systems. As Marcel Duchamp observed, the camera was for Man Ray "a mere instrument in the service of the mind."

Despite the innovative, cost-cutting manner in which Man Ray's painting were hung—frameless, set flush into a false wall made of cheesecloth to stress their concern with two-dimensionality—his debut in the New York gallery world was as disappointing as it could have been. The critics were unanimously negative with respect to the newer work, preferring the less threatening, tradition-rooted landscapes.

In early November, the show over, the snow swirled in Ridgefield, and Man Ray began to dig in for a long winter of withdrawal. He was dejected to the point of turning his back on everyone and everything connected with the city. Not even news of Sam's marriage to the beautiful Lena Nash could bring him back into the fold: "We cannot come this week," he flatly informed his brother.

The day the Daniel exhibition closed, Man Ray had received a letter from John Weichsel inviting him to participate in the People's Art Guild exhibition opening later that month at the University Settlement on Eldridge Street. The Guild, "organized . . . for the socialization of art and consequent broadening of its scope and patronage" was attempting to bring more new art to the attention of unschooled audiences.

Man Ray informed Dr. Weichsel, whom he'd known through his erudite weekly lectures at the Ferrer Center, that he had "decided after all to keep out. I have enough work and attention demanded of me under present conditions." Still smarting from the wounds of critical ignorance, he continued, "As an atom in your scheme, I shall not be missed—in my scheme of things the world is an atom." Man Ray, the fledgling existentialist, concluded in his meticulous, copperplate hand, "and I enjoy a comfortable nullity therein."

These dark thoughts were brought to an end when, "puttering around one morning" in the cottage, he received an urgent telephone message from Mr. Daniel. Arthur J. Eddy, a prosperous Chicago attorney, had stopped into the gallery while Man Ray's paintings were leaning temporarily against the wall prior to being crated and shipped back to New Jersey. Eddy picked six works and offered a quick two thousand dollars for them. Daniel, ever supportive, told Man Ray he would waive his commission.

Eddy's choice of works was significant for more than economic reasons. He was an immensely cultured man, presciently having purchased Manet and Whistler long before they became popular, and was the author of an enthusiastic book published the previous year, *Cubists and Post Impressionism*. Eddy had taken an exceptionally informed look at Man Ray's work, aware of the origins from which it had sprung, and he had seen in the young, untried painter great promise for the future. Man Ray's stock rose meteorically in Daniel's assessment with this windfall. He would give him a second show a year later and a third to follow.

The infusion of cash, more than he had ever seen in his life, and in a concrete way a validation of his work—most important, of his newest work—precipitated an utter reversal in Man Ray's thinking. He told Adon now was the time to move back into the city, to be where the action was, to make more connections. He would cut back on the McGraw Company job to three days a week to provide time for expression of his new artistic ideas.

Man Ray rented a studio in midtown Manhattan, across the street from Grand Central Station. It was about as public and tumultuous a location as he could find and one vastly different from Ridgefield, where only birdcalls punctuated the silence. He was pushing to the other extreme, seeking to immerse himself in the crowd after several years of being off to the side. Meanwhile, recovered from the flurry of newspaper articles and parties that had heralded his arrival in New York, Man Ray's newfound friend Duchamp had moved out from under the Arensbergs' protective wing at 33 West Sixty-seventh Street to a forty-dollar-a-month downtown studio— away from the midtown hubbub, in the Lincoln Arcade Building on Broadway. He had purchased two huge plate-glass panels, each one more than four feet by six feet and weighing close to two hundred pounds, several wooden trestles, oil, varnish, lead foil, lead wire, silvering, aluminum foil, and glue, and was beginning to focus all his energies on a project that would occupy him obsessively for the next eight years, *La mariée mise à nue par ses célibataires, même* (The Bride Stripped Bare by Her Bachelors, Even), or more familiarly, *The Large Glass.*

Duchamp took a subsistence-level job as a librarian at the French Institute. His English had improved to the point where he was composing experimental poetry to edify his friend Walter Arensberg. He had formulated his plans for the *Glass* in France two years earlier, and they coalesced in the new milieu. Duchamp was able to bring together and summarize a wealth of varied elements in the work, which he described as "juxtaposing mechanical elements and visceral forms . . . geometrical designs as in [his] earlier painting of 1914, *Chocolate Grinder* . . . and forms of uniforms inside moulds . . . made with lead wires fixed onto glass by drops of varnish, the *Cemetery of Uniforms and Liveries.*"

Only a modern, frenetic city like New York could give Marcel Duchamp the feeling of mystery and license he required. In New York, he could come to terms with the pressures and frustrations that were pushing him ever farther away from conventional painting. Like Baudelaire's *flâneur,* the observer who strolls through the crowd but is not really part of it, Duchamp used New York's dense social fabric as an opportunity to lead an increasingly dandified life. The city was a perfect place to parade in and yet remain apart.

And it was Baudelaire, mystically anticipating Duchamp's glass piece, who had written that "he who looks outside through an open window never sees as many things as he who looks out through a closed window." In its earliest stage of creation, *The Large Glass* lay on its side across wooden horses, as Duchamp, with what his enthralled visitor Man Ray observed as "the patience and obstinacy of a spider reweaving its web," painstakingly laid down a network of wires meant to reveal *and* obscure a window into the problem of unrealized and unfulfilled love. Trying to portray the lyrical relationship of mechanically inspired forms, Duchamp repeatedly enacted on the glass surface the theme of separation. The bride, on the panel above, was barred forever by a firm line of metal from her bachelors below. They would never connect. The act of love was portrayed as a "nonact" between machines prevented from union.

Two years earlier, Apollinaire had peered astutely into Duchamp's deepest motivations when he had described him as "detached from aesthetic preoccupations." If only he could have stopped by the Broadway studio to find his predictions realized to such an extreme!

"When one goes to see people," Duchamp said, "one is influenced even if one doesn't think about it." On those late afternoons when Man Ray paused by the dim studio to assess his friend's progress, he saw a monumental effort built up by meticulous increments. He saw Duchamp, with every move, using art purely as a conveyance of thought. Duchamp's glass welcomed the spectator to look into and through it, an ironic window into the perceptions of the viewer, who by its contemplation became part of the work.

Duchamp and Man Ray passed many evenings at the Arensberg salon; for, indeed, that was what the opulent duplex had become. Virtually every night was open house for a constantly shifting cast of characters—the artists Jean and Yvonne Crotti; painter Francis

Picabia and his wife, Gabrielle Buffet-Picabia; Cubist painter-philosopher Albert Gleizes and his wife, Juliette Roche; the composer Edgard Varèse, who'd arrived, like Duchamp, on the SS *Rochambeau* at the end of 1915; the painter Joseph Stella; Beatrice Wood, the actress; the psychiatrist Elmer Ernest Southard; eccentric Baroness Elsa von Freytag-Loringhoven; artists Charles Sheeler, Charles Demuth, and Morton Schamberg; William Carlos Williams; Wallace Stevens, when he was in town; Mina Loy and her husband, Arthur Cravan, the man who would challenge world heavyweight champion Jack Johnson to a boxing match. The evenings of drinking, dancing (Louise was a piano player), feasting (Louise was also an indefatigable concocter of hors d'oeuvres), art-ogling (the walls were filled with Walter's acquisitions), and fighting (like the time Isadora Duncan knocked out Walter's front teeth) stretched into marathon sessions, given Walter's predilection for all-night wrangling and debating.

These were not events at which an éminence grise or charismatic hostess presided, perched upon a regal armchair, posing questions à la Gertrude Stein. Rather, there was a free-for-all ambience, in keeping with the spirits of the host and hostess and the guests. As a matter of fact, one did not even have to be invited to attend. Newcomers came and departed throughout the night with the same aplomb as veterans. Attendance was as impromptu and spontaneous as Lou Arensberg's piano improvisations, played regardless of whether anyone was listening.

The drinking often continued as Duchamp, Louise Norton, Man Ray, and Adon sampled the bars along Broadway, then repaired to a little café just inside Central Park for breakfast at dawn. Adon by his side, nodding in agreement, Man Ray chatted enthusiastically about his new work in collage and his experiments with flattening the pictorial frame. Although one was free to call upon Duchamp in his studio to view his glass-in-progress, he never referred to it in public. Over coffee, Duchamp had a habit of sitting with his back to the park greenery. He sipped slowly, observing that after a night on the town one's hands were invariably dirty—"drinker's hands," he called them. Man Ray slipped away in time to be at work downtown. The rest of the group retired to bed and slept until noon.

MAN RAY. *THE ROPE DANCER ACCOMPANIES HERSELF
WITH HER SHADOWS*, 1916. OIL.
Collection the Museum of Modern Art, New York, gift of G. David Thompson.

THE ARTIST
AS TIGHTROPE
WALKER

UNLIKE DUCHAMP, who kept his notes for *The Large Glass* on various odd-size scraps of paper covered with indeterminate scrawls, hieroglyphics, and sentence fragments—shopping list reminders to himself of what he must be sure to do next—Man Ray decided early in the game to codify his theories in a coherent and organized fashion. Despite his avowals to the contrary later in life, Man Ray was a careful and deliberate writer, who issued a running commentary on his attitudes toward his work, where it was heading, and what its intended function in the world was to be. "Learn to be articulate" was one of his favorite bits of advice to the few students who worked with him (including his sister Elsie's daughter, Naomi), and he heeded his own credo to the letter.

At the beginning of one of Man Ray's most fertile creative periods, 1916–1917—a time when his improvisations and sorties into new and different media came so thick and fast it is almost impossible to establish a reliable chronology for them—he set down his first true "manifesto" in a self-published booklet called *A Primer of the New Art in Two Dimensions*. "Just as the lens sacrifices actual space to focus all of that space upon the plate," he wrote, with significant reference to his newfound tool, the camera, "so the artist must condense the time and space element to create life's equivalent." In defining his *painterly* principles and relating them to the particular conditions under which the *photographer* operated, he was illustrating the synthesis between the arts. "Each of the arts," he stated, "has a characteristic factor that is static and containable in the flat plane." The goal of every mode of expression was the same: "The new two-dimensional medium is not merely painting any more than it is merely drawing or color. It is a most universal"— note that term—"and concentrated form of expression. With it the artist can really begin to create, which is the highest and most joyous form of expression."

We are limiting ourselves, Man Ray believed, if we persist in categorizing and compartmentalizing the arts, dwelling upon their differences instead of noticing and accepting similarities. The statement was really not as objective as it sounded. Rather, it was Man Ray's defense of his experiments with a variety of artistic modes for making imagination concrete.

In early spring 1916, Man Ray again exhibited a favorite painting he had shown at the Daniel Gallery, *Invention-Dance,* this time as part of the "Forum Exhibition of Modern American Painters" at the Anderson Gallery. Organized by Alfred Stieglitz, Robert Henri, John Weichsel, and Willard Huntington Wright— all Man Ray devotees—the show used the work of seventeen artists to trace developments in American art during the three years since the Armory Show. That the Armory Show had brought excitement and new ideas to American art was evident at the Forum Exhibition in the works of Arthur Dove, Marsden Hartley, John Marin, Morgan Russell, Abraham Walkowitz, Man Ray, and others.

Each artist was represented in the catalogue by a brief statement. Here again, Man Ray reaffirmed his commitment to working out "on a single plane as the instantaneously visualizing factor... motives and physical sensations in a permanent and universal language of color, texture, and formal organization. He [the artist] uncovers the pure plane of expression that has so long been hidden by the glazings of nature imitation, anecdote, and other popular subjects."

The statement reflected Man Ray's idealistic attempt to meet the Cubist challenge, working within the boundaries of a flat surface, recognizing that a painter deceived himself if he thought of his legitimate field of action as otherwise. What could be done to make that plane *live?* Man Ray took the intellectual high road, playing it off against the joyous manipulation of color and shape.

MARCEL DUCHAMP. *THE BRIDE STRIPPED BARE*
BY HER BACHELORS, EVEN (THE LARGE GLASS), 1915–1923.
OIL ON LEAD WIRE ON GLASS.
Philadelphia Museum of Art, Bequest of Katherine S. Dreier.

His works from this period are frequently characterized by dance and movement imagery. The articulateness of his ground rules is a fresh complement to their exuberance.

The many-faceted figures of *Invention-Dance* boasted arms and legs raised and splayed in all directions, intersecting with a companion figure off to the side that looked as if it had walked straight off the *MCMXIV* canvas. It was but a hop, skip, and jump to the four-feet-by-six-feet *The Rope Dancer Accompanies Herself with Her Shadows,* Man Ray's second monumental work. From that, he moved through yet another threshold into sophisticated collage, clichés-verre, airbrush painting, his first "object/assemblage," and his earliest sculpture—all within the space of one ecstatic year.

How appropriate to Man Ray is the image of the "rope dancer," the tightrope walker he had seen in a vaudeville show, so much a metaphor for the young artist who also takes risks with every step, moving farther and farther away from the comforting poles (or polarities) of convention, out to the middle of the wire, where there is nothing to protect him except his wits, no net below to catch him should he fail to keep his balance by continuing to move forward and create. There was more than a bit of the exhibitionist in the rope dancer. Man Ray understood the impulse to play the daredevil in front of a crowd, because that made the role all the more delicious to savor.

The Rope Dancer expressed Man Ray's current intrigue with Synchromist painting, concerned with the juxtaposition and display of pure areas of color for the highest visual impact. His romance continued with Cubism, so attractive because of its refined theoretical basis and the complete license it gave to the artist's imagination. The work also illustrated Man Ray's irrepressible playfulness, his lack of fear for his materials, the looseness with which he "played around" while making something.

One possible impetus for moving to a larger field may have been the sight of Duchamp's glass, each of its two panes the same size as *The Rope Dancer.* Man Ray hints that he was also flush with new funds from Mr. Eddy's purchase and able to "go out and buy a few hundred dollars' worth of colors and canvas." The painting had its beginnings, he said, in "a very mechanical drawing of a dancer with a violin scroll in the foreground like an old Degas, a pastel . . . the orchestra being more Toulouse-Lautrec." This first step was schematic, relying on mechanical instruments from Man Ray's workplace. He then transposed the drawing, tracing it onto "various pieces of spectrum-colored paper, with the idea of suggesting movement not only in the drawing but in the transition from one color to another." Man Ray then cut out the shapes and began to slide them around, using the color areas like a storyboard for the ultimate canvas. At this juncture, the thought crossed his mind that it might be interesting to use spray-painting techniques instead of brushes. But that prospect struck him as "too decorative . . . it would make a nice curtain for the theatre, for a musical comedy."

Man Ray looked down at the discarded scraps of colored paper strewn around the floor of the studio—now more commodious surroundings at 11½ West Twenty-sixth Street—and saw in them, rather than in the polished, deliberately planned forms, "an abstract pattern that might have been the shadows of the dancer." He picked up the outtakes for the rope dancer and instead manipulated them, bit by bit, "so that [he'd] get the colors contrasting next to each other, orange against blue, purple against yellow, using [his] scientific knowledge of color" and his Synchromist awareness of color relativities to achieve the desired effect. He was finally ready for the application of pigment to canvas, copying the layout "with precision, yet lavishly"—so lavishly, in fact, that he soon used up all his newly purchased colors.

What began as an ambitiously large blank canvas—the act of stretching it having posed the challenge before the idea was worked out—ended up as a study in primary colors topped by a fanciful, wide-skirted female figure, her arms and legs scattering every which way. Man Ray had moved through a whole range of instinctive as well as deliberate "tries" until he hit upon just the right combination of planning and chance, of formal knowledge and a measure of desired ignorance. Each filament of rope reaches out to a different color area (or "shadow") and pulls it back to the dynamic woman in motion. The painting in final form was meticulous and very polished; paint had been thinly applied, and the surface was lacquerlike in its sheen. The "dancer" herself is outlined by a white border that makes her stand out against the startling color scheme.

Man Ray used airbrushing to create a "photographic quality" in his work, which he found thrilling. He also liked the inherently dangerous idea of painting at great speed without having to touch the surface of the canvas, or cardboard, as was most often the case in the full-scale airbrush works he began the following year.

In the aftermath of *The Rope Dancer,* Man Ray began a new

series of works that emerged from leftover paper shreds and his ingrown reluctance—no doubt stemming from his father's similar attitude toward materials—to see anything with potential use go to waste. At an earlier point in his painting life, Man Ray had seen the entire visual world as a fit subject for the canvas. He was moving further from that now, into more abstract areas, but he still believed that materials for making art could come from anywhere—even from the gutter.

Revolving Doors, ten serial images, went through a number of incarnations with Man Ray's rapid diversification. They began as collages, then became oil paintings; then prose poems were written three years later to accompany some of the images; then a *pochoir* (stencil) edition of the collages was published in Paris in 1926; and, finally, recreated paintings were executed in Hollywood in 1943. Man Ray was reluctant to let go of any of his works. He rarely felt their iconography was exhausted at the point of completion, and he often remade favorite works he feared were lost, referring to them as his "children." Once he sent them off into the world, Man Ray's works were forever attached to him by a slender filament, the way *The Rope Dancer* was tied to her shadows. Man Ray kept meticulous card-file records of every work he made as well as every idea for possible works and an ongoing record of the provenance of each piece, remembering when it was sold and to what collector or museum. He knew which works were damaged and which ones were available for barter.

The evocative titles of the *Revolving Doors* images reflected several of Man Ray's emerging themes: his interest in gesture and movement (*Mime*); in music (*Orchestra*); women (*Jeune Fille,* a nice play upon words, with its strands—*fils*—reaching out); Duchamp (*Concrete Mixer,* an homage to his friend's painting, *Chocolate Grinder*). In their first incarnation, they also investigated the problem of planar fidelity with thin sheets of colored paper that were affixed to white cardboard, interpenetrating brilliantly.

"While these works did not have the finished and imposing quality of oil paintings," Man Ray later conceded, "I considered them equally important." He was well aware of the eternal hierarchy that assessed painting as the ultimate achievement and test of any real artist.

Man Ray and Adon continued to help each other toward new levels of literary expressiveness. He hand-lettered and published her anarchistic, sound-poetry broadsheet, "visual words / sounds seen / thoughts felt / feelings thought" out of his one-man company at "11½ West 26th Street—N.Y.—U.S.A.—Jan 1917." The primal poems were handsomely presented on blueprint paper in a handy folio.

She wrote the preface to the exhibition catalogue for Man Ray's second show at the Daniel Gallery, which took place during December 1916 and January 1917. Her epigraph from Axel Borg denied the myth that only children are possessed with a clear and fresh perspective about nature. The eye that reaches the highest level of development—the artist's—also sees the world anew every day. Adon went on to promote the primacy of "the idea" in all art, "includ[ing] the picture painted . . . the substance itself; color; and from the color—the subject—ideas and matter are one in painting." A poet herself, Adon was willing to concede that "words . . . will never [be] as expressive as the gesture."

This important show of Man Ray's work exemplified his wife's endorsement of the "gesture," the poetic possibilities ready to be released by the artwork's physicality. It included a *Self Portrait,* his first publicly exhibited art object, one that pointed out the distance between Marcel Duchamp's readymades and Man Ray's more aggressive management of materials. Against a black-and-aluminum-paint background rested two electric bells and a push button. When the curious spectator pressed the button, nothing happened. "That made them livid," Man Ray recalled with a laugh, years later, "and they said I was a bad workman." Another work nearby, *Portrait Hanging* was hung crookedly on purpose. A second nail, placed strategically, prevented any well-intentioned visitor from naturally enough trying to straighten it. "It swung back like a pendulum," said the artist, who "wanted the audience, the visitors, to participate in the creative act," to feel some sense of what Adon meant by "gesture." These were Man Ray's humorous but generous efforts to use his work to reach out and *engage* the audience. Throughout his artistic career he believed "humor was the best communication of all."

As soon as he achieved an intimate knowledge of the interplay of paint on canvas, Man Ray moved away from formal painting and into the application of paint with palette knives, airbrushes, and the like. As soon as he knew he was more of a *maker* than just an applicator of paint, he moved to embody his ideas in assemblages of miscellaneous items, sometimes resting them on a flat surface, as if to imply that this was where they had originated; other times as freestanding forms. As soon as he had codified the realm of *two* dimensions to his complete intellectual satisfaction, he broke through into the *third,* through writing.

As soon as Man Ray, the mechanically apt former student of architecture, had come to terms with the intricacies of the camera, he wanted temporarily to do away with it. In 1917, he created his first cliché-verre, both a photograph and a print. The earliest versions of clichés-verre were executed by etching lines on glass plates and allowing light to pass through to create an image upon photographically sensitive paper. The glass was usually covered with a "ground" of thick emulsion that was pierced with a needlelike etching tool. The artist was then able to print from this handmade negative. Man Ray, however, preferred to draw on exposed film, or even onto the negatives of old photographs. It was quick, it was a process receptive to his facility with the line as a draftsman, and it allowed him to bypass the technical routes allied with straight photography. Again, a subversive manner of creating became a perfect complement to the traditional one. Man Ray could take absolutely unadorned, entirely representative, documentary pictures of his work, and that of other artists, to help New York collectors like John Quinn and Henri-Pierre Roché in their record keeping. And he could just as easily discard the camera for his personal manipulation of photographic material.

An artistic storm was brewing overseas, as yet undetected by Man Ray and other American iconoclasts. The eye of a hurricane is meant to be an area of calm. But the Cabaret Voltaire, no. 1, Spiegelgasse, in neutral Zurich at the peak of World War I, could hardly be called aesthetically tranquil or uncommitted. For it was here, on February 5, 1916, that a group of young artists in disillusioned exile from the war "formed a centre for entertainment . . . run on the principle of daily meetings where visiting artists will perform their music and poetry," proclaimed cofounder Hugo Ball.

With poet and physician Richard Huelsenbeck, Marcel Janco, Hans Arp, Emmy Hennings, and the monocled, frenetic, pint-sized Bucharest poet Sami Rosenstock (better known as Tristan Tzara), Hugo Ball was spearheading an effort to create a literary explosion deafening enough to drown out the din and clamor of guns and cannons.

This wild and extremely erudite movement of *je m'en foutisme* ("thumbing their noses at the world" as wordsmith Tzara labeled it) came to be called "Dada" in April of that year. The origins of the name are uncertain. Huelsenbeck claimed that he picked it at random from a Larousse encyclopedia, the French word for *hobbyhorse*. Others said it echoed the sound of two Romanians, Janco and Tzara, in enthusiastic agreement, "da, da—yes, yes"; that it was derived from the slang for *good-bye* in German; or, according to Tzara, that it was an African tribal word for *the tail of the sacred cow*. Whatever the derivation of its name, the movement originated as a "writers in performance" series. The *littérateurs* emerged from their garrets and, at a dark time in history, claimed the cabaret stage as their territory.

Disgusted by senseless carnage, the artists believed they had a moral imperative to use the power of language to arrest, disturb, and provoke. Nothing less than a systematic derangement of the senses would do. "Order = disorder; self = not-self; affirmation = negation," Tzara wrote, in an early manifesto, "ultimate emanations of absolute art. Absoluteness and purity of chaos cosmically ordered . . . I love an old work for its novelty," he said. "It is only contrast that attaches us to the past."

The Cabaret Voltaire became a nightclub unlike any the world had ever seen. Poets declaimed from scraps of paper pulled out of coat pockets to the accompaniment of cowbells and fists banged upon tables. "Negro rhythms" were the rage. As tom-toms pounded, the esteemed Dr. Huelsenbeck donned an African mask and sang of "The bladder of the swine/Vermilion and cinnabar/Cru cru cru . . ." As wineglasses crashed to the floor, Tzara screeched and howled that "you should put out the light in your window as you would spit out the pit of an apricot . . . dip little chickadees in ink and clean the face of the moon."

Hanging on the walls of the Voltaire were colorful, cut-out wood assemblages by Hans Arp, jigsaw-puzzle paintings by Marcel Janco, and, later, works by Klee, Kandinsky, and de Chirico, an arresting visual counterpoint to the bizarre activities on the stage— recitations of abstract, phonetic poetry: "gadji beri bimba glandridi laula lonni cadori," Hugo Ball intoned, "gadjama gramma berida bimbala . . ." and so on.

To Tzara and his colleagues, poetry was "a living force in every respect, even antipoetically." Dada's main goal was to free art from codified notions of what each art form was supposed to be, by destroying the boundaries between genres. There were no limits to the world of fantasy if the artist was serious in his dedication to the cause. When he broke language down to its component parts—and Kurt Schwitters carried the practice to its ultimate, espousing the letter itself as the sonic basis for diction—or broke forms in painting into shards of barely recognizable reality, the artist made a statement about his prophetic power to remake the world.

Harking back to his earliest days at the Ferrer School, long before his exposure to Dada, Man Ray had been a follower of anarchist philosophy. As late as 1919, he said that he still considered himself an "out and out anarchist" and proved it by collaborating with Henry S. Reynolds and Adolf Wolff on the publication of the first and only issue of *TNT* magazine. In an edition of one thousand copies, selling for fifty cents each, *TNT* included sound poetry by Adon Lacroix, as well as her play *Pantomine;* Man Ray's narratives to accompany *Revolving Doors* collages; writings by Walter Arensberg, Philippe Soupault, and Marcel Duchamp; and a drawing by Charles Sheeler. *TNT* had "a very radical slant . . ." Man Ray said, "it was a tirade against industrialists, the exploiters of workers. . . ." Working along parallel lines in New York City, Man Ray would have undoubtedly been attracted to the principles informing the Dada movement.

Man Ray had been an anarchist in art, too; a traveler with an unlimited passport, he had shifted styles and métiers in his search for the mode that most immediately expressed his needs. America may have remained untouched by the scourge in Europe, but Man Ray had sensed the ricochets of bullets and had given graphic vision to his own antiwar feelings—all long before a copy of Tzara's book, *La première aventure céleste de Monsieur Antipyrine* (The First Celestial Adventure of Mr. Fire Extinguisher) reached Marcel Duchamp, long before the first issue of *Cabaret Voltaire* magazine reached Marius de Zayas, long before Francis Picabia, on one of his frequent transatlantic voyages, brought news of happenings in Zurich to New York in the spring of 1917, imparting it over chess games and hors d'oeuvres at the Arensbergs.

Man Ray had had the Dada spirit long before the movement took brief but forceful hold in New York. He had pulled his new and important painting, *The Rope Dancer,* out of the first exhibition of the Society of Independent Artists at New York's Grand Central Palace that April, in protest against the Society's suspension of their jury-free "rule of no rules." They had rejected his friend Duchamp's readymade porcelain urinal, submitted as a sculpture by the pseudonymous "R. Mutt." What began with a radically democratic Academy-scoffing attitude that "every artist is welcome to show in alphabetical order" with no jury and no prizes ended, paradoxically, with much the same furor it had been designed to avoid. How far could the boundaries of freedom be stretched? In the spirit of Dada, upstart magazines like Picabia's *391*, *The Rogue* (Allen and Louise Norton's short-lived venture), *Rongwrong* (its title reputedly the result of a printer's error), and *The Blind Man* set out to document the rights of audacious artistry. "Whether Mr. Mutt with his own hands made the fountain or not had no importance," an anonymous writer scolded in *The Blind Man,* published predominantly as protest against the Society's actions. "He *chose* it. He took an ordinary article of life, placed it so that its useful significance disappeared under the new title and point of view—created a new thought for that object."

Man Ray and Marcel Duchamp were still far removed from calling themselves New York Dadaists. They did not need to. Duchamp chose a urinal—and a metal dog comb inscribed with a nonsense phrase, a ball of twine screwed between two brass plates, and an advertisement-sign for Sapolin Paint—and designated these objects, all assisted by him to a small degree, as phenomena to be intellectually considered and, perhaps, chuckled at. Man Ray went some steps further in his constructed pieces by depriving the viewer of emotional payoffs.

Man Ray's first efforts at object-making—mirrors that did not reflect, buttons that did not work when pressed—advocated a new idea of artistic freedom and became Dada after the fact.

THE *OTHERS* GROUP, RUTHERFORD, N.J., APRIL 1916.
FROM LEFT, SEATED: ALANSON HARTPENCE, ALFRED
KREYMBORG, WILLIAM CARLOS WILLIAMS, AND
SKIPWITH CANNELL; *STANDING:* JEAN CROTTI, MARCEL
DUCHAMP, WALTER ARENSBERG, MAN RAY (?), R. A.
SANBORN, AND MAXWELL BODENHEIM.
The Poetry/Rare Books Collection, University Libraries,
SUNY, Buffalo, New York.

MAN RAY,
PROFESSIONAL
PHOTOGRAPHER

BY THE TIME Man Ray and Adon moved, once again, to 147 West Eighth Street, their marriage was under strain. Economics played a part in the rift, for he was working only three days a week at McGraw. His growing interest in chess—under the tutelage of Duchamp—was also becoming a problem. Man Ray was spending many evenings away from home at the Marshall Chess Club on West Fourth Street. And up the street to the east was the formidable Brevoort Hotel. Louise Varèse remembered its quintessentially Parisian bar, a veritable "Paris in New York . . . the waiters were so [French] that they never bothered you but clustered together out of earshot to talk politics after they had put the bottle of whiskey or absinthe, with its ritual accessories, on the table, leaving you to pour your own drinks! and to uninterrupted conversation." There, around a table, Man Ray joined in the animated conversation of the wealthy dandy Francis Picabia—"*J'ai horreur de la peinture de Cézanne,*" was one of his more shocking pronouncements, "*elle m'embête.*" (I'm horrified by Cézanne's paintings; they bore me.)

Juliette Roche and Albert Gleizes, Joseph Stella, and the composer Edgard Varèse lived upstairs from the bar. Varèse became one of Man Ray's first formal photographic subjects. With his high forehead crowned by an abundance of wavy hair, dark skin, and thick brows curved over deep-set eyes, Varèse's face was imposing and strong, full of allure to Man Ray. "What interested me mostly were people," Man Ray recalled, years later, looking back on this bohemian period. "I didn't want to *paint* portraits anymore. . . . Portrait photography relieved my depression about painting, especially as I was being so attacked by the critics for doing abstract painting."

Man Ray began to bring subjects home to his studio, actually a corner of the living room, further disrupting a domestic scene made more problematic by Adon's flirtations with other men and her all-night absences and by Man Ray's bouts of self-destructiveness. He even went so far as to create a canvas titled *Suicide,* behind which a gun was to be rigged up, its trigger pulled by a string the despondent artist held. Such art was designed to eliminate, rather than imitate, life. Where once Man Ray's work and new acquaintances had been shared with his wife, they now became a mounting source of tension and rivalry.

Man Ray was not without woman friends. Through Duchamp, he met a shy, "thin, interesting and pallid young girl . . . her gaze fixed like the eye of a dazed camera . . ." who had arrived in Greenwich Village in February 1918, and was sharing a flat at 86 Greenwich Avenue with Djuna Barnes, Malcolm Cowley, and Kenneth Burke, paying six dollars a month for a triangular room. Her name was Berenice Abbott, and she had left home in Springfield, Ohio, to make the pilgrimage to the big city in hope of beginning a career as a journalist. Instead, she dropped out of Columbia University, worked as a waitress and yarn dyer, acted in minor roles at the Provincetown Playhouse in New York, and took up sculpting.

Man Ray, Duchamp, and Abbott used to go out drinking, dancing, and, as she said, "toot around the Village together and have fun." Abbott "admired Man Ray's work very much, especially his portraits of men." He was "a quiet sort, very gentle" to her, and she was in awe of his ability to achieve such results with a camera, especially since Man Ray did not have a dark room.

Berenice's roommate—before Abbott got her own place on "Clothesline Alley," off Christopher Street near Sixth Avenue—Djuna Barnes, managed to make a career for herself in newspaper writing. She began as a feature writer for the Brooklyn *Daily Eagle* and by 1916 was writing drama and short fiction regularly, like Alfred Kreymborg, for the *New York Morning Telegraph Sunday*

Magazine. Barnes was another important photographic subject, with her long neck arched swanlike, exquisitely chiseled profile, and ever-present cigarette in its holder. She would turn up at Man Ray's place with her good friend Mina Loy, also living in the Village, fair-haired and similarly aristocratic in bearing, dressed in light colors to contrast with the black Djuna wore.

With the departure of Duchamp to visit his sister in Buenos Aires and America's entry into the war, Man Ray's social life slowed down. He was lonely—his marriage had finally broken up—and retreated more deeply into his work. He welcomed the occasional weekend visits of his cousin, "Mage" Levinson, Jenny's elder son from Philadelphia, a lad nine years his junior. The two traveled up to Ridgefield for day trips, where Man Ray—still proud that "in under four minutes" he could produce evocative likenesses— dashed off multicolored pastel drawings down by the water, sketches of sailboats at rest offshore in the Hudson. Back in town, they strolled over to the chess club or rode the train to Brooklyn for a meal at the Rays', where Mage entertained the family after dinner with his syncopated piano playing. Man Ray tutored the boy in the mysteries of the new art and, in turn, asked his cousin for interpretations of particularly obscure works around the studio. No matter what reply was offered, if intelligently produced after careful thought, Man Ray's rejoinder was consistent. He smiled and said, "That's your opinion; that's good."

Man Ray had by this time made a permanent transition away from still lifes and toward graphic work in aerographs, especially, and portrait photography to maintain his cash flow. However, there remained at least one collector resolutely interested in the artist's Ridgefield period. Ferdinand Howald was a retired coal merchant from Columbus, Ohio, who when in town lived in an eight-bedroom apartment on West Seventy-second Street, which was filled with pictures.

"A florid gentleman," Man Ray observed, "with a white moustache, very distinguished-looking, not very talkative," Howald had been one of the earliest frequenters of the Daniel Gallery and was dedicated to supporting the young native modernists even while there was an overwhelming preference for the publicized French masters. Over the course of twenty-five years, drawing heavily upon Charles Daniel's collection, Howald amassed a huge and richly representative assortment of American art at its best: Demuths, Hartleys, Marins, Prendergasts—and Man Rays.

Early on, he purchased a simple yet deftly composed 1914 *Madonna,* a beatific smile on her averted face as she holds her infant, and several primitive object-studies that reflected the tranquil domesticity of life in the country, one complete with snoozing cat contentedly curled upon a pillow. Daniel later reflected that Howald was the kind of collector who "grew in his understanding of art. . . . If you told him something, he'd listen and mull it over." Retiring, sensitive, and courtly in manner, he was willing to progress in his tastes and actually did acquire, from Man Ray's third one-man show at Daniel's at the end of 1919, a fine aerograph, *Jazz*—a marked departure from previous affinities.

Howald did not actually meet Man Ray until a few days before the young artist left for Paris in July 1921, when they shared an important lunch in the paternal benefactor's opulent apartment.

For the time being at least, Man Ray's mind was made up: he "photographed what [he] did not wish to paint." And his photographic work during the final two New York years prior to his departure for Paris dealt with concerns he had addressed in his early paintings. Instead of sitting by the window of his Brooklyn bedroom and re-creating on canvas the vista of brownstones, fire escapes, and laundry hung out to dry, he turned his lens toward the backyard of his Eighth Street house, snapped a windblown procession of bedsheets fixed by clothespins billowing in the breeze, and called it *Moving Sculpture.* Instead of spiriting young women into his parent's home to paint from models, he photographed a woman with her left hand on her hip, dreamy eyes in soft focus half looking at the camera—and saved the image to use as a double-exposure backdrop for a portrait made during his first year in Paris. Where he might once have painted everyday domestic objects in a traditional still life, he wrapped a sewing machine in burlap, tied it tightly with string, and photographed the assemblage in homage to the memorable line in Lautréamont that Adon had introduced to him all those years ago—*L'énigme d'Isidore Ducasse* as the image was called.

Rather than asking his friend Berenice Abbott to come and sit for him over a period of days and different sessions, Man Ray took her picture as she looked at him over her left shoulder, capturing the mildness in her eyes and the slight petulance on her lips, melding little girl innocence with womanly awareness. He entered the print inconspicuously in John Wanamaker, Inc.'s, Fifteenth Annual Exhibition of Photographs in Philadelphia where, as *Portrait of a Sculptor* (for that is what Abbott was at the time; photography came later, under Man Ray's influence), it won honorable mention, a ten-dollar prize, and ran in the local newspaper. The lens allowed for a more empowering distance between the photographer and his subject, and Man Ray liked the feel of it.

A new Man Ray, the artist as professional photographer—for he had finally screwed up the courage to quit his job at McGraw and devote himself full time to portraiture and documentation—greeted Marcel Duchamp upon his return from a year and a half abroad. After Buenos Aires, where he had worked on drawings for *The Large Glass,* tried to put together a Cubist exhibition, and further polished his game of chess, Duchamp had moved on to Paris, taking up residence with Picabia and mixing with the Dada crowd. The Dada movement had traveled, too—from Berlin, Cologne, and Hanover to Paris. At the Café Certa, Paris's Dada watering hole, Duchamp had exchanged ideas with the writers André Breton, Louis Aragon, Paul Eluard (Eugène Grindel), Philippe Soupault, and Georges Ribemont-Dessaignes.

Duchamp brought back a distinctively Dada gift for his friends the Arensbergs, a glass ampoule from a pharmacy in which was forever sealed "50 cc. of Paris Air." To Man Ray, he presented a less tangible, far more important gift—inspiration, to push ever deeper into photography and explore its particular relevance to the documentation of Duchamp's renewed activities in New York. The two began an unbroken chain of collaborative projects.

As a warm-up exercise, Man Ray photographed Duchamp's studio. Dingy, other-worldly, and abandoned looking, the place retained an empty quality. Duchamp was absent from the picture but still provided atmosphere. *The Large Glass* had been positioned near the studio window, left open a few inches during the time Duchamp had been away, so that New York dust would pour in constantly and provide an urban coating to the work. "While the bride lay on her face decked out in her bridal finery of dust and debris, I exposed her to my sixteen-candle camera," Man Ray remembered, referring to the camera that he rarely took out of the studio, and "within one patient hour," while the two slipped out for a bite to eat, leaving the lens open and the glass illuminated by the light of a naked bulb hanging overhead, "was fixed, once and for all, the *Domaine de Duchamp.*" After the photograph was made, Duchamp carefully cleaned off the dust, except in one section where, he noted, he had mixed dust with varnish to create "an effect of blond, transparent cones which I never would have obtained with paint." To Man Ray, the finished image, with its slanted perspective, as if one were swooping down upon the thing from a great height, looked like a "picture taken from an airplane." Duchamp named the photo with emphasis upon the *process* that had given birth to the image in the first place: *Elevage de poussière,* or "Raising Dust," in the same sense, he said, as "Raising Pigs." Wrote Man Ray, twenty-five years after the fact, with glee, "Didn't we raise the dust, though, old boy!"

That was far from all. At Duchamp's studio, Duchamp and Man Ray built and then attempted to document—with nearly catastrophic results—the *Rotary Glass Plates,* Duchamp's first motor-driven artwork. Three progressively wider tiers of glass propellers, looking like a triple-decker windmill on its side, were mounted on a shaft to be whirred circularly by an electric motor. On each pair of glass "wings" were painted gently curving parallel lines, meant to create, once the wings were set in motion, the illusion of a spiral. Man Ray set up his tripod slightly to the right in front of the construction, and he managed to make an exposure when the apparatus was switched on. But the shaft revolved at such high speed that the elastic belt connected to the propellers snapped off, catching the glass and spraying splinters all over the room.

Besides "R. Mutt," Duchamp had yet another persona-project: the creation of a feminine alter ego, Rose (later Rrose) Sélavy (*c'est la vie*), who was Duchamp himself dressed in drag—complete with makeup, perfume, jewelry, and lavish furs. Rose Sélavy never appeared in public. She was a hidden, artificial person who existed exclusively in Man Ray's imagery, photographed *only* in his studio, but who did manage to create a number of artworks and readymades. Who was she, friends speculated—"a Mona Lisa taking the readymade existence of Duchamp? . . . a way for [him] to incorporate the Femme Fatale into himself? . . . a mediumistic being . . . from the labyrinth beyond time and space?"

Rose Sélavy's most celebrated appearance was as the bizarre cover girl for the one and only issue of *New York Dada* magazine, which Duchamp and Man Ray coedited in April 1921. Tristan Tzara was attempting to stir up greater interest in Dada on the American side of the Atlantic and had written directly to Man Ray earlier in the year, after a thick and fast correspondence with Walter Arensberg. While Duchamp insisted in the ultimate Dada manner that "Dada was nothing. . . . It is destructive, does not produce, and yet in just that way is constructive. . . ." Man Ray viewed Dada as "a state of mind . . . the tail of every other movement." He understood the nature of the beast and had himself adopted it. The magazine synthesized the different attitudes of the two friends. Duchamp-as-Rose graced the cover, in a portrait superimposed on a bottle of perfume. Stieglitz contributed a photograph of a woman's foot in a shoe that was clearly too tight, even while insisting he was "definitely *not* a Dadaist." Tzara came through with a lengthy "authorization to name your periodical Dada," saying that "Dada belongs to everybody. . . I know excellent people who have the name Dada. Mr. Jean Dada; Mr. Gaston Dada; Francis Picabia's dog is called Zizi de Dada . . . Dada belongs to everybody. . . Like the idea of God or of the tooth-brush . . ." and, Tzara added, he looked forward to the acceptance of Dada on the most universal and widespread level, nothing less than "Dada-globe."

In a send-up of the typical daily newspaper society page, readers of *New York Dada* were promised that at the forthcoming introduction of the Marsden Hartleys and Joseph Stellas to New York high-life, Mina Loy would preside, and "before the pug-debs are introduced," the article proclaimed, "she will turn a gold spigot and flocks of butterflies will be released from their cages. They will flitter through the magnificent [Madison Square] Garden, which has been especially decorated with dust for the occasion. . . . " On its fourth (and final) page—actually, the magazine was one large sheet folded—this unusual periodical displayed a raucous poem by Marsden Hartley in praise of *saltimbanques* (acrobats) and front and side views of the ubiquitous queen of New York Dada herself, the Baroness Elsa von Freytag-Loringhoven, star of the film coproduced by Man Ray and Duchamp, *Elsa, Baroness von Freytag-Loringhoven, Shaves Her Pubic Hair.*

"There was only one issue," recalled Man Ray. "The effort was as futile as trying to grow lilies in the desert." Two months after the magazine's publication, he reported to Tristan Tzara that " . . . all New York is dada, and will not tolerate a rival—will not notice dada—dada in New York must remain a secret." And in the last interview he gave in his life, to the collector and scholar Arturo Schwarz, Man Ray was asked if it was true, as he'd been indicating all along, that "there was no such thing as New York Dada." He replied, "Absolutely! There is no such thing. I would discourage it entirely. You can put me down as having said that. I don't think the Americans could appreciate or enter into the spirit of Dada. . . . They are on their own." It was more comfortable for Man Ray to deny the existence of the Dada movement than to admit that he preferred to maintain a stance outside it.

Perhaps Francis Picabia understood this aspect of Man Ray's personality—the artist off to the side—when he drew a schematic chart of the Dada movement, published in *Anthologie Dada*, Paris, 1919, in which more than thirty-five names were listed, beginning with Corot and Ingres (tradition breakers in their own right), spiraling all the way up to Tzara, Arp, Duchamp, de Zayas, Stieglitz, Arensberg—the whole gang, but Man Ray was not to be found, conspicuous by his absence. Katherine Dreier sensed this inclination away from groupism, when the inspired founder of the Société Anonyme in New York listed Man Ray in her first annual report of 1921 as among the artists "belonging to no school, but imbued with the new spirit in art."

With the inception of the Société Anonyme in the spring of 1920, the collaborative efforts of Man Ray and Marcel Duchamp achieved international proportions. Katherine Sophie Dreier, the organization's driving spirit, had been born in Brooklyn Heights, the daughter of the representative of a London iron merchant's firm. She grew up comfortably, attended art schools as a child, then Pratt Institute and studio classes in Paris. Two of her paintings were on view at the Armory Show. In addition to her love for art, she possessed a strong social activist streak, had been involved in the womens' suffrage movement, and worked tirelessly for more progressive labor legislation.

Dreier met Duchamp through the Arensberg group at the time that plans were being made for the Society of Independent Artists Exhibition, and, in the wake of the inflammatory "R. Mutt" incident, she tried to get Duchamp to reconsider his precipitate resignation. She also began to take French lessons from him, and she commissioned his last major oil painting, *Tu'm,* for her New

York apartment. Like Duchamp, Dreier traveled to Buenos Aires during the First World War. Later, she saw Duchamp in Paris while on a trip to Europe to see her German relatives. She was eager to meet dealers, visit galleries, and steep herself in new work, and Duchamp introduced her around, indoctrinated her into Dada, and took her to Rouen to meet his family.

Thus, Duchamp and Dreier were old friends by the time she conceived of a much-needed American organization predicated upon the slogan that "traditions are beautiful—but to create—not to follow." The statement had been made by German painter Franz Marc, founding member with Kandinsky of the Blaue Reiter group in Munich. The Société was dedicated to "heralding a new era in art" at a period when, Miss Dreier declared, "the men most sensitive to the coming new influences must in the very nature of things express themselves differently from the past." Dreier summoned Duchamp to her apartment at 135 Central Park West for a preliminary meeting to lay the groundwork for New York City's first "museum of modern art." Duchamp, in turn, did not make a move without his old accomplice, Man Ray.

Over cups of tea, Miss Dreier began the meeting by requesting suggestions for a name for this pioneer venture. She had seriously been considering "The Modern Ark," playing upon the symbolic implications of bringing art into the present moment, saving it from the flood tides of conservatism. Man Ray had an idea, too, having come across a phrase in a French magazine that intrigued him: Société Anonyme—which he thought meant Anonymous Society. Duchamp found this amusing, since in fact the expression was the French equivalent of *incorporated,* used in connection with large companies. The name stuck.

On April 29, 1920, the Société Anonyme was incorporated "to provide a public, noncommercial center for the study and promotion of modern art." The artist, not the art historian, was to be the chronicler of art's new era. The organization did not sell any works exhibited under its auspices, because Miss Dreier insisted upon its primary function as educational. But it would "gladly bring any prospective buyer directly in touch with the artist." Miss Dreier had rented three rooms in a brownstone at 19 East Forty-seventh Street, just across Fifth Avenue from the Daniel Gallery. The first exhibition took place there, that May and June. Duchamp supervised the interior decoration and Man Ray designed the lighting.

Five more shows followed, made up of works from Miss Dreier's collection, as well as loans from the Arensbergs, Arthur B. Davies, and other dealers in town. Der Sturm, the Berlin gallery, supplied additional works—including those of Paul Klee, Kandinsky, Campendonk, Gabo, Pevsner, Brancusi, and Schwitters.

In later years, Man Ray occasionally wondered why he had been so readily accepted as part of such a prestigious effort. It was clear from Marcel Duchamp's evaluation of Man Ray's work, published in the Société's first catalogue raisonné of 1949 (edited by George Heard Hamilton) that Duchamp saw, early on, the importance of his friend in the context of the Société's goals: "His paintings of 1913 and 1914 show the awakening of a great personality in his own interpretation of cubism and abstract painting," Duchamp wrote appreciatively and went on, "He took on photography and it was his achievement to treat the camera as he treated the paintbrush, a mere instrument at the service of the mind."

Miss Dreier understood that Man Ray was interested in photography as a means of making a living, and she took him at his word. His duties as vice president of the organization centered upon publicity. He designed the Société's banner, which hung proudly outside the building during exhibitions. And he photographed her own extensive art collection, as well as works on exhibit, which were then made into postcards for sale. Occasionally Miss Dreier had to remind Man Ray of approaching deadlines for shows—"I hope you can get up here soon to take the pictures," she wrote, in one rather snappy note. The few postcards that survive—*Figure,* by Duchamp's brother Jacques Villon; *Regarder d'un oeil, de près, pendant presque une heure,* Duchamp's miniature glass work; *Mlle. Brancusi,* by Constantin Brancusi; and Man Ray's own *Lampshade*—show that the images were primarily serviceable.

Lampshade, one of Man Ray's most whimsical efforts, was on display at the Société. An elongated spiral of paper hanging by an armature, the original artwork was supposedly inadvertently discarded by a janitor in the building the night before the exhibition was due to open in January of 1921. Miss Dreier was extremely concerned and, by Man Ray's account, was at a loss for how to replace the object. He then got the idea of dashing out to a tinsmith, creating a replica out of metal, and spray painting it white in time for the opening, or so he wrote with clear self-satisfaction in his autobiography.

But their correspondence reveals a different story: "I was wondering," Miss Dreier wrote to Man Ray on January 19, 1921, "whether it would not be better to make the Lamp Shade scroll out of metal, which would keep its form. You saw by the way it was shown yesterday that a certain limpness had gotten into the paper. . . . How much do you think it would cost to make this out of tin?" Miss Dreier ended up keeping the work for her personal collection. (It was placed on exhibition in a memorial show at Yale University Art Gallery in February 1953, after Miss Dreier's death in March of the preceding year.) She also owned a number of Man Ray's paintings, including his bird's-eye-view depiction of the Arc de Triomphe purchased in 1923, which also remained with her until her death.

It was a contentious though mutually respectful relationship. Thirteen years Man Ray's senior, portly and imposing in stature, blunt and authoritarian, Katherine Dreier was a woman used to getting her own way, possessed by a mission for her entire working life. Man Ray trusted her. In one of his rare bursts of self disclosure, at a particularly vulnerable time when he was making the transition from painting to photography and trying to justify it to himself as well as to others, Man Ray told Miss Dreier that he was "still in the experimental state in photography and the results are still largely accidental. This is also due to limitations under which I do the work." No doubt he was painfully aware of his poor circumstances, which prohibited him from having a darkroom and forced him to do all his developing at night. Perhaps, also, he was responding to one of her repeated proddings that he not forget his duties to the Société.

He went on, "I am trying to make my photography automatic—to use my camera as I would a typewriter—in time I shall attain this and still avoid the irrelevant for which scientific instruments have such a strong penchant. In working for the truth," the still idealistic Man Ray concluded, "one is apt to get too much of it, or get it a bit exaggerated."

When Miss Dreier trusted Man Ray to take more of a leadership role in the Société, however, the results could occasionally be less than she'd expected. On February 16, 1921, the Société opened the first one-man exhibition in America of the works of Russian-born American artist Alexander Archipenko. Man Ray, appropriately enough, was asked to speak at an inaugural symposium. As usual, he did not prepare formal remarks beforehand, but simply approached the podium as the event got under way, and launched into a circuitous story about his role as a photographer. "The other day," Man Ray told the assembled multitude of artists, critics, and general public, "while I was photographing other painters' paintings in the gallery, a man kept walking up and down in front of the camera, between the canvases and the lens." It turned out, Man Ray fabricated to his listeners, that the man's thoughts became imprinted upon the photographic plate! And, when developed, they were none other than "an attack on dealers, collectors, galleries, and people who live by the works of artists and never allow artists to make a living from it"—another sensitive issue for Man Ray, jobless, getting by on his wits and photographic aptitude. "The audience was entertained and not bored," Man Ray recalled, but Miss Dreier was not terribly amused. As soon as he had finished speaking, she got up and said, "Now I shall say a few *serious* words. . . . "

Nor was she very pleased when, under the official auspices of the Dada movement, Man Ray's friend Joseph Stella disrupted the gallery's first public gathering on April 1, 1921, by talking loudly during a reading of Swinburne. The woman who was lecturing was trying to make a case for the poet as primal Dadaist. "I wish that man," she announced indignantly, pointing to Mr. Stella, "would say something. He has been annoying me during my reading by laughing." All was not frivolity, however. Distinguished critics sympathetic to the Société's cause, like Henry McBride, Sheldon Cheney, and Christian Brinton, were active members and speakers. And Marsden Hartley's address on "The Importance of Being Dada," delivered for the occasion, was a well-considered and argued piece.

By June, Man Ray's path was becoming clear. His correspondence with Tzara was a lifeline pulling him to Paris, city of his childhood dreams. The art he had seen at the Société Anonyme's revolving series of shows was also seducing him. The museum was about to close up shop for a year and a half, while Miss Dreier traveled to Europe and China. Duchamp, his stays in New York City limited by the terms of his tourist visa, sailed mid-month for Paris on the SS *France,* off to stay with his repatriated friends the Crottis, expecting that Man Ray would soon follow.

Man Ray no longer had any entangling alliances with Adon

and was unemployed and fancy-free. Charles Daniel had had enough of his newfangled work and demonstrated no interest in photography. His old paintings no longer seemed to possess any relevance to Man Ray, who had feelings for only a few canvases. He made a house-of-cards funeral pyre with the landscapes and literally sent them up in smoke. Man Ray was drastically short of funds for his passage and, on the advice of Alfred Stieglitz, made a luncheon appointment with Ferdinand Howald, who agreed to give him five hundred dollars as an advance against the purchase of new paintings to be produced in Paris over the coming year. Neither man realized at the time that this would soon prove to be a point of friction between them.

It only remained to say farewells to the Ray family, now living in larger quarters on Kosciuzsko Street. The day before his ship was due to sail, Man Ray paid a quick call to Brooklyn, bringing his camera along. In the kitchen, Minnie did not even look up from her customary position bent over a large pot on the stove, as Man Ray captured Sam and Lena, married nearly six years now, with their two dark-eyed, dark-haired daughters—little Helen, a babe in arms, and her older sister, Selda, standing by. They were a beautiful tableau. Out in the backyard under a tree, sister Dora, also married, cradled her four-month-old daughter, Florence, as husband Israel Goodbread looked on with a smile. Ever mindful of her big brother's financial straits, and with a touch of regret that she very well might not see him again for a long time—if only she knew how long!—Dora slipped a five-dollar gold piece out of her dress pocket and gave it to Man. "For your trip to Paris," she whispered.

948. PARIS — *La Rue*
Campagne Première C. M.

Here's where I live
$25 per month *swell place!*

MAN RAY'S POSTCARD TO HIS PARENTS ANNOUNCING
THE MOVE TO 31 BIS, RUE CAMPAGNE-PREMIÈRE, JULY 1922:
"HERE'S WHERE I LIVE, $25 A MONTH—A SWELL PLACE!"
Private collection.

T O P|A R I S

MERVYN, THE adolescent hero of *Les chants de Maldoror,* embarked upon a voyage of discovery and growth made possible, he believed, only by the renunciation of "father, mother, Providence, love, and ideals." Man Ray, the young hero of his own self-created saga, resolved to plot his own course, and he set forth for Paris with little more than a hundred francs in his pocket, a steamer trunk filled with paintings, aerographs, and objects, a few carefully chosen glass photographic plates, and a brief note from Duchamp, promising that he would try to be at the train in Paris when Man Ray arrived and would try to gather some other friends, like Berenice Abbott. "I have arranged for a room for you in a little hotel where Tzara lives," Duchamp wrote Man Ray reassuringly, having laid the groundwork for his friend's arrival.

By the time Man Ray made his break for Paris, he was fully formed as an artist. He had been rigorously trained on native ground and gained some renown as a portraitist, painter, collagist, object-maker, and poet. Now, at the age of thirty, he was committed to leaving his past behind, traveling light in more ways than one. In subsequent years, when visitors to his studio probed his ethnic origins or took stabs at guessing his "real" name, he always made the same reply: "That's not me, I'm Man Ray."

His existential persona began to take form as he was on

shipboard. No one in Paris would know where he was born. His new acquaintances among the Dadaists would be told that he "almost was not born at all," a veiled reference to the odd circumstances of his parents' first meeting in America and their nearly immediate separation. This attempt to make himself anew was reflected in several references Man Ray made in early letters home to family and friends as feeling like "a new-born baby."

Like James Joyce's hero, Stephen Dedalus, Man Ray was trying to awake from the nightmare of history—in his case, attempting to spring free from *personal* history and the traditions of his background, free of entangling alliances, as John Russell has written, of "a certain rhythm of life, a certain circumambient culture; himself and one suitcase would have to be enough."

The day before his scheduled arrival at Le Havre, Man Ray wrote a postcard to brother Sam admitting that he was "just a bit lonesome." Their correspondence continued for much of the first year Man Ray was abroad; more often than not it had to do with the elder brother's constant need to replenish his funds. Man Ray was attempting to make a clean break from what his family represented, rather than from his family as people. That was a distinction easier to describe than effect. The first collage he made upon arrival in Paris was called *Transatlantique*. It showed a photograph of burned newspaper shreds surrounded by spent and broken matches above a section of a Paris street map. One can just barely discern the American text in the scraps of newsprint, not yet entirely obliterated.

Duchamp was at the Gare St. Lazare when Man Ray's train pulled in on the afternoon of July 22, 1921, and he took his culture-shocked, non–French-speaking pal to a Right Bank hotel at 12, rue des Boulainvilliers. The room cost all of three dollars a week. *"Je te remercie, mon vieux, je te dois beaucoup,"* Man Ray told Duchamp more than twenty years after the fact, remembering so well those first hours in a strange city, where he would have been lost without a guide. Their next stop after the quiet Passy neighborhood was the Café Certa, Dadaist meeting place, secreted away at 11, passage de l'Opéra, just off boulevard des Italiens. An expectant group, writers all, awaited the much-heralded new arrival from America: André Breton, Louis Aragon, Paul Eluard, Philippe Soupault, and Jacques Rigaut were the literary welcoming committee, *"Tous les critiques si bien disposés envers moi"* (All the critics who admired me so much).

Between sips of the Certa's renowned port wine, Soupault immediately broached the subject of having a Man Ray exhibition at his bookstore, the Librairie Six, on the avenue Lowendal, that coming fall, if it could indeed be pulled together by then. The refugee from "New York Chaos," Man Ray's pet name for the purported "New York Dada" movement, was thrilled at the prospect.

Man Ray spent his first several weeks getting acclimated geographically—"It's as difficult to get about in as Brooklyn," he wrote in a letter to Sam—and linguistically, with the help of Duchamp. He was particularly taken by café life, marveling at the cheap food and fast pace: "Everything is gay and moving, everyone is on the streets—it is a big Greenwich Village, but with wine and beer everywhere," he wrote Sam, after a visit to the Café Petit Grillon, another favorite Dada venue next door to the Certa. "If you don't order a bottle of wine with your meal, they think you're crazy—and so would I, now—when it's ten cents! . . . Something is surely going to happen to me soon," he went on. "People are more interested than I expected."

There was a lot to get used to in Paris beyond the high life—the food was good and inexpensive, and the jazz in "a real American negro club where they drink nothing but champagne" was the kind he had never heard the like of in New York. The conversation was heady—albeit interpreted by Duchamp. Deeper into the summer, on a visit to Marcel's family home at Puteaux, Man Ray was embarrassingly conscious that he was still not speaking French.

There was also, Man Ray soon realized, the volatile artistic-political climate. Dada was coming to an end. Superficial signs were already present: Tzara had been going head-to-head with Breton and insisted upon maintaining a more intentionally frivolous attitude toward the movement. The flamboyant half-Cuban, half-French Francis Picabia was also making a point of downgrading the "honest workman" attitude toward art among French painters. Picabia, who drove around town in his sleek, powerful car—one of a dozen of them he owned in his lifetime—and veered off into the countryside at a moment's notice, wasn't much for punctual attendance at meetings of the kind Breton favored. He was generous to Man Ray, supplementing the young American's income at a crucial time in his career by contracting him to photograph his burgeoning art collection.

The years 1922 to 1924, in fact, are often referred to in the history of the Parisian avant garde as *"l'époque floue,"* the "indistinct period of transition," according to William S. Rubin, "during which young poets dialectically transformed moribund Dada into the new movement." Philippe Soupault, looking back, pinpointed the period just previous to Man Ray's arrival as the most explosive time for Dada—when Tzara made his triumphant appearance on the scene and "critics, journalists, academicians, professors, mobs, middle-class Frenchmen, all were required to fall under his disquieting spell, placing all accepted values in question . . ."

Man Ray, so continuously dependent upon the kindness of strangers, could not afford to take sides, to alienate either Breton or Tzara. And even as the years in Paris passed, Man Ray was known as the one member of the circle who never feuded with anyone, the one member of the old guard even after it evolved, as it soon would, into the more codified Surrealist effort, who could remain on speaking terms with both Breton *and* Tzara. Man Ray did not feel threatened. The only American of the lot, he enjoyed privileged status, but never took advantage of it, except by ingratiating himself with people on all sides of the table.

Barely a month had passed since his arrival when Man Ray realized to his chagrin that he could no longer afford to reside at the hotel. Luckily there was a maid's room unoccupied on the sixth floor of 22, rue la Condamine, home of Yvonne Chastel (now divorced from Jean Crotti) where Duchamp had stayed during his temporary sojourn in Paris. Once again, Duchamp took Man Ray under his wing. Increasingly guilty about his need to live off others, Man Ray's preoccupation with his lack of funds made it difficult, at first, for him to concentrate on his work. And Mr. Howald was waiting, back home, for some signs that his investment had not been in vain: "I am not producing," Man Ray confessed, from his new digs, "but undergoing the painful process of acclimitization [*sic*]. . . ." He tried to take the philosophical high road in explaining his temporary idleness: "The clumsiness and awkwardness we see in many modern works," he advised Ferdinand Howald, "is the result of tackling a new view point, and not so much calculated—that is— in the best works. I have the same experience now in person. I am an infant here!"

It was an honest revelation. Man Ray was waiting for the new cultural stimulation to work its way through the receptive and fertile terrain of his imagination. Although living on the edge—pleading

MAN RAY'S STUDIO, RUE CAMPAGNE-PREMIÈRE, 1924–25.
ON THE LEFT WALL IS THE AIRBRUSH PAINTING, *SEGUIDILLA*,
1919; ABOVE THE CHAIR IS *PORTRAIT OF RROSE SÉLAVY*, 1923.
Collection Timothy Baum.

with his family in Brooklyn for a few more dollars and sleeping in a
borrowed room—Man Ray also possessed enough faith in his own
staying power to know that natural inventiveness and resourceful-
ness would eventually save him. The trick was not to make a false
step that might damage his credibility. He successfully negotiated a
series of additional payments from Howald, fifty dollars per month
over a six-month period extending into the new year—
demonstration, for the time being, of his benefactor's faith that
eventually Man Ray would snap out of his "down" period and
begin to produce innovative and original work. Should Mr. Howald
get the wrong idea, Man Ray assured his patron, "I love the
mellowness and finish of things here, and the sombre aspect does
not touch me. I have too much of America in me for that."

There was so much America in Man Ray, in fact, that his
initial attempts to find a gallery to represent him proved futile,
setting a pattern that persisted throughout his life as a working
artist. The exhibition at Librairie Six had been put off. It was still a
sure thing, but very much a one-shot affair. After all, Soupault was a
writer (Man Ray had published him in the short-lived *TNT* back in
New York), not a dealer. Man Ray approached the collector and
dealer Léonce Rosenberg to handle some work through his gallery,
L'Effort Moderne, but Rosenberg's priority remained art in the
classic Cubist vein, and he was not enthusiastic about Man Ray's
brand of American Cubism, the kind exemplified by the few pieces
he was able to bring over, and even less impressed by the
aerographs. Man Ray also received invitations, later in the fall, to
show in Brussels and Germany but was hesitant—again, displaying
sagacity even in the face of economic pressures—to leap into an
opportunity elsewhere in Europe, wanting to "make [his] first show
in Paris, so that [he] would not appear provincial. It must be New
York or Paris to begin with!"

Gabrielle Buffet-Picabia, like her husband, recognized Man
Ray's particularly marketable skills. Times may have been thin for
"real" art, but here was a top-flight photographer languishing. She
seized the moment, the onset of the fall couture showings, to
introduce her American friend to Paul Poiret, dress designer
extraordinaire. This was the man Janet Flanner was soon to acclaim
"the sartorial genius of Paris," one of the first couturiers to become
a perfumer as well, naming his two fragrances "Martine" and
"Rosine," in honor of his daughters.

A great entrepreneurial spirit, Paul Poiret had begun his career as an umbrella salesman and passed through several incarnations as playwright, painter, actor, merry-go-round designer, and theater owner, before opening his showroom. On its foyer ceiling was painted the constellations in the sky at the time of his birth. It was said of Poiret that every garment he wore was made to order, even his hats. He believed quite adamantly that fashion should be "the privilege of the elite."

Poiret was an eccentric original and Man Ray naturally gravitated toward him immediately. His first assignments, to photograph the offerings of the season, highlighted Poiret's expensive, opulent, Orientally influenced fashions: silk, crêpe, and lamé designs that were heavily decorated with satin, panther fur, beads, gilt, and tassels; and his scarlet, flowing tuniclike hand-painted gowns reminiscent of decadent harem life. In the years to follow, Man Ray was often called upon to photograph guests at Poiret's legendary dinner parties, affairs where the bejeweled aristocracy of Paris sat at seventy-five-foot-long tables and were serenaded by parrots.

A prominent sign hung over the entrance to Paul Poiret's private office in his *maison de couture:* "Stop and Think / Ask Yourself Three Times / If You Should Disturb Him." The forbidding message was an important one for Man Ray in his early days in Paris. He, too, eventually cultivated an intimidating mien designed to scare away the timid and challenge the bold. Poiret cut an imposing figure, full-statured, usually dressed in pastel-shaded suits, taciturn and brusque on first encounter, but capable of welcoming guests into the sanctum of his country home with charm and gourmet cooking. And visitors to Man Ray's studio invariably commented upon the gruff greeting giving way to warmth and even sentimentality as he understood they came to admire his work. In fact, people dropping by for short courtesy calls often found it difficult to tear themselves away, so insistent was Man Ray upon making them feel at home.

Yvonne Chastel lived in the exclusive Seventeenth Arrondissement on the Right Bank of the Seine, all the way across Paris from Montparnasse, which was fast becoming the American quarter. The area had gotten its name in the seventeenth century when students retreated to what was then a mere hill south of Paris to recite poetry freely in the open air. Located between the Observatory and the railroad station, not far from the old city walls, Montparnasse was the former home of Baudelaire, Verlaine, and Rimbaud, and now welcomed refugees from all countries. Man Ray, bent on assimilation, felt cut off from the community's creative atmosphere. To Sylvia Beach, proprietress of Shakespeare & Company, the bookshop on the rue de l'Odéon that soon became a showplace for Man Ray's portraits, Montparnasse was a "ghastly . . . hangout for pederasts." Apollinaire referred to it as *"le quartier de loftingues"* (the eccentrics' district). To André Breton and his more austere companions, Montparnasse "had a reputation for promiscuity and doubtful connections." And Virgil Thomson, one of the Americans descending upon Paris in those early years, shunned the quarter because it was too much like Greenwich Village. Indeed, the Café du Dôme, a cavernous meeting place for Americans on the boulevard du Montparnasse, strongly resembled an outdoor version of the Brevoort Bar on Man Ray's familiar Eighth Street.

Late in 1921, Man Ray decided to make his move, heartened by an upswing in his fortunes through the slow but steady growth of his reputation as a journeyman photographer. He took a room at the Grand Hôtel des Ecoles, 15, rue Delambre, in the very heart of Montparnasse. Gertrude Stein was one of Man Ray's first visitors there, and she commissioned him to be her "official" photographer (as well as portraitist of her beloved dog, Basket), a decision that ultimately landed them in an unresolvable dispute. "He lived in a cubicle-like small room," Stein wrote, under the byline of her companion, Alice B. Toklas, who accompanied her on the excursion to this out-of-the-way part of the city, "but I have never seen any space, not even a ship's cabin, with so many *things* so admirably disposed. He had a bed, he had three large cameras, he had several kinds of lighting, he had a window screen and in a little closet he did all his developing."

It was all very well and good, and necessary, to sit and sip at the Café Certa with the intelligentsia. But it was likewise comforting for Man Ray to know that just across the street from his hotel was the Dingo Bar, where Jimmy the Barman and his associate "Joe the Bum" made "lost generation" statesiders feel a little more at home. La Coupole, Le Select, La Rotonde, and Le Trianon were within walking distance, up and down the boulevard, or on nearby side streets. And the district's social life began to heat up the following year when Hilaire Hiler, a multilingual American painter and musician, opened his Jockey Club on the rue Campagne-Première. Hiler, who according to contemporary accounts looked "rather like a handsome frog, dark and sorrowful, with brooding eyes and a big mouth," could be found every night at the piano, regaling guests with vintage jazz songs imported from back home. *The Little Review* was making a reputation for itself as publishing the best avant-garde art and literature. Its editor, Jane Heap, claimed Hiler's club as her stomping ground, as did Mina Loy when she and her daughters, Fabienne and Joella, arrived in 1923, the widowed American patroness Mary Reynolds, and Duchamp as well.

Man Ray's first one-man show in Paris opened on December 3, 1921, a blustery, wet day. Thirty-five works, most of them brought over in his steamer trunk from New York, crowded the walls of the Librairie Six. Although attendance the first week was good, nothing sold. Paintings like *Legend, Love Fingers,* and *Percolator,* and aerographs like *Suicide, My First Born, Anpor, La volière,* and *Seguidilla* (this last published the previous month in Harold Loeb's new magazine *Broom*) made a gloomy impression. The stylish exhibition brochure featured a detailed map showing the exact location of the bookstore, and it included short statements by Man Ray "welcoming committee" members—Louis Aragon, Jean Arp, Paul Éluard, Max Ernst, Georges Ribemont-Dessaignes (an astute critic who was to write the first monograph on Man Ray's work), Philippe Soupault, Tristan Tzara—and the featured artist himself.
   "La lumière ressemble à la peinture de Man Ray comme un chapeau à une hirondelle, comme une tasse de café à un marchand de dentelle, comme une lettre à la poste" (Light resembles Man Ray's paintings the same way a hat does a swallow, a coffee cup does a lace salesman, a letter does the mail), Soupault free-associated. Man Ray, disinclined to go public with a philosophical blurb of the sort that used to grace his Daniel Gallery catalogues in the old days, jumped into the Dada spirit, too, with a mock recipe for a fish dinner made by carving up a *"carpe de Seine,"* and a description of a mock survey of 281 artists to determine how they were fed as babies: *"il n'y en a que 4 qui sont nourris au sein"* (only four among them were breast-fed). Not a word about his attitude toward art.
   There was an additional work, however, nestled among paintings, aerographs, collages, and objects, that was not listed in

the catalogue, because it was created spontaneously on the afternoon of the opening. Standing out in the gathering of the younger set at the Librairie Six that day was "a strange, voluble little man in his fifties," Man Ray observed, "who looked like an undertaker or an employee of some conservative bank" and who also, fortuitously, spoke fluent English. He was the avant-garde composer Erik Satie. As the afternoon wore on, the two men repaired to a nearby café to talk. His confidence boosted and imagination ignited by a few rounds of whiskey, Man Ray stepped into a hardware store on the way back to the gallery. "I picked up a flat iron," he recalled, and "asked Satie to come inside with me, where, with his help as an interpreter, I acquired a box of tacks and a tube of glue. Back at the gallery I glued a row of tacks [fourteen, to be precise] to the smooth surface of the iron, titled it *Le cadeau* [The Gift] and added it to the exhibition. This was my first Dada object in France."

In recollecting the event, Man Ray neglected to mention that he photographed the iron, a "gift" for poet Philippe Soupault, proprietor of the gallery, almost as if intuiting that something might befall it; by the end of the day, the object had disappeared. In fact, most of the hundreds of objects Man Ray assembled over the next fifty-odd years were created to be photographed. Once a record had been made, the object was either destroyed or "lost."

Simultaneously ominous and playful, *The Gift* is iconoclastic and important, but Man Ray did not want to take it too seriously. He was fond of saying that anyone could *make* an iron adorned with a row of tacks, but only one person could have come up with the original *idea*. In Man Ray's eighty-third year, an edition of five thousand *Cadeaux* was manufactured under his approval, signed, and sold for three hundred dollars apiece.

Man Ray's attitude toward objects was different from his friend Duchamp's. For Duchamp, it was usually enough to rest his "unaesthetic" attention upon the chosen, designated thing. However, for Man Ray, juxtaposition was the key: "I need more than one factor, at least two," he insisted. "Two factors that are not related in any way. The creative act for me rests in the coupling of these two different factors in order to produce a plastic poem." One need merely contemplate the laboratory retort filled with ball bearings, or the cello neck from which hangs a hank of horsehair, or the loaf of French bread painted blue resting on a scale, or the pipe rack interlaced with plastic tubing, to understand this statement. No

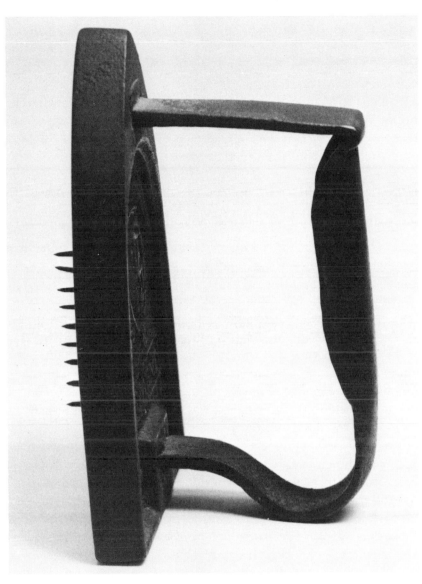

MAN RAY. *CADEAU* (GIFT), 1963. GALLERY IL FAUNO
EDITION OF 1921 OBJECT. FLATIRON WITH TACKS.
Courtesy Sotheby's, New York.

matter what he fabricated, no matter what the materials, Man Ray's objects, he said, were always "designed to amuse, annoy, bewilder, mystify, inspire reflection, but not to arouse admiration for any technical excellence usually sought or valued in objects classified as works of art."

Despite Man Ray's ongoing insistence that his objects had no import or intent beyond the immediate edification of the viewer (or the creator), *The Gift* does intrigue, particularly in light of Man Ray's conflict about the function of art in the marketplace. This commercial arena presented him with problems as he struggled to come to terms with creating art for making a living versus art as blessing, as an item for barter, as a simple, unadorned gesture. "Truth in making is making by hand," wrote William Morris, "and making by hand is making by joy." Man Ray, the tailor's son, had trouble keeping his restless hands still. When seated on a couch in a friend's living room, for example, he could not resist sketching a drawing of a nude upon the paper matchbook cover he was toying with, and presenting it straightaway to his hostess as a "gift." He delighted in the *act* of making, and in what the Germans call *sachlichkeit,* the rich "thingness" of the world around him. He encircled himself in what at first came across as a clutter of handmade furniture and gadgetry. It was only when the visitor to his atelier became properly oriented that he or she discerned the method in the madness, the reasons why Man Ray's objects, his "dumb, beautiful ministers" had to be in attendance. This was true *bricolage*—the term used to describe the skill that makes a billiard ball rebound from a cushion with sufficient force, which evolved to mean the surprising, imaginative use of the sort of objects that are likely to collect in an attic. Man Ray even went so far as to characterize this capacity to create *objets gratuits* as what distinguishes our species from others. Bricolage—tricky, quirky, spontaneous manipulation of familiar and mundane materials—allowed Man Ray to practice a democracy of ideas.

There was something inherently American about Man Ray's desire to subvert the utilitarian function of his objects. They often possessed a useful basis, and we find ourselves protesting—as the hardware-store owner remarked on that fateful December day— "But you'll ruin the shirt if you put tacks on there!"

Historically, *The Gift* anticipated André Breton's first *Manifeste du surréalisme* by a good three years. In that essay, the chief articulator of the movement spoke of "the poetic consciousness of objects" and endorsed the artistic rightness of "manufacturing objects seen in a dream." Breton always believed the proper province of Surrealist painting to be the replication of the artist's inner landscape.

The Gift likewise predated Fernand Léger's seminal essay of 1925, "The Machine Aesthetic: The Manufactured Object, the Artisan, and the Artist," in which the artist told his readers to pay more attention to "the arrangement of saucepans on the white walls of their kitchens," ultimately more worthy of artistic measuring than works housed in sacrosanct retirement "in the official museums." "Utility," Léger wrote, "does not prevent the advent of a state of beauty." Man Ray used utility as his springboard to the whimsical realm of improvisation: "Let us refresh ourselves with forms that are not Art," wrote the Dutch artist Theo Van Doesburg, pioneer of the De Stijl movement, in 1926, "The bathroom, the bathtub, the telescope, the bicycle, the auto, the flat-iron."

With a resilience fast becoming part of his new, cosmopolitan self, Man Ray accepted the complete lack of sales from the Librairie Six exhibition. This kind of failure was the emerging artist's rite of passage. He resolutely told Ferdinand Howald, eager for some word of his protégé's success, that "my exhibition . . . has placed me sort of apart from the huge mass of daubing that goes on here. Even the few recognized or 'arrived' painters regard me either in a spirit of conciliation or quiet fury. You have no idea," Man Ray the insider wrote Howald, "of the jealousy and intrigue that goes on here in the art world. But that is merely a sign of its vitality." He was toughening up—or at least doing a good job of sounding that way.

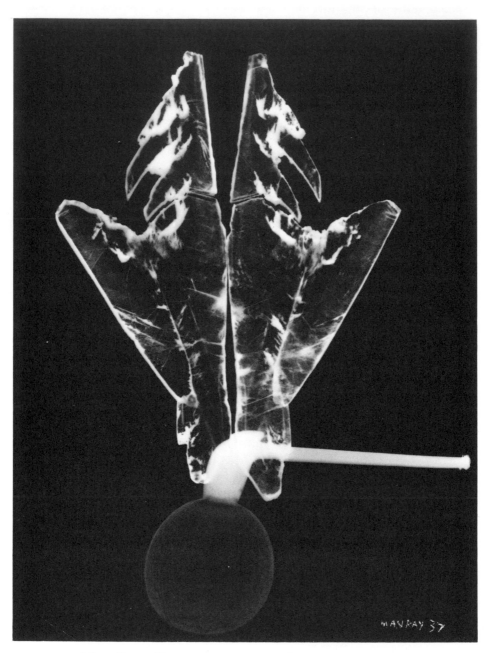

Man Ray. Rayograph, 1937. Incorporates the
clay pipe with glass bubble assemblage, *Ce qui manque
à nous tous* (What We All Lack), 1927–1935.
Private collection, Berkeley, California.

P A I N T I N G
W I T H
L I G H T

IN THE NEW year, Duchamp departed on the SS *Aquitania* for New York to make contact once again with *The Large Glass,* eternally awaiting him there. *"J'ai fait revenir mon verre et je travaille un peu dessus"* (I've reacquainted myself with my glass and I work a bit on it), Duchamp wrote Man Ray after his arrival in the States. The guardianship of the American-in-Paris shifted to Tristan Tzara, who moved into a room on the same floor as Man Ray in the Grand Hôtel des Ecoles. *"Embrasse Tzara pour moi"* (Hug Tzara for me), Duchamp concluded his newsy note, satisfied Man Ray was well provided for spiritually, even without the protective Rose Sélavy.

Tzara was as single-mindedly dedicated to his poetry as Man Ray was to his new artwork. Gertrude Stein saw the two men as birds of a feather. It was not simply because they were both of Jewish origin, barely over five feet tall, and given to effervescence and warmth, or that they saw eye to eye on artistic matters and preferred to err on the side of humor. Tzara possessed a streak of healthy self-deprecation that appealed to Man Ray. He knew when it was better to laugh at himself than to keep his dissatisfaction pent up within. As he himself expressed in an autobiographical poem:

> Take a good look at me!
> I'm an idiot, a clown, a mystifier!
> Take a good look at me!

> I'm ugly, I have an inexpressive face,
>   I am small.
> I'm like all of you!
> I wanted to give myself
>   a little publicity.

That winter of 1921–22, Tzara was the first person to lay eyes on one of Man Ray's most sensational discoveries. Although for several months it had no name at all, this groundbreaking new image ultimately became known as the "rayograph." Developing contract fashion work for Paul Poiret, at night as usual, Man Ray "mechanically placed a small glass funnel, the graduate and the thermometer in the tray on the wetted [with developer] photographic paper." When he turned on the light in the tiny bathroom adjacent to his bedroom at the hotel, "an image began to form, not quite a simple silhouette of the objects as in a straight photograph, but distorted and refracted by the glass more or less in contact with the paper and standing out against a black background, the part directly exposed to the light."

Man Ray, of course, did not invent the photogram process. William Henry Fox Talbot in England in 1835 had been the first to make what he called "photogenic drawings," or cameraless photographs, harnessing the energy of sunlight on a sheet of fine paper spread with nitrate of silver to cause, he wrote, "natural objects to delineate themselves without the aid of the artist's pencil." The shadowy traces of a fern leaf would leave their ghostly impression where the sun's rays could not go. In 1918, Christian Schad had created contact prints with flat objects laid directly onto photosensitive paper. One of the major qualities distinguishing static "Schadographs" from Man Ray's technique was the factor of motion. Man Ray not only moved the light source, shining it at angles through objects, he also shifted the objects around in space above the paper, adding dynamic depth and a variability of tone often including all manner of grays, not simply blacks and whites.

Man Ray had learned from Alfred Stieglitz long ago that what others supposed to be the limits of the photographic medium should never be accepted. While he may not have made photographs in the *style* of Stieglitz, Man Ray was influenced by Stieglitz's urge to challenge the givens of picture making, to go beyond the limits of what camera and film were thought capable of by the keepers of the status quo. Stieglitz's unforgettable image of a snowstorm on Fifth Avenue in the dead of night provided the basis for Man Ray's studies of the boulevard Edgar Quinet. Stieglitz's example had enlarged photography for Man Ray. Now, in a cramped hotel bathroom, the young photographer punctuated the plane of the paper, dispelled whatever impression of flat imagery remained, and veered into unplotted spatial territory, making light an instrument as subtle as the brush had once been in his hands.

The first rayographs were tantalizing enigmas, combining household imagery of the kind Léger referred to—drinking glasses, kitchen utensils, combs, keys, a grater, tongs—with unrecognizable objects, all seeming to float in amniotic fluid, unborn, coalescing, mysterious, but never horrifying. Rayographs were, by their nature, made rapidly and repeatedly, as the effect could be determined in a matter of seconds. Once the exposed paper was dipped in the developer and had the chance to swim there, and the image rose gradually to the surface, awakening, Man Ray would decide if it bore any resemblance to what he had hoped for. Or he might throw some items together without a care for the result and be pleasantly surprised. There was, in any case, no such thing as a "mistake."

The dark bathroom where Man Ray worked in solitude was a place filled with a continuing sense of discovery. His efforts were powered by the potential for endless variation. His options were infinite. He flashed the light sources off and on and played light over the objects from above and from the side. He might begin by placing all the objects in the planned scene upon the paper, then, by removing them one by one, create a spectrum of ghosts and shades. He might leave the emerging print in the developer for varying periods, thereby influencing the degree of contrast in the final image. He might discover that only the top half of the photogram held an image worth keeping, in which case he was free to print, trim, and rephotograph it and reprint only the desired area. The "instantaneous" impact of the rayographs was often a well-crafted illusion, the result of many tries. All his instincts came into play, and play it was, as Man Ray became caught up in the thrill of being able to determine what he had made more quickly than in any easel painting. Painting now seemed static, primitive, and tame. To Man Ray, the chemical factor was paramount, the idea that the selected "objects were consumed by flames ... oxidized residues fixed by light...," that in fact images were seared into paper by a convulsive interaction of silver and salts, light and water.

Tristan Tzara brought all his verbal gymnastic skills to bear upon Man Ray's photograms: "Is it a spiral of water or the tragic glitter of a revolver, an egg, a shimmering arch, or a dam of reason, a thin ear with a mineral whistle or a whirlwind of algebraic formulas?" he speculated wildly. Tzara had seized upon the iconographic rhythms in Man Ray's work: the spiral, always a favored image, a symbol of cyclical continuity; the revolver, first apparent in Man Ray's 1920 photograph, *Compass,* then in the *Suicide* picture; the egg, to Man Ray the most perfect form in nature. All these "deformations," Tzara went on, were "filtered like hair through a comb of light . . . the projections, surprised in transparency, in the light of tenderness, of dreaming objects that are talking in their sleep."

To the visionary Tzara, there were "submarine views, pebbles of clouds, flights of sharks through waves of applause, retinas of sails, dawns of crustaceans in glass . . . crumpled papers that disturb the stars . . ." in Man Ray's flights of photographic fancy. Tzara was extreme and eloquent in his praise, as was another poet-friend of Man Ray, Robert Desnos, whose poems would soon serve as inspiration for the photographer's audacious film work. Writing in the Parisian newspaper *Le Journal,* on December 14, 1923, Desnos described Man Ray as a kind of prophet, a guide to heretofore restricted and concealed perceptual universes: "Following him, we will descend these toboggans of flesh or light, these pointed slopes, we will search for the key to hidden cellars."

The 1920s are understood to have been a time when the race to be first in everything reached manic proportions. In the early years of the decade, even as Man Ray was taking his exploratory steps away from painting and into photography, Laszlo Moholy-Nagy, the Hungarian Constructivist abstract painter working in Berlin, and his wife, Lucia, were making photograms in a more static style, likewise using ordinary kitchen objects as the basis for their imagery. Fifteen years later, Moholy would say that he had become caught up in "the great responsibility of the real photographer," but his initial flirtations with the medium emphasized its explosive potential. In the middle twenties, in fact, during his Bauhaus years (1923–28), Moholy moved on to reject "all hand-produced textures, gave up painting, and called for 'drawing with light,' 'light in place of pigment.'" In a letter to Beaumont Newhall on April 7, 1937, Moholy stated that he "made [his] first photograms in 1922," giving them to Harold Loeb and Matthew Josephson to be published in Paris in their magazine *Broom,* "because they heard from Tristan Tzara that I made photograms. I did not know in this time," he went on, apparently wanting to set the record straight, "neither about Talbot's and others' shadowgraphs nor about [Man

Ray's] Rayographs." Contrary to Moholy's recollection, Tzara had indeed taken some rayographs to Moholy to show him. And five years after the letter to Newhall, Moholy slightly modified his earlier version, saying that "Man Ray and I, independent of each other, reinvented the photogram. . . . Reversing the habitual way of selecting photographic views for their black and white values . . . a new hidden world arises out of night scenes, settings in contrasts, glowing with sublime magnificence, a play of radiating light sources enveloping the objects with an aura. . . ." Finally, in Chicago, dying of leukemia, asked by his friend, the art critic Katharine Kuh, if he had been "influenced by Man Ray," Moholy-Nagy replied, "Very much."

"*Je suis enchanté,*" Duchamp wrote Man Ray from New York, "*de savoir que tu t'amuses bien et que surtout tu as lâché la peinture*" (I am pleased you're having such a good time, and that, above all else, you've dropped painting). With impetuous excitement, urged on by Tzara, Man Ray had related the news of his latest discovery to his friend across the seas. He had wanted Duchamp's endorsement and had gotten it. Marcel was never one to criticize another's work, and with Man Ray he exhibited even more than his customary restraint.

Man Ray was far less ebullient in telling Ferdinand Howald of his latest photographic adventures: "You may regret to hear it," he eased his way in by saying, "but I have finally freed myself from the sticky medium of paint, and am working directly with light itself. I have found a way of recording it. The subjects were never so near to life itself as in my new work." Then, digging an even deeper hole, Man Ray observed that if he could "make an income and have a couple of friends to enthuse with me over ideas and things, I should never enter the art market and never exhibit."

Howald shot back with a burst of admonition and advice. Expressing polite, cautious interest in Man Ray's "new process," he warned the young man against casting aspersions, as he had been of late, on Charles Daniel, one of Man Ray's earliest supporters. "The dealer cannot *make* people buy pictures," Howald wrote. And he went on, very tellingly, "I think you will be well-advised to exhibit in New York as frequently as possible. The American artist living abroad by dropping out of sight drops out of mind, unless he shows his work often." How true those words turned out to be in the decades to come, as the subtle balances of achievement and failure in Man Ray's diverse career tipped this way and that.

For the present, Man Ray had no choice but to defend himself against Howald's well-reasoned but nevertheless stinging rejoinder. He hoped it would matter to his patron that none other than Jean Cocteau, after seeing the rayographs, had gone on record that Man Ray had "delivered painting . . . set painting free again." It must also mean something to Mr. Howald that just the previous week, the illustrious editor of *Vanity Fair* magazine, Mr. Frank Crowninshield, had paid a call to the cramped studio and handpicked four recent works for the forthcoming November issue. And surely Mr. Howald would be impressed to know that *Les feuilles libres* magazine in Paris had just published another new work, which, Man Ray tried to explain yet again, "looks like photography. . . is done with photographic materials . . . without a camera." Man Ray had hoped that Howald would continue to choose freely from the stock of canvases left in the back room at Daniel's place. Howald eventually did so, but not before expressing dissatisfaction that there was clearly not going to be any fresh work in that genre for the foreseeable future.

On December 7, 1921, Man Ray was in the capacity audience at Adrienne Monnier's bookstore across from Sylvia Beach's place on the rue de l'Odéon, when James Joyce read selections from his soon-to-be-published novel, *Ulysses*. The crowd had been duly warned by Valéry Larbaud "that certain pages to be read are bolder than is common and might justly offend readers." Poet, Whitman aficionado, and creator of the fictional A. O. Barnabooth, Larbaud translated Joyce's words into French, as the Irishman declaimed in his nasal, tenor voice.

In the new year, Miss Beach, who was Joyce's publisher, sent him over to Man Ray to have his portrait made for wide distribution. Joyce was uneasy in the presence of the camera. Still recovering from an eye operation (followed by no-less-arduous leech applications around his eyes), he wore thick glasses and, in a gesture of tiredness and frustration, shrouded his averted eyes with his hand. When Joyce did manage to look into the camera, it was with a furtive glance. Posed before a simple burlap curtain, his dark suit and bowtie set in relief by its muted tones, the author comes across as appropriately pensive.

What was Man Ray's portraiture method, he was often asked. How did he "get" that essence of the person into his work, time after time? Speed was one key. He had been schooled by Robert Henri in quick portraiture and was completely prepared when the subject arrived: lights in place, camera standing on its tripod a fair distance from the chair, so as not to intimidate. Man Ray did not overly instruct the sitter. He told Gertrude Stein, for instance, that she could "move all she liked, her eyes, her head, it is to be a pose, but it is to have in it all the qualities of a snap shot." Other friends such as the English painter Roland Penrose recalled that sitting for Man Ray "was as quick and casual as bantering with him in a café. All he used to say was, 'Show your teeth' . . . he didn't fiddle forever with the lens or the lights," but he never said, "smile" per se, however, knowing that command invariably gave rise to a stilted grimace.

Man Ray the portrait photographer projected a calm exterior, a quiet authority. He always remained self-possessed, giving the impression of knowing precisely what he was doing as he labored to make his work natural. "This method," he wrote, "is the only one that gave me good results; the only thing is, that it sometimes takes years of study to know how to recreate unaffectedness!"

Man Ray often fell back upon "hunting" expressions on those rare occasions when he did convey what was going on in his mind during a session. He stalked his prey subtly, quietly, motivated by deep curiosity about the structure of the human face, caring little about his subject's thoughts, fame, or fortune. His mind-set was that of the sportsman out for a day in the field. He preferred not to "give the impression of working. When my clients leave my studio they often tell me, 'I never had such an easy sitting.'"

Man Ray's off-the-cuff sensibility opted against "finish," against *"la belle matière,"* and in favor of the quality he most admired about Matisse, the painter who did not *"fignoler"* (touch up) or become finicky with his paintings. Man Ray used soft, coarse-grained, rough-surfaced paper to achieve a down-to-earth cast to the photographic image. Better, he felt, to spend more time in the darkroom later or on the setup beforehand—just lounging, smoking his pipe, as he often did before a subject arrived, playing the session through mentally before it occurred—than to create an anxious atmosphere with the other person present in such an intimate way. Paul Poiret also noticed the effectiveness of this technique in the fashion context, where timing was of the essence, for Man Ray was more concerned with getting the model's facial expression into a "ravishing, divine" ambience that would then succeed in glorifying her body.

In many of Man Ray's best portraits, there is a predominance of grays, middle tones resulting from overexposure, which he believed was "very kind to the face." Man Ray shunned the darker end of the spectrum, observing that "blacks give no more strength to a photograph than 'strong' drink gives strength to a man. I have never put any alcohol in my image. An image is not a cocktail."

He exhibited consistent and marked disdain for fancy technology, too. In a letter to Katherine Dreier, Man Ray once compared the camera to "a typewriter." Another day, he compared it to "an old shoe." Late in life, he delighted in asking his students—excited about a well-turned image they'd produced with their spanking-new cameras—whether they were certain they'd done the work, or had it been "Mr. Zeiss"? "It's not the equipment that matters," Man Ray was fond of saying, "it's the person who pushes the button."

Man Ray's personality and sensibility meshed with the medium beautifully. Roland Barthes has written of the "great portrait photographers as great mythologists." Man Ray was in the process of mythologizing his past life as he moved more deeply into photography, and the other-wordly tone of his early portraits, their ever-so-slight haziness, made his subjects look as if they had sprung from a past of the photographer's fabrication.

Like his nineteenth-century predecessor, the great photographer Nadar (Gaspard Félix Tournachon), Man Ray captured the likenesses of the young artists and writers of the bohemian crowd who flocked to his door. He had a talent "to produce an intimate likeness rather than a banal portrait, putting himself at once," as Nadar insisted, "in communion with the sitter."

The photograph was a document. Man Ray began as a record keeper of other artists' work, then made the natural transition to record keeper of Paris in the 1920s. He referred often and proudly to his voluminous "files," claiming to have "taken" virtually everyone of note in town or passing through. There were even Americans in London who advised travelers on their way to the Continent to seek out Man Ray.

Beyond keeping a faithful record of an experience, photography served the purpose of keeping the photographer, himself, at a well-defined distance from his subject. The photographer needed to interpose that distance in order for the image to be successful. Contemporaries remember Man Ray as quiet, reserved, always "around," but often in the wings, certainly capable of having as good a time as the rest of them. He was more at ease in his studio, where the balance of power was in his favor. Man Ray's camera served as protection, a kind of social insulation. He seemed prescient during shootings, as if he knew before snapping the shutter what would work and what would not. Even when others took pictures of him, Man Ray would call the shots, laughingly predicting when an exposure would not come out. And he was invariably right.

The photographer was endlessly engaged in decision making. More than the desire to exercise control, Man Ray craved the restless mental state, the fluidity of ideas, apertures, focal lengths, judgments of light and shadow interrelating with each other. His live American intellect had an antipathy to idleness.

During his first year and a half in Paris, Man Ray photographed Gertrude Stein, James Joyce, Henri Matisse, Francis Picabia, and Fernand Léger. Toward the end of 1921, Ezra Pound moved to Montparnasse, taking a flat on the rue Notre Dame des Champs, and working on his long poem, *The Cantos*. Pound and Man Ray were cordial neighbors, little else; but other authors were to become steadfast friends and subjects—among them, Paul Eluard, who collaborated with Man Ray in 1937 on *Les mains libres,* a book of drawings with poems based on them. Eluard later joined the Communist Party and then the Resistance during World War II. Raymond Radiguet was another early subject. Touted as "the new Rimbaud" in the 1920s, the novelist killed himself in 1923 after producing two brilliant works of fiction by the age of twenty. Max Jacob, poet and painter, close friend of Picasso and Apollinaire, looked dapper in his tweed jacket and dark vest, bushy eyebrows raised inquisitively over his bright eyes, domed forehead fairly bursting with ideas. Picasso and Braque were photographed in their studios. Composer Francis Poulenc chose to stare straight at Man Ray, right hand against his cheek, the familiar burlap cloth behind him.

By early summer 1922, Man Ray had photographed the Marquise Casati, unintentionally double-exposing her face so that it looked as if she had two pairs of eyes—so thrilling her that "she ordered dozens of prints and sent them . . . all over Paris; sitters began coming in—people from more exclusive circles." Man Ray's career finally developed enough momentum to allow him to move out of the Grand Hôtel des Ecoles, and over to 31 bis, rue Campagne-Première, a large mansion at the corner of the boulevard Raspail conveniently situated next to the Métro station. His studio there consisted of one large room with plenty of natural light and a staircase leading up to a balcony, off which there were a bedroom and darkroom, where his assistant—for it wouldn't be long, another year, before he was able to hire the first of many helpers—could make prints while he busily photographed. All in all, "a swell place," he wrote in a quick postcard to his parents.

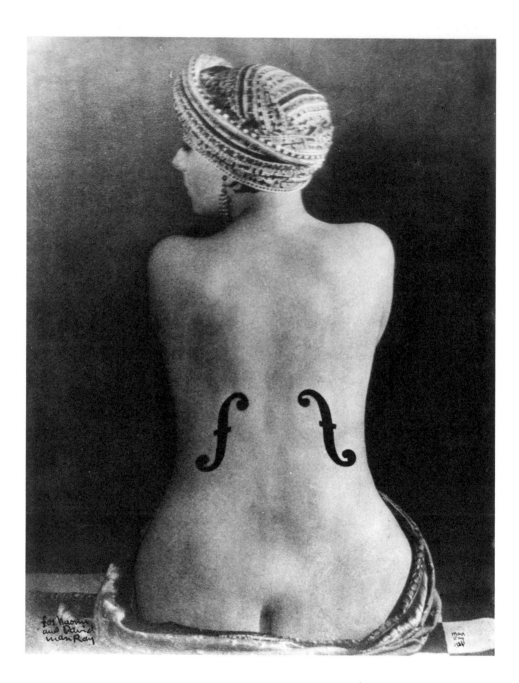

MAN RAY. *LE VIOLON D'INGRES*, 1924.
Collection Naomi and David Savage.

LOVE AFFAIR
WITH THE
FEMALE FORM

M A N   R A Y could not believe the torrent of invective pouring from the rosebud lips of the woman across the café on the avenue du Maine, where he sat drinking with his friend, the artist Marie Wassilieff. Evidently the *patron* had informed that beauty with the dark, sculptured coiffure that she and her friend were improperly attired—no hats, alas—and would have to leave. Man Ray heard the word *merde* more than once, and as glasses and chairs were tossed, he intervened, saying he knew the two women, and he invited them to sit at his table.

Meeting Kiki—for that was her name around the quarter, Marie told Man Ray—completed Man Ray's initiation. After dinner at La Rotonde, they took in a movie, *Folies de femmes,* by Eric von Stroheim, during which, like a smitten teenager, he furtively grasped her hand in the darkness. That night, Man Ray also learned the story of Alice Prin, who was like him a name-changer, a chameleon personality. She had been born October 2, 1901, in Châtillon-sur-Seine, Burgundy farm country. She was fond of saying her mother literally bore her on the street, and there Kiki remained, urchinlike, for the rest of her life.

One of six daughters, she never knew her father and had been raised by kindly grandparents. Her sorely pressed mother went off to Paris, sending money back home periodically. By the time she was twelve, Alice, too, had made the voyage out, and she became accustomed to hard labor. She scrounged jobs at factories during the war years and worked at a bakery. By the age of seventeen, she had become Kiki of Montparnasse, a familiar gamine at La Rotonde, dressed up in men's clothing (which gave her a Chaplinesque aura). Artists bought her drinks and quick meals of fried eggs when she was starving, and she posed for them in their studios— Mendjinski, Kisling, Foujita, Utrillo, Soutine. Her body was like a Maillol sculpture. She was firm and petite, her breasts beautifully rounded. In one of Kisling's portraits—she posed for him more than a hundred times—Kiki's brow is fringed with her trademark crown of dark bangs, and her head is tilted as she peers coquettishly upward. To the Norwegian painter Per Krohg, she was more seductive, her tiny lips pursed pouting, and one leg jauntily propped against the base of a fountain of Pan, to whom she bears no small resemblance. Foujita was drawn to her wide-set eyes and aquiline nose. He pulled her hair back behind the ears to emphasize Kiki's high cheekbones and pure skin tones.

Kiki loved to *feel* love. "*Je me tue avec l'amour,*" she told Man Ray. She might give herself to a man if it meant she didn't have to return late at night to her tiny, subterranean room on the rue de Vaugirard. She, too, was an exile from a simpler life, and she wanted to be held. All the better if she served as some kind of muse for these artists who prostrated themselves before her insolent, cheery beauty.

Man Ray sensed that Kiki's loneliness would connect with his own. The night they met, he presented himself to her as a photographer, the first artist she'd known who was not a painter. "La lumière peut tout faire," he told her in his broken French. "L'ombre travaille pour moi. Je fais l'ombre, je fais la lumière; je fais tout avec le caméra." (Light can do everything. Shadows work for me. I make shadows. I make light. I can create anything with my camera.)

Despite his entreaties, Kiki was reluctant to pose for Man Ray. Perhaps she feared the machine he'd use to capture her image. Yes, his odd accent pleased her, she thought, but he had a mysterious air. Yes, he was soft-spoken, but he could also be distant, "dreaming of new ways to take pictures," not focused enough on her as a woman.

When she finally emerged from behind the screen in his studio, modestly trying to cover herself with her hands, Man Ray saw the source of Kiki's hesitation, the secret she'd been hinting at: she had no pubic hair. He draped the lower part of her body with a petticoat and asked her to raise her right arm and rest it crooked against the side of her head, one of his favorite poses, reminiscent of antiquity, accentuating the curve of her body and right breast; the other arm curved down across her belly, her left wrist adorned with a single gold bracelet shining dully against the white fabric. Her shyness mirrored his, and the confidence just barely peeking out from beneath that reserve reflected Man Ray's, too. In the studio she was less brazen, the private Kiki, the Kiki he loved. She lived with him for six years, and, though they never married, she showed her sense of belonging by referring to herself as "Kiki Man Ray."

The public Kiki also came under Man Ray's stylizing spell. He took her many steps beyond the primitive charcoal eyebrow-pencil she used for makeup as a teenager. They followed the same ritual every night before going out. After her obligatory hour-long bath, he designed Kiki's face and painted it on with his own hand. First Man Ray shaved her eyebrows completely, and then he applied others in their place, varying the color, thickness, and angle according to his mood. Her heavy eyelids, next, might be done in copper one day and royal blue another, or else in silver or jade. A tiny cap with a brocaded veil, a beaded dress with a plunging neckline—a rose positioned strategically, to be removed at the height of the festivities and placed between her gleaming, perfect teeth—would complete the preparations, and they'd be ready, invariably accompanied by Kiki's steadfast companion Thérèse Treize. Thérèse and Kiki met during the three-day national holiday festivities during the summer of 1922, and Thérèse took a room near Kiki and Man Ray's in the Hôtel Istria, at 29, rue Campagne-Première, next door to the studio. When Man Ray was off on fashion shootings out of town, Thérèse shared Kiki's bed. Nights in Paris when the three of them were together, accompanied by Tzara or Robert Desnos, their haunt was Hilaire Hiler's Jockey Club at the end of the street. Kiki played chanteuse and Thérèse passed the hat.

Outside, the Jockey was distinctive, its huge, modernist murals painted by Hiler himself, depicting Indians with feathered headdresses astride rearing steeds. Inside, the dance floor measured little more than a few square yards. To Hiler's piano accompaniment, Kiki belted out peasant songs from Guernsey and her native Burgundy "in a voice as hoarse as that of a vegetable hawker," the writer Kay Boyle observed, "her hair smooth as a crow's glistening wing." One might find in the smoke-fogged room Montparnasse luminaries as various as Jean Cocteau, Ezra Pound, and interior designer Curtis Moffat united in their adoration of the one and only Kiki. "Viens par ici / Viens mon p'tit homme," she sang to them,

> Y'a pas trop de merdes
> On n'y voit rien,
> mais tu verras,
> je serai cochonne,
> t'amuserai bien!

(Come closer, come here, my little man; there's nothing can harm you; I may not look like much, but you'll see, I can get sleazy, I can show you a good time!)

When she wasn't thrilling the arty set, Kiki would break from the mob, rejoin Man Ray and Thérèse at their table, and count her money. She felt free at any time to interrupt a conversation with her own loudly expressed opinions. She could leap across tabletops with the ease of a gazelle, and, through it all, Man Ray remembered fondly, "She was incorruptible, had her steady man, and sang for the fun of it."

Behind the artful, kohl-decorated mask was always a vulnerable child. Behind the model's bravado and the showiness of the performer, lay a shy, insecure little girl, desperate to please people. "Life is *au fond* so limited, so *diabolique* . . ." she told Djuna Barnes once, in a rare confession of unhappiness.

Man Ray had found more than a model and mistress who adored and inspired him. In the early 1920s he still spoke French idiomatically, and visitors to his studio or friends who spent an evening with the couple recalled Kiki as an invaluable "bedside dictionary." In the late fall of 1922 Man Ray fell seriously ill. He told his parents it was merely "a nasty cold," but in fact he was severely depressed, even to the point of considering suicide. He was fortunate to have Kiki by him to bring him things to eat, heat his studio, cook his meals, and fetch the daily papers.

Thanks to Kiki's vigilant care, Man Ray was able to pull himself out of the studio long enough to photograph Marcel Proust on his deathbed. The great author died in his chambers at 44, rue Hamelin, just off the exclusive avenue Kléber, at 5:30 P.M. on November 18, 1922.

His longtime maid, Celeste Albaret, was in attendance, as were his brother, Dr. Robert Proust, and, the following day, other friends and admirers, including two of Man Ray's photographic subjects and friends, the Vicomtesse de Noailles and Jean Cocteau. At Robert's invitation, most probably suggested by Cocteau, Man Ray came on Monday, November 20, to make portraits of the author's majestic head and folded hands.

The following week, with excuses for having "been in bed since Monday suffering from headaches, etc.," Man Ray managed to send two new photographic prints—demonstration rayographs for his forthcoming book *Les champs délicieux,* with an introduction by Tristan Tzara—over to Ferdinand Howald. But that mere effort alone sent him "back to bed" again. Man Ray was ordered by his physician to go on the Hay Diet, much in vogue at the time, and Kiki made sure he kept to a nonalcoholic regimen.

But all was not harmonious between Man Ray and Kiki. Problems arose out of the flowering of Kiki's own talents as an artist, writer, and actress. Although he encouraged her abilities, Man Ray was collapsing with jealousy—but his pride made him hide it from everyone. Despite the fact that she was an indispensable support, Man Ray insisted that Kiki stay away from the studio in the afternoons while he was working. And when he was in the company of Tzara, Man Ray assumed a bleakly playful, demonic pose, pretending to be cynical about love and romance. Kiki found this behavior perplexing, as she did the intentionally irrational manner of some of Man Ray's other intellectual friends. Man Ray knew this highbrow playacting was threatening to her. Perhaps naïvely, she confided in Tristan Tzara (or "Zara" as she called him), sending him long, confessional missives when she was visiting her grandmother in Châtillon-sur-Seine—confidences he blithely converted into grist for the mill of his own novel, *Faites vos jeux* (Place Your Bets).

Complaining that it was too hard to break into the French cinema because only languid blond beauties were wanted, Kiki left Man Ray in the fall of 1923 to try to make a career for herself in American movies. But after a disappointing tryout at the new Paramount studios in Astoria, Queens, handicapped by her lack of facility with English, she returned to Paris. She was hoping "to do grotesque slapstick," a local, English-language newspaper in the Quarter reported; " . . . she has been one of the best laugh-getters in the Quarter since she first landed in Montparnasse as a kid. . . ."

An exhibition of Kiki's primitivist, pastoral canvases filled with images from her countryside childhood—"flat" cows and pigs, stiffly smiling peasants—and her whimsical line drawings (including one where she depicted herself posing nude for a beret-clad artist) sold out completely later in the year. Some of the sketches subsequently adorned her autobiography, published in French by Editions Broca, and then in English by Edward Titus under his Black Manikin Press imprint, with a laudatory introduction by Ernest Hemingway.

Man Ray has left many images of Kiki. Clothed, she is fashionable, chic, and demure, the whites of huge eyes like searchlights penetrating the mysterious darkness around her as she looks to the side at some invisible distraction. Impeccably coiffed and made-up by her in-house stylist, the photographer himself, she is the veritable epitome of the "roaring twenties" as she hikes her skirts up to mid-thigh and sets her lips in a leering grin that speaks of her abandon and carefree nature. Nude, her body bathed in Man Ray's delicate lighting, Kiki intrigues with her ability to pose as if only partially conscious of what flesh can do. She was a great model because she followed instructions but always revealed a small—and significant—measure of defiance and autonomy to remind the viewer she was as independent as the man taking her picture.

Of all the images of Kiki by Man Ray, there is none quite so notorious and powerful as the one in which her smooth, naked, curved back is adorned with the two curlicue "f"-holes of a violin, *Le violon d'Ingres,* (1924), first published in *Littérature,* no. 13, June 1924. Its most obvious resonances are purely visual; in Ingres's *Baigneuse de Valpinçon* the model looks to the right, whereas in the photograph Kiki looks to the left. And there is also the play upon words in the idiomatic title, the "hobby" of Ingres, who insisted that visitors to his studio listen to his inferior violin playing instead of looking at his superior canvases.

Ingres was one of Man Ray's first idols. While still in New York, he had been introduced to the work of the master by Marius de Zayas, among others, who had alerted him to the evolution of modernism in French art "from the classicism of Ingres . . . studying form as it exists objectively, static, measurable, in itself." De Zayas placed Ingres squarely at the beginning of a tradition extending straight through to Matisse.

Jean-Auguste-Dominique Ingres and Man Ray had other points of convergence. The painter glorified odalisques, houris swooning languorously. The photographer took equal delight in the contours of the flesh. Like Ingres, Man Ray was chronically eclectic. Both admired the Oriental style, as well as visual aspects of the Middle Ages; both drew from many periods of art for their iconography, and both were critically condemned for this practice. Both experienced brief formal educations but did not let their artwork suffer from it. Both emerged from humble upbringings. Both remained victimized by the critical assessment that their imagery was too enigmatic.

There is far more than double entendre in Man Ray's image of Kiki's back. The inclusion of extra imagery in a picture predicated upon "real life" makes *Le violon d'Ingres* a classic Surrealist work. It is also an outright act of homage, yet another example of Man Ray's awareness that what came *before* fueled him in his role as an artist of the *present,* an iconoclast who had not forgotten tradition. And the photograph is *playful,* in all senses of that word. It plays with ideas of photography as Man Ray's "hobby"/violin. It plays with the idea of woman, but does not degrade her. It possesses the woman, makes her—almost—into an object, yet maintains respect for the classicism of the female form.

"Having brought [*The Large Glass*] to a state of incompletion" in New York, Marcel Duchamp signed the work and returned to Paris in February, 1923, feeling that "after eight years, it was monotonous" to attend to it any longer. "I wasn't bothered by it," he took pains to explain, "there were simply other things happening in my life then," namely, chess training and competition, perfection of his revolving optical disks (phonograph-record size, with obscure slogans printed on them), giving French lessons to Americans in Paris, writing puns— and inventing a new system of roulette gambling.

Duchamp also met and soon became close with Mary Reynolds, now living near the Observatoire in an apartment she had made beautiful with maps pasted on the walls and earrings hung as adornment instead of paintings. Duchamp added further decorative touches by painting one wall deep blue, pounding tacks into it at jagged angles, connecting the tacks with white string, then painting the tack heads white and illuminating the tableau with a lamp he fashioned from a mattress spring.

Mary Reynolds and Duchamp were seen frequently in public together, and they took holidays in Villefranche throughout the twenties. They made a striking couple—Duchamp was tall and lithe, while she, too, was dark, elegant, beautifully shaped, with soft eyes. She was the only person in bohemia with any money, Peggy

MAN RAY. KIKI DE MONTPARNASSE (ALICE PRIN), 1926. A
VARIANT OF THE PHOTOGRAPH *NOIRE ET BLANCHE*,
SHOWING KIKI WITH HER HEAD AGAINST A TABLETOP, ALSO
SOMETIMES ENTITLED *COMPOSITION*.
Private collection, New York.

ABOVE: MAN RAY. KIKI, 1922.
BELOW: MAN RAY. KIKI, 1923. CLICHÉ-VERRE.
Private collection.

Guggenheim observed, "yet she was always broke because she lent it or gave it all away the minute it arrived from America." During her thirty years of serious involvement with the avant garde, Mary Reynolds purchased many of Man Ray's works and became an experimental bookbinder who favored elaborate and exotic materials, "a great figure in her modest ways," said Duchamp, with his characteristic reserve.

Duchamp took a room on the same floor as Man Ray and Kiki in the Hôtel Istria. The rue Campagne-Première was becoming the liveliest locale in Montparnasse. Yet by 1923, Man Ray was ambivalent about remaining in Paris. In letters home, and in conversations with visitors, he expressed a desire to establish a dual residency, like Duchamp, and be able to travel back and forth between New York and Europe.

In the fall of 1923, via Florence, Vienna, and Berlin, Mina Loy finally came to roost at 15, rue Campagne-Première. Using seed money from Peggy Guggenheim and her husband Laurence Vail, Mina set herself up in the business of making and selling lampshades. Many of her designs were revolutionary, certainly in league with Man Ray's metal spiral from his Société Anonyme days, including the use of bottles, globes, and decorated clear plastic. Mina's eighteen-year-old Joella managed the daily affairs of the shop on the rue de Colisée, charming the *haut monde* clientele who threaded their way through the cramped quarters. Mina designed all her own clothes as well as the children's things, and wrote poetry. Her first major collection, *Lunar Baedeker,* was brought out by Robert McAlmon through his Contact Publishing Company, which also published William Carlos Williams, Ernest Hemingway, Gertrude Stein, Marsden Hartley, Djuna Barnes, and H.D., among others. Loy's literary reputation was on the upsurge, and her readings at various soirées in the Quarter were always crowded, lively affairs.

It was at one such gathering that Man Ray, a neighbor down the street, noticed Joella and told her he thought she had a very classical face. Six years after he'd photographed her mother in Greenwich Village—her head thrown back in profile, right ear adorned with a thermometer pendant—he invited Joella to his studio for a session. Quick and spontaneous, as was his style, Man Ray moved around a lot and made no attempt to pose her. He chose as his final version a profile from the left side (opposite to Mina's), her wavy hair swept back behind her ear and slightly solarized to give it silvery highlights, her lips gently pursed. Seven years later, back in Paris on a purchasing expedition with her husband, New York art dealer Julien Levy, Joella's chiseled features were once again immortalized by Man Ray when he executed a plaster cast of her entire head, requiring her to breathe through straws stuck into her nostrils. This he "antiqued" with brownish-red shoe polish. However, Salvador Dalí got hold of the work and altered it by tinting Joella's hair orange and painting half her face to represent a brick wall, the other half a heavenly blue sky with clouds afloat.

Yet another member of the old Greenwich Village crowd had appeared at Campagne-Première that spring looking for work: Berenice Abbott. She had left New York in 1921 four months before Man Ray, spent time in Paris and Berlin occupying herself with a variety of odd jobs before returning to her sculpture studies, and in general had been knocking about on the edges of insolvency, by her own admission "leading a rather perilous life."

It just happened that Man Ray was having trouble getting along with his current assistant, a young man who thought he knew everything, and Abbott blithely confessed that she, on the other hand, was in complete ignorance as far as photography was concerned. "What about me?" she asked, hoping her lack of experience would make her a less threatening prospect. Man Ray was at first hesitant to hire her, but then finally said, "Why not?"

The studio was two-tiered with strong northern light on the lower floor (which was also the first floor of the building—the *rez-de-chaussée*) and a partial balcony above. Man Ray's tripod and view camera, chairs, and a simple screen and lights were set up below. Upstairs, next to a small bedroom, was an even smaller darkroom where Berenice Abbott, for fifteen francs a day, spent long hours "doing everything after Man Ray took his picture"—from developing and printing, which she learned quickly during just a few weeks of practice under Man Ray's subtle teaching-by-doing instruction, "to mounting, which wasn't fancy," she recalled, "just a strip of glue along the top of the back of the print. We didn't go in for dry mounting in those days."

The following year, just before she left for a brief holiday in Amsterdam, Man Ray lent her a simple box camera to take along. He pressed it into her hands, in outright encouragement that she try to take some pictures of her own. Here, too, Man Ray's instruction was low key and inspirational, rather than prescriptive. Berenice Abbott had no idea of becoming a photographer. However, her abilities in journalism (for that had been, after all, a very early career dream), her keen eye for detail, and her handiness, nurtured by years of sculpting, combined to make Abbott to her surprise and shock a natural at the craft.

In 1925, Berenice Abbott for the first time caught sight of the photographs of Eugène Atget in Man Ray's studio. Their direct and humble qualities touched a documentary nerve in her: "There was a sudden flash of recognition—the shock of realism unadorned," she remembered, "the real world, seen with wonderment and surprise, was mirrored in each print." Urged to tell her something about the old man, Man Ray dismissed him abruptly as "a primitive." At one point, Man Ray had tried to teach Atget how to use a Rolleiflex, to provide an alternative to the old man's method of haunting the streets at dawn before they were populated. But Atget "complained that '*le snapshot*' went faster than he could think, '*Trop vite, enfin.*'" Abbott knew she had to meet this man, who lived just a few houses up the street, at number 17 bis.

Mounting five flights of stairs, stopping before a sign that declared, DOCUMENTS POUR ARTISTES, she encountered the "slightly stooped . . . tired, sad, remote, appealing" seventy-five-year-old pioneer. She was impressed first of all by his refusal to adapt to the latest gimmickry, and equally by his steadfast, noncommercial philosophy. Even on her—by now—twenty-five-francs-a-day wage, Abbott managed to scrape together enough money to acquire a few prints, which turned out to be the first of many she would purchase in the ensuing years.

Atget's penetrating realism—studies of street after Parisian street charged with a bright, animal attentiveness and a lithe energy—was in jarring contrast to Man Ray's ethereal portraiture. Where Atget was the celebrator of the exterior, Man Ray was the interiorizing artist.

Taking pictures of friends and acquaintances, Abbott built up a clientele in much the same way that Man Ray had developed his own following. Although Abbott never intended to learn what she could and then simply go off on her own, never meant to "use" Man Ray, she soon developed an independent reputation, and the two "became unwitting competitors."

May Ray was at the height of his power and reputation as a portraitist and able to command one thousand francs for a sitting (which got him into difficulties with old friends like William Carlos Williams and Gertrude Stein, who expected a "break" in their fees).

That Abbott charged at first much less also helped to make her popular. She consciously tried to portray women more "as people, not still-lifes." Stylistically, Abbott went for a harder edge. She had no interest in rayography, or in infringing upon Man Ray's territory. The crunch came when both photographers realized she was paying more into a prorated share of the studio rent and materials than he was paying her in assistant's wages; and that, consciously or not, Abbott was undercutting Man Ray's commercial attractiveness. Abbott, for her part, did not want her name forever linked to his. And she was tiring of the frenetic pace in the Quarter. Never an habitué of the Dôme to begin with, she hungered for her own place in another part of town. Early in 1926, after much soul searching, Berenice Abbott left the employ of Man Ray, whom she still thought of, without rancor, as a good friend, and set up shop at 44, rue du Bac.

It had been an important apprenticeship. Although Man Ray, in accordance with his belief that a work of art should not be criticized, virtually never made an evaluation of Berenice Abbott's work, he had changed her life. He had taught her through the sheer example of his relentless pursuit of opportunities. Abbott and Man Ray rarely went out together. He had been quiet, self-involved, and businesslike with her—but never cold.

She quickly achieved recognition as the "other" portraitist of "The Crowd." The walls of Sylvia Beach's bookshop were covered with Abbott's photographs as well as Man Ray's. To be "done" by Man Ray or Berenice Abbott meant you were rated as somebody. And by mid-1926, Abbott's "somebodies" included James Joyce, Jean Cocteau, Djuna Barnes, Marie Laurencin, and André Gide, photographed with austere clarity and mysterious luminosity.

She was the first of four major assistants to Man Ray in the important years of the 1920s—followed by Jacques-André Boiffard; the Englishman Bill Brandt; and the blond, blue-eyed model from Poughkeepsie, Lee Miller.

Berenice Abbott and Eugène Atget were not the only photographers who shared Man Ray's disdain for elaborate equipment. Gyula Halász Brassaï also appeared on the scene in 1923, a Transylvanian who had attended art schools in Budapest and Berlin. Thanks to the friendship of André Kertész, another photographic simplifier, who was to use the first Leica in Paris in 1928, Brassaï came to rely almost exclusively on his Voigtlander Bergheil. This reductive urge likewise carried over into the number of shots he took of any given subject—two or three, so that, when they succeeded, true photographers felt, as Brassaï put it, that "they had really made the picture themselves, not won it in the lottery."

The Romanian sculptor Constantin Brancusi believed equally in the new aesthetic of simplicity. Although he had begun taking pictures as early as 1905, when he was twenty-nine years old, Brancusi solidified his theory about the proper function of the camera when he met Man Ray, soon after the American's arrival in Paris. Brancusi's studio at 8, impasse Ronsin, a mazelike cul-de-sac just off the boulevard St. Michel where he lived from 1917 through the late 1920s, was the backdrop for nearly his entire photographic oeuvre.

Like Man Ray, Brancusi insisted that he alone could document his work correctly, and, imperatively, in a particular setting—a whitewashed atelier, where the only touch of color came from several canary-yellow cushions scattered about. Huge, slanted, skylightlike windows let light into the entirely handmade environment, creating "friendly shadows," among which the sculptor labored to the sound of African tribal music played on an old-fashioned Victrola, by two needles resting simultaneously on the record. The statues, rough-hewn and smooth, each one polished by hand, populated the other-worldly landscape, posed as if walking over the cement floor littered with dust and stone chips. In the center of the space, on a huge wood-burning stove, Brancusi cooked his tasty peasant dishes, unadorned and spare as his work; two large mushrooms steeped in their own juices with no superfluous seasoning would typically be more than enough lunch for the artist and a visitor.

Only a few of Brancusi's photographs afford a glimpse of a leaf-laden tree limb, seen through the studio window. If Brancusi did venture out with his camera, it was to capture his monumental *Endless Column* in the countryside, bathed dimly in moonlight, top and bottom artfully framed by vegetation.

Man Ray helped Brancusi come to terms with photography's potential to document work, as well as to give life to the artist's vision. Brancusi's mission was to create a "printed memory." He liked to walk around the work displayed on its pedestal and take a series of shots from different sides. At Man Ray's instigation, Brancusi would also shoot a few feet of movie film of a work, then select the best frame to print from. Man Ray took Brancusi shopping for equipment for the darkroom the sculptor built in the studio, painting its outside walls white so as to blend with the rest of the room. It was impossible for Brancusi to bathe in his bathtub once he became engrossed in photography, for it was used instead as a washbasin for prints.

The two artists shared the conviction that one's work was never done—an endless column or an inexhaustible supply of images. Both held a healthy skepticism about showing work at conventional art galleries. They gravitated toward primary, elemental forms in nature. Brancusi's "egg" imagery in works such as *The Beginning of the World* (1924) resonates perfectly with Man Ray's own glorifying references to the form. Both adored the female figure ("Mlle Pogany" could never be sculpted enough, Kiki could never be photographed enough), and both maintained a reverence for the sanctity of the studio, where the *real* work occurred.

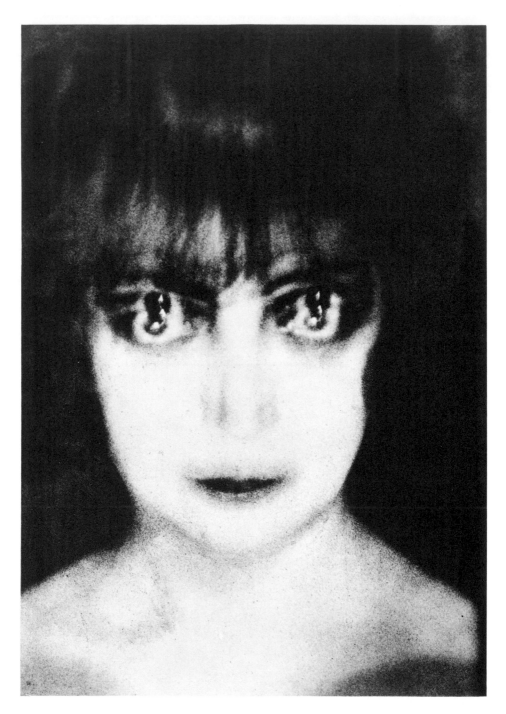

MAN RAY. *THE MARQUISE CASATI*, 1922.

F R O M   D A D A

T O

S U R R E A L I S M

BY THE TIME of the tumultuous public showing of Man Ray's first film, the battle lines between Tristan Tzara and André Breton had been firmly drawn for a year or more. Tzara's magazine, *Le coeur à barbe,* was inordinately eclectic. Its cover for April 1922 displayed iconography of the most disturbing kind—razors, hot-air balloons, and steamships cohabiting with mussels, snakes, and camels. Breton, meanwhile, initiated a new series of the more serious journal *Littérature,* moving away from what he perceived as Dada's outmoded idiocy and toward nonliterary Surrealism, insisting that "one knows what my friends and I mean by [the term] . . . which is not our invention. [It had first been used by Apollinaire in 1917.] We mean to designate a certain psychic automatism that corresponds rather closely to the state of dreaming."

Dada was about to pass through its final, convulsive agony, and Man Ray became swept up in the drama despite his reluctance to be part of an ideological controversy. It was Tzara's doing. He approached Man Ray on the spur of the moment, knowing well his friend's love of improvisation.

On Thursday, July 5, 1923, Tzara informed his neighbor Man Ray that the gala Dada-arts soirée planned for the following two nights at the Théâtre Michel, on the rue des Mathurins near the Opéra, still lacked the right kind of cinematic ingredient. Already set for the bill were Hans Richter's *Rhythmus 21* and Charles Sheeler's *Manhatta,* two short films, as well as musical compositions by Stravinsky, Milhaud, Auric, and Satie. Poetry would be provided by Cocteau, Soupault, Tzara, and the book designer Ileas Zdanévitch. Georges Ribemont-Dessaignes would be reading from his text, *Mouchez-vous* (Blow Your Nose), and Tzara's play *Le coeur à gaz* would be performed. Could a Man Ray movie be produced on twenty-four hours' notice?

Tzara would have had to understand that Man Ray was not a great fan of standard feature films. At a conventional showing he might on a good day be able to find two or three minutes' worth of sustained excitement. Man Ray believed that film, like any other art form, failed if it was not a kind of *liberté-machine* orbiting the viewer into new sensual spaces. And the only films worth seeing— and making—were short ones.

It did not take long for Man Ray to transform twenty meters of celluloid into an event. He cut the stock into manageable lengths and pinned them down on his work table, then began systematically to treat each segment as if it were a special dish at a banquet of unsurpassed variety. Some strips were seasoned with salt and pepper, others with nails. Yet others were made up of composites of still images from Man Ray's photographs and rayographs—a light-striped torso, an egg crate revolving. After each section of film was modified or altered, the image was fixed in exactly the same manner as a rayograph would be, then developed. The next day, lacking anything remotely resembling splicing or editing equipment, Man Ray glued the whole chain together to form a reel of less than two minutes' running time.

Tristan Tzara introduced his friend the following night and in soft, soothing tones, described his nonpartisan stance. Man Ray was perceived by parties in all different camps of Dada as *"hors de toute polémique"* (outside all political dialectics), some said by virtue of his allegiance to Duchamp. Tzara knew full well Man Ray's resistance to the storms of argument rising up on all sides of him; still, he *had* been crafty enough to co-opt Man Ray's work for that special evening.

The audience reacted to Tzara's words with an audible sign of relief—in this segment of the presentation, at least, they might be free from conflict—but their false security disappeared as soon as the first images of Man Ray's film were projected, pinpoints of light like snowflakes flying upward, an epileptic dance of pins and tacks. The film, ironically titled *Le retour à la raison* (The Return to Reason), represented a breaking away from the constraints of yet one more art form. Man Ray had torn down another icon, rebelling against linear narrative in film. "All the films I have made have been improvisations," Man Ray declared forty years later. "I did not write scenarios. It was automatic cinema . . . I don't like films that show what happens in life."

The evening at the Théâtre Michel ended in an uproar. Most of the audience never even saw the end of Man Ray's film. Tzara's play, meant to be the capstone of the evening, did not make it through to completion either, as André Breton leaped up on the stage and began to berate the actors, who, "hampered by Sonia Delaunay's solid cardboard costumes, were unable to protect themselves and made efforts to flee with tiny steps," recalled the poet Georges Hugnet, also present that night. "Breton boxed Crevel's ears roundly and broke Pierre de Massot's arm with his walking-stick." Louis Aragon and Benjamin Péret soon joined the fray, as did the usually docile Paul Eluard when he realized that his poems had been included in the program without his permission. Never had so many poets fought in one spot with such relish. Overwhelmed by other members of the audience while fiercely attacking Tzara, Eluard collapsed into the footlights, smashing several lamps. Police were called in to break up the riot and clear the hall, leaving the little theater in this normally respectable bourgeois quarter of Paris with rows of seats hanging loose or torn open.

A year later the ideological smoke had cleared. The fragments of Dada sorted themselves out in ways that revealed their proponents' varying positions. Tzara's simple pronouncement that basically "the true Dadas were always separate from Dada" was borne out. Picabia had become the founder of "Instantanéisme . . . the value of the instant," and to this momentary cause he devoted the final issue of his magazine, *391,* no. 19. Breton published his first Surrealist manifesto in October 1924 and provided the movement's formal and refined definition, "Pure psychic automatism, by which one intends to express verbally, in writing or by any other method, the real functioning of the mind . . . based on the belief in the superior reality of certain forces of association heretofore neglected, in the omnipotence of dreams, in the undirected play of thought."

Man Ray admitted that although he was flattered by Breton's early designation of him as a "pre-Surrealist," by virtue of his subconsciously derived, refracted visual imagery, he still had to earn a living, when all was said and done. He enthusiastically reported to younger sister Elsie back home that he had now added a glossy, high-paying magazine to his quiver, in addition to *Vanity Fair*: "I am working for *Vogue*." On assignment in Biarritz, he'd hobnobbed with the likes of the Marquise Pierre de Jaucourt, who, the caption intoned, "figures prominently in both the French and Spanish contingents of exclusive society at Biarritz, where her husband is President of Polo"; the Countess Françoise de Chevigné, whose chalet, as photographed by Man Ray, was "very pure in style"; and Miss Louise M. Clews, who "spends much of her time in Europe, and particularly in Biarritz, where she lives during the season."

Man Ray was devoting himself to reaching a wider and more various public with the versatility of his work. Fashionable readers of *Vanity Fair* and *Vogue* saw the side of Man Ray that made wealthy society women appear properly chic and "in the mode." At the same time, the more literary-inclined readership of Margaret Anderson and Jane Heap's *Little Review*—"A Magazine of the Arts, Making No Compromise with Public Taste," transplanted from Chicago to Paris, via New York—found in the autumn 1924 edition and continuing over the next two issues, an array of ever-more-daring rayographs (one mysteriously titled *Rose Sel à Vie*), drawings (one based on the 1922 photograph of the multieyed Marquise Casati), watercolors (including a simplifed and dynamic update of the famous *Rope Dancer* of 1916), and photographs of "objects to be destroyed."

Man Ray was equally at home in the drawing rooms of the rich and powerful (where he was increasingly being summoned for portraiture) as he was in his darkroom fashioning rayographs. As long as he could sneak into a fancy dress ball wearing cuff links in the shape of red electric lights that flashed on and off, he would capitulate to the conventions of social style. It was as if he had embarked on a publicity campaign to prove that he was a three-ring circus unto himself, "what with abstract and portrait photography, movies, and now and then a painting. . . . But it's all one thing in the end," he reported excitedly to his friend Katherine Dreier back in New York, "giving restlessness a material form."

■   ■   ■

Man Ray may have renounced all attempts to label or categorize him, but from the days of the first *Manifesto,* he was nevertheless numbered by André Breton as a leading proponent of the Surrealist aesthetic in the arts, in the same august company as Ernst, Masson, de Chirico, and Duchamp.

But Breton was a chronic appropriator, as everyone knew; one was not politely asked if he wanted to be on the list. In the presence of Man Ray, Breton once even tried to corral Henri Matisse into the Surrealist ranks. "I thought it delicious," Man Ray gossiped the next day to Gertrude Stein, "to hear Matisse speak of drawing hands that look like hands and not like cigar butts. Breton, expecting to find a sympathetic iconoclast, found himself facing an instructor in painting! And as they talked, it seemed that the two men were speaking entirely different languages."

As quickly as an artist could be swept *into* the Surrealist group, so also could he be cast *out.* Breton was capable of stunning reversals of opinion about his friends. They could be transformed from "men above reproach, to cretins" overnight. Robert Motherwell observed of Breton's immeasurable and seemingly immutable authority that "although he does not always seem to have been right (even from a Surrealist point of view) somehow he always *was* Surrealism, and no one wanted the leadership from him."

André Breton had founded his first club, an avant-garde group called "Les Sophistes" while still a student at the lycée. With his long, wavy hair habitually pushed back behind his ears and his large, protruding lower lip, Breton gave the impression—one he did not strive much to correct—of being arrogant and standoffish. "About him," observed his ambivalent colleague, the critic Georges Ribemont-Dessaignes, "there always lurked the odor of the secret society."

The dream was the underlying theme behind Surrealism; as a medical student, Breton had been strongly impressed by Sigmund Freud, with whom he'd had a brief audience in October 1921. In the aftermath of a war in which the phenomenal world had been forever changed, Breton advocated turning inward and giving vent to the unconscious. Surrealism had arisen, phoenixlike, out of Dada's ashes and was dedicated to the overthrow of authority. Thus, like the followers of Dada, the Surrealists developed an obsession with not talking about their childhoods. Personal history was irrelevant. For these young men, the critic Alain Jouffroy has said, family was "nothing more than an immense pile of dead leaves." Rather, one remade oneself, invented a new life, even (perhaps) invented a new name, and, in the process, denied one's true origins.

Declared artist and sound-poet Kurt Schwitters, "The medium is as unimportant as myself. What is essential is only the *idea.*" Thus did Man Ray and the Surrealists enjoy an uneasy marriage, points of convergence as clear as points of difference. Breton detested the jazz Man Ray loved—in fact, he shunned all music—and Man Ray's flirtations with astrology and spiritualism must have struck Breton as signs of weakness in character. The atmosphere of a crowded, smoke-filled bistro no doubt appealed to Breton, while the quiet of his high-ceilinged atelier, broken only by the click of the camera shutter, held fascination enough for Man Ray.

To be sure, Man Ray and André Breton had their personal disagreements, but the first issue of *La révolution surréaliste* (December 1924) was nonetheless adorned by Man Ray's photograph *L'énigme d'Isidore Ducasse,* made what seemed like an eternity ago, in 1920 in New York. Wrapping a sewing machine in burlap and tying it with rope, Man Ray had created a startling iconography based on Lautréamont's lines. For the nine issues to follow, the magazine's covers and illustrations were predominantly by Man Ray.

It was also in *La révolution* that Man Ray's very first "luminograph" appeared in 1924—a panoply of blurred lights caught by leaving the shutter open on the boulevard Edgar Quinet at midnight. There was a Futurist impetus underlying much of Man Ray's work at this time. The automobile imagery infiltrating his photographs over the following two years reflected the fact that he purchased his first car in 1926 as financial worries somewhat dissipated. Had not the Futurist movement's founder, Italian artist F. T. Marinetti, declared in 1909 that "the beauty of a car at full speed [was] greater than that of the Victoire de Samothrace"? Futurism was inspired by Marinetti's dedication to "the object in motion," the "new connections between modern man and the machine." Man Ray always had taken special pride in his speed of execution. There was too much to be done, and not nearly enough time to do it.

"This is Sunday and about the only time I have to write," Man Ray began a letter to sister Elsie, with what was fast becoming a standard apology. By his own admission, he was increasingly "leading a double life . . . the isolated creative one of the artist, and the busy social life which my photography forces me to live." Likewise, the ever practical side of him rhetorically wondered, "How many who had devoted themselves exclusively to their art had ended tragically?"

During these peak, frenetic, and productive years of the 1920s in Paris, as Man Ray reached surer ground in his art while he broadened his contacts at magazines and in society, the artist himself was not the only one to notice his double-edged existence. Georges Ribemont-Dessaignes had already published, with Gallimard in 1924, the first monograph about Man Ray's work, in celebration of his painting. Now, in the May–June 1925 issue of the magazine *Les feuilles libres,* this sensitive critic gave further evidence that public awareness of Man Ray was expanding: "Look at the simple and tranquil Man Ray," he declared, echoing the widespread impression held by artists and socialites alike. Here was a "quiet, hardly loquacious young man," who had "unlocked the entry to a shocking universe" with his rayographs, while continuing to "pursue journalistic fidelity in his photographs," and maintaining "a pleasing facility" in his paintings.

André Breton, in his book, *Le surréalisme et la peinture* (1928), also paid homage to Man Ray's unique ability to move in so many directions so well. A painting could only succeed, Breton wrote, when it acted "as a window giving onto an appealing landscape." Man Ray's photographs attracted Breton in this way. He spoke of their classically Surrealist reverence for the female form, which expressly avoided any degradation of that shape. Breton rhapsodized over "the extremely elegant, extremely beautiful women who reveal their luxuriant hair to Man Ray's intense lights. . . . A string of pearls gleams on naked shoulders on the white page. . . . Are we seeing golden hair, or angels' hair?" Breton's description validated such glamorous subject matter, and he gave further approval by making a pointed analogy between the work of Man Ray and Max Ernst. There was no more concrete illustration possible of the seriousness with which the American's oeuvre was viewed at this crucial point in his career.

Anyone who considered Man Ray's pictures done on assignment placed side-by-side with his more exploratory studies could see his intuitive understanding of the medium. The back-lighting, the sidelong or downward glance, folded hands or slightly raised arms, fingers intertwined, mouth with the wisp of a smile—the evident time taken to imagine the woman in a pose just a fraction different from what convention dictated—such factors came into play no matter what the circumstances.

By adding simple touches, like a double-direction shadow, a Byzantine sculpture, or a vase of pansies, their heads drooping delicately, Man Ray transformed what would have been ordinary models posing to show standard couture into what *Vogue* editors appreciated as "a catechism in chic . . . a daring way with the mode." His highly stylized and instantly recognizable fashion work populated the pages of editions of the magazine on both sides of the Atlantic during the twenties. For example, he back-lit the Hon. Mrs. Reginald Fellowes to capture the delicate curve of her neck. Mrs. Fellowes had achieved permanent renown in Parisian society by throwing a party, cohosted by Elsa Maxwell, at which guests were asked to come dressed like people everybody else knew. Showing the same sensitivity with which he draped Kiki, Man Ray pulled Mrs. Fellowes' crêpe shawl down below her right shoulder to provide just a hint of pale arm.

He posed the Princess de Faucigny-Lucinge, only daughter of the Baron and Baronne Emile d'Erlanger, so that the whites of her eyes dominate the center of the frame. His studies of chalets in Biarritz display a distinctively Atgetian perspective, unpeopled, full views with archways subtly shaded.

After Dorothy "Dody" Todd, editor of British *Vogue,* sat for her portrait, she also gave Man Ray plenty of work. In the American edition of *Vogue,* Man Ray joined the heady company of Edward Steichen, Arnold Genthe, Nickolas Murray, and Charles Sheeler. And Man Ray scored his biggest journalistic coup of all when he was commissioned to document the Exposition Internationale des Arts Décoratifs et Industriels Modernes in Paris, held from April to October 1925.

The French Exhibition, as it was known to American readers, occupied dozens of specially constructed halls, stretching across the heart of Paris from the Place des Invalides on the Left Bank to the Champs Elysées. A design competition, it marked the explosion of Art Deco onto the international scene in every form possible—from jewelry to furniture to architecture. The *esprit nouveau* aesthetic—Le Corbusier's art of beautiful utility—had been born at the outset of the decade. The French Exhibition was a paean to technology and machine-made art. Cubism was at the heart of Art Deco, perhaps best exemplified by Sonia Delaunay's sensational *"Robes-Poèmes,"* on view at her boutique on the Pont Alexandre III. Her coats were flowing paintings, patterns of squares and triangles in bright colors, repeated on her accessories. One could even buy an open car with its exterior painted to match the design on the garments.

Man Ray was eminently comfortable with this art-by-design, long ago having accepted technological intervention in the art-making process. And his personal appearance—lately he'd been affecting dark suits, pure white or plain blue broadcloth shirts sent by Elsie from New York, and somber ties—mirrored the pared-down principles of the French Exhibition. The refined and functional form of Man Ray's dress harmonized with his deliberate physical movements. No gesture was superfluous. Even when he found himself to be "busy as a cockroach," he never became stirred into a breathless frenzy. He was as cool and smooth-surfaced as the mannequins *Vogue* sent him to photograph.

The fashions by Lanvin, Callot, Worth, Paquin, and Jenny on display at the Pavillon de l'Elégance were highly sheened, close to the body, with just-short-of-daring, deep *V*'s down the back, narrow off-the-shoulder straps, and occasional hints of sequins and ruffles. They caused far less of a stir than the mannequins designed by André Vigneau. Made of wax painted silver, gold, and "Egyptian red," these other-worldly presences were positioned in graceful, natural stances. One local newspaper columnist expressed his disdain by likening their facial features to Brancusi's sculptures. Some mannequins were completely bald, others wore bathing-cap–like coiffures. Gazing blankly and disquietingly into nowhere, they were perfect subjects for the inventive eye of Man Ray, who treated readers of the September 1, 1925, issue of *Vogue* to a richly detailed assortment of photographs.

Meanwhile, the daring Paul Poiret chose to show his fashion line aboard three barges moored at the quai d'Orsay: *Amours* (Loves), *Délices* (Delights), and *Orgues* (Organs). Asked why he had selected these particular names, he replied, "Women, always women." *Amours* featured Poiret's perfume piano, which, when played, directed a variety of scented breezes toward visitors. *Délices* was an epicurean restaurant. And a series of fourteen color illustrations of the designer's current fashions, by Poiret's close friend Raoul Dufy, hung prominently on the walls of *Orgues*. It was fashion in the Fauvist mode, bright splashes of color in jagged patterns, forthright, but even so, *près du corps* in the slimmer style of the day.

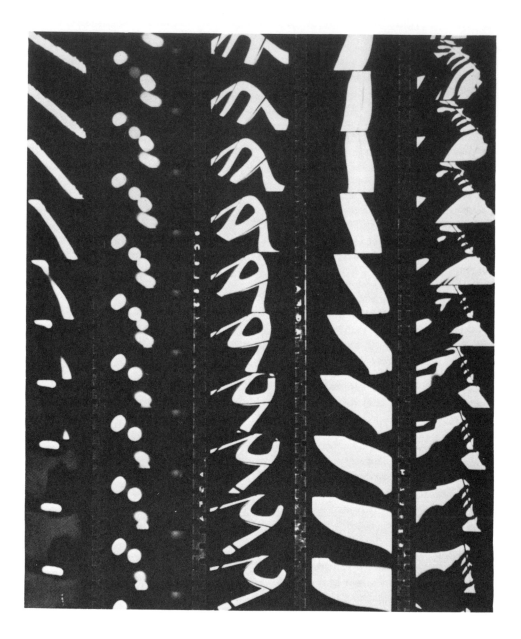

MAN RAY. FRAMES FROM *EMAK BAKIA*, 1926.

CINEMATIC
ADVENTURES

A T   A   T I M E when one could live quite well in Paris on one hundred
dollars a month, Man Ray was receiving upwards of five hundred
dollars for a picture spread in *Vogue*. Ten years later, he would be
commanding seven hundred and fifty dollars per picture from
Harper's Bazaar. Business success brought with it financial complex-
ity, as the variety of sources from which Man Ray derived income
increased: clients from other countries passing through Paris,
German art and fashion magazines as well as those in America,
England, and France. Early in the new year, 1926, Man Ray began
to plan for a bank account in New York City at the Trust Company
of North America, where he could, again through the efforts of sister
Elsie and her husband, Sam Siegler (conveniently enough an
accountant), "have some money put away for when I come back to
New York or if an emergency happens here." The emergency would
not come for another dozen years when war broke out, but Man
Ray's foresight proved sagacious indeed. Meanwhile, he asked
sitters to pay him in dollars whenever possible. In the spring,
wealthy young American patron Arthur Wheeler, the behind-the-
scenes producer of Man Ray's second and far more ambitious film,
Emak Bakia, gave him the generous sum of three thousand dollars to
help make this avant-garde effort a reality—and it all went straight
to Elsie for deposit in New York.

The New York nest egg, besides quickly becoming a hedge

against the vicissitudes of a free-lance future, also made it easier for Elsie to purchase American photographic supplies for brother Man, who was distinctly dissatifsfied with the quality and availability of equipment and paper in Europe. His explicit requests brought Elsie from her home in Jersey City to Willoughby's Camera Store on West Thirty-second Street to acquire such exotic but necessary items as "100 sheets double weight Vitava Athena Old Master paper"; "a folding Korona tripod no. 2," with the advice that she tell the clerk he "works for the magazines, etc., and that I'll have to pay duty on it—to get the best price possible"; "a half-dozen print blotting books 10 by 12 inches or larger; a half-gallon can of Probus Paint . . . it's a waterproof paint for trays, etc."; and "the Heliar lens, 4.5-36 centimeters focal length." To this order Man Ray added, as he occasionally did, a call for "half a dozen pairs of good but not too expensive stockings, one pair black and the others nice flesh tints, for between a dollar and one-fifty, smallest size," for his model-companion Kiki. Throughout his career as a photographer, Man Ray made light of sophisticated equipment, the unnecessary trappings of his art. He even constructed his own backs for his large-format view camera, doubling up on the film frame so as to obtain two exposures from one plate. His requirements were simple.

Man Ray flatly states in his autobiography that as soon as Arthur Wheeler came across with the backing for a new film meant to be "in the nature of an experiment," rather than—heaven forbid—a traditional feature, he "went to work at once, neglecting other photographic commitments." There was, however, a two-month hiatus during which the artist addressed two other pressing concerns. Since December 1925, he had been preparing for a large exhibition at the Galerie Surréaliste. It opened on March 26, 1926, and, more in the nature of a retrospective, included a host of paintings, airbrush works, and objects, New York exports from Ridgefield days and before, still unsold and of personal importance. The old skin of the past had not been wholly shed.

Etude dated from 1908, *Un rêve, Paysage,* and the important *MCMXIV* from 1912, 1913, and 1914 respectively. These were beginning to take on the appearance of vintage canvases in the Man Ray oeuvre. And *Revolving Doors,* the rainbow-hued collage series of 1916–17, was issued in a new, multiple *pochoir* edition of ten sheets each. Over the years, Man Ray gave away virtually all of them.

Springtime in Paris, with its fresh light and sudden downpours, was also a season when Man Ray took to the streets more often, producing a rare series of neighborhood snapshots he'd promised Elsie ever since his arrival. The rue de la Paix in rain, with the Vendôme column looming grayly in the background; a cobblestoned courtyard washed in sunlight, seen from the gloom of a carriageway, an old woman hunched reading a book against one wall; the Moulin de la Galette; the old Bullier dance hall opposite the Closerie des Lilas on the avenue de l'Observatoire near Man Ray's Montparnasse home—all were printed postcard-size and used freely by Man Ray for communiqués to the home front. Again, the spirit of his formidable neighbor Atget lurks in these unprepossessing views taken in the course of Man Ray's wanderings. To Berenice Abbott, he had denied being influenced by the old man's work. But that disclaimer, like so many others, did not hold up under scrutiny. Man Ray was hanging Atget's pictures in his studio and singing his praises at café gatherings.

Man Ray stockpiled an assortment of film "takes" of Paris that were to figure prominently in his next opus, and he cautioned Arthur Wheeler that the project had to be viewed as purely speculative, no guarantees given as to final quality. Now he was ready to start in earnest on the movie, which he expected to finish in the fall. His projections proved accurate. *Emak Bakia* premiered in November.

Exterior shooting was done at Wheeler's estate in Bidart, Basses Pyrenées, near Biarritz. There, enjoying the sparkling summer weather and the break from Paris—swimming and lounging on the beach by day and dance parties at night with Kiki by his side—Man Ray doubled up on assignments from *Vogue* and also pursued whimsical ideas for his film. Along with the poet Jacques Rigaut in one key sequence, Kiki was the undeniable star of her lover's new film.

It was collagist's work, incorporating snippets from *Le retour à la raison* in the form of moving rayographs; street-scene montages culled from previous months of Parisian rambling; near-realistic sequences, one particularly startling, in which Man Ray's trembling handheld camera, during a high-speed open car trip with his hostess, Rose Wheeler, flies through the air over a herd of sheep crowding the provincial country road. In another segment, Jacques

Rigaut liberates from a suitcase torn shirt collars, which flap upward like a flock of crazy doves.

Man Ray was adamant that there be no script for *Emak Bakia,* no discernible narrative progression, in keeping with his belief that there generally was no progress in art. Nevertheless, there *are* motifs in the film, repetitions of patterns of light as Man Ray paints with light, exploring more deeply dazzling contrasts engineered to stir the viewer's emotions. Ever since the 1911 *Tapestry,* Man Ray had been obsessed with the placement of dark objects upon light backgrounds; light faces against dark backdrops; dark words against light paper. Indeed, Man Ray conceptualized *Emak Bakia* as a cine-poem, assembling the film the way a poet composed, bit by bit, word by word, striving for effect through words resonating with one another, rather than by literal, or expected, meaning. To Man Ray, the film was "a whole that still remained a fragment."

The final image of *Emak Bakia* is its crowning statement, and it establishes an undeniable connection between the film and mainstream Surrealist theory. Kiki's eyes are shut, but eyes have been painted on her eyelids, so that, as she closes her false eyes, her real eyes shine forth. The Surrealists put much stock in the blurred boundary, so easily dissolved, between sleep and waking. Man Ray was hopeful this visual statement would go over well with them. It turned out, however, that Rigaut's presence in the film undercut whatever legitimacy *Emak Bakia* would otherwise have attained. He was among the borderline members of the group, not in high favor at the time, and his performance was thought to smack of grandstanding.

The premiere audience at the Théâtre au Vieux Columbier—albeit only fifty people, including the Wheelers—went along with Man Ray's unusual standards. This time, there were no riots. *Emak Bakia* enjoyed a successful run, traveling on to London and Brussels in January 1927.

In late February, after hinting that he wanted above all else to have a hit show in New York, Man Ray took the film to America, and his star actress, Kiki, went along. It was Man Ray's first trip home since his departure in 1921, and naturally the whole family flocked to see him. On March 7, the night of the gala premiere, Man Ray and Kiki went first to Max and Minnie's place on Kosciuszko Street in Brooklyn, where the ebullient Kiki sat on Mr. Ray's lap, her lovely legs displayed, and had her picture taken from all angles, laughing and smiling as she tried without much success to carry on a coherent conversation in English with everyone. Minnie was particularly taken with Kiki. She noticed how reserved and gentlemanly her son Man was in the presence of this prepossessing and warm French girl.

From the elder Rays' apartment everyone then moved on to the new place where sister Do and her husband lived on Quincy Street. Lena, Sam's wife, in the midst of preparing a big dinner, called to say that she lacked a soup ladle. Do offered to bring hers over. As the group marched to DeKalb Avenue, Kiki snatched the silver ladle from Do's hands, held it up like a baton, and led a jolly procession down the street, singing the *Marseillaise* at the top of her lungs. Coming to a hydrant in her path, undaunted, she hiked up her skirts, in a well-practiced motion, and leaped over the obstruction—to the great delight of all—calling out some deliciously risqué argot expression at the same time.

The Guild Theater on West Fifty-second Street in Manhattan was packed for the exotic double-feature, *Emak Bakia* preceded by Marcel L'Herbier's *The Living Dead Man,* based upon Pirandello's *The Late Matthias Pascal.* Readers of the playbill were cautioned, in exhaustive notes "by the noted modernist artist Man Ray," that "if you like, *Emak Bakia* is a pause for reflection on the present state of the cinema, and to the author an indicator of a future plan of action noted down in haste," a signal that he was contemplating subsequent films to build upon the current one. While he had told the Parisian preview audience that *Emak Bakia*—the name of the Wheeler estate—was an old Basque expression for "leave me alone," New Yorkers were informed, in an addendum to the program notes, "it was chosen because it sounds prettily and means"—a barb aimed squarely at critics—"Give Us A Rest."

Aside from a few squeals of alarm from five-year-old Florence, Do's younger daughter, frightened by the choppy imagery, the film was met with polite interest. However, critic Gilbert Seldes was in the audience that night, and in the March issue of *The New Republic* he picked up the gauntlet, dismissing the L'Herbier film as "dull," then moving on to attack "Man Ray's film [as having] gone straight to hell with good intentions." Except for "rare moments" when "a few feet of film create a startling, almost ravishing effect," Seldes intoned, "the whole and most of its parts lack significance. There is almost no relation between any hundred feet of film and the preceding or subsequent hundred." This "effect," the lack of transitions, the story vacuum, was, of course, precisely the writer-director-cameraman-editor's intention. Once again, Man Ray's work seemed to be a direct challenge to the inbred capacities of the critical establishment.

What he ultimately was after, Man Ray told an interviewer in New York, was "to [have the spectator] rush out"—*not* in disbelief, incredulity, or suspicion—"and breathe the pure air of the outside, be a leading actor and solve his own dramatic problems" after experiencing the film. "For that way, he would realize a long-cherished dream," Man Ray's dream as well, "of becoming a poet, an artist himself, instead of being merely a spectator." As with the provocative objects displayed at his exhibitions, meant to goad and anger the visitor into action (or an even more extreme response, as in the *Object to Be Destroyed* metronome of 1923, which actually *was* destroyed at an opening in 1954), Man Ray's films, unlike Hollywood movies, were intended to raise the viewer from his customary absorptive role.

This seductive plastic medium held few inherent frustrations, and after *Emak Bakia,* Man Ray would make increasing use of it. The ultimate technological Futurist art at this crest of the machine age, film was the serial extension of photography, the mode of expression Man Ray knew so well. In film, he set up a rhythm of fragments, of randomness coexisting with "beats" of parallel imagery.

Where *Le retour à la raison* had been an impromptu sketch drawn at a moment's notice as a favor to a friend, *Emak Bakia* took Man Ray six months, a long time in his scheme of things. He allowed himself to improvise upon earlier compositional principles and work them through. In the process, he paved the way for his next film, the only one he ever made with a narrative based upon an actual text.

While *Emak Bakia* continued to cause a stir in Paris, Man Ray's paintings and rayographs were on display in his native territory. The Société Anonyme mounted its biggest exhibition ever, at the Brooklyn Museum, from November 1926 to January 1927. The artists were listed by nationality, and Man Ray could be found in the "United States" category. His painting *Arc de Triomphe,* a bird's-eye view of the monument, which continued to be a personal favorite of

Katherine Dreier's, was one of only eight works illustrated in the catalogue, out of 307 pieces by artists from twenty-three countries. Duchamp's abbreviatedly titled *Glass* was also on view, in a pristinely smooth condition. After the show, dismantled into its two panes, crated carelessly, and jostled continuously during the forty-mile trip to Miss Dreier's West Redding, Connecticut, home, *The Bride* arrived cracked. Its creator, however, was not disturbed: "It's a lot better with the breaks, a hundred times better," he said. "It's the destiny of things."

Duchamp was becoming quite the art entrepreneur. In addition to his fieldwork assembling items for the Société Anonyme exhibition, under the guise of Rose Sélavy he sponsored a sale of Picabia's works in Paris. He also arranged a Brancusi show in New York and helped his old friends the Arensbergs build up their collection, in large measure by buying back his own works dispersed over the years, wanting, he said, "the whole body of work to stay together."

Duchamp met the young Julien Levy in New York City at the time of the Brancusi exhibition at the Brummer Gallery. Levy, at the encouragement of his wealthy father, purchased a sculpture. Harvard dropout, erstwhile experimental filmmaker and photography aficionado, Levy had at that time no thought of opening a gallery. But he thirsted for the stimulation of Paris, and he accepted Duchamp's invitation to sail there with him at the end of February 1927, at the very time Man Ray was on his way to New York for the opening of his new film. Following an exhibition of recent paintings and photographic compositions at the Daniel Gallery in March and April, however, Man Ray did return to Paris, and Levy—who'd been an early admirer of the rayographs—paid him a visit at the rue Campagne-Première.

It was at Man Ray's studio that Julien Levy, like other photography connoisseurs before him, including, of course, Berenice Abbott, first laid eyes upon Eugène Atget's work. He was immediately seduced by it. During the few months Levy lived in the neighborhood, just around the corner from Man Ray, he purchased as many photographs as Atget permitted. It was during this spring, too, that Levy met and married Joella Loy, Mina's daughter, still at work in the lampshade factory.

Atget had clearly been in decline. Berenice Abbott was taking the old man's portrait often toward the end, and she described his face as "looking more and more like that of a tired actor." He was still going out on shoots every morning at daybreak, his tripod and view camera resting heavily upon his stooped shoulders as he trudged through the Paris streets. One early August day, Abbott arrived at Atget's studio on the rue Campagne-Première and dashed up the stairs intending to show him prints from their latest sitting. She was shocked to discover he was gone. The concierge informed her that Atget had died. His collection of more than two thousand glass plates and eight thousand prints were in the possession of his old friend, André Calmettes, director of the municipal theater in Strasbourg. From that moment onward, Abbott devoted as much energy to the cause of advancing Atget's reputation as she did to her own, eventually purchasing a huge amount of his work in order to save it for posterity.

"For twenty years," Calmettes told Abbott, his friend Eugène "had lived on milk, bread, and bits of sugar. . . . In art and in hygiene he was absolute. . . . He applied this intransigence of taste, of vision, of methods, to the art of photography." That kind of austerity, and a passion for the straight, unmanipulated image, pulled Berenice Abbott toward him.

The review of the First Salon of Independent Photographers, May–June 1928, praised Abbott and panned Man Ray. She was so upset, she hid from everyone for a week. No one in the show—not even Hoyningen-Heuné, Kertész, Nadar, or Outerbridge—received the kind of critical attention Abbott did. Her portraiture was compared to Holbein; "with the most naked, the most modest, the least pretentious truth," gushed a reviewer in the weekly magazine *Chantecler,* "this human representation evokes a spiritual emotion." Her fame was established once and for all. Eight months later, Berenice Abbott returned to America.

"For years I knew your eyes like those of a great brown moth," reminisced Kay Boyle affectionately of her poet-friend Robert Desnos, "and your brown suit, as transparent from awe as a moth's threadbare wing. You were twenty-eight then, and you lived to become a metaphor for a totally unconceived France." He commanded awed affection from Man Ray as well. Robert Desnos was a true visionary, given at any moment to trances during which he would recite long poems and anagrams in a distant voice. In Man Ray's photographs of the young writer, who made his living as a journalist and critic, Desnos is seen slouched in an armchair, his heavy-lidded eyes half closed or half open, as if he is either going into a deep, surreal sleep or creeping slowly out of one.

Desnos had been among Man Ray's earliest admirers. In a piece for *Le Journal,* published in Paris on December 14, 1923, he wrote a frequently reprinted appreciation, "The Work of Man Ray," a lyrical, free-associative tribute tracing the photographer's roots in literary tradition, reminding readers perhaps still unfamiliar with the American's oeuvre that "whatever his initiation, Man Ray springs from poetry, and it is under that spirit that I have come today into his domain, which is as open as eternity." Desnos was familiar with Man Ray's exercises in media other than photography, and in the course of the article ran down the list from painting to object-making. But he claimed it was in the realm of the written word that the two found common ground. Desnos was echoing the intuitions of the other French poets including Cocteau, who had called Man Ray "the poet of the darkroom." Man Ray easily embraced this interpretation, avowing, in *Paris Soir* of May 23, 1926, that he "preferred the poet. He creates, and every time man has raised himself in the moral order, he has done so by creating something, be it a machine, a poem, or a moral attitude."

When Desnos was about to depart on a journalism assignment to the West Indies for two months in the winter and spring of 1928, Man Ray and Kiki threw a dinner party for him. It was a bittersweet affair; great quantities of wine were consumed. At the end of the meal, the guest of honor arose rather shakily from his chair and began, as was his custom, to recite. Producing a crumpled sheet from his pocket, the poet revealed a poem he'd written that day. Man Ray was struck by the dramatic imagery in "*La place de l'étoile,* " and brazenly told Desnos that he'd just put the idea for a new film in his head. He promised that by the time his friend returned from abroad, the work would be completed.

That night, his imagination stirred by Desnos's poem, and no doubt motivated by his own reckless promise, Man Ray defied his dictum against the use of scenarios for short films by jotting down some notes in bed. As the years passed and he became a lighter and lighter sleeper, Man Ray rigged up a swiveling platform by his bedside so that if inspiration struck at any hour he could set to work in the Proustian mode, writing or sketching without even getting out of bed.

The film was eventually divided into thirty-three segments, each one described in sparse phrases and sentence fragments on the left-hand side of the page ("Un homme et une femme dans la rue. Marche leurs jambes. Les jambes de la femme. Elle s'arrête."). On the right, the intended musical accompaniment to the silent film was laid out, everything from the popular song *"Plaisir d'amour (ne dure qu'un instant)"* and a tango, to *"O sole mio"* and, finally, one of Man Ray's enduring favorites, a Bach aria.

The poem, changed to *"L'étoile de mer"* (The Starfish), is interpreted very precisely. Man Ray's visual conception of the movements of the characters is intercut (a favorite device) by brief flashes of imagery ("des journaux emportés par le vent . . . un train qui passe . . . un bateau" [newspapers blown by the wind . . . a passing train . . . a steamship]). Occasional subtitles dropped in make a composite, running subtext: "Qu'elle est belle / Après tout / Si les fleurs étaient en verre / Belle, belle comme une fleur en verre / Belle comme une fleur de chair / Vous ne rêvez pas!" (How lovely she is / After all / If the flowers were made of glass / Lovely, lovely like a glass flower / Lovely like a flower of flesh / You're not dreaming!) The scenario thus evolves into a collaborative, imagistic poem. It anticipates Man Ray's joint effort of 1937 with Paul Eluard, *Les mains libres*.

By the time he is a half dozen segments into the film, Man Ray begins restlessly and cubistically to move elements around so that when he reaches the seventeenth take, in which a nearly nude woman is surrounded by broken bottles with wine flowing out of them, he also intercuts images of the actual *étoile de mer*. The star of the sea thus provides thematic unity to the poem, and, by extension, to the film.

The starfish was a key symbolic concept for Desnos, suggesting, according to the poet, "the very embodiment of a lost love, a love well lost—without this sea star purchased as a talisman from a second-hand dealer on the rue des Rosiers, I would not have kept a memory of the affair. It is under the star's influence that I have written, in a form propitious to the apparitions and to the ghosts of a scenario, what Man Ray and I saw as a poem, simple like love." The sea star, the starfish, inhabits liquid depths as well as heavenly reaches and possesses a double destiny, in keeping with Surrealist mysticism, also appealing to Man Ray's habitual affinity for ambiguous objects. "Man Ray has constructed," Desnos said, "a domain that no longer belongs to me, and that was not totally his," merging dualities to achieve a work blending oral poem with visual imagery.

L'étoile de mer is an erotic film: a couple meets, they caress, then part, without making love. It is a disturbing work, because Man Ray never lets the viewer settle into any chain of events for more than a few moments. The collaborators originally planned thirty-three scene shifts within the space of a half hour, then cut the film down to half that length.

Kiki returned for another appearance as the female lead,

MAN RAY. CHÉRUIT DRESS. GEOMETRIC PATTERNS MADE
POPULAR BY THE ART DECO INFLUENCE. *VOGUE*, MAY 15, 1925.
Courtesy Vogue. *Copyright 1925 by The Condé Nast Publications, Inc.*

opposite the tall, blond André de la Rivière, a young man who was Desnos's neighbor. The poet enjoyed a cameo role, taking Kiki away from her supposed lover at the end of the film. Reflecting Lautréamont's influence once more, Man Ray juxtaposed highflown praise for a woman's charms with jarring imagery calculated to confuse and, therefore, to snare the viewer's attention. The film's truncated love scenes; jarring images of machines and mirrors breaking accompanied by the ironic refrain of "How lovely she is"; windblown newspapers symbolizing transitoriness and fragility of daily events; and Desnos's instructions at the end of the scenario that the film conclude as it began, with the *"Plaisir d'amour"* refrain now altered to declare that *"chagrin d'amour dure toute la vie"*—love's pleasure lasts but a moment, its resulting depression lasts a lifetime—all make a statement about the evanescence of love. Was it merely coincidental that a year after the film's premiere at the Studio des Ursulines in May 1928, Man Ray and Kiki would be on the verge of breaking up their six-year liaison?

L'étoile de mer was an autobiographical statement, bringing several identity themes into focus. Kiki was the relentlessly active woman in the film, expressing herself through her body, using it to enthrall the methodical and passive man who made pretenses at being her lover but who—with his distant expression, plain demeanor, and slow, ponderous walk—spent more time bidding her *adieu* than making love. Repeated images of departure, trains and boats fading into the distance, underscored the ambivalence of the supposedly intimate relationship. Many scenes in the film were shot through glass, or depicted artifacts of glass, emphasizing the precarious nature of the romance. The woman was left alone at the end, having lost her dark love. She was spirited away by the tall, fair, Desnos-figure, seduced into disappearance by a writer. This image, too, turned out to be prophetic.

In its unsparing admiration for Kiki, the film expressed Man Ray's doubts about being able to keep her. Man Ray was the artist who made this woman, his Galatea, come alive with beauty every night before emerging to face the world of café society. Ironically, his talent at transforming her was so formidable he succeeded in making her doubly attractive to others. Perhaps he never really wanted to keep Kiki forever, but rather he was creating something solely for the purpose of being photographed that, like one of his fantastic objects, could then be lost to him.

Man Ray's first three films all served to recapitulate earlier iconography, and they recycled past motifs that the artist struggled his whole life to exorcise: *Le retour à la raison,* in only sixty feet of celluloid, managed to be a mini-retrospective. Imagery of spirals recalled Société Anonyme days, when Man Ray improvised his lampshade for Miss Dreier at the last moment. Snatches of rayographs subliminally flashed on the screen—*Danger/Dancer* appeared, partially obscured by a mist of cigarette smoke. Carousel lights blurred by overexposure recalled Man Ray's recent photograph *Boulevard Edgar Quinet at Midnight.* The film stock itself was a moving rayograph. He even wrote his name on the film in hurried script. At the end, the nude torso of an anonymous and voluptuous woman turned laboriously in a half circle before a pattern of stippled light, bright and dark tones reversed. The woman had no face, no name; she served only as an "object of affection."

Emak Bakia was likewise a study in spirals. The camera moved vertiginously, recalling Man Ray's whimsical cine-poem experimentation with Duchamp, also completed in September 1926—*Anemic Cinema.* The calm, slowly spiraling optical disks of *Anemic Cinema,* some with elaborate puns upon them, some without, resonated with the swaying daisies and dizzying seascape of *Emak Bakia,* transforming the landscape around Arthur Wheeler's estate into a dreamworld. Man Ray's earlier work again took cameo roles in his film. The astute viewer could spot *Invention/Dance,* one of the abstract, figurative paintings first displayed at Charles Daniel's gallery in New York, as well as Man Ray's *Fisherman's Idol* (1926), a dignified icon assembled from bits of cork gathered on the shore; the rest of the world saw detritus and abandoned fragments.

Premiering with *The Blue Angel* at the Studio des Ursulines on May 13, 1928, *L'étoile de mer* was greeted, not unexpectedly, with critical confusion. Man Ray chose recordings of Cuban dance music to accompany the film at the last moment, discarding his elaborately plotted orchestral scenario in favor of a more disruptive and violent background. A columnist in *Variétés* regarded the characters in the film as "circulating in a kind of Milky Way. . . or appearing as if one had taken hashish. Everything dissolves and then is reborn, evolving arbitrarily. . . ." Another writer had difficulty understanding the occasional lines of Desnos's text projected as subtitles at arbitrary intervals, arguing that they became self-defeating and ultimately "lost meaning and unraveled."

Man Ray insisted throughout his career that poets enjoyed a special perspective on his work. Robert Desnos, even before his participation in *L'étoile de mer,* was part of the select literary audience with a taste for Man Ray's imagery. Desnos's enthusiasm was fired by Man Ray's incessant willingness to take risks. The poetic text for *L'étoile de mer* had evolved spontaneously, in classic Surrealist fashion. It was no accident that Man Ray photographed Desnos asleep (or, at least, feigning sleep) in a softly upholstered armchair, for the poet and the filmmaker shared a conviction in the power of dream life, the netherworld where true creation occurs: "Man Ray derives neither from artistic deformation," the poet declared, "nor from the servile reproduction of 'nature.'" Eight years after Man Ray arrived in Paris, his film work was embraced by Desnos as the most magical manifestation of his talent.

Man Ray's restless desire to make his mark in as many art forms as possible continued to drive him forward. He allowed two stills from *L'étoile de mer* to appear in *transition* one month after the film began its extended run, but the photographs, one of Kiki's bare foot, the other of her sleeping face, were titled, simply, *Film.* In the same issue of the French-English magazine, edited by Eugène Jolas, Man Ray published a photograph of his *Danger/Dancer* aerograph on glass from the New York years (1920) posed on an easel next to a section of Brancusi's *Endless Column.* In *transition* no. 15, half a year later—timed to coincide with Man Ray's "Photographic Compositions" show at the Arts Club in Chicago, the first major exhibition of such works stateside—a portfolio of rayographs was featured, coyly referred to by the artist as "photographic studies." The cover of this special *transition* displayed a stark rayograph, and the eight images within were more fixed, static, and "flat" than earlier examples. The lengths of string Man Ray employed in several of the rayographs lend them a more figurative air. Informed observers such as *Vanity Fair* editor Frank Crowninshield, now a member of the founding board of directors of the new Museum of Modern Art in New York, pointed out that, like Man Ray, "more and more the American photographers are being touched by so-called Modernism . . . more and more they are yielding to the beauty of cubes; to sharply-opposed effects of shadow and light. . . ." Crowninshield (or "Crownie," as he was known to his friends) had noticed Man Ray's experimental imagery long before any other American editor, and he had been the first to give the artist's new photographs exposure in the United States.

The critical climate back home was improving, reflected in Man Ray's important exhibition in Chicago. And a nagging dispute was brewing with New York gallery owner Charles Daniel about which of the canvases Man Ray had left behind were available for consignment. Man Ray admitted to sister Elsie that he was "getting very homesick after my visit last year." A new niece, Naomi, had been born, and Man Ray confided to Elsie, after receiving a photograph of the baby, that he thought she "resembled [him] . . . one way or another the family is being perpetuated, it seems!" However, despite all these enticements, he was unable to make a crossing, much to his beloved sister's disappointment.

MAN RAY IN THE RUE CAMPAGNE-PREMIÈRE STUDIO,
EARLY 1930S. *Private collection.*

ATELIER
MAN RAY

THE TWO-TIERED studio at 31 bis, rue Campagne-Première, just off the busy boulevard Raspail, was handsomely situated. The building boasted fine friezework and sculpted details, multicolored inlaid brick, stately windows, and two voluptuous muses adorning the frosted-glass double doorway. Man Ray's studio was identified by a large plaque simply stating his name—no title. The name Man Ray, by 1929, was enough. "The doorbell," a journalist observed, "scraped like the legs of a cicada or the cry of a cricket." Once inside, the environment was much the same as in Man Ray's cramped room at the Grand Hôtel des Ecoles, first described by Gertrude Stein. The artist was "surrounded by his little world of wood and iron, chess, cubes, cones, pyramids, and scrolls. A difficult stairway," reporter Ferdinand Powey told readers of the August 25, 1929, *L'Européen,* "leads to the path of dreams."

It was a busy time for Man Ray. Constant requests for interviews from the Parisian press eager to explain this mysterious little man with the American-flavored French accent were cutting into his work time. Visitors to the studio, no matter who they were, were greeted with impatience. Man Ray was quick, often gruff, not even taking the time to pause from his work, murmuring a mere "Hello," then crossing his arms over his chest and waiting, his heavy-lidded, dark eyes open wide, "with the look of an orphan," some friends said, or "the gaze of an owl with a cigarette clamped in his mouth."

There was not only the problem of intrusive but well-meaning visitors; there were also fissures in Man Ray's relationship with Kiki that were making times at home unbearable. Now that his reputation as a photographer was beginning to oppress him, Man Ray was feeling, too, a powerful pull toward painting, and he finally decided to seek a separate studio in a quieter neighborhood.

As Man Ray tells it in his memoirs, he was taking one of his daily strolls in and around his beloved Jardin du Luxembourg, this time meandering up boulevard St. Michel to the north and east of the Quartier, when he "came upon a To Let sign on a quiet street." It was 8, rue Val-de-Grâce, in the Fifth Arrondissement, near the Sorbonne, and equally near the imposing dome of the Observatoire. Halfway down the street from the seventeenth-century Val-de-Grâce church, with its dominant, colonnaded entrance and wrought-iron gate, was an intimate block of flats, across from a charming, quiet courtyard, where ancient maple trees were set amid meticulously groomed islands of grass and bright flower beds. Val-de-Grâce was a welcome change from the hustle and bustle of Montparnasse, yet only a ten-minute walk from Campagne-Première.

The studio was smaller, and Man Ray designed and built highly veneered leather, metal, and canvas furniture to fit, setting aside an area near the window for painting. He did install a telephone, a concession to his concern for maintaining commercial contacts; a gramophone, so he could listen to beloved jazz records while he worked; and a small desk in another corner for correspondence. On the walls the works Man Ray displayed were, as usual, mostly his own, with some examples from his growing collection of African masks. The painting studio was clean, spare, and coolly minimal, in marked contrast to the systematic clutter of the other place.

Man Ray spent mornings at Val-de-Grâce while the light was best. Then, after lunch, he'd race back to Campagne-Première, where his assistant, a young woman named Natacha, had covered calls, appointments, and work in the darkroom. Among the first works Man Ray achieved in his new studio were prefigurations of what he called two decades later *peintures naturelles*. In the current Surrealist mode they became known as "automatic painting." Onto canvases that had been expensively treated with silver and gold leaf, Man Ray squeezed gobs of color, improvisationally, directly from the tube. He was still in a hurry.

By unanimous acclaim, Kiki was the most convivial, outspoken person in Montparnasse night life, and the most conspicuously glamorous, towering over Man Ray—she was a head taller and far more flamboyant. He became more muted than ever in her presence. In mid-1928 friends noticed that their public arguments were becoming frequent and violent, with chairs and bottles being thrown across rooms. Kiki often ended up leaving on the arm of another man or retreating for a few days of solace to the flat of one of her fellow-models.

In 1928, through Man Ray, she'd met Henri Broca, for the two were working together on *Paris-Montparnasse*, a monthly news sheet distributed around the quarter. Man Ray says he encouraged Kiki to begin writing her memoirs; Broca claims likewise. Meanwhile, unknown to both of them, she had been unofficially working on her life story, commissioned by Edward Titus, husband of Helena Rubinstein, publisher of Black Manikin Press, and proprietor of the bookstore by the same name on the rue Delambre, just a few blocks away from Man Ray's studio toward the carrefour Vavin, hub of Montparnasse. It wasn't long before Kiki moved in with Broca, whom Man Ray promptly branded as "a drinker and a drug addict, subject to hallucinations." One of Broca's fantasies, no doubt, was that he could capitalize upon Kiki's fame and make it his own fortune. In this assumption he was correct, for the French version of *Souvenirs de Kiki de Montparnasse* was brought out by Editions Broca in early 1929, to immediate acclaim. Soon after, Kiki left Broca for her accordian-playing accompanist. Man Ray, for his part, was spending more time out of the quarter and summering in the south of France.

The following year, Titus published an English-language edition of *Kiki's Memoirs*, ably translated by Samuel Putnam, the American poet, with a rave introduction by Ernest Hemingway that romanticized the 1920s and placed Kiki at the center of that romance, the ultrafeminine symbol of "an Era that is over." Discussing her lovers in a series of charming, primitive, and revealing vignettes, Kiki shifted with ease from Chaim Soutine to Modigliani, Kisling, Utrillo, Foujita, Per Krogh, and Man Ray

("He has an accent I like and a kind of mysterious way with him"). Titus advertised the book in the pages of his esteemed magazine, *This Quarter:* "Kiki! Kiki! Kiki! loud and hearty rings that name wherever she appears in the streets and haunts of Paris" ran the bombastic copy, describing her writing style as "straight-from-the-shoulder, humanly and . . . as truly to the manner born as Villon, Rabelais, or Montaigne."

The fact that the book sported an introduction by Hemingway—the only one he'd ever written in his career—made a great impression on the American community. Kay Boyle's tribute was typical of the response to Kiki among habitués of Montparnasse at the end of the twenties: "When you knocked at Kiki's white, strong flesh for entry," Boyle recalled, "she opened wide her heart and moved the furniture aside so that you could come in."

Despite himself, Man Ray continued to attract wealthy patrons who were no longer satisfied with merely a still portrait. In midwinter 1929, Vicomte Charles de Noailles, impressed by the virtuosity of *L'étoile de mer,* approached Man Ray with a commission for what was originally intended as a glorified home movie. Noailles wanted to own a documentary of himself, his wife, Marie-Laure, and a dozen or so friends carousing and enjoying themselves at his château in Hyères. Having underwritten films by Cocteau and Buñuel, he was no stranger to the avant garde and was open to a loose interpretation of the word *documentary.* Noailles therefore kept the terms unspecific, giving Man Ray complete freedom. The result was a film that began straightforwardly, bearing all of the trademarks of objectivity, according to the terms of their agreement—and ended fantastically: *Les mystères du château de dés* (The Mysteries of the Château of Dice).

Man Ray's filmmaking assistant, Jacques-André Boiffard, figured prominently in the work. He had helped with the camera on both *Emak Bakia* and *L'étoile de mer* and had picked up his own surreal style of photography simply by being around the studio for five years. Like André Breton, Boiffard had had medical training but had dropped out of professional school as he became more involved in Surrealism. With Paul Eluard and Roger Vitrac, Boiffard had written the preface for the first edition of *La révolution surréaliste* in 1924. Four years later, he executed a series of photographic illustrations for Breton's novel of the Paris streets, *Nadja.* During the mid-1930s, Boiffard returned to medical school and became licensed as a radiologist.

In the film's opening scene, Man Ray and Boiffard toss dice to decide whether or not to leave Paris for an all-night journey southward. Their trip by car down twisting roads to the château is assiduously recorded. Once arrived, they made an exhaustive record of the place, which is devoid of people. The film insists upon noting exterior reality faithfully, until the other characters enter— their identities concealed by stocking masks—and dance, play, swim, and cavort self-consciously for the camera. The viewer observes Noailles and his friends in action, but comes away knowing nothing about them personally. With its insistence upon chance and concealment, the film is an important statement of themes close to Man Ray.

The Noailleses' château was designed by the Belgian architect Robert Mallet-Stevens in Cubist fashion, massive blocks of stone set at odd angles. The stark, geometric shape of the building reminded Man Ray of the imagery in Stéphane Mallarmé's "*Un coup de dés jamais n'abolira le hasard*" (A Throw of the Dice Will Never Abolish Chance). Written in 1897, the poem was one Man Ray had first read long ago in Ridgefield, when Adon Lacroix had pulled the slim volume out of her steamer trunk. Mallarmé was revered by the current generation of Surrealists; "*Un coup de dés*" was the immediate forerunner of Apollinaire's "*Calligrammes,*" which in turn had occasioned Man Ray's earliest experiments with concrete poetry. In *Le surréalisme et la peinture,* André Breton singled out Lautréamont, Rimbaud, and Mallarmé as quintessential models for Surrealist language. To Mallarmé, the "game" of poetry was the artist's ultimate effort, representing the highest imaginative plane upon which, if he dared, he could triumph. Like Man Ray's film   a reflexive commentary, as are all his films, on film itself— Mallarmé's poem "*Un coup de dés*" is a commentary upon poetry itself.

Noailles was delighted by the film, which he saw at a private showing in June 1929, and he at once proposed financing a full-length work by Man Ray with no strings attached. The offer was followed immediately by a series of disparaging denials by Man Ray, calculated to dampen any future backer's enthusiasm for his cinema. "I wonder if I must continue to make films," the ever contentious artist said in an interview the following day. "Sound cinema will completely oust ordinary film, won't it?" The advent of "talkies" meant the death of cinema as Man Ray conceived of the art, and he wanted no further connection. "I don't believe that making a photograph talk gives to the cinema a really interesting realistic aspect," he went on, "personally, I haven't the slightest desire to show a klaxon and to make people hear the exact sound simultaneously." Two months later, Man Ray responded even more bleakly when a reporter for the magazine *L'Européen* asked him about the current state of film: "Something is going to die," he replied. "Today's cinema will be replaced by talking pictures, in color, in relief. Today's cinema is finished. Let's not mourn over it."

Man Ray even managed to convince Noailles to suppress the public showing of *Château de dés* until a full four months after the film was completed. It finally began a run at the Studio des Ursulines in October 1929, against the artist's wishes. Friends were respectful but mystified. Man Ray pleaded with André Breton not to go see the film because he felt it had too much of a home-movie air about it. Breton had to satisfy himself with hearsay and with Man Ray's chance remark that he was anxious about the film's minimal appeal to a broad audience. However, Man Ray's old friend from Greenwich Village days, the composer George Antheil, wrote from Vienna that word had spread there of *Château de dés* as "the greatest step forward that film has made in the last ten years." Would Man Ray be interested in selling rights to have it shown in opera houses around the Continent, starting with the Urania Kino in Vienna? Man Ray ignored the offer. He responded instead with a tentative proposal to collaborate on a new film with Antheil. Four years later, no progress had been achieved and the film was never made, despite Antheil's encouragement and pleading.

Man Ray discovered it was not easy to shrug off a reputation as if it were an old coat and step lightly into a new one, especially when friends persisted in coming around to the studio and showing him off. One such visitor toward the end of 1928 had been Man Ray's former Montparnasse neighbor, Ezra Pound, now living in Rapallo. Pound's parents, Homer and Isabel, were visiting their son as part of an extended holiday in Europe following the elder Pound's retirement from the United States Mint in Philadelphia. While father and son were staying at the Hôtel Foyot, Pound sent Man Ray a striking photographic portrait done in Vienna that past spring by a young man named Bill Brandt, with a brief covering note endorsing Brandt's talent: "Brandt is quite a good chap," Pound scrawled. "If you have time and space for a hemale [*sic*] pupil, you might send him 'conditions' etc.—E.P."

Pound was a friend of the Brandt family in London and had promised to find work for the twenty-four-year-old diabetic Englishman, recently arrived in Paris after four years' recuperation from tuberculosis in a Swiss sanatorium. Brandt had once entertained the idea of becoming an architect, but he'd taken up photography during idle stretches of his recovery. Like Man Ray, he assumed the stance of an outsider, partly as a result of his fragile nature, partly because he resisted the middle-class mold.

Man Ray took the young man on, offering him little more than a place to sleep. Brandt was an admirer of Man Ray's work and no doubt expected to be classically instructed, but this was not to be. "Man Ray was not very much a teacher," Brandt reminisced more than fifty years later, "and he was difficult to get on with"—as Berenice Abbott might have warned him. Brandt left the Campagne-Première studio after a mere three months, but not before exploring the place from top to bottom. When Brandt photographed Man Ray a few years before the master died, Man Ray asked him, "What did you learn from me? How did you do it?" aware that for days at a stretch he had been away, shooting in the south of France, at work on *Château de dés,* on assignment for Condé Nast, or secluded at his painting studio. Brandt confessed to Man Ray, "Whenever you went out, I opened all your drawers, I looked at everything in the studio," fearing that Man Ray would be angry, but, in fact, "he was delighted. 'That was the right way to learn,' he said."

Bill Brandt stayed on in Paris for two years after his brief encounter with Man Ray, supporting himself with occasional reportage assignments for *Paris Magazine,* while publishing his experimental work in the Surrealist journal *Minotaure.* Following in the path of Atget, whom he also revered, Brandt wandered through the Paris streets early in the day, photographing, he said, "signs and shop dummies, statuary and funerary monuments, and odd, archaic corners" of the city. He developed a cryptic and hybrid style, a surreal variant on "straight" documentary work, shooting from eye level with a tripod. His unique chiaroscuro developing technique gave the images a highly charged, eloquently foreboding air. The portrait of Ezra Pound that first caught Man Ray's eye zeroed in extra-tightly on the face, cutting off the top edge of Pound's hat. The poet's glance comes across as an anxious and vulnerable expression seized on the run, snared between moods.

After their work with Man Ray, both Bill Brandt and Berenice Abbott—who had never met the young man following in her footsteps—chose the photojournalist's path, turning away from Man Ray's cerebral imagery, deciding to direct their energies forcefully toward the hard truths of the outside world. They chose to employ photography as a medium through which to make a more compassionate statement about the human condition. Brandt spent the next two decades constructing a record of the panorama of English society. He passed solitary weeks at a stretch delving into gritty, out-of-the-way neighborhoods in London's East End and the worst slums of northern industrial towns, Rolleiflex always at the ready. Brandt's first two books, *The English at Home* (1935) and its dark complement, the unabashedly Brassaï-like *A Night in London* (1938), provide a portrait of England and its people in social and economic crisis, with imagery spanning deep blacks, grays, and bleached-out whites.

Abbott, meanwhile, embarked upon a comprehensive portrait of New York City from the Battery to the George Washington Bridge, in dense, busy, celebratory style. Her photographs are filled with the iconography of street signs, with shopkeepers staring vacantly. As Abbott reached for the grand image, her picture frames were almost bursting, compositionally packed. There are looming buildings, networks of structural steel before a blank sky, impassive and window-studded walls, and gridwork under an elevated subway. She loved New York as much as Man Ray said he hated it.

Both photographers did learn from Man Ray what he in turn had learned from Stieglitz: to be daring and ruthless in choice of subject matter and to take their cameras wherever imagination dictated. Even as he was enduring his own sea-change, Man Ray stood as an example of the sensibility photographers needed to have. He opened the door to photography for Berenice Abbott and Bill Brandt and then allowed them to step across the threshold at their own risk. The subject matter in any picture was of secondary importance to celebrating the *idea* of taking it. Excitement must be found in the *act* of making the picture, in the decision to seize this or that instant via a discriminating eye—and then to live with the choice made.

"Photography can never grow up if it imitates some other medium," Berenice Abbott declared. "It has to walk alone; it has to be itself." And, to Bill Brandt, "atmosphere was the spell that charged the commonplace with beauty. . . . It is a combination of elements . . . which reveals the subject as familar and yet strange."

Influence takes many forms. Man Ray would have approved of both credos.

With Kiki off the scene, Bill Brandt established on his own, Jacques-André Boiffard gone, and Berenice Abbott departed for America, the atmosphere at 31 bis, rue Campagne-Première was eerily quiet. The summer of 1929 deepened. Many residents of the Quartier headed south for the strong Mediterranean sunlight, perfect for *en plein air* painting, and the active nightlife at the Hotel Welcome in Villefranche and other popular points along the Mediterranean coast.

Disconsolate and footloose, Man Ray was about to leave for a long-overdue vacation in Biarritz with his patrons and friends the Wheelers. It was a balmy evening in July. He strolled over to a favorite bar, Le Bateau Ivre on the boulevard Raspail, for a farewell drink. Ordering his customary white wine—unlike most of his acquaintances, Man Ray was a moderate social drinker—he slowly mounted the wrought-iron spiral staircase separating the crowded bar downstairs from the quieter tables above.

Seated at a round table with the proprietor of the place was a strikingly beautiful young woman—she couldn't have been more than in her early twenties—drinking Pernod with plenty of ice (she was an American, perhaps?). As Man Ray approached, the patron gestured excitedly toward him and said to the ravishing blonde, "her pale hair cut short so that she looked like a sunkissed goat boy from the Appian way, 'This is Man Ray.'" The short, compact man with dark hair and darker eyes and the slashlike, unsmiling mouth held out his hand to shake hers. Years later, she would recall the economy and spareness of his movements, and his square, work-man's hands, "not dry, noticeably hot with almost a magnetic heat . . . and very soft, silky skin." "What's your name?" the photographer asked this tall, slender, blue-eyed creature, glancing up and down at her perfect figure, considering her prospects as a future model. "My name is Lee Miller," she replied boldly, with a trace of upstate twang, "and I'm your new student." "I don't have students," Man Ray the nonteacher shot back tersely, "and, besides, I am leaving for Biarritz tomorrow." "So am I," Lee said, not thinking, simply relying, as she so often did, on her impulsive instincts.

They were together for three years, in an affair and partnership unsurpassed in Man Ray's life. Born in 1907, Elizabeth Miller was the daughter of a Canadian mother and an American father. Theodore Miller was an engineer and a serious amateur photographer who passed along his love of things mechanical to both the daughter he adored and her younger brother by three years, Erik. Lee's classic beauty had not gone unnoticed. By sixteen, she had moved from Poughkeepsie to New York City, modeling for Edward Steichen and Arnold Genthe in the studios of Condé Nast. For two years, 1927–28, she studied at the Art Students League.

Deciding to further their educations in painting, Lee and a friend, Tanja Ramm, sailed for Italy in the spring of the following year. There, contrary to idealistic expectations, Lee experienced what she called a "revulsion against classical art. Instead, [she] had been working up to this idea that Steichen had put into [her] head of doing photography." In Rome, Lee and Tanja parted ways. Lee set off for Paris, determined to track down and connect herself with the best in the business, Man Ray. She'd heard about him from Frank Crowninshield and the rest of the Condé Nast group. Her goal was not to model for Man Ray but to learn from him. Luckily, Lee had not been put off by the unfortunate news from Man Ray's concierge that monsieur had already left for the summer. Instead, she plucked up her courage and took the chance she would find him at one of the places he was known to haunt nearby. She got more than she bargained for.

For the first half year they were together, Lee Miller lived with Man Ray and served as his darkroom assistant and receptionist. Unlike Berenice Abbott, who worked alone in the darkroom, Lee labored there by Man Ray's side. Visitors to the studio, such as Madge Garland, assistant editor of British *Vogue,* were "greeted by a vision so lovely they forgot why they had come." Lee favored unadorned, neutral-tone outfits, such as pale gray wool pullovers with matching straight-legged velvet trousers, which set off her natural good looks. Her skin was flawless and quite fair, her eyes light and languid, her straight hair cut short to just below the ear.

She made a dramatic contast with the small, dark man with a torso like a bull. To George Antheil, who dined with Man Ray whenever his frequent travels took him from Vienna to Paris, Lee Miller was an "extremely beautiful and increditable [*sic*] and sylphlike creature . . . a decor by herself."

Lee enjoyed telling new acquaintances that her father was a cowboy and that she was descended from American pioneers. She quickly had the other American women in Paris wild with jealousy. In a much-gossiped-about incident at one of Armand de la Rochefoucault's famous soirées soon after Lee's arrival, Bettina Bergery (née Jones) stubbed out her cigarette in Lee's feather boa and the wrap caught fire instantly. Considering the dramatic extent of Lee's décolletage, exposing her pure-white back, it was surprising she was not badly burned—and all because Bettina was convinced Lee was having an affair with her diplomat-husband, Gaston.

At first, Man Ray did not seem to mind Lee's quick rise to attention, either in the eyes of other women or other photographers, such as George Hoyningen-Heuné, who at the time was working in Paris for *Vogue*. From Hoyningen-Heuné and his assistant, Horst P. Horst, Lee picked up invaluable tips on studio lighting and photographic technique while she modeled. This new knowledge stood her in good stead in her collaboration with Man Ray.

Indeed, Lee Miller's professional relationship with Man Ray did not linger long on the mere assistantship level. She was quick, ambitious, and talented. Pressed shoulder to shoulder in the little darkroom, which "wasn't as big as a bathroom rug," Lee recalled, they "worked at a wooden sink lined with acid-proof Probus paint, a big print developing basin and a tank above that where the water could run through and rinse. Man Ray was absolutely meticulous about how photos were fixed and washed." At one end of the tiny room was a cupboard where he kept his film, nine-by-twelve-centimeter glass plates, and an enlarger with a mercury light to blow up his images, which he'd print on coarse-grained paper, then scrape away imperfections from the surface with a fine, sharp miniature knife. Whether it was the extremely cramped environment or simply the fact that they were of like minds aesthetically, Lee felt that it was often difficult to distinguish who had produced which image. Many pictures attributed to Man Ray over the years were, Lee often claimed later, actually executed by her.

Notable among these photographs with ambiguous origins was the lustrous nude first published in the third issue of *Le surréalisme au service de la révolution* in December 1931, *Primat de la matière sur la pensée* (Primacy of Matter over Mind). The reclining nude woman with eyes closed appears to be sleeping in midair. The print is noteworthy as much for the drama and sensuousness of the image as for its technique: solarization. Lee Miller took credit for the discovery of this "edge-reversal" method and said she had first used it two years earlier, with Man Ray's portrait of Suzy Solidor, dated 1929. Suzy stands with her hands cupped over her breasts, looking modestly off to the side. Lee was in the darkroom developing this print when, as she liked to tell the story, something—a mouse perhaps—ran over her foot. She screamed and turned on the light. In the tanks at that instant were a dozen nearly ready negatives. After they'd been "flashed," the unexposed sections of the negative, which had been black, were developed, turning white, and "came right up to the edge of the white, nude body. But the background and image couldn't heal together," Lee remembered, "so there was a line left which Man Ray called 'Solarization.'"

It was a magical halo, an aura. Living by his dictum that "the tricks of today become the truths of tomorrow," Man Ray subtly seized credit for the discovery six years later, when his first full-length collection, *Photographs 1920–1934*, was published by James Thrall Soby. Viewers—professionals and otherwise—were baffled by the sight of profiles against a white ground shaded in such a way that the outline of the face was emphasized by a heavy black line, as if drawn by a crayon. "This process was the result of an accident," Man Ray explained a few years later to expatriate publisher William Bird who interviewed him for the New York *Sun,* "that took place in the darkroom." He did not elaborate on the nature and cause of the accident, nor did he state who was actually *in* the darkroom at the time. Rather, Man Ray said, "I was in despair, as my sitter had left town, and could not pose again." He finished the developing and was pleasantly surprised to arrive at an unexpected result. "I have been experimenting with similar 'accidents,'" Man Ray continued slyly, "and have now learned how to produce them at will."

Lee realized it was one thing to be able to make an accidental discovery and another to evolve ways to control it. Here, Man Ray was the acknowledged master. If he knew while he was actually shooting a portrait or a nude that he intended to solarize the image later in his darkroom, Man Ray would arrange the lighting so that minimum contrast resulted in the negative. Eventually, he systematized the method and refined it further, making a print from a negative onto soft bromide paper, rephotographing it onto high-contrast paper, then developing it normally, stopping the process before the shadows became gray. He drained and sponged the surface with dry cotton, then "flashed" the negative for three seconds, with a forty-five-watt bulb that was three feet away. Development would occur in the sensitive emulsion slowly, after about two minutes; there was no need to dip the paper into the developer. Finally, the image was fixed in the usual way, and a print was then made on matte paper. The image could be diffused if Man Ray chose to increase the size of the silver grains in the paper coating.

As often was the case in Man Ray's work, solarization involved a subtle and delicate mixture of intervention, restraint, and action.

At about the time of the solarization "accident," Lee Miller moved into her own apartment at 12, rue Victor Considérant, near the Cimetière du Montparnasse. She set up a studio and darkroom there and began to produce portraits that were, like Berenice Abbott's early work, very much in the mode of her teacher. She had met Cocteau, Picasso, Max Ernst, Paul Eluard, and Stravinsky through Man Ray. She, too, worked for *Vogue* and for the important couturiers Patou, Schiaparelli, and Chanel. She, too, explored blatantly Surrealist imagery: a woman sits with her back to the camera, her right hand massaging the hair on the back of her head, bringing to mind the *Star Tonsure* iconography in Man Ray's photograph of Marcel Duchamp's haircut from a similar angle. In another, striking soft-focus print, a nude woman is bending so far forward her head reaches below the bottom edge of the picture frame, and for a moment one is disoriented, confused about which direction she is facing. In this aspect of her work, more than any other, she demonstrates her debt to Man Ray.

Lee was interested in shadows—those cast by a network of iron bars for instance—and in silhouette, shown by a hand reaching toward the white sky in despair. Two decades later, she shot some evocative cityscape portfolios of postwar Dublin for London *Vogue*. Her style by then had simplified and she demonstrated her documentary side with lyrical shots of the River Liffey and the shimmering reflections of buildings lining the riverbank. School-

LEFT: MAN RAY. PHILIPPE SOUPAULT, 1921. *Collection Timothy Baum.*
RIGHT: MAN RAY. JEAN COCTEAU, CA. 1924.

boys at play in the courtyard of Belvedere College were caught in moments of unabashed joy and naïve unselfconsciousness, as if the camera were invisible.

Man Ray struggled with Lee Miller's headstrong nature and unshakable insistence upon having her own place (even though they spent most nights together), own clientele (even though most of them had already been photographed by him), and most difficult of all, other lovers as well. At the same time, he was grappling with problems arising from his inability to control the course of his reputation. Perhaps the best example of this was the Gertrude Stein rift.

Man Ray and Gertrude Stein had made a strong impression upon each other at their very first meeting in the artist's Montparnasse hotel room nearly eight years before. In an odd little story published within months of the encounter, "Didn't Nelly and Lilly Love You," Stein sought to characterize the intrepid American artist seeking to become part of Parisian bohemian life: "I return the line and they incline to reproduce the time," she wrote. "In this way we say that the hand leads the way. This is a description of Mr. Man Ray."

LEFT: MAN RAY. CONSTANTIN BRANCUSI, 1930.
RIGHT: MAN RAY. COCO CHANEL, CA. 1935.

Indeed, Man Ray did try to lead the way for her during the lean years. For Gertrude Stein, these were most years. Despite her unchallenged central position in all of Paris when it came to bringing people together, her work was largely ignored. Man Ray generously volunteered to act as her agent with his contacts at British *Vogue* and other magazines, but with no success. In the early to mid-twenties, Man Ray could not find publication outlets for Stein's work.

While Gertrude Stein let it be known that Man Ray had exclusive rights to photograph her, she did not think very highly of him as a painter. As far as Man Ray was concerned, Stein fell into the category of his "sitters," as opposed to his "models." He had trouble reconciling portrait photography as a job—where he was employed, even for a few minutes, by someone paying a fee for service—with his more authoritarian role as a manipulator of the human form for aesthetic reasons. He preferred having the power to control, and most women who posed for him caught on to the fact soon enough, or they found themselves not posing for him much longer.

"Haven't you understood yet," Miss Stein said increduously

to Eugène Jolas, editor of *transition*, "that the leading British-language writer today is myself, Gertrude Stein?" To which the ever undiplomatic Jolas replied, "Miss Stein, you will excuse me, but I do not agree with you." This was in the very early 1930s, when most readers shared Monsieur Jolas's response. Meanwhile, Man Ray, by his own admission, was "getting known and had the reputation of being a very expensive photographer perhaps because [he] sent out bills more often when [he] thought sitters could pay something."

The young artist on the ascendancy, breaking into every glossy fashion magazine as well as the respected avant-garde and Surrealist literary and art journals in several languages, figured it was time for Miss Stein to produce payment for the portraits he had made of her and her dog, Basket. On the afternoon of February 12, 1930, Man Ray sent her a bill for "500 frs. for the last series of photographs" he had taken. This action struck Miss Stein as forward and singularly devoid of respect. She wrote back to him on the same sheet of note paper:

> My dear Man Ray:
> Kindly remember that you offered to take the last series of portraits the first time you saw my dog. Kindly remember that I have always refused to sit for anyone to photograph me in order to give you the exclusive rights. Kindly remember that you have never been asked to give me any return for your sale of my photographs. My dear Man Ray, we are all hard up but don't be silly about it.
> Always,
> Gertrude Stein

They never spoke to each other again. The bill was never paid. And the bitterness never left Man Ray. Forty years later, Perry Miller Adato was in Paris to work on her documentary of the life of Gertrude Stein, *When This You See, Remember Me*. She tracked down many survivors of those Lost Generation days, and succeeded in convincing them to reminisce for her camera. Only Maria Jolas and Man Ray refused to be interviewed. Man Ray was "acerbic" over the telephone with Adato when the subject of Gertrude Stein came up, recalling as if it were yesterday that she wasn't interested in his "real work"—his painting—but only in using his photographs "for publicity purposes.

. . . She was falling all over those other young painters," Man Ray said with anger, "but all she could see me for was simple portraiture." To complicate matters, in her *Autobiography of Alice B. Toklas,* published in 1933, Gertrude Stein had written of Man Ray with insight and warmth.

The Gertrude Stein incident was not the last time Man Ray would have trouble sorting out the knot of his feelings about being renowned in one context while simultaneously yearning for recognition in another. Fellow-artist and neighbor on rue Campagne-Première (where he founded his Atelier 17 studio for printmaking) Stanley William Hayter remembered Man Ray in those troubled years as "the photographer who thought he was a painter." In fact, by 1930, Man Ray's first painting breakthrough of his mature period was not all that far off. The irony would be the circumstances plunging him into the most monumental canvas of his life.

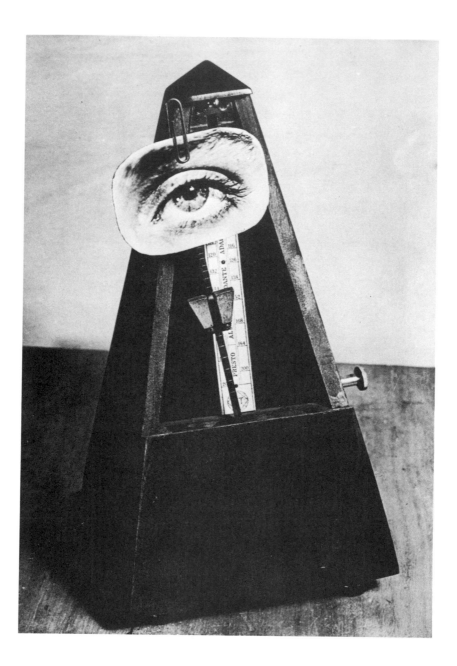

MAN RAY. *OBJECT TO BE DESTROYED*, 1932.
A PHOTOGRAPH OF LEE MILLER'S EYE IS AFFIXED
TO THE METRONOME.

THE LVERS

MAN RAY and Lee Miller were a photography team much in demand on the spring social circuit. One of the most noteworthy events during the 1930 season was the White Ball given by Mr. and Mrs. Pecci-Blunt (she was the niece of Pope Leo XIII). Guests could come in costume or not; the stipulation was that they had to wear white. Jean Cocteau and Christian Bérard created white plaster masks and wigs for the occasion. A white dance floor was laid in the garden of the estate. The orchestra played behind bushes.

Man Ray was hired to provide extra-special effects. The day before the ball, browsing in a flea market on the Right Bank, he discovered some discarded, hand-colored film, which he projected onto the white costumes from a window overlooking the crowd, so that the guests became a moving screen. Lee said it worked even more effectively when they projected black-and-white film, some of it with captions, creating the impression of a circus of letters arbitrarily moving together. Years later, she recollected that she had borrowed a white gown from one of the couturiers she worked for, Mme Vionnet, to wear to the Pecci-Blunt party. But Man Ray insisted that she had been "dressed as a tennis player in a very smart shorts and blouse," making her irresistible to the male guests who could not take their eyes off her shining blond hair and shapely legs. Lee did not spend much time by Man Ray's side that night. She was too busy dancing with anyone who asked her, having fun while Man Ray worked.

Lee and Man Ray often went out socially with people who came to know them first as portraitists. That summer of 1930 was also notable for the appearance on the scene of William Seabrook, an American writer Man Ray described as a "sort of Marco Polo" with a penchant for the exotic, both geographically and sexually. He always seemed to be en route either to or from the West Indies or Africa. His wanderings provided fuel for books and magazine serializations, for which he was paid extremely well; *Ladies' Home Journal* offered Seabrook thirty thousand dollars for a multipart article on Africa after he returned from Timbuktu. He also amassed a distinguished collection of African masks at a time when primitive art was in vogue among the Surrealist crowd.

Seabrook's other exotic interest lay in tying up or otherwise adorning and encumbering young women and then asking Man Ray to photograph them. He even went so far as to present his wife, Marjorie, with a silver dog collar designed by Man Ray. In this dubious area the two were true collaborators. One of Seabrook's many notes sent to Man Ray by *pneumatique* mail from the Hôtel Place de L'Odéon (where he always stayed while in Paris) goes into rapturous detail, enumerating a shopping list of costumes to grace the female body: "I've got some additional tentative ideas to go along with the black mask," Seabrook breathlessly wrote Man Ray one morning, in anticipation of their meeting. "A black priest's robe and priest's shovel hat. . . . Concealed beneath it a wasp-waist hour-glass corset finished either in some glittering fabric that looks like polished steel, or in black leatherlike material to match the mask. Also boots or slippers with fantastically high heels. . . . Unless I hear from you to the contrary," he wrote, "I'll bring the young woman by your studio for a little while around five-thirty this afternoon."

Man Ray and Lee and Seabrook and Marjorie quite enjoyed one another's company even though Lee refused Seabrook's entreaties (for he, too, found her seductive) to participate in the dress-up photo sessions. She was content to watch. She did agree to pose nude for Man Ray, although his studies of Lee's body are strikingly less explicit than those of Kiki, who stared into the camera straightforwardly. Lee is always seen from the side, soft-focused and romantic, her legs demurely crossed, her eyes downcast.

Jean Cocteau, however, succeeded in drawing Lee Miller into a dramatic role, much to Man Ray's distress. Cocteau had fallen out of favor with Breton and had been, in effect, excommunicated from Surrealist ranks. Backed by Charles de Noailles, Man Ray's benefactor for *Château de dés,* Cocteau was assembling his cast for *Blood of a Poet* in 1931, darting around from table to table at the Dôme, looking for the right female to play a part in his first film, when he discovered Lee. Noailles once again had come through with no-strings-attached funding. The two had originally agreed it might be amusing to make an animated cartoon. This idea was soon dropped in favor of what Cocteau called "a film as free as an animated cartoon, choosing faces and places which would correspond to the freedom a designer has when inventing a world of his own."

Cocteau recreated the Temple of Eleusis in Greece on film, and he populated his spectacle of antiquity with human statuary. Covered from head to toe with pastelike makeup so that she would resemble marble, then draped in white robes, Lee nearly suffocated from the complete blockage of her pores. Man Ray was livid—he was resentful of missed opportunities now that he had (perhaps foolishly) announced his divorce from film—and accused Lee of being disloyal. He was jealous of Cocteau for having placed Lee in the spotlight and angered by her long hours away from the portrait studio while shooting was in progress.

On the many occasions over the three years they were involved with each other when Lee, ever the free spirit, went off for brief spells with other men, Man Ray wrote long, convoluted letters to her, which always followed the same pattern, one he had shown before with Kiki and Adon. Although he gravitated toward talented, outgoing women, he had trouble keeping them close to him. Man Ray encouraged his women to follow their own paths but then dissolved into anguish when they went astray. He conceived of himself as giving power to the women he loved, then would accuse them of abusing that power and turning their backs on him. "I have tried to make of you a complement of myself," he wrote to Lee when she became embroiled in a quick affair with the Russian interior decorator, Zizzi Svirsky, early in 1931, "but these distractions have made you waver, lose confidence in yourself, and so you want to go by yourself to reassure yourself." Thus he analyzed what he saw as Lee's inability to handle the autonomy he believed only he could confer on her. "But you are merely getting yourself under someone else's control," Man Ray continued, "much more subtle and indispensable. . . . You know well, since the beginning I promoted every possible occasion that might be to your advantage or pleasure, even where there was a danger of losing you."

Man Ray's crucial mistake with Lee Miller was this assumption that her strong will, sense of direction, and headstrong nature existed only insofar as they were handed down from him. Even when Lee met the man she ultimately married, the wealthy Egyptian Aziz Eloui Bey, Man Ray honestly believed that if he refused to let her go she would not have the inner strength to effect a permanent break. He threatened to do her harm, and he let word out around the quarter that he had a pistol and just might use it. When Lee did not come back, Man Ray degenerated into extended, graphic complaints on paper, defacing drawings of her image with erratic scrawls and scribbles. He retreated into "breaking her up" by fragmenting the visual representation of her body. Her eye was a favorite target. When Man Ray found that Lee finally had no intention of returning to him, that she was moving in with the Egyptian even after Bey's wife had killed herself in despair, Man Ray drew Lee's eyes and mouth in his notebook and then wrote her name on top of them so many times they were unrecognizable.

In Edward Titus's important magazine of the period, *This Quarter,* v. 1, September 1932, Man Ray published one of the most striking images of his artistic career, a drawing of a metronome with a cut-out photograph of Lee's eye clipped to the stem. The instructions in the caption to the drawing, called *Object of Destruction,* which later became an object, told the whole story: "Cut out the eye from a photograph of one who has been loved but is seen no more," Man Ray began poignantly, as if he hoped readers would identify with him and thereby annihilate his loneliness. "Attach the eye to the pendulum of a metronome and regulate the weight to suit the tempo desired." Intriguing advice; he was referring to progress— or lack of it—in a relationship. "Keep doing to the limit of endurance," precisely what had happened with Lee; she had reached her limit many times over, whereas he still felt driven to her. "With a hammer well-aimed," the artist concluded, "try to destroy the whole at a single blow." But obliterating what he had created— godlike—was another question. It was not that simple to block out the memory of a three-year affair in one fell swoop.

A few months earlier, he had encapsulated a photograph of

Lee's eye, larger than life, in *Boule de neige,* a paperweight in the shape of a glass ball filled with water; the image drowned in a swirl of floating white flakes when the paperweight was shaken. This object caused a great sensation in New York at Julien Levy's first Surrealist Exhibition in January 1932. Perhaps the "eye" of Lee Miller was the photographer's eye, and by separating it from her body, Man Ray was reclaiming authority over her sovereignty as an artist. In a photograph taken around the same time—not of Lee, but of a professional model—called *La résille* (The Hairnet), the woman is seen through the black, spider-web sections of the net, so that her face and hands are broken up into hundreds of tiny sections. Once again, in Man Ray's aggressive, classically Surrealist iconography, a woman is fragmented and therefore rendered less powerful.

"Accounts never balance one never pays enough," Man Ray wrote Lee towards the end, distraughtly wondering why he was abandoned after having paid with so much of his soul. "I am always in reserve," he confessed, with a tinge of pathos, in a note to Lee in October 1932. Finally, in December 1932, Lee Miller shut down her Paris studio and sailed for New York.

The night Lee left was cold and rainy. Man Ray began the evening at the Café du Dôme, where he ran into Jacqueline, one of his favorite models at the time. Also drinking solitarily, she was in the throes of breaking up with her lover, the sculptor Mayo. In his disconsolate mood, Man Ray opened up to Jacqueline as he never had when she was posing for him. She was accustomed to Man Ray as a taciturn artist who communicated with a nod of the head or an economical wave of the hand when they were in the studio.

But this gloomy night, Man Ray was compelled to talk. He spoke of Lee as the woman who came closest to making him change his fundamental attitude toward women. He said he would have married her and had asked many times, but she had always gently but firmly refused him. In a way, Man Ray reflected, the Cocteau film incident was a decisive factor. Their relationship never recovered equilibrium after Cocteau chose Lee for *Blood of a Poet.* She had become a rival, and a talented one.

Man Ray and Jacqueline left the Dôme at such a late hour there was no place else open in the neighborhood to have another drink. "Let's walk," he said, taking her arm. They strolled slowly through Montparnasse Cemetery, making a circuit that took them past the corner of rue Victor Considérant, where Man Ray could just barely discern the outlines of Lee's apartment house through the mists. Back at the boulevard Raspail, they were two blocks from the studio. "Let's work," Man Ray said, clutching at the activity he knew best to take his mind away from his troubles. Jacqueline recalled that Man Ray "had the look of an orphan" that night. His dark eyes shining, he assembled what he called "suicide paraphernalia" on a table in front of him: a noose, a knife, a pistol. He wanted to capture *"un état d'âme,"* the mournful spirit of a moment when, Man Ray and Jacqueline concurred, they would both "dearly love to be dead." They began to photograph each other in mock-suicidal poses. At one point, as the past-midnight rain pounded furiously against the tall, opaque windows of the rue Campagne-Première studio, Jacqueline peered through the camera viewfinder: Man Ray, a sardonic smirk on his face, held the pistol to his head. She was terrified, not knowing whether the gun was loaded.

In the space of three weeks after Lee left, Man Ray wrote Elsie, he "lost about fifteen pounds due to worry, and also following the Dr. Hay diet," one of Lee's last legacies, prescribed in a book her mother had sent her called *Health and Food.* Dr. Hay's restrictions on food were such that "you could never eat potatoes or starch on the same day as you ate fruit, or fruit on the same day you ate meat." This regimen also called for a radically increased consumption of liquids, especially Perrier water and orange juice. Man Ray now wholeheartedly adopted Dr. Hay's taboos, as he had on earlier occasions, in an attempt to purge himself of all vestiges of corrupted life. His complaints of chronic loneliness, delivered with an habitually dour expression, were exceeded only by endless descriptions of various and sundry stomach pains, to such an extent that many friends thought he might be suffering from an ulcer. Habitués of the quarter knew to steer clear of him.

That dismal winter of 1932–33, Man Ray deprived himself of social intercourse, went to bed early, slept in late, and spent less time working, turning down jobs because he was unable to concentrate. He indulged himself with bitter feelings about Lee's apparently successful photography studio in New York, set up with her brother, Erik. Man Ray bristled at the news that—according to clippings sent by his family—the Millers advertised themselves as "representing the Man Ray school of photography." Man Ray assured his sister that he hoped "in time to disconnect my name from all these publicity hunters, because my real living is made through private channels."

In January 1933, almost immediately after her arrival in New York, Lee Miller's first one-woman exhibition of photographs appeared at Julien Levy's gallery at 602 Madison Avenue. Man Ray had shown his portrait photographs, rayographs, solarizations, and objects there a year before. Lee had made a complete break, and her show proved her independence beyond a doubt.

The self-proclaimed champion of "equivocal, ambivalent, anti-plastic, accidental . . . anti-graphic photography. . . of the cause of photography as a legitimate graphic art," Julien Levy naturally gravitated toward a kind of photography that was too sophisticated to make an impression on the marketplace. Even at the absurdly low price of twenty-five dollars a print, the works of Abbott, Atget, Brassaï, Coburn, Cunningham, Evans, Kertész, and Man Ray did not sell. The first three seasons of the gallery were almost completely flat, but Levy managed to keep his enterprise afloat with a financial cushion left him by his mother at her death in 1925.

Photography was struggling for acceptance in the fine-arts arena. A true believer like Levy could hang the works in a manner that attempted to place them on the same level as paintings, but it did not necessarily follow that photographs presented in an historical context—as he did with thematic shows such as "Portrait Photography" (1933) or Beaumont Newhall's "Photography, 1839–1937"—would succeed commercially. Yet, no other dealer was willing to keep work on consignment for years, in endless hope that times would change.

Lee Miller and Man Ray would not see each other again for five years. But after an initial silence, the bitterness died, and they began an exchange of tender letters. All during her brief marriage to Aziz in 1933, Lee yearned to be reunited with her former lover: "Darling," she wrote him on her honeymoon voyage to Cairo, "please come to Egypt like Aziz says—but soon . . . still always your Lee."

Man Ray found one way to hold on to Lee Miller, using the same vehicle he had employed with Adon two decades earlier, and with Kiki: his work. Adon had been immortalized asleep in the

Ridgefield cabin. Kiki's back had been forever emblazoned with "f" holes. Lee's lips were now abstracted from her body to hover in the Parisian sky dirigiblelike, lurid and red. The canvas was eight feet long and over three feet high, and it took Man Ray two years of meticulous, daily work to get it right.

A l'heure de l'Observatoire—Les amoureux (Observatory Time—The Lovers), or, as it has become more familiarly known, The Lips, has been described as the quintessential Surrealist painting, a supreme example of biomorphism, the use of organic forms oddly and obliquely referring to man, in a kind of fastidious, realistic illusionism—the unifying theme in mainstream Surrealist art in the heyday of the 1930s. Its title exemplifies Gertrude Stein's insistence upon embodying "time in the composition."

The Lips relied on a reference central to Surrealist philosophy, the devouring woman. It was the latest in a distinct series of big paintings, stretching back to MCMXIV of the Ridgefield period and The Rope Dancer and anticipating by a half dozen years Le beau temps. Every time Man Ray reached for the dramatic, grand statement in his paintings, he succeeded. The bigger canvases forced him into a deliberateness of gesture and drew him away from the slapdash approach that ultimately (permanently, some critics would say) undermined his reputation as a painter.

Man Ray's complete absorption in the task of painting The Lips also enabled him to forget his deepening hatred of photography ("the drudgery of [his] professional work," as he called it) and to escape into the preferred "high and exacting plane of Surrealist activity." Surely it is no accident that Lee's lips in the painting are flying through the air—reveling in sublime height, set in a faint smile, redder than any lipstick-reddened lips could possibly be. Indeed, the color of The Lips is as emancipated as its subject: the woman gone, the woman flown.

It is not known whether Man Ray was also recalling the evil lips of Maldoror, the "sapphire lips" of Lautréamont's poem, that satanically lyric work that had made such an enduring impression upon him in his American Dada period. The monumental painting is—like Lautréamont's poem—truly startling in its impact. Once again, as he had done so often in his photographs, making him the darling of the Surrealist writers, Man Ray set out to reinvent the female anatomy, in much the same manner as one of his earliest exemplars, Ingres. He wanted to prove himself with The Lips, to

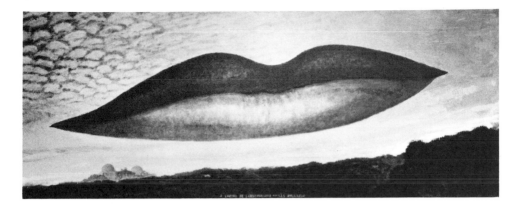

MAN RAY. *A L'HEURE DE L'OBSERVATOIRE—LES
AMOUREUX* (OBSERVATORY TIME—THE LOVERS),
1932-34. OIL. *Private collection.*

MAN RAY AND PAUL ELUARD, 1939-40.
Collection Timothy Baum.

demonstrate that he could take on a vast terrain and keep control of it. The work is figurative, yet mystifying.

Peter Gay could just as easily have been writing about Man Ray when he observed of Mondrian (another obsessive stylist) that "painting was the aesthetic correlative for his repressions, his way of coming to terms with himself—at once an expression of his problem and an embodiment of his solution." *The Lips* was the ultimate gesture of sublimation, as autobiographical a work as any in Man Ray's corpus up to that time, an attempt to lay claim to a lost love.

The contours of Lee's lips, vaguely resembling a man and a woman locked in sexual embrace, are the contours of Man Ray's deepest fantasy. What he could no longer possess in the flesh he shaped on the canvas. "Your mouth becomes two bodies," Man Ray wrote in his journal, in a text meant to explicate, at least tentatively, the signs of the painting, "separated by a long, undulating horizon. Like the earth and sky, like you and me." The relationship with Lee was scarcely over before he was striving to reconstruct it each spring morning in 1932 in his Val-de-Grâce studio. "Every stroke required a high pitch of tension and interest," the artist recalled, equal in intensity, he might have hoped, to the feeling he would have had if Lee herself were beside him. Few admirers of the work knew that the painting began as an idea based upon a photograph of Kiki's lips. He never got around to executing it in the aftermath of that parting. He had to wait until the powerful impetus of the disintegration of his affair with Lee.

In the far left-hand distance of the painting, past the unmistakable and familiar tree line of the Luxembourg Gardens, the twin domes of the Paris Observatory can be discerned. *The Lips* dispels any doubts about Man Ray's autobiographical tendencies in his work, for the domes effectively "fix" the painting geographically. It was a short walk from his studio to the corner of rue Val-de-Grâce, then left down boulevard St. Michel to reach the seventeenth-century observatory. Its walls oriented to the points of the compass, the unusual building was constructed without metal (so as not to disturb the magnetic compasses within) or wood (to avoid fire). The Paris Meridian time line passed through the observatory. There, scientists and astronomers first calculated the true dimensions of the solar system. Since 1919, it had been headquarters of the International Time Bureau.

"The admirable thing about the fantastic," André Breton

declared, in his extensive, explanatory essay, "Surrealism: Yester
day, To-Day, and To-Morrow," translated by Edward Titus and
published in the special Surrealism number of *This Quarter,*
September 1932, "is that it is no longer fantastic: there is only the
real." The memory of Lee's lips was as real as the daily sight of that
permanent locale of time, the Paris Observatoire. Man Ray's
characteristic bravery, his drive to forge onward into new territory
just when he touched a low ebb, enabled him to confront the space of
Lee's absence, even more vibrant and filled with artistic promise
than her presence had been. Together, Lee Miller and Man Ray
had fought constantly. In her absence, she inspired him to his great
midlife work.

Photography could never serve the same high purpose of
painting in helping Man Ray understand himself. This unavoid-
able truth made Man Ray's ensuing struggle to become accepted as
a painter all the more painful.

MAN RAY, NEW YEAR'S, 1933. *Private collection.*

LEE MILLER. *SELF PORTRAIT*, 1933. TAKEN AT HER
PHOTOGRAPHY STUDIO IN NEW YORK.

MIDDLE

LIFE

MAN RAY's aversion to taking the easy path, no matter what the context—romance, art, or commerce—was characteristic of his volatile and unpredictable personality, endearing him to the Surrealists even as it caused problems with the women in his life. And where family was concerned, Man Ray's elusiveness, compounded by his absence, was continually irksome.

Both generations of Rays were proud of this bohemian son and brother cut from a different cloth. During the 1930s, Minnie Ray served on the board of directors of Beth Moses Hospital in Brooklyn, where she did volunteer work for many years. At one board meeting in the fall of 1934, a friend of Minnie's mentioned having seen a selection of Man Ray's work in the Sunday rotogravure section of the *New York Times,* an excerpt from his collection, *Photographs 1920–1934.* How unusual and impressive the pictures were! Minnie was surprised and thrilled. "You're the first person in Brooklyn to say anything to me about my wonderful son," she told her friend as they walked home along Stuyvesant Avenue. "He's a genius and he's living in Paris, and we never see him anymore," Minnie added, expressing sadness in her quiet way.

Man Ray's two sisters and brother shared their mother's ambivalence. Elsie, of course, was Man Ray's primary contact. He wrote most often to her, always managing to mention "the folks,"

177

usually in the final paragraph, and occasionally slipping in a few dollars to be passed along to Max and Minnie. Elsie and her husband, Sam, served as intermediaries between Man Ray and his parents. As the years passed, they had very little direct contact with their son. Man Ray's father suffered in silence, as always. His mother bore the weight of her oldest child's distance stoically, except when she lost her patience. Man Ray's repeated promises that he would "come over soon" began to lose their meaning. Five years later on, when war in Europe threatened, Minnie would worry incessantly about her Emmanuel's safety, most evenings sitting by the parlor bay window and gazing out into the Brooklyn darkness for hours on end.

Brother Sam, the soft-spoken poet, did not achieve the success he had hoped for in his working life. As the private secretary of a well-do-do import merchant who speculated in real estate, Sam led an uncertain existence during the Depression years, and he eventually lost his job. He and Lena and the two girls, Selda and Helen, had to move in with Max and Minnie. Sam never recovered from these reversals, and he suffered several nervous breakdowns, "with midnight calls for the doctor," he wrote in a personal memoir, "rows of medicine bottles, needles and blood-lettings." When Sam died of heart failure in 1935 at the age of forty-two, his older brother sent regrets but did not attend the funeral. Growing up in Brooklyn, Sam and Emmanuel had had endless conferences about how they would take care of the folks when they were older, married, and settled down. The two boys agreed they would chip in regularly and help foot the bills. Man Ray may have had the resources to hold to his word on this boyhood pledge, but family reminiscence indicates he did not do so. Sam, faithful and close at hand, desperately wanted to help Max and Minnie, but was not even able to keep his own house in order.

Do and her husband, Israel Goodbread, a fellow with a flourishing mustache, had relocated to Philadelphia, where Minnie's side of the family still lived, with their daughters, Florence and Nancy. However, the Goodbreads, too, had problems making ends meet in the late twenties and early thirties, and so, for a time, they put all their belongings in storage and moved in with Max and Minnie in the big house on West Sixth Street in Brooklyn.

"I'm getting quite broke again myself," Man Ray complained to Elsie, "the slump is beginning to have its effect on me. Am counting on a series of orders as a result of the ad I did for Knox hats (September *Vogue*) with my new process." The Ray clan would look back on those troubled times with bitterness and bewilderment, and one night especially stood out in sharp relief, when their anger and questions about the true status of Man's finances first crystallized. It was a Sunday evening at "Pop and Mom's," a generally melancholy reunion around one of Minnie's memorable dinners. The three siblings who out of loyalty and necessity had chosen to stay close to home realized with heartfelt pangs how old and thin and gray the folks were getting. Their regret was intensified by the fact that Max, who was still working, was once again helping to support his children: "Pop gave me $10 more last week," said Sam. "Me, too," chimed in Elsie, "although I hated to accept it." "But what can we do about it?"—hopelessly from Dorothy—"we haven't any of us got a cent. And Pop is always saying he'd rather spend his few, hard-earned, saved-up dollars on us now, while he is alive, than leave it to us after he's gone, when we may not need it so much—and we certainly can never need money more than we do right now."

The doorbell rang. Max arose slowly from his armchair and went to answer it, returning to the anxiously awaiting group with a cablegram in his hand, trembling, for it was from Paris. What could this mean at such an hour? There was only one person who could have sent it. Sam snatched the yellow envelope from his father and tore it open: "DEAR FOLKS: AM WELL CAN YOU WIRE ME FUNDS LOVE MAN."

At midlife, Man Ray found himself at the convergence of a curious and unexpected set of circumstances. His great romance had ended. After two years, he had still not fully recovered. There was no woman consistently in his company. Having completed the most important painting of his career, he had not shown it beyond the confines of the Val-de-Grâce studio. He had achieved an ambivalent estrangement from his family. At the age of forty-four, Man Ray told Elsie, thanking her for remembering his birthday, "I don't watch the years pass . . . and I haven't any gray hairs yet." He denied interest in marrying again, especially as he found himself embroiled with Adon in a dispute over financial arrears. She had surfaced after fourteen years, with a claim that her now-famous artist-husband owed her money. It turned out they had never officially been divorced. In view of the current argument, it was just as well they'd not had children together, yet Man Ray frequently mentioned his young niece Naomi, who seemed to be developing artistic inclinations: "Tell her I'll teach her photography when I come over," he promised Elsie.

The most complicated arena of all was photography, the talent Man Ray could not deny, the career he might wish away yet that persisted as his very life's blood. The profession was devalued by the critical establishment and adored by the emerging school of bold magazine art directors, and by a few forward-looking diehards, the Julien Levys and Frank Crowninshields of the world. They were joined, in 1934, by an exciting curatorial group at the Museum of Modern Art, then a mere five years old. Under Alfred Barr's leadership, the fledgling institution shook the staid art establishment to its foundations during the 1930s.

James Thrall Soby was also among the true believers. This "son of wealth," the scion of an old Hartford family, visited Man Ray in Paris at Barr's urging and subsidized the publication in the fall of 1934 of a dramatic, opulently produced collection of photographs from the first fifteen years of his mature output. Soby had left Williams College after only two years and used his family's money to pursue his first and only love: art. He had become a discerning collector while still in his teens; his first deep interests were Matisse and Derain. In 1930, through A. Everett ("Chick") Austin, another risk taker (as director of the Wadsworth Atheneum in Soby's hometown of Hartford, he mounted the first full-scale Surrealist exhibition in America), Soby was introduced to Alfred Barr and Julien Levy, and his taste assumed a new direction. At a time when any kind of support was so hard to come by, Soby acquired a 49 percent interest in Levy's gallery and became an important financial backer of the avant garde. Publication of Man Ray's work was followed the next year by a critical study, *After Picassso*, in which Soby discussed what he called the "Neo-Romantic" painters, including Man Ray as a painter as well. In the late 1930s, Soby became an influential member of MOMA's advisory committee. Man Ray remained, however, Soby's first and closest friend among the Surrealists.

Photographs 1920–1934, Man Ray's 1934 collection, was a carefully assembled survey, a tribute that, through its format and choice of texts, revealed much about the artist's conception of himself. It was primarily an expression of Man Ray's documentary urge.

"Nothing can destroy the word," he once wrote, "it will always remain on record, just as a book cannot be destroyed by burning it." Time and again, Man Ray also pointed to language as a primary form of bearing witness. The survival of objects, and by extension works of art, was "one of his consolations." A book was the ultimate form of the legacy artists were meant to leave behind. *Photographs 1920–1934* was Man Ray's most cogent statement to date, an assembled chorus of statements and images, a summary that was also a valedictory.

The book's introductory image was a pen-and-ink sketch of Man Ray by Picasso, executed January 3, 1934. An artist Man Ray admired his whole working life, beginning with his formative years at Stieglitz's, Picasso did the drawing as repayment for the exquisite album of photographs of his pre-Cubist canvases Man Ray had assembled when he first arrived in Paris. It was a blotted, gloomy study of Man Ray wrapped in an overcoat against the chill of Picasso's drafty studio on the rue la Boétie, but there was no mistaking the pensive, dark eyes, the hair without a streak of gray, the aggressive stance. Man Ray liked the idea that Picasso struggled with the sketch, working away for more than half an hour, "clumsily, like a student who was drawing for the first time . . . squatting down on a small stool with a quart bottle of ink on the floor beside him and a pad on his knees."

The book was organized into five sections, reflecting the areas of Man Ray's interests in photography: objects and scenes in nature; nude studies and fragmentary renderings of women's bodies; portraits of women (all unnamed, except one—Gertrude Stein); portraits of men; and rayographs.

In Man Ray's introductory text, "The Age of Light," he grappled with the artist's known and unknown motivations. The question, "Why create?" was one Man Ray always believed worth asking, but the issue seemed particularly acute at this point in his life. The primary justification was simple and not surprising to anyone who knew his work: the desire to keep active, take risks, and defy convention in apparent violation of society's implicit rules. The pursuit of freedom had to be maintained at all costs, or art would suffer. It was an impulse that had driven Man Ray forward at every crossroad. And this pursuit, he pointed out, had to have a powerful energy pushing it, or the goal would never be realized. "From the first gesture of a child pointing to an object and simply naming it," Man Ray wrote, "but with a world of intended meaning, to the developed mind that creates an image whose strangeness and reality stirs our subconscious to its inmost depths, the awakening of desire is the first step to participation and experience." It was as close to a straight autobiographical résumé as he had ever come, and a far cry from the playful obfuscation in the catalogue for his very first exhibition in Paris at Philippe Soupault's Librairie Six more than a decade before.

He went on, pointedly, with a slap at the critics who persisted in labeling him a mere experimenter or trickster and devalued his rayographs in particular, by asserting, "It is in the spirit of an experience and not of experiment that the following autobiographical images are presented." The heat and light of the photographer's vision were unleashed upon the thing in the world and resulted in "the undisturbed ashes of an object consumed by flames." This was an important metaphor, an expression of creation arising out of destruction. It had roots in the pure chemical reactions of photographic development, the mingling of ingredients, the breakdown of metallic molecules, set in motion by the imagination.

Were the women unnamed because to Man Ray one woman was expressive of all women, or was there a less poetic interpretation, such as the one put forth decades later by Joella Bayer (at the time her photograph was taken—it appears on page 47 of *Photographs*—she was the eighteen-year-old Joella Loy), who said that Man Ray did not want everyone who read the book to know who his girlfriends were? Kiki was well represented, as was Meret Oppenheim, the young Swiss artist (of *Le déjeuner en fourrure* fame) Man Ray met through Giacometti in 1932; and Jacqueline, his model and companion the night Lee Miller left; and literati Iris Tree and Natalie Barney. The men of Man Ray's life were presented with no regard for anonymity—among them, Dalí, Tzara, Joyce, Eluard, Derain, Breton, Braque, Picasso (taken in 1932 at the same session that resulted in the image of Man Ray, with Picasso's hands like strong shovels, one cradling his cheek, the other flat on the table), Brancusi, and Antheil.

There were testimonial assessments of Man Ray from a roster of longtime friends and appreciative critics. Paul Eluard's poem described the essential solitude of the photographer, "Dans la chambre noir ou le blé même / Naît de la gourmandise / Reste immobile / Et tu es seule" (In the dark room where even the wheat itself / Is born of greediness / Remain unmoving / And you are alone). André Breton, who understood Man Ray intimately, even at times when the photographer was apart from the Surrealist fold, declared his portraits to be "the real Ballad of Woman of the Present Day." Aptly drawing upon the predatory image to describe Man Ray's approach to women, Breton attested that his friend possessed "the eye of a great hunter, the patience, the sense of a face, between dream and action . . . to dare, beyond the immediate likeness." Indeed, the snapshot—the quick impromptu photograph—derived its name from the hunter's term for a rifle shot fired quickly, from the hip, out of faith in a chance mark being struck.

Tzara's piece, "Quand les objets rêvent" (When Things Dream) had originally been published in 1922 on the occasion of the first appearance of rayographs, but it continued to be one of Man Ray's personal favorites. "You people this ocean which you accompany with your supreme silence," the voluble Tzara praised his quiet companion. Tzara credited Man Ray with having the intuitive capacity to penetrate to the heart of things, recreating them so that they seemed to speak to the viewer with a language uniquely their own.

Man Ray had high expectations for the book's success. He secretly hoped that royalties from its sale would enable him to make a long-overdue trip to New York. French reviewers were lavish in their praise. But the word from stateside was decidedly harsh. In early October 1934, soon after the book's publication, Man Ray rushed to buy a copy of *The New Yorker,* where Lewis Mumford, in his column "The Art Galleries," had assessed the book. Alas, it was the same story all over again. Man Ray was neatly categorized as "an extremely adroit technician, who had done almost everything with a camera," Mumford suggested, "except use it to take photographs . . . I cannot think of a single trick anyone has done during the last fifteen years that Man Ray does not show in his book." To Mumford, Man Ray was no more than an "imitator" of Brancusi, Renger-Patzsch, Eisenstein, and Paul Strand. He was wasting his time "photographing calla lilies so that they will look like drawings by a second-rate academician."

Dejected and angry, returning home late on a Saturday night from an aimless round of café-hopping, Man Ray picked up the phone and called his friend, *New Yorker* correspondent Janet Flanner, who, since 1925, had been filing biweekly "Letters from Paris" under the pen-name "Genêt." He had photographed Flanner several times. She lived nearby on the rue Bonaparte and was someone in whom he could trust and confide. Most important of all, she had always respected Man Ray's work. Flanner rallied to Man Ray's defense, and she pointed out the difficulty that Americans (in America) chronically experienced in coming to terms with the advanced state of European culture. "Many American citizens are suspicious now," she told Man Ray the next day, in an emotional letter meant to cheer him up, "of anything that doesn't look real, natural and if possible all right for little Mable, aged 8, to drink deep of." She tried to show Man Ray that his subversion of photographic technique was "a threat to the American Conception of mechanics." To Flanner, Man Ray's work brought out "the other side of art, i.e., new perception of old materials . . . like the behind-side of the canvas, a state of consciousness (coming from unconsciousness) on the artist's part and not just the funnyness of Bohemianism." She believed that Mumford had missed precisely the point Man Ray was attempting to make; the work, though different from anything preconceived or expected, was not—emphatically not—a trick. It was not one more gloss, one more safe sortie at *"Blague-*ing and *épater-*ing the bourgeois." The work was deadly serious.

Rrose Sélavy (Duchamp had recently, for mysterious reasons, added another *r* to her name) had gone on record in *Photographs 1920– 1934*, as fully in accord with her old friend Man Ray's intentions. Her statement, though typically opaque and all the more mysterious because it was the only text published in German, shone with praise for Man Ray as the consummate portraitist of men who, "insolent, serious and conscious of their looks . . . turn around to face the world."

While Man Ray had been based in Paris for the past five years, Marcel Duchamp had been traveling in pursuit of the ideal chess tournament. He was not a brutal player. A concern for aesthetics, for the beauty of the game, prohibited ruthlessness. Duchamp engaged in chess dispassionately. In the late twenties, he had begun work on a book about the endgame, the resolution. His competitive play in Hyères, Paris, The Hague, Marseilles, Nice, Hamburg, Prague, La Baule, and Folkestone occasionally resulted in what were, to Duchamp, gratuitous victories. In 1930, he played to a draw with the American champion, Frank Marshall, and in 1932 he won the Paris chess competition. But Duchamp always insisted that winning was not the point. He wanted to get away from winning so that he could comprehend chess in the same way he had gotten away from painting, so that he would not fall into the trap of becoming an addict to the smell of turpentine. To be seduced by the act of art was tantamount to losing one's ability to comment intelligently about it.

Aside from continuing to arrange art exhibitions for the Société Anonyme that furthered Constantin Brancusi's career, and playing chess, Duchamp's major preoccupation during this time was bringing together the diverse theories and methodologies of composition he had arrived at over the previous twenty years. He went about this activity deliberately and cheerfully, unaffected by André Breton's accusation in the *Second Surrealist Manifesto* (1930) that he had abandoned art for chess.

Duchamp's personal/artistic history took form as a series of "boxes," beginning in 1932 with his treatise on the endgame in chess, *L'opposition et les cases conjuguées sont réconciliées* (Opposition and Sister Squares are Reconciled). Notes, proofs, and diagrams for what eventually became a book were "prepublished" (or, more Duchampian, "not-published") in a cardboard box bearing the label of a Paris department store, Old England. This was called *The Box of 1932* and served as the prototypical form for his major *Green Box* of 1934. In February of 1932, after returning to Paris from setting up a Brancusi show in New York, Duchamp began work on this project, intended as a companion piece to *The Large Glass*, which had been languishing at Katherine Dreier's home in Connecticut.

Man Ray was intrigued by his friend's "preoccupation with putting his earlier work on record, making it permanent . . ." and the two of them moved forward on their respective missions, for Man Ray's book of photographs was at this time also beginning to take shape. *The Green Box* consisted of one color plate and ninety-three facsimiles of manuscripts, drawings, photographs, notes, sketches, and studies for *The Large Glass* drawn from the formative years of that work, 1911–20. He intended that the Box be consulted when viewing the *Glass*. Duchamp made a template for each scrap of paper and painstakingly tore reproductions one by one, to create three hundred regular and twenty deluxe editions. His concern with the most utterly faithful reproduction of his old notes was nothing short of fanatical. He rigorously preserved the type and grade of paper, the color of the ink, and the irregular shape of each fragment. However, the final selection was mixed together loosely in the box. There was no coherent order to the notes; that responsibility lay with the reader.

In September 1934, *The Green Box* made its appearance at the same time as Man Ray's volume of photographs was published by James Thrall Soby. Duchamp began immediately to concoct another box work, *The Box in a Valise,* meant to be a portable museum, a mini-retrospective of his important efforts. "Rrose Sélavy Editions" at 18, rue de la Paix became a busy cottage industry. Production of the *Valise* took nearly six years. Each example contained sixty-eight miniature objects, reproductions of such works as *The Large Glass, Nine Malic Molds,* the *Glider, Air de Paris, Traveler's Folding Item,* and the ever controversial urinal sculpture by "R. Mutt," *Fountain.*

Although he was on the road a good deal, Duchamp was never out of touch with Man Ray. There was always time for dinner when he was in Paris, or for an informal get together at Duchamp's flat at 11, rue Larrey. When Katherine Dreier passed through town, the three enjoyed a reunion. Man Ray was no longer active in the Société Anonyme, but Duchamp knew that Miss Dreier still thought of the photographer with fondness.

Man Ray was spending too much time in solitude—summers in Paris could be deadly—and Duchamp was especially sensitive to his acute loneliness after the breakup with Lee Miller. Duchamp invited his friend to visit him in the Catalonian fishing village of Cadaqués, where he shared "an absolutely delightful little house" with companion Mary Reynolds, as well as with Salvador Dalí and Gala. Urging Man Ray on with promises of "ideal weather by the sea," Duchamp had more than social graces in mind. Dalí had been commissioned by *Minotaure* editor Paul Eluard to write an article about the "modern style" architecture of Barcelona. Eluard and Duchamp had convinced Dalí (who, at first, typically thought to take the pictures himself) that Man Ray was the ideal person to provide the photographs. The five met at Cadaqués and left soon after for a quick vacation and shooting session in Barcelona in mid-September 1933 before swooping back to Paris. Man Ray's appropriately "beautiful and terrifying" pictures (the terms were Dalí's) appeared in *Minotaure*'s December double issue (no. 3–4).

Man Ray was not in the least put off by Duchamp's calling upon him to provide what were essentially documentary photographs to accompany Dalí's imaginative text. Man Ray agreed with the Bauhaus ideal of the artist as exalted craftsman. He also shared

Matisse's view, expressed in an early issue of *Camera Work,* that "if it is practiced by a man of taste, photography will have the appearance of art. . . . Photography should register and give us documents." Man Ray would have rather spent his time making a record of the architecture of Barcelona—or, as he'd done earlier on assignment for *Vanity Fair,* the elegant homes of Biarritz—than acquiescing to the whims of portrait clients in his studio. In documentary photography, facts and their primacy shared importance with the artist's desire to create a subjective interpretation of the world. "Documentary," declared a critic of the period, "is an approach, not a technique; an affirmation, not a negation."

On the infrequent occasions when he did turn his lens outward, Man Ray demonstrated an iconography remarkably similar to his work in portraiture. He let trees, buildings, and quiet city spaces speak for themselves. In *Au château tremblant,* one of a group of 1930s views of Paris, for example, two lovers stand framed in the dark window of a cheap hotel separated only by a fence from a dingy stretch of railroad tracks winding into the murky distance. The camera seems to empathize with the relentlessly gray setting and the angle, slightly higher than the cityscape, subtly implies the photographer's gentle but undeniable superiority.

Man Ray was never content to accept the conventional distinction that placed documentary photography on the same side as "straight" or "objective" depiction, apart from pictorial experimentation and expressionism. He had no use for labels and did not know the meaning of objectivity. James Thrall Soby recalled with delight the time when, six years after the publication of Man Ray's *Photographs,* he was showing a serious documentary photographer a group of Man Ray's inimitable pictures of "the high social and intellectual world of Paris. 'Why,' the documentarist exclaimed, 'these are documents too!'"

Man Ray professed no political ideology, either. As a matter of fact, in the later thirties, with rumbles of war in the distance, he became known for his decided absence of political credos. Man Ray's documentary style was visionary, grounded in the imagination rather than in a set of closely held and inflexible political values, or a social conscience.

While Man Ray was summing up his noncommercial photographic work of the past fifteen years, he was also directing a final surge of energy toward his fashion portfolio. Condé Nast, a steady client since Man Ray's first rayographs had appeared in *Vanity Fair,* was struggling through a succession of editorial changes, and the canny free-lance photographer was sensitive to them and able to make his move at the right time. In mid-1934, Carmel Snow resigned as editor of *Vogue,* where she'd given Man Ray many assignments, and joined *Harper's Bazaar* as fashion editor. Soon after, at a New York Art Directors Show, she met Alexey Brodovitch, who at the time was head of the advertising art department of the Philadelphia Museum School and after four years was looking for a change. Snow hired Brodovitch as art director of *Harper's Bazaar,* where he remained for twenty-five years, transforming the look of the magazine and influencing fashion art direction for decades to follow.

Meanwhile, *Vanity Fair* was in trouble. One year after Carmel Snow had left, *Vanity Fair* folded and was incorporated into *Vogue,* signaling the end of Frank Crowninshield's presence as an advocate for Man Ray at Condé Nast. Crowninshield's insatiable taste for the new and instinct for the modern had helped Man Ray break into the New York magazine and museum worlds.

However, Man Ray's lack of editorial affiliation was short-lived. Alexey Brodovitch had arrived in Paris, an exile from his native Russia, in 1920 and had known Man Ray during the decade of the twenties. Brodovitch was quick to make his mark at *Harper's.* Within months, photographs by Man Ray—as well as by Bill Brandt, Dalí, Cocteau, Dufy, Chagall, Derain, Munkacsi, Christian Bérard, and Léonor Fini—began to appear in the pages of the magazine. And for the next several years, Man Ray received the most lucrative and visible fashion assignments of his life.

Alexey Brodovitch has been called "the art director of the century," and for good reason. He was the first of his profession to introduce the concept of movement into a fashion magazine, the first magazine art director to combine pictures and text with a fearless use of white space, and the first to plan spreads of art and photographs rather than merely single pages. He allowed scandalous freedom to his photographers, conferring with each one even about cropping and layout. He respected their individual styles and never tried to coerce them into conforming to an overall editorial concept. Some of the most idiosyncratic work of Brassaï, Cartier-Bresson, Lisette Model, and Hoyningen-Heuné to be found anywhere was introduced in *Harper's*. "The disease of our age is boredom," Brodovitch said, "and a good photographer must successfully combat it. The only way is by invention—by surprise."

Richard Avedon credited Man Ray with "breaking the stranglehold of reality on fashion photography." But this radical departure would not have been possible without Brodovitch's support. Brodovitch wanted to feel shocked by a photograph before giving it editorial prominence. He shared Man Ray's desire to make something new without debasing the image through trickery or ostentatious displays of virtuosity. Like Man Ray, he had turned away from traditional modes of studying art at an early age, so he was not prejudiced by academic expectations. Like Man Ray, Brodovitch hated to repeat himself, either in the layout of *Harper's Bazaar*, or in his own equally controversial photography, especially of the Ballet Russe. Man Ray and Brodovitch were also akin in their nondidactic teaching methods. His Design Laboratory at Philadelphia was noted for a consistent absence of transmitted information. Rather, Brodovitch simply ignored photographs his students brought to him that were of no excitement. Class discussions usually did not center on photography, but branched out into the other arts; students were trained to think about taking pictures in a broader context.

Brodovitch is best remembered for his command to Cocteau when the artist's whimsical drawings were first commissioned for *Harper's:* "Astonish me!" This credo informed the pages of the magazine he art directed and was based on the same trust he had placed in his students.

By 1935, Man Ray preferred to make fashion photographs in his own studio and have the couturiers send models with gown changes to him. He was proud, he told Elsie, that he "never went to the dress houses." There was a practical reason for working this way; it was not out of vanity or self-importance. Man Ray had designed a unique lighting system of "photofloods," mounting a line of 60-volt lamps plugged into 110-volt circuits which were, in turn, placed upon lightweight tripods for easy movement. He attached this contraption to a rheostat, which permitted a steady, bright light that burned out quickly but gave him the quality of manipulation he needed and created the multiple-shadow effect found so often in his photographs of this period.

MAN RAY. BOULANGER AND SCHIAPARELLI GOWNS.
HARPER'S BAZAAR, MARCH 1936.
Copyright 1936 by The Hearst Corporation. Courtesy Harper's Bazaar.

Man Ray's *Harper's Bazaar* photographs are distinguished from those of other photographers by the unadorned quality he was able to achieve at Campagne-Première and, in 1937, when he moved yet again, around the corner at rue Denfert-Rochereau. Rather than constructions of imitation palm trees and beach scenes, Man Ray preferred that if there were any backdrops or sets at all they be of original art. One of his most compelling images presented an elegant model in evening wear seated in a satin-lined wheelbarrow designed by the Surrealist artist Oscar Dominguez.

In the same way that Paul Poiret had become a studio "sitter" as a result of Man Ray's photographing his seasonal shows, Coco Chanel and Elsa Schiaparelli came to the studio themselves. Man Ray succeeded in cultivating the powers of the *beau monde* fashion houses, who benefited greatly from the kind of exposure their designs received in *Harper's*. Within two years of Brodovitch's ascendancy at the magazine, Man Ray was ensconced in larger studio quarters and had purchased a new Peugeot, as well as a second home in the suburbs at St. Germain-en-Laye. There also began to be a noticeable polish to his wardrobe. While always fastidious in appearance, Man Ray had come to favor somewhat bohemian clothing topped by a beret. During the flush years of the mid-to-late thirties, however, he indulged in suits custom-made by Knize on the Champs Elysées, although he never abandoned his preference for American broadcloth shirts—16 collar, 33 sleeve—special ordered from New York through sister Elsie.

For a succession of springs, Man Ray received the plum assignment, the dream of every fashion photographer: exclusive coverage of the Paris openings. These were lush six- and eight-page spreads of the latest styles, eagerly awaited by American readers. In presenting the new designs of Schiaparelli, Mainbocher, Molyneux, Rochas, Lelong, Boulanger, Reboux, and Balenciaga, Man Ray consistently avoided the extreme contrast, the stark and sometimes harsh style characteristic of his *Harper's Bazaar* colleagues George Platt Lynes and Hoyningen-Heuné. He posed his models with a sense of romance, rather than outright drama, and he softened contours. One floor-length gown by Louise Boulanger, "a new cut and a new white crepe satin splashed with pansy browns and yellows" appeared in a triple-exposure, the same model posed three ways, to show the dress from the front and both sides, black space between each image creating the effect of the woman watching herself, eyes downcast and unfocused, as if she were dreaming, or had stepped out of the photographer's dream.

Elsa Schiaparelli's gown of "stiff pink Ducharne satin, cut empire, with a train and red and yellow roses" was revealed in the same way: a blond model instead of a brunette turned to the left in the first take, faced the viewer in the central take, and turned her back to the reader in the third. Man Ray skillfully played the flounced gathers at knee level against one another so that the whole assemblage seemed to swirl. When photographing single-exposure illustrations, he fixed the models in Spanish-dancer-like poses, one hand resting lightly on the waist, the other gracefully extended into space at a forty-five-degree angle, fingertips lightly curled. The model's hair was pulled back sharply from her forehead, her eyebrows penciled to create a thin, expressive line, lips pouting and eyes melancholy, while the multicolored panels of her A-line dress made a downward sweep to balance the lofty curve of her arm. A black Rochas gown ornamented with satin ribbons crossing the bodice; a "fan" made, as close examination revealed, out of a cluster of black gauze orchids; a handful of real flowers clutched to the model's breast, created an operatic impression.

The exterior, on-location shootings Man Ray had frequently done for *Vanity Fair* and *Vogue* were of the past. Virtually all his work for Brodovitch had a rarefied, interior, sparse cast. The photographs inhabited another world. There could be no mistaking the dreamlike, abstracted quality of a Man Ray fashion layout.

And there was no question that the Surrealist aesthetic was exercising a strong influence on the fashion statements of 1936–37. Illustrated in the magazines were white eyelids and green eyelashes, blue fingernails and mauve toenails; an evening dress with a larger-than-life-size red lobster print; buttons resembling anything from a crab's claw to fighting monkeys; extreme evening hats reminiscent of bird cages; and, of course, the famous Schiaparelli-Dalí black felt hat in the shape of a shoe, with its shocking pink velvet heel.

There are precious few glass-plate negatives of Man Ray's fashion work surviving today. The more in demand he was for commercial work, the more he axiomatically professed to "hate photography, to want to do only what is absolutely necessary to keep me going, and produce something that interests me personally. All these reproductions you see," he confessed to Elsie, who received the full brunt of Man Ray's feelings, "do not thrill me in the least, it's part of the unfortunate medium I employ.

"I have painted all these years," he continued, "and if I brought over my things to New York I could fill a respectable gallery, but these one-track minded Americans, the Modern Museum and others, even after having visited my place, and seen my work, have now put me down as a photographer."

He went on to hint at his commitment to live on in Paris long after many of his compatriots who came over in the original twenties wave had retreated home: "Do you wonder that I stay in Europe? I have here enough friends who support my work and exhibit it, and the fact that I do photography for a living instead of trying to sell paintings, does not lower *their* estimation of my output." Unlike Eluard, Breton, Tzara, and Picabia—who had inheritances and trust funds to keep them alive so that they were able to spend the greater part of every afternoon and evening gathered around long café tables in dialectical discussion—Man Ray had to work continuously to support himself. He referred obliquely to setting aside some "pin money" in the event he had to make an emergency trip to the States. By the latter part of the decade, Man Ray was not the only expatriate in Paris with an intimation of this necessity.

In 1922, rayographs had come into being to balance Man Ray's contract photography for Paul Poiret. The art, the "other work" existed to validate Man Ray, in spite of the energy he had to divert into laboring to make a living. In the 1930s, the construction of objects continued unabated, with the same motivation. Man Ray left a trail of fetishes throughout his studio. In almost all cases, they were made for a small circle of intimate friends, the Surrealists who understood (as Breton insisted time and again) the necessity of the struggle to free objects from their names and lift them above mere cultural artifacts to the level of art. To the Surrealists, objects had souls: they lived and died like people.

One object among the multitude produced during this fertile time in Man Ray's life is an apt metaphor for his dual existence. *Ce qui manque à nous tous* (What We All Lack), originally created in 1927, was reincarnated in 1935 to be shown at the important *"Objets surréalistes"* exhibition in the Galerie Charles Ratton (actually Ratton's apartment) in Paris in the spring of 1936. It was simple in design: a clay pipe, the title inscribed neatly upon the stem, graced with a glass soap bubble. The object was created partly in response to the challenge André Breton put forth in the preface to the exhibition catalogue: the artist must strive to bring arbitrarily selected disparate elements together in such a way that the synthesis produced a "change of role" for the newborn thing in the world. Only thus, through the celebration of the *trouvaille* (found object), could Breton's "crisis of the object" be instructively cured. These new, synthesized objects gave the viewer hope in man as maker.

The structure of Man Ray's life at this singularly important juncture of his career in 1935 conformed to Surrealist doctrine. Opposing and incongruous elements were forced by circumstances to coexist in jarring juxtaposition. However, they did so to the endless discomfort of the artist himself. The more Man Ray responded to the drive to create—he was helpless to do otherwise— the more he boxed himself into a cyclic pattern of anger against the medium of photography, ironically providing him with the economic wherewithal to carry on making art.

MAN RAY. *THE SURREALISTS*, 1930. *LEFT TO RIGHT:*
TRISTAN TZARA, PAUL ELUARD, ANDRÉ BRETON,
JEAN ARP, SALVADOR DALÍ, YVES TANGUY, MAX ERNST,
RENÉ CREVEL, MAN RAY.
The J. Paul Getty Museum.

SURREALISM
ACROSS
THE SEAS

THANKS TO an intrepid group of London poets who began to meet regularly on Friday evenings during the winter of 1935–36 at the Leicester corner pub in Leicester Square, Surrealism finally made its way across the Channel from France. Before their ideological split, André Breton and Paul Eluard did much to further this internationalization, traveling to London for the movement's early exhibitions there.

David Gascoyne was the youngest member of the London group and by common consent the most enthusiastic. He had seen a show of Man Ray's photographs at Lund, Humphries & Co. in London in 1934 and was now writing a short history of Surrealism. In the study, Gascoyne traced the Surrealist movement's precursors, from de Sade to Baudelaire, Lautréamont, Mallarmé, Charles Cros, Huysmans, and the fin de siècle; then through Jarry, Wyndham Lewis, Apollinaire, Raymond Roussel, and Jacques Vaché in more modern times. "I think we can say," Gascoyne observed judiciously, "that the development from dadaism to surrealism was *dialectical* . . . a new declaration of the rights of man." He was sensitive to the delicate nature of the movement's current internal politics, and he was not the first to recognize that Man Ray always managed to remain outside the struggles, whether grand or petty. Gascoyne had even gone so far as to compose a manifesto for

the nascent English effort. He cannily approached Man Ray first,
writing him with refreshing directness that "surrealism is very
much needed here in England, at present we have only, on the one
hand, the dogmatism and orthodoxy of the English branch of the
Writer's International . . . and poets like Cecil Day Lewis and
Stephen Spender, who approximate most nearly, I suppose, to the
present-day Aragon;—and, on the other hand, individualists,
stylists, the littérateurs." Gascoyne, Herbert Read, and Roland
Penrose were laying the groundwork for a definitive exhibition of
Surrealist art at the New Burlington Gallery in the coming summer.
Man Ray became their primary contact in Paris, because he was in
the unique position of being a liaison with the Surrealists, without
completely belonging to their group.

Man Ray had known Roland Penrose, who had arrived in
Paris a little more than a year after him, since the early 1920s. Born
in London in 1900, Penrose came from a family that was a fortunate
blend of artistic ability and great wealth. His father was an
academic painter of Irish descent, his mother the daughter of a
successful banker who inherited her family fortune. Coming down
from Cambridge in the fall of 1922 and, he wrote in his diary,
"determined to free [himself] . . . from the stifling restrictions of
[his] puritanical upbringing," Penrose made the Paris crossing and
"was born again."

Man Ray and André Breton became Penrose's closest friends
among the Surrealists; however, Max Ernst was his first strong
artistic influence. Penrose set up a studio near the Seine on the rue
des Saints Pères. His independent means allowed him to travel
widely, spending summers at the cottage on a hillside near Cassis he
shared for some years with his French wife, the poet Valentine
Boué; Eluard especially admired her work. Penrose's paintings in
the Ernstian mode, grotesque figures set against primitive, lurid
dreamscapes, were displayed at his first one-man show in Paris in
1928. In the mid-thirties, his marriage ended and he returned to
London, immediately joining Gascoyne's circle, which soon widened to embrace the painters Humphrey Jennings and Paul Nash,
sculptor Henry Moore, and others.

The New Burlington Gallery show was supported by Penrose's
generosity with funds and his natural ability as an organizer and
mediator. For two months before the exhibition opened on one of the
hottest days of the year, June 11, 1936, Man Ray shuttled back and
forth continuously carrying artworks between London and Paris.

He also provided the official photographs of the assembled works for the press. Bill Brandt mingled with the crowd, taking pictures of the luminaries at the opening, and he managed to catch André Breton delivering the welcoming address, in a photograph that conveys his bombastic style. The walls of the huge East End gallery were covered with the works of Tanguy, Dalí, Magritte, Miró, Bellmer, de Chirico, and Dominguez. Man Ray's paintings, photography, and rayographs were in good company. The huge *Lips* floated above a doorway, just as it did in its usual home, the Val-de-Grâce studio. His beloved *Rope Dancer* also made a rare public appearance, as did the *Mathematical Objects,* a series of photographs of items created in the 1880s by a physicist attempting to render algebraic formulae correctly. Max Ernst had taken Man Ray to see the objects on display at the Poincaré Institute in Paris, and he had photographed them in a deliberately impressionistic style.

In all, more than sixty artists from fourteen different countries were on display at the exhibition. As a result of the show, which ran through July 4, attracting fifteen hundred people a day, the *International Surrealist Bulletin* was born in London, officially certifying the ever greater influence of the movement. The exhibition was nothing short of a sensation, and the *Weekly Bystander* noted, it "set more tongues wagging in passionate disagreement than any exhibition since the Post-Impressionists first bewildered London."

Unfortunately, part of the "passionate disagreement" around the show emanated from Breton and Eluard, who could not coordinate their feelings about yet another monumental exhibition already in the planning stage for the following winter at the Museum of Modern Art in New York, under the guidance of Alfred Barr. Barr was putting together a show that he wanted to call "Fantastic Art, Dada, Surrealism," following the example of the Burlington House effort, but bigger and more compehensive, going as far back as seventeenth-century art to illustrate the tradition and roots of the modern movement. Breton would have none of this. The show had to be exclusively Surrealist, or there would be no deal. Breton enlisted the partisan energies of an old ally, the poet Georges Hugnet, who agreed with this stance. Eluard was, as usual, more willing to compromise.

Each poet owned extensive art collections. Barr sought to be definitive and so had found himself in a quandary. On the one hand, he needed the official sanction of the movement's spiritual leader, Breton. On the other hand, he was determined to make this show—

as he had done with the "Cubism and Abstract Art" exhibition at the museum the preceding spring—part of what critic Russell Lynes called Barr's "public course in the history of the modern movement with the Museum as his blackboard." Following Gascoyne's diplomatic approach, Barr likewise appealed to Man Ray's judgment: "I regret more than I can say this difference of opinion with the surrealist poets," he told Man Ray. "In any case I wish to concentrate the exhibition upon the principal dada and surrealist artists without including much of the rank and file." Breton's incorrigible habit of bringing in and then booting out artists and writers from the Surrealist fold made it difficult for anyone to know from one month to the next just who the rank and file really were. Hence the meaninglessness of such distinctions, especially for Man Ray, who made it his custom to ignore them and concentrate on his work. He was pleased to help Barr assemble important works for the exhibition, with the caveat that, "You can take your chances, but I can't foretell the outcome."

Man Ray and Alfred Barr had met during the early summer of 1935 on one of Barr's yearly European art-hunting trips with his wife, Margaret (known to close friends as Daisy). These expeditions were part of the agreement Barr had made with the museum when Harvard art professor Paul J. Sachs, founding trustee of the Modern, hired him in 1929 as its first director. Barr was a Man Ray partisan from the beginning, and he planned to represent the artist grandly in the "Dada and Surrealism" show. He was impressed by the range of rayographs and paintings he had seen in Man Ray's studios. After visiting the Burlington Gallery exhibition, Barr added several more pieces to an already lengthy list that included well-chosen examples from all of Man Ray's media: *Theatr,* a newspaper collage dating from pre-Paris days; airbrush paintings; objects; *The Lips,* to hang most prominently, as befitting its stature; pen-and-ink drawings from Man Ray's collaborative book in progress with Paul Eluard, *Les mains libres;* photographs, including the *Mathematical Objects* series; and rayographs, one especially chosen for the cover of the extensive exhibition catalogue.

Barr also borrowed works by Breton's wife, Jacqueline, René Magritte, and Marcel Duchamp from Man Ray's personal collection—and one in particular by Meret Oppenheim. The Oppenheim piece caught Barr's imagination so strongly when he first saw it at the Burlington Gallery that he eventually purchased it for the museum's permanent collection. Called *Le déjeuner en fourrure*

(Breakfast in Fur)—the title was Breton's idea, meant to resonate irreverently with Manet's *Déjeuner sur l'herbe*—it was a fur-lined teacup, saucer, and spoon.

Born in Berlin-Charlottenberg, in 1913, the daughter of a German physician and a Swiss mother, Meret Oppenheim grew up in Bern and Basle and moved to Paris at eighteen, already an accomplished artist. She studied for a while at the Académie de la Grande Chaumière, dropping out to labor on her own as a collagist, painter, and poet. At the Café du Dôme one day in the late spring of 1932, she met the sculptor Alberto Giacometti, fellow-Swiss and (it turned out, after some conversation) also fellow abandoner of the academy, who was living now in the rue Hippolyte-Maindron across a courtyard from his brother Diego, a furniture craftsman. "Sculptor-in-residence" for the Surrealist group, extravagantly praised by Dalí and Breton, Giacometti was a wiry fellow, a vivacious talker who, at the time he came to know Oppenheim, was deeply involved in making dream-inspired objects.

Through Giacometti, Oppenheim was introduced to Hans Arp and Max Ernst, who invited her to show in the Salon des Surindépendants exhibition of 1933. And Giacometti also intro duced Oppenheim to Man Ray, at the time engaged in taking pictures of the sculptor's recent creations for a comprehensive article by Christian Zervos to appear in *Les cahiers de l'art,* nos. 8–10.

Man Ray took numerous nude studies of Meret Oppenheim in the privacy of his studio before asking her to help with an ambitious series of photographs he was preparing for *Minotaure.* Against a foreboding backdrop, the huge iron flywheel of painter Louis Marcoussis's etching press, Man Ray posed Oppenheim nude except for a simple band around her neck. In some of the images, her arm was blackened with printer's ink. In others, Marcoussis, sporting a false beard and formal attire, expressionlessly attempted to blot her arm and fingers clean. Her limber, white body fairly shone in such a gloomy setting. "He told me he wanted to photograph me against a kind of machine," Oppenheim recalled. ". . . It was certainly with a rebellious spririt that I allowed him to reproduce those poses in *Minotaure.*" Like other models who worked with Man Ray, Oppenheim did not have to be coaxed: "Man Ray gave the directions and I followed them," she said.

During his heyday at *Harper's Bazaar,* Man Ray kept in touch with Oppenheim. She too, was attempting to diversify and interest several of the large couture houses in costume jewelry design. It was through Man Ray that she was able to sell her idea of "winter jewelry"—a band of fur glued on a simple brass bracelet—to the designer Elsa Schiaparelli. A frivolous discussion at the Café Flore with Pablo Picasso and Dora Maar, who admired the bracelet and thought it quite original, led to some free-associating about what else could be covered with fur. "This teacup and saucer I'm drinking from right now, for instance?" Oppenheim thought. She strode off to Monoprix department store and bought a cup, saucer, and spoon, which she then decorated with Chinese gazelle fur. André Breton took the piece for the seminal Galerie Charles Ratton exhibition of objects in the spring of 1936, and then it went on to the London Burlington Gallery show. The furry cup has since been called "the ultimate disturbing object, and a brilliant summation of the Surrealist idea of fortuitous juxtaposition."

The critic and philosopher Herbert Read, one of the most partisan advocates of Surrealism in England, recalled that the Burlington Gallery show came "after a winter long drawn out into bitterness and petulance," during "a month of torrid heat, of sudden efflorescence, of clarifying storms." With all the political factions and groups of artists not speaking to one another, it was a miracle that the exhibition came off as well as it did.

Paul Eluard, for one, found himself exhausted after the show. He urged Man Ray to join him and Picasso, as well as a few others, for a stay at Mougins, a hilltop village a few miles from Cannes in the south of France. It would be a time for rest and withdrawal from London's hothouse atmosphere. The poet was eager to continue working with Man Ray on the book of verse and pen-and-ink drawings that they had begun in earnest a few months earlier.

Picasso was now most often seen in the company of Dora Maar, a beautiful Yugoslavian photographer who had approached the artist at the Café Deux Magots on the pretext that she had been commissioned to write a story about him. She was a sultry-voiced, compelling presence, her deep blue eyes set beneath unusually thick eyebrows. That summer, as the civil war raged in Spain, she never left Picasso's side, even during his protracted conversations with Eluard, as he questioned the nature of his allegiances—to Spain, art, or both. Succumbing to subtle arm-twisting by Eluard, he had consented to show at the Burlington Gallery. But Picasso fancied himself a "dissident Surrealist," one who, like Duchamp, did not mind being affiliated in principle with the movement but who

fundamentally kept his own counsel. Picasso established connections with other artists on the basis of personal affinities rather than
aesthetic principles or causes.

"Le Maître Picasso," as Apollinaire used to call him, was the
center of the group that summer, which included at various times
art dealer Christian Zervos and his wife, Yvonne, poet René Char
and Paul Rosenberg, Eluard and his wife, Nusch, and Man Ray
and his first serious companion since Lee's departure, Adrienne
("Ady") Fidelin, a dancer from Guadeloupe. The daily routine was
languorous and did not vary. Picasso liked to begin with a leisurely
swim at the beach, after which he and Man Ray would take long
walks by the rocks in search of driftwood, shells, and sun-bleached
bones. Picasso, too, was fond of *bricolage* and fascinated by Man
Ray's spontaneous skills at creating it. Man Ray, dressed in a beret,
old corduroy trousers, and a baggy Breton blouse (sleeves occasionally rolled up to his shoulders), would pause every hundred yards to
snap a few shots with his trusty 35mm camera. Contrary to one of
his self-perpetuated myths, he *did* carry a camera outside the studio.
He cut a jaunty figure with a trademark little cigar clamped
between his teeth for extra effect and his beret poised at an angle.

Lunch was under a grapevine-shaded pergola in back of the
Hôtel Vaste Horizon, cypress trees arching over a terrace where
several tables were pulled together so that friends and visitors could
eat communally. Like Man Ray, Picasso could not keep his hands
still; lunchtimes invariably became creative times. A paper napkin
was torn and twisted into the shape of some strange creature before
the admiring eyes of the assembled group. One memorable portrait
of Nusch was constructed with crayon, coffee, lipstick, and wine on
a paper tablecloth. Picasso, attracted to Man Ray's cameraless
interpretation of photography, asked him that summer to teach him
the cliché-verre technique, and he became able to etch designs into
photographic plates without the use of a camera.

After lunch, the couples "retired to their own respective rooms
for a siesta and perhaps lovemaking." Following their work
sessions—during which Picasso liked to spring out onto the terrace
with completed paintings that seemed to emanate fully executed
from his magic hands—favorite diversions included drives to St.
Tropez or La Garoupe for sightseeing and more picture taking.

Man Ray's fame preceded him to New York City. *Harper's
Bazaar* had published his portrait of Wallis Simpson, friend of King

Edward VIII and "the most talked about woman in the world," and when he finally arrived in November of 1936 for the opening of Alfred Barr's pièce de résistance at the Museum of Modern Art, "Fantastic Art, Dada, Surrealism," the artist was touted by the press as a "surrealist prophet." Perhaps his friend Salvador Dalí had the edge: not only did he manage to dive through the window of a Fifth Avenue department store, he also made the cover of the December 14 issue of *Time* magazine. But who, after all, had taken the atmospheric picture that made Dalí look like a cross between a matinee idol and a matador? None other than Man Ray.

Reporters were curious about Man Ray's audience with Mrs. Simpson, caught at three-quarters view, wearing a high-necked dress by Schiaparelli with white embroidered piping around the throat, and an ethereal gaze. He was evasive: "I cannot talk about one person when I speak about photography," Man Ray told Helen Worden of the New York *Herald,* settling back even more deeply into the cushions of the white plush sofa in his white-walled twenty-sixth-floor room bathed in stark north light at the Barbizon Plaza on Central Park South. "My meeting with Mrs. Simpson was purely commercial," Man Ray went on, drawing the defensive shade down one more notch. "She is only one of a thousand women I have photographed. It was routine work." Pause. There was again an echo of Man Ray's pretense that photography was not art. He wanted to shift the subject to Surrealism, "the movement," Miss Worden warned her readers, "which those who belong to the cult declare will sweep the United States this year." She persisted on the more glamorous theme of Mrs. Simpson. "They ask me if a woman is beautiful—" Man Ray began, about to improvise on the endless Surrealist obsession with the female form; "Which brings us back to Mrs. Simpson," Miss Worden, the veteran interviewer, interjected, seizing an opening once again. "But Man Ray refused to be sidetracked into talking about the beautiful lady from Baltimore. He lapsed into a clamlike silence." It was the silence of a man who respected confidences.

"Surrealist fever" did seem to be living up to its hype in New York. "You aren't going to be able to find a solitary place to hide from Surrealism this winter," *Harper's Bazaar* breathlessly intoned. Chic shops around town decorated their windows with bizarre displays. Even the *Saturday Evening Post* departed from its staid image for the occasion, publishing a selection of experimental fiction. "The town is practically crawling with Surrealist exhibitions," Lewis Mumford observed from his perch at *The New Yorker*. He trained his sights on the current exhibition at Curt Valentine's gallery on Fifty-seventh Street, where some of Man Ray's new drawings for his work-in-progress volume with Paul Eluard were on view. Julien Levy and Pierre Matisse also mounted shows to coincide with the Museum of Modern Art's extravaganza. The show had become Alfred Barr's "appalling task. How he suffered over that!" recalled Monroe Wheeler, at that time of the museum staff.

Barr did appear more fragile, thin-lipped, and intense than usual on opening night at 11 West Fifty-third Street, the brownstone that became the museum's home in May 1932. Barr's anxiety was not surprising when one considered that more than seven hundred items had been assembled, dating from the fifteenth and sixteenth centuries, through and past "the War." Dürer, Holbein, and da Vinci pointed the way to Tanguy, Dalí, and Breton. Miracle of miracles, Man Ray presided over them all. Entering the museum through double glass doors—before reaching the fifty paintings by Max Ernst upstairs, before encountering Hans Arp's two dozen pieces, Meret Oppenheim's teacup, or Marcel Duchamp's encaged marble sugar cubes embellished with a thermometer, *Why Not Sneeze Rose Sélavy?;* before marveling at folk art, art by the insane, and art by mainstream Dadaists—the visitor had to come to terms with *The Lips,* facing every one of the fifty thousand people who came to the show during its three-month run. The museum trustees were shocked at the prominent location of the painting, but Barr refused to move it.

One enthralled art lover the night of December 2, 1936, was Helena Rubinstein, wife of Edward Titus, who begged Man Ray to let her borrow *Observatory Time—The Lovers* for display in the window of her New York City salon at 8 East Fifty-seventh Street. He graciously agreed, secretly hoping *My Lovers,* as he was fond of calling the picture, would be sold. Other viewers were nowhere near as awestruck. Perhaps hungering for a confrontation, Man Ray stationed himself squarely in front of *The Lips* that night, hands thrust firmly into the pockets of his dinner jacket. James Thurber, on assignment for his *New Yorker* "Talk of the Town" column, heard himself daringly ask "Mr. Ray" what his painting meant. "Ordinarily," the artist replied, wit always at the ready, "when somebody asks me to explain a painting, I ask him to explain a tree—and he's always stumped." Even the customarily droll Mr. Thurber was momentarily stalled. "This painting," Man Ray obligingly went on, "is half a dream and half a sort of conscious representation of the whole idea of love." Fair enough; and, unexpectedly, a rather straight reply. "However, if you wish," the artist added, immediately undermining the apparent seriousness of his response, "if you wish to give it any other interpretation, you are welcome to."

Alfred Barr would have nodded assent had he been eavesdropping on this exchange. Barr had pushed hard for the show, because he saw and acknowledged the same two dimensions in Surrealist art that Man Ray referred to in his statement to Thurber. It was, to be sure, outrageous and iconoclastic, evoking extreme responses. It was antirational, founded upon the dream life's penetration of waking life.

To Alfred Barr, Surrealism was also the most modern of modern arts precisely because it lacked definition and had succeeded in subverting the surface clarity and Platonic value system of Cubism. Surrealism reflected the inherently foundationless and anxious sentiment of the day. And so it made a deadly serious declaration about the lack of reliability its proponents saw in "the conventions and standards of established society," Barr observed, "holding society responsible for a variety of social, political, and economic follies . . . a spectacle of madness." Surrealism avoided definition because the world from which it sprang lacked any reassuring clarity. This Man Ray understood so well that he lived and breathed it. Man Ray was a Surrealist *person,* not merely an artist.

A rayograph was chosen for the cover of the exhibition catalogue published by the museum. But rayographs were in a class by themselves, a special breed. Man Ray continued to produce them long after he had officially ceased practicing any form of commercial photography. Rayographs were exempt from his endless moral twistings and turnings about photographs. Man Ray's argument with himself took a further step with the publication of *Photography Is Not Art,* in Paris, at the same time as the Museum of Modern Art show. The book-size portfolio included twelve of Man Ray's photographs with a preface by André Breton.

In this brief book, Man Ray staked out a position diametrically opposed to the one he had taken six years earlier when he had tried to explain to Francis Picabia the motivation behind his exhibition of photographs at the Galerie Alexandre III in Cannes. Man Ray had believed then that the time had long since arrived for photography to be shown in precisely the same way that art was shown, in galleries usually dedicated to the display of painting and sculpture. Picabia had eloquently described Man Ray as "the man with the sadness of the profound ideal." Time and circumstances had proved Man Ray to be overreaching himself. Now, he was more prone to view photography as "nine-tenths mechanics," as far from the methodical and deliberate mode of making art as possible.

In *Photography Is Not Art,* Breton christened Man Ray "the man with the magic lantern head," who transformed pure imagination into images calculated to shock and surprise—like fruit, hanging on branches, clothed in paper bags. With this new book, Man Ray took photography as far as he dared into its own world, as if to update Marius de Zayas's long-ago pronouncement in *Camera Work.* "Photography is not art," de Zayas had written in 1913, "it is the plastic verification of fact," as opposed to Art (with a capital *A*), which "is the expression of the conception of an idea." The critic added the qualifier that although photographs were not, perhaps, "art," they could "be made to *be* art" through manipulation, not trickery.

By placing paper bags over fruit on branches, Man Ray was recalling Paul Strand's work, which he had seen often at Stieglitz's gallery. Strand had taken de Zayas up on his challenge and photographed a table tipped on its side, harshly lit by the sunlight in such a way that it avoided looking like a table except under intense scrutiny. He intervened, always respectfully, in the world of things, manipulated it, and created an image that showed—the way brushstrokes did in a painting—the intervention of the human hand. By essentially reorganizing, however slightly, the supposedly objective world, Strand made his resulting chiaroscuro photograph "un-straight," or "artistic." Fidelity was not art. The mechanical, all-seeing lens, allowed to do its work, could not—so the critics heatedly said—be accepted as an instrument of art.

Man Ray continued the debate, nearly a quarter century later, that had begun when photography was born, for Baudelaire at that time had condemned the "photographic industry," which he saw as the refuge for painters *manqué,* too lazy or inept, or simply not gifted enough to achieve their goals in true art. To Baudelaire and other serious critics of the era, photography was useful to sketch from—a "poor stepchild" of painting, not much more.

Perhaps photographs would never have the same acceptance, the same critical imprimatur that paintings and sculptures automatically received. Perhaps the fact of reproducibility separated photography from the mainstream of artistic tradition, and it needed to be discussed and evaluated on its own terms, quite apart from painterly considerations. And perhaps those terms had not yet been invented and, ironically, might not be during Man Ray's lifetime.

Daisy Barr did not like the "Christmas snapshots" Man Ray had taken of her in New York and, after a long delay, finally returned the proofs ("I have long since passed the photographic age. *Il n'y a rien à faire avec cette tête là* [There's nothing you can do about that face] and you were sweet to try...."). However, except for that brief embarrassment the stateside visit was a success. The exhibition catalogue for the Surrealism show quickly went into a second printing, assuring Man Ray's rayographs even wider circulation. He also managed to complete some *Harper's Bazaar* assignments while in New York.

Man Ray returned to Paris just in time to accompany thirty-three of his paintings to the Palais des Beaux Arts in Brussels for a major show with Yves Tanguy and Max Ernst, "Trois peintres surréalistes." Except for what was absolutely necessary to keep the rent paid at the new flat at 40, rue Denfert-Rochereau just by the Observatoire, he cut back on portraiture commissions. Man Ray consolidated his resources by abandoning the rue Campagne-Première and Val-de-Grâce studios.

Meanwhile, Lee Miller, freshly divorced from her Egyptian, swept back into Paris for the first time in five years. It was a summer night. An elaborate *bal masqué* had been planned by Marcel Rochas. The Surrealist crowd turned out *en masse*. Man Ray created a sensation, dressed as a pirate, naked to the waist, with flared pants and a turban. Ady was with him as his willing slave, breasts exposed. Max Ernst also came shirtless in deference to the heat, having dyed his hair blue and painted little eyes all over his chest. Eluard, René Char, Léonor Fini, the Vicomtesse de Noailles, Michel Leiris, and Julien Levy were also in attendance. Lee Miller outdid them all, choosing the utter simplicity of a floor-length robe in contrast to rampant outrageousness.

Roland Penrose was struck by the unusual beauty of this woman he'd never seen before, and he asked Man Ray to introduce him to Lee: "Blond, blue-eyed, and responsive, she seemed to enjoy the abysmal contrast between her elegance and my own slumlike horror," Penrose recalled. Lee "caught [him] in her cup of gold," just as she had snared Man Ray eight long years before. Man Ray brought together two people he cared for and in doing so revived his dormant friendship with Lee.

After a sojourn in Cornwall, where Man Ray continued work on his sketches for *Les mains libres*, the three couples—Eluard and Nusch, Lee and Roland, and Man Ray and Ady—joined Picasso and Dora Maar for another idyllic stay in Mougins. The view from the Hôtel Vaste Horizon was especially lovely that summer of 1937—down a hill thickly populated with olive trees and cypresses to the deep blue of the Bay of Cannes, across to the purple hills of the Esterel and the snow-covered Provence Alps. The lovers sipped a local rosé wine under their favorite arbor and breathed deeply of flowery fragances that hung heavy in the air. To honor Picasso's great, passionate painting completed that spring in angry response to the senseless Nazi bombing attack that killed two thousand people in the Spanish town, Eluard composed his poem, "Victory of Guernica." Picasso painted portraits of the women; drives to Nice to visit Matisse were highlights of the fertile summer. Man Ray shot his absolutely last movie, in color, starring Picasso and Eluard. Deferring his return to Paris until the end of September, Man Ray rented a flat in Antibes and converted it to a painting studio. Back at 40, rue Denfert-Rochereau, he found to his relief a letter finally authorizing his divorce from Adon Lacroix.

"In these drawings, my hands are dreaming," Man Ray said of his haunting pen-and-ink sketches in *Les mains libres*, published November 10, 1937, by Jeanne Bucher in Paris. To commemorate this milestone in the artist's career—"They are the sum of all my experience, in photography as well as painting," he told New York *Sun* critic Henry McBride—there was a festive show of the drawings at Bucher's boulevard Montparnasse gallery.

The last two years had seen Man Ray on the move constantly. He had kept a notebook by his bedside wherever he traveled. At night, before retiring, if an idea occurred to him, he made a quick drawing for possible use in the book. And the following morning, when he woke up, if he had had a dream, Man Ray sketched an image from it immediately. An extended exercise in automatism, *Les mains libres* met with Breton's enthusiastic approval.

Far more than a Surrealist travel diary, the book was a tribute to the friendship between an artist and a poet with roots in the earliest years of the 1920s. When Man Ray first arrived in Paris, he had met Paul Eluard at the Café Certa, remarking to himself at the time that the poet with the high forehead and pursed lips bore an uncanny resemblance to the young Charles Baudelaire. There was no one in the Surrealist circle as soft-spoken, conciliatory, and persistently romantic as Eluard.

Man Ray appreciated the tension between the well-wrought outward polish of Eluard's poems and their subversive content. Eluard was attracted to Man Ray's thirst for solitude, and he said so in his poem "Man Ray," published as part of the Soby collection. Man Ray could not take enough pictures of Eluard's wife, the "Berlinoise" Nusch, whom the poet had met on a train in March 1929 and had married in 1934 after his divorce from Helena Diakonova—better known as Gala. She, in turn, became Dalí's lifelong muse. In 1935, poet and photographer had collaborated on

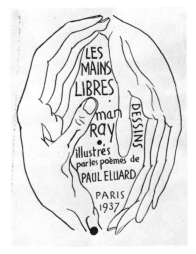

MAN RAY. FRONTISPIECE, *LES MAINS LIBRES*, "DRAWINGS BY MAN RAY ILLUSTRATED WITH POEMS BY PAUL ELUARD." EDITIONS JEANNE BUCHER, PARIS, NOVEMBER 1937. *Private collection.*

Facile, Man Ray's homage to the sensuous contours of Nusch's body complemented by Eluard's hymns to her love.

On matters political, however, the two men parted ways. Eluard joined the Communist Party and then the Resistance during World War II, while Man Ray quit the scene entirely. On matters artistic, they remained joined by their faith in the power of imagination: "The poet," Eluard declared, "is he who inspires rather than he who is inspired by others."

Man Ray and Paul Eluard shared a belief in the purifying capacities of art and poetry, in the wealth of imagery available to the artist able to plumb the depths of his "waking dreams," in the necessity that the artist no longer see himself as an omnipotent god, but rather as a mere mortal, who was, in Eluard's terms, "daring to kiss beauty and love on the mouth." Above all, Man Ray shared Eluard's belief in *"la fraternisation"* as a way of bridging the artist's essential solitude. Men as artists must work together, in an exalted brotherhood of the spirit. This solidarity had been the major theme of "L'évidence poétique," the poet's speech at the Burlington Gallery Surrealism show in London on June 24, 1936. Man Ray had listened attentively from the audience and leaped into action; progress on *Les mains libres* finally picked up speed. The two traveled and worked together the entire summer, in London, St. Raphael, and Mougins in July; Salins, St. Tropez, and Mougins again in August; and back in Paris in September.

The frontispiece of *Les mains libres* explicitly declared that "drawings by Man Ray" were "illustrated by poems by Paul Eluard." The poet placed himself in the background, presenting Man Ray in the introduction to the book as "a man who reveals himself, who gives us his eyes, his hands . . . Man Ray draws so as not to forget himself, to be present, so that the world shall not disappear from his eyes. He draws to be loved."

In *Les mains libres,* a dream journal, Man Ray gave expression to his fantasies with a free, unrestrained hand. Women were portrayed in a succession of supplicant, powerless, and, at times, endangered poses: head thrown back, hair descending in cascades; kneeling down, looking up, hands clasped to the neck in fear, shock, or surprise; eyes half closed in agony; nude, grasped by a giant's hand; being formed by a paintbrush on a string, collapsible, portable at will; lying beside a life-size fish or about to be eviscerated by scissors. If Man Ray was drawing "to be loved," it was out of anger inspired by love spurned, or as Eluard tellingly observed, "always out of desire, not need."

The poems did not serve as captions for the drawings. Rather, they played against or in counterpoint to them, as in *"Le Tournant"* (The Bend in the Road), a sketch of a hand reaching around a treacherous hillside by the sea. "I hope / for what is forbidden to me," states the accompanying poem in its entirety. In *"Rêve"* (Dream), we see the view Man Ray undoubtedly saw from his twenty-sixth-floor room at the Barbizon Plaza while he was in New York for the Museum of Modern Art show, except that hurtling down over the buildings lining Fifth Avenue and heading for a crash landing in the Central Park Wildlife Sanctuary is a Futurist steam locomotive chugging upside-down through the air. The poem reads "At dawn / I return//The Eiffel Tower is leaning / The Bridges twisted / The street signs dead//In my ruined house / In my home / Not one book remains//I undress."

The book concluded with Man Ray's sketch for an "imaginary Portrait of D.A.F. de Sade."

Man Ray's fascination with Sade (1740–1814) had roots in his pre-Paris days. Adon Lacroix had introduced him to Apollinaire's writings about the marquis. And when Man Ray moved into his rue Campagne-Première flat, he discovered that the scholar Maurice Heine, a next-door neighbor, had recently published an article on Sade in *Der Sturm*.

Heine, respectfully known as "the inventor of Sade," had actually made a pact with Apollinaire to search out and publish Sade's uncollected works. Apollinaire's premature death put an end to the joint project, but in spite of poor and failing health, Heine devoted himself to the task for the next two decades. The popular story goes that when Heine remarked to Man Ray that no portrait of the mature Sade existed, the artist set out to discover all he could about the man, even going so far as to visit the château in the Vaucluse where Sade had been raised.

Paul Eluard had spoken at great length about Sade during his June 1936 lecture at the Burlington Gallery, noting, too, that "we do not have a visual image of Sade." Sade, he continued, "desired to give back to civilized man the full force of his primitive instincts."

Man Ray's sketches of Sade for *Les mains libres* followed soon after Eluard's speech. Dated 1936, they foreshadowed two oil portraits he subsequently executed in 1938 and 1940. In the first, the Bastille is in flames in the background, while figures writhe in agony in the foreground. The whole is dominated by a massive profile built from stone blocks, the marquis with an impassive expression on his face. In the other, the background is calmer. The crisis has passed.

The hellishly vibrant 1938 *Portrait imaginaire de D.A.F. de Sade* presents him as if breaking forcibly from the stone confines of his body, and includes a telling inscription from Sade's writings about his explicit wishes for an unmarked grave. Sade's epigraph subtly summarizes Man Ray's conflict as an artist. He used his personality to draw attention to the work, hoping that finally the work would survive any vestigial memories of him.

Sade had taken a path leading from the erotic, dominant sexual behavior that satisfied his need to overwhelm women to at least one *grande passion,* his sister-in-law. Like Sade, Man Ray cherished most of all the possibility of a final, tranquil, and comforting love. Sade found such love with Marie-Constance Quesnet, the woman who shared the last twenty years of his life. Man Ray was, in 1938, not very distant himself from achieving that enduring, romantic bond.

Man Ray admired Sade because he had "spent twenty-seven years of his life in prison for his beliefs," yet while incarcerated composed his most important works. Man Ray frequently made reference to Sade's passion for "total liberty." His friend Henry Miller would later observe, "This was . . . Man Ray's religion. . . . He was a believer without a church."

One of the heroes of the Surrealists, Sade was the rebel and revolutionary, the atheist, the apostle of love. He was the exponent of a defiant individualism, the outcast who said and did what he thought, with little care for the opinion of others. He could be cruel or he could be kind in the gratification of his desires, but those desires invariably came first. He believed in the sovereignty of pleasure, and he was omnivorous in fulfilling his needs. "You will know nothing if you do not know everything," he wrote in *The 120 Days of Sodom,* one of Man Ray's favorite books. "If you are timid enough to stop with nature, nature will escape you forever." Indeed, Man Ray's work during the late thirties is filled with attempts to resolve his anxiety about this truth. While living happily with Ady, a self-effacing young woman with modest needs, Man Ray continued to express the other side of his nature with imagery of dominance, frequently manifested by objects in bondage. There were created, for example, many variations on the theme of Venus bound, the torso tied with rope, her head in a net, or deformed and wearing makeup. Man Ray's mannequin for the Surrealist exhibition in Paris in January 1938 bore glass tears on her face and glass soap bubbles in her hair. She was a perishable representation of woman. And *Les mains libres* was a veritable catalogue of supplicant women.

The book was a study in ambivalence: *Paranoia, Oui ou non, Le peur, L'angoisse et l'inquiétude* (Paranoia, Yes or No, Fear, Anxiety and Restlessness) were works well suited to the particular fluidity of Man Ray's pen-and-ink line. In *Les tours d'Eliane,* the dark, central door of a castle is also a vaginal opening, and an intrepid, tiny Don Quixote stands poised to enter, fearful of the consequences of becoming sexually overwhelmed. Man Ray wanted to imagine woman, as in another drawing, *Femme portative,* formed from spiral upon spiral and suspended by a string that he could maintain or release at will. Such is the artist's power.

During the period following the publication of *Les mains libres,* Man Ray made good his promise to himself and others to become more of a painter and less of a photographer. He had made a statement with *Photography Is Not Art.* He had brought out a book that demonstrated his virtuosity with the ink pot. In early 1938, simultaneous with the Sade portrait, Man Ray severed his ties with *Harper's Bazaar* (it would be for a period of more than two years) and embarked upon an ambitious session with the easel in his rue Denfert-Rochereau studio, as well as (spring and summers) in the delightful setting of Antibes. *La fortune* (Chance), a study of a pool table on end, billiard balls ready to find their own paths toward the pockets; *Le malentendu* (The Misunderstood One); *Le mur* (The Wall), in which dancing shadows of men chased jagged shadows of women; *La femme et son poisson* (The Woman and Her Fish), sketched in *Les mains libres* and fleshed out in paint, a study in anthropomorphism; and the tricky *Peinture de chevalet* (Easel Painting), which—artifice within art—portrayed a painting of a woman resting on an easel, all emerged from Man Ray's palette before the end of the year. He proclaimed proudly in letter after letter to sister Elsie that he was passionately involved in the true artist's calling, free of the constraints of the marketplace, and back in league with his painter-colleagues, Dalí, Ernst, and Wolfgang Paalen.

The Exposition Internationale du Surréalisme in the Galerie Beaux-Arts in Paris during January and February 1938 was organized around the theme of store mannequins dressed by painters. The "generator-arbitrator" of the show was Marcel Duchamp, who contributed a mannequin of his own design named Rrose Sélavy, and who made a point of leaving for England on the day of the opening. Duchamp came up with the idea of lining the gallery ceiling with twelve hundred coal sacks resting above a small grating through which a dim light filtered from far above. Man Ray, as he had done for the Société Anonyme shows in New York, assumed his natural role as master of lighting, *maître des lumières,* and handed each visitor a flashlight when he came into the opening-night festivities. This was an effective way to subvert the see-and-be-seen mentality of these affairs. Man Ray was enjoying his realignment with the libertine Surrealist brotherhood.

He contributed more than a dozen illustrations to the *Dictionnaire abrégé du surréalisme,* an ambitious compendium published to accompany the exhibition, a veritable "who's who" of the movement. Breton was characterized therein as *"le verre d'eau dans la tempête* (a glass of water in the storm); Eluard was *"la nourrice des étoiles"* (star-nurturer); Ernst took on his familiar persona, *"Loplop, le supérieur des oiseaux"* (King of Birds); and Man Ray *"peint pour être aimé"* (paints to be loved).

Man Ray managed, with Elsie's help, to resolve a dispute that had been going on for nearly a decade regarding payment due for pictures the Daniel Gallery had sold. Elsie contracted with a distant relative, lawyer Samuel Sootin, who was able for a cut-rate fee of fifty dollars to obtain release of all Man Ray paintings held in storage by Charles Daniel in the warehouse of W. S. Budworth in New York City. The works were sent to Elsie's home in Jersey City. From that time onward, Elsie Siegler became, in addition to her brother's lifeline business contact, the primary archivist for his precious work in the United States.

MAN RAY AND MARCEL DUCHAMP ON
HOLLYWOOD STAGE SET, 1949.
Private collection.

E S C A P E   T O
A M E R I C A

MAN RAY was planning to spend half a year with Ady in Antibes, where he could paint at will, enjoy the company of friends, and turn his back on photography. He would be producing a new kind of canvas in the Surrealist idiom and retreat comfortably into the rich territory of his dreamscape imagination. The paintings manifested that realm.

It was an idyllic time for Man Ray. And so he had difficulty accepting ominous signals of conflict. His news home from abroad during the prewar years contained a chain of denials. "Don't worry about the war," he reassured Elsie, "it's not half as bad as you think.... There will always be a chance to get away in time." Meanwhile, Léon Blum's Popular Front—a coalition of the left and center, bringing together Communists, socialists, and radicals— could no longer hold up against the incursion of Fascism in France and the rise of Mussolini and Hitler. Man Ray nonetheless insisted, "All the threats of war are bluff... I am staying on here until there is real discomfort—so far it's all in the air—except for the poor wretches in Germany and Italy." The prevailing feeling in Paris was that war must be avoided at any price. Pacifism seemed the best path to follow. Man Ray was not the only one wearing blinders.

"Staying on" was especially important to Man Ray, not only because of his long-held belief that Paris was the proving ground for his artistic innovations. Nor was it only due to the powerful accretion of seventeen years' adjustment to one place. His warmth toward Paris was also balanced by a residual bitterness toward America. It surfaced briefly one warm May evening at Café Flore on the boulevard St. Germain, a popular Surrealist roosting place. Eluard, Arp, Giacometti, Max Ernst and his lover, the English painter Leonora Carrington, and Man Ray were sitting at a group of tables outdoors toasting the imminent departure of Max's nineteen-year-old son, Jimmy, off to New York to seek his fortune. Man Ray could not restrain himself as he listened to Leonora's tête-à-tête with the boy: "You're teaching that boy British English," he barked. "They'll laugh at him all the way down the gangplank. Here is what you're supposed to say," Man Ray continued, turning to Jimmy with a dark smile, "and listen to my pronunciation." Talking slowly so that Jimmy could understand, Man Ray reverted to his mock-gangster intonation, hard-edged, deliberate, tough: "Listen, kid, I was born in Philadelphia. That's where they say that they pull in the sidewalk at eight o'clock at night. I moved, of all places, to New Jersey," he went on, in his typical fashion leaving out details of fact as it pleased him, "New Jersey? . . . Forget it.

"America is just a very, very big place," he said, "and you'll be surprised how much room there is for doing things and even thinking about them. You'll find people to whom you can talk. I found Stieglitz, and from then on it was like a pebble dropped into a lake. I didn't want to wait for any more little waves, and I came over here."

Jimmy had no way of knowing these common themes in Man Ray's view of America—his disdain for its provincialism and narrow attitudes, and New York's overwhelming way of intimidating artists who were trying to make a splash before their rightful time had come. "I've gone back a few times," he went on, "and it's a mess, and you'll have to learn to do some swimming and hold your nose. Just look at what you're leaving behind." There lay the nub of the argument. In the young Jimmy Ernst, Man Ray may have seen a glimmer of himself at an earlier age, making a similar choice to move, in the opposite direction. If he could not dissuade or protect Jimmy now, perhaps Man Ray could use the situation to crystallize the complex of his sentiments about his homeland.

"If we're still here in ten years," Man Ray said, "come to visit us." Within the invitation resided his veiled hope that the circle would, somehow, impossibly, remain unbroken for a decade. Alone among the Surrealists, however, Man Ray would choose not to rejoin the group, haphazardly and desperately reestablished in exile in New York during the war.

Two years earlier, Man Ray had tried to dissuade André Kertész from making the transatlantic crossing. One day before the photographer was due to leave, he ran into Man Ray in the Café du Dôme. "I'm going tomorrow to New York, but only for one year, a contract with Condé Nast," the Hungarian said. He'd been in Paris for a good eleven years, and it was time for a change. The promise of money was too good to refuse. "Don't go!" replied Man Ray, "I'm an American, and I'm telling you—don't go; it's not the right place for an artist!" but Kertész did leave, never to return, and in later years he admitted that "Man Ray was right."

The two photographers did not see each other very often during the time they were living in Paris. They staked out separate territories and stayed clear of each other. When the Vicomtesse de Noailles wanted her portrait made, she went to Kertész first, but he immediately referred her to Man Ray: "He did what he wanted, I did what I wanted, and I knew he was the portrait maker *extraordinaire.*" The point of convergence between Man Ray and Kertész, however, lay in their willingness to stretch the possibilities of photography in ways it had never been tested before. Kertész's notorious "distortion nudes"—images of women distended and wavelike, as if viewed in a fun-house mirror—were "amusing to create, a kind of game" to him, just as Man Ray's rayographs proclaimed a spirit of liveliness and humor. Tristan Tzara, who counted both men as his friends, saw that common quality immediately.

"Don't go," Man Ray had pleaded with Kertész. "Just look at what you're leaving behind," he had gently chided Jimmy Ernst. And yet, as many historians have since observed, the 1930s marked the beginning of a period of political and social instability in France that has not yet closed. Her army crumbled, deteriorating in six short years from the world's strongest to Europe's most disorganized force. Her system of alliances, which had guaranteed the Versailles settlement, collapsed following 1936. Her parliament, which had survived democratically for over sixty years, was in a state of paralysis by 1938 and dissolved by 1940. Her economy was stagnant.

In general, the political climate in France was characterized by polarization and confusion during the years 1935–40, and a pacifist and meek attitude toward Germany on the part of the government. There was a strong desire to avoid a repeat performance of the Great War, which had decimated the society. The economic malaise of France between the wars was in many respects traceable to the aftereffects of World War I. More than 1.3 million Frenchmen had been killed. France was "a nation of old men, widows, and *mutilés de la guerre.*"

"Bread, peace, and liberty" was the motto of the Popular Front. Its leader, Léon Blum, who counted many of the intelligentsia among his friends, including Man Ray, denounced the practice of compulsory military service, espousing pacifism as the only answer, as Hitler moved to invade the Rhineland in March of 1936, and general strikes and a precipitous devaluation of the franc served to weaken further other European nations' faith in France's ability to save herself. The following spring, frustrated by its domestic policy and paralyzed in foreign policy, the Popular Front collapsed. Blum made a return to power in March of 1938 but was soon ousted.

Man Ray's savings from his lucrative work with *Harper's Bazaar* had been accumulating in his bank account in New York City. He could withdraw money in dollars, and throughout the chaos in France, he was therefore not prey to the vicissitudes of the franc. Just as crucially, he remained resolutely apolitical. He was not, as were others of his Surrealist colleagues, seduced by Communism. "I wasn't getting myself mixed up in politics . . ." he wrote years later, looking back on those volatile times, because it "might create some misunderstanding by leading people to think I was politically minded." Every artist of the period had to decide about the extent to which he was going to become *engagé,* or remain detached in the world of ideas.

Ray family lore reflects back to the fact that Man Ray's father had left Russia in order to avoid military service. Antiwar feelings, relatives have insisted, ran deep in the Radnitsky past. One must also remember Man Ray's gravitation toward the teachings of Emma Goldman, and when he was only in his twenties his earliest cartoons during World War I, for *Mother Earth News,* expressing empathy for oppressed people and hatred for the huge systems that conspired to devour them on a far-off continent. The Dada movement itself was inherently pacifist. The sheer force of Dada at its inception was a reaction against the patent absurdity—the absolute ludicrousness—of man creating war. And as the conflict died, Dada's swan song began. Wrote Richard Huelsenbeck, one of Dada's founding fathers, "We loathed the senseless, systematic massacre of modern warfare." It is not surprising that Man Ray, one of Dada's standard-bearers, would hew closely to his antipolitical doctrine, and that he would react, in the spring of 1939, with another monumental painting, harking back to August 1914 and the scale of the *MCMXIV* canvas of Ridgefield.

Man Ray had taken on a certain patina of irony in the intervening twenty-five years, so that when he set out to illustrate graphically that all was not right with the western world, he entitled the seven-foot-by-six-foot canvas *Le beau temps* (Fair Weather), and, he wrote, "using all techniques from Impressionist to Cubist and Surrealist," he described "the dream of mythological animals at each other's throats." This painting had as its starting point a sketch of two gargoyles, fantastic beasts—countries?—locked in mortal combat. They were reminiscent, in their fury, of Man Ray's similar representation of a two-headed dragon for the cover of *Mother Earth News,* many years past.

It was the loveliest, most limpid springtime in Paris, while guns to the east heralded Germany's invasion of Czechoslovakia. At home in Saint-Germain-en-Laye, Man Ray cherished his temporary removal from all the fracas and painted through his deeper terror. The central figure in *Le beau temps* is a harlequin with a lantern instead of a face (*"l'homme avec la tête du lanterne magique"*—Breton's description for Man Ray) about to cross a bloody threshold and move from the light and airy side of the landscape to a decidedly darker side. While the beasts struggle atop the roof of a modernistic house, two shadowy lovers are embracing, oblivious—or trying to be—to the struggle going on all around them. Man Ray brought back the image of the tilted pool table from *La fortune,* injecting a note of hope into the otherwise bleak scenario. Broken walls and naked, pitchforklike trees, unnavigable landscapes and darkening skies add to the ambience of gloom. The whole is underscored by the trickiness of the title, which should perhaps be pronounced with a mocking tone: "Fair weather, indeed!"

Le beau temps took its place in the succession of big paintings that loom like signposts in Man Ray's work. Engendered by a frightening dream, *Le beau temps* was set firmly in Surrealist ideology. It was a painting in which Man Ray made a decision to bear down and work with the surface of the canvas in a more polished manner. He more than justified his repeated declarations to Elsie that he had "gone seriously back to painting."

Man Ray was so entrenched in his new artistic persona that as the months passed he wrote to his sister more frequently than ever, almost as if the repetitiveness of his denials would stave off the conflict he so deeply wished away. "Everyone is doing a lot of barking here," he told her, "but no one wants to bite first." After *Le beau temps,* he assured her (and, clearly, although her side of the correspondence is lost, Man Ray was receiving a blizzard of concerned letters from stateside) that "all the newspaper talk [the headlines Elsie must have been reading that spring] is rot—no one wants war here, and it's all a political game, like chess. There will always be time to act," he said, "if things really get serious."

After a quiet summer in Antibes, Man Ray returned to St. Germain-en-Laye—a heavily wooded suburb to the west of Paris, past Neuilly, Puteaux (family home of the Duchamp-Villons), and Chatou. Set amidst the Marly woods, the château was originally built in the twelfth century by Louis VI and partially destroyed and reconstructed in 1539 by François I. It was a quiet, out-of-the-way place where, in that fateful autumn of 1939, Man Ray could detect "no sign that France was at war." Yet, with the partition of Poland and Hitler's violation of the Munich accord, France had no choice but to join England in entering the war. The events of the following eight months became known as "The Phony War," because Germany took no aggressive action against France. However, Man Ray seized the opportunity, a mere three days after "war" was declared, to drive six hundred miles back to Antibes, where he gathered all his canvases to take to St. Germain-en-Laye for safekeeping. At this point, he honestly believed he would endure the war and manage to hang on near Paris. As he wrote Elsie with the candor he seemed to reserve for her alone, he was nearing fifty years of age and getting tired of so much moving around.

Early in the new year, Man Ray was approached for one more fashion shooting by the editors of *Harper's Bazaar,* who proudly proclaimed in the March 15, 1940, issue, filled with views of the spring showings, that "Man Ray, the American painter and photographer, who has been in retirement in the South of France, had returned to Paris expressly to photograph once more" for the magazine. *Harper's Bazaar* even managed to round up the photographers and staff artists who had been mobilized and were serving in the French army. Photographer Jean Moral, Cassandre (the poster artist who designed so many distinctive covers for the magazine), Vertès, the artist, and Louise Macy, the Paris editor (now "devoting her free time to French war charities") joined Man Ray in a rush of day and night sittings in studios with windows taped to avoid shattering should the dreaded bombs fall. During the preceding two years, other credits had supplanted Man Ray's in the fashion spreads. Readers had become more accustomed to the work of Hoyningen-Heuné, George Platt Lynes, and Louise Dahl-Wolfe. It was Man Ray's final session. The Diana Vreeland era had begun.

Once again, the telegram from Paris was terse, clipped, and to the point: GREETINGS TO ALL HEALTH FINE AM PRETTY SAFE DON'T WORRY MAY COME OVER SOON BROTHER MANRAY. Elsie, Sam, Naomi, and Elaine had reason to be concerned about Brother Man on June 8, 1940, the dismal day the message arrived in their home in Jersey City. Following invasions of the Netherlands and Belgium, the end run around the Maginot Line, and the evacuation of Dunkirk, German motorized columns began their advance to the City of Light. The last members of the government fled the capital on June 10. Paris was declared an open city. The Republic had failed, and Man Ray, at the last possible moment, joined the odyssey southward, with little sense of his ultimate destination, except that he figured Spain was his safest bet. It was a desperate, panicky, and catastrophic moment unequaled in the history of France. Paris had become a ghost town. The capital of modernity and individualism was now a spiritual wasteland.

Man Ray was part of a human avalanche, terrified refugees surging south on choked roads under sporadic strafing. Parisians were joined by more than a million Belgians and perhaps two hundred thousand Luxembourgers, Poles, Dutch, and Jewish refugees from the Reich. All told, more than eight million people were uprooted that summer. Léon Blum was also part of the throng. In his journal, he vividly described the horror: "The great highway," he wrote, "including its shoulders and its bicycle paths, was completely covered to the very edge of the houses and fields. . . . My imagination would not have been able to conceive anything like the spectacle that met my eyes. . . ."

To Man Ray, inching along in his Peugeot 402 with Ady by his side and little in the way of possessions, the "exodus from Paris took on a Biblical character." His first destination was the west coast, a small town called Les Sables-d'Olonne, just north of La Rochelle. Passing through Rambouillet, Chartres, and then westward, away from the major flow of human traffic, through Tours, he made it in under three days. Once in the beach resort, he would have heard the news that the French government in exile had moved to Bordeaux. On June 22, as part of a crowd huddled around a radio in a café, Man Ray listened to General Pétain declare that an armistice had been reached. The Vichy demarcation line was in place, effectively splitting the country. In Foch's railway carriage of 1918, which had been extracted from a museum and put in its old resting place in the forest of Compiègne, northeast of Paris, Hitler dictated an interim settlement (a holding action until he completed the conquest of Britain), placing his occupying troops in all of northern France, including Paris, and down the western coast. The southern zone— the Mediterranean and the Pyrenees—remained unoccupied. The French government moved on to Vichy and was given the power to administer both zones, subject to Germany's occupying authority.

Picasso at this time was in Royan, farther south along the coast, and Duchamp, with Mary Reynolds, was still more distant, in Arcachon. Man Ray was not permitted to visit his friends, despite his declaration "in a loud voice" to German troops in Sables that he "was an American." He was told to return to Paris, whence he had come. Both towns were within the occupied zone, but the Germans who briefly detained Man Ray may have suspected he might try to cross the dividing line.

By the time Man Ray returned to the sanctity of rue Denfert-Rochereau he had decided, reluctantly, to repatriate. His rationale was that "in such a climate, it was impossible for [him] to do any work; besides," more crucially, "no one came to the studio; all [his] friends had disappeared." Nearly two decades had passed since Man Ray first arrived in France, boldly turning his back on America. Until the last possible instant, with seeming disregard for international circumstances and ignorance of the potentially dangerous consequences of attempting to persist any longer, Man Ray pronounced stridently and often that he was an American, and therefore neutral. It cannot be determined to what extent the fact that Man Ray was Jewish also proved to be a motivating factor in his decision to leave. Because Man Ray did not adhere to any organized religious or political/ideological system, he would not have described himself as Jewish, as a matter of ingrained principle. However, that qualifying attitude would have made no difference to a German officer asking probing questions, for example, especially as anti-Semitic policies in Vichy France were codified with startling rapidity.

Man Ray's primary project during his four final weeks in Paris was to secure the safety of his artwork. This he did by leaving his paintings in the care of his longtime friend, the paint dealer, Maurice Lefevre-Foinet. The inventory included two monumental efforts of the 1920s, *A l'heure de l'Observatoire—Les amoureux* and *Le beau temps,* as well as *Legend, La retour à la raison, Peinture de chevalet,* and *Femme noire.* He also left a separate case of twenty of his smaller paintings, one watercolor and nineteen oils, including a painting by Le Douanier Rousseau. Man Ray loved Le Douanier's style and identified with his determinedly naïve approach.

Ady, who elected to stay with her family in Paris, took responsibility for her lover's other effects. She sold a Tanguy painting, a de Chirico, several deluxe first editions of *Les mains libres,* and a few other items to Paul Eluard, who two years later, in turn, sold them again, handing the funds over to Ady, who responsibly sent the twenty-five hundred francs to Man Ray. He also permitted her to sell off some photographic lenses for him, including two Dallmeyers and a Zeiss.

After a quick, nostalgic visit to his old stomping ground in Montparnasse, where he bade farewell to Kiki and Giacometti, Man Ray packed a small valise with rayographs, watercolors, and an etching by his friend Picasso, *Minotauromachy.* He also grabbed a couple of cameras and was off to Biarritz by train. It was toward the end of July when Man Ray made his third and last trip southward; this time, he wondered, for how long?

Man Ray told friends and family his goal was to get as far away from the war as possible. His destination, he avowed, was some idealized point far beyond New York. Tahiti was most often mentioned, and seriously. Indeed, to Man Ray, as to many other artists of his day, Gauguin had effected the ultimate escape for a Surrealist, underscoring the connectedness of primitive society and self-realization. Man Ray often said that he was not a person who enjoyed changing locales too often—but the great instability

MAN RAY. ADY IN ANTIBES, SUMMER 1938.
Collection Timothy Baum.

brought about by the virtual collapse of French society, coupled with the fact that he did not have a concrete plan about his ultimate resting place, helped to liberate him. Man Ray's dream of Tahiti, distant symbol of happiness, had first surfaced in a drawing in *Les mains libres*. It was no coincidence that in these troubled times, just a few months before Man Ray took his leave of Paris, a major canvas by Gauguin, *A Tahiti,* sold for an astronomical price at auction.

Arriving in Biarritz, he immediately sought the American consulate, recently reopened in the state of emergency requiring the quick exit of so many Americans. He applied for a visa. There he ran into an old friend not seen for some time, Virgil Thomson. The two decided to continue their travels together.

Man Ray and the American composer had first met in Paris in the summer of 1921, introduced by Mary Reynolds when both were newly arrived from New York. Thomson had always admired Man Ray's inventiveness. He was impressed initially by the sight of *Tapestry* hanging on the artist's studio wall, recalling it years later as a "cubist quilt."

During the twenties and thirties they saw each other now and then at Sylvia Beach's bookshop, at Gertrude Stein's salon, at the Reynolds/Duchamp flat, and at Thomson's place on the quai Voltaire. But the antipathy to music among Surrealists may have contributed to some distancing in the later 1930s.

The new Vichy laws and dicta against Jews were enacted simultaneously with the forming of the new government in July 1940, well before any German ordinances or prohibitions were published. Jews were overtly encouraged to emigrate. Vindictiveness characterized early Vichy actions against the Jews that inhospitable and tense summer, adding to the atmosphere of shock and dislocation. Man Ray was not unaware of this tense climate, although he did not write home about it. In fact, he just missed, by less than two months, a Vichy law of October 1940 allowing for internment of foreigners of Jewish race and the establishment of special camps for Jews in France.

Neither Thomson nor Man Ray had any American money, but they figured that once they made the trip to Lisbon, they could wire America for funds. They also managed to borrow some cash from a Quaker woman who was returning to the U.S. after distributing money to Americans. Granted permits to enter Spain, the two had one tense moment at the border crossing from Hendaye to Irún.

Although Man Ray was traveling very light—two small suitcases and a couple of cameras slung around his neck—Thomson had brought all his earthly possessions with him because he was relocating in New York to take up employment as music critic for the *Herald Tribune.* In all, he had fourteen pieces of luggage, including six trunks filled with original music scores—Thomson called them "his capital, so to speak,"—work he hoped to have performed in the States. The German border guards who inspected Thomson's trunks were suspicious that the scores might be a secret code, a common practice in wartime. *"Nein,"* the quick-witted Thomson told them, *"sonaten von Mozart!"* *"Ah, Mozart!"* the guard said with a sigh, waving the two men through.

Man Ray and Virgil Thomson took a sleeper train from Irún, a small town on the Spanish border, straight through to Lisbon, arriving on July 25. And then the waiting game began. The city was, Man Ray wrote Elsie, "a madhouse filled with refugees from all over Europe," all with the same purpose, to find a scarce berth on one of the steamships and get out, quickly. Staying with Thomson at the Hotel Francfort, Man Ray wrote to his New York bank, the Trust Company of North America, authorizing the release of four hundred dollars from his account to pay for a ticket at the American Export Line offices there.

Gala Dalí was also in Lisbon, trying to arrange passage for herself and her husband, while Salvador paid a farewell visit to his father in Figueras, Spain, and then spent a week in Madrid. The Dalís had followed much the same route as Man Ray, fleeing Bordeaux before the bombings began there.

Finally, on August 6, the *Excambion,* of the American Export Line, departed for New York. Among the illustrious passengers were Man Ray, the Dalís, Thomson and Suzanne Blum (an attorney and longtime friend), and film director René Clair and his wife, Brogna. Although Man Ray had optimistically hoped for a berth, he and the others were forced by overcrowding to sleep on mattresses arranged on the floor of the ship's library.

It was not the most joyful crossing for Man Ray. He slept with his cameras under his pillow. Despite this precaution, they were stolen, and he was unable to get them back. While Dalí regaled the group with his endless stream of jokes, Man Ray was quiet and pensive, concerned about the artwork and possessions he had left behind and worried whether he would ever reestablish himself in

Paris again. He did not join the others for drinks in the evening, but rather spent much of his time reading: "An artist should avoid alcohol and permanent attachments," he told Thomson on one such occasion. Man Ray was moving from a place where everyone knew him, where he'd been supremely comfortable working, where he'd almost always had a woman on his arm, and where he'd had a lively social life. He was moving to a place he had left with bitter feelings, the scene of his first break with a past holding very few happy memories.

On August 16, 1940, the *Excambion* docked at Hoboken.

MAN RAY. *MR. KNIFE AND MISS FORK*, 1944.
ASSEMBLAGE. INSPIRED BY A BOOK
BY THE POET RENÉ CREVEL, *BABYLONE*, 1931.
Private collection.

BEAUTIFUL
PRISON

SISTER ELSIE and her daughter Naomi were at the pier waiting with excitement for Man Ray's arrival. A horde of journalists and photographers were also in attendance because news had spread that the flamboyant Salvador Dalí was on board. "He's a famous man—don't you want to get his autograph?" Elsie asked her daughter, but Naomi only had eyes for her uncle, who had been encouraging her artistic abilities from afar for so many years. Man Ray strode down the gangplank, oblivious to the crowds, politely declining Dalí's request that he help interpret his French to the press. "I don't want any of that. No publicity for me!" Man Ray muttered under his breath to Elsie, as the three slipped away to the Sieglers' home at 115 Fairview Avenue in Jersey City.

During his brief visit for the Museum of Modern Art show just three years earlier, Man Ray had known his stay was temporary. This time around, he had absolutely no idea how long the sojourn would last, and he was in a self-absorbed, morose frame of mind, "overcome," he admitted, "with a feeling of intense depression."

Man Ray had a love-hate relationship with New York City and would occasionally refer, half in jest, to the intimidation someone of his modest stature felt next to the tall buildings. One of the reasons he liked Paris so much was because, he would explain, the architecture was more sympathetic to his just-over-five-foot height.

Now he was leaving twenty years of progress and success

behind him to return to the place of his early struggles. New York critics had not been kind to Man Ray at the start of his career. He was one of the few artists in those times who actually sat down and wrote to the daily critics refuting their views. That forthright behavior had not helped to advance his reputation in the New York gallery circle.

But there were deeper reasons for Man Ray's spiritual crisis. Long before the Surrealist movement had taken hold, he had been internalizing a Surrealist selfhood. One of André Breton's credos was "always for the first time," the necessity that a true Surrealist create a new future through a new persona, the Yeatsian "myself I must remake." Man Ray's return to America only served to underscore the existence of the "self" he had been working so hard for more than two decades to erase. The reconstruction of Emmanuel Radnitsky's identity may be said to have been officially begun on the day when he and his brother, Sam, decided to change their last name. More than one visitor to Paris from stateside had looked up "Emmanuel Radnitsky" from Brooklyn days, bearing a message from home, and had been flatly told, "No, I am Man Ray."

The classic Surrealist image—in literature and the visual arts—was a tribute to ambiguity, a testimony to the vibrancy of change, but always as an expression of mental freedom. The Surrealist spirit was adventuresome. Voyages outward were necessary whether they were literal, such as Desnos's occasional, unannounced forays to exotic lands, or imagined. They were meant to be in search of fresh truths—"*le merveilleux,*" like the hands of *Les mains libres* or Breton's hymn to "fidelity to what one has freely chosen"—not retreats occasioned by the need to escape danger or cramped, uncomfortable sojourns on the library floor of an ocean liner. Man Ray's voyage out was regressive, disconcertingly open-ended, and unwilling. Unlike the first brushstroke onto virgin canvas with its promise of renewal, or the first faint glimmerings of a photographic image rising to the surface in the developing tray, Man Ray's voyage on the *Excambion* ended in disappointment.

It was to be a quiet, uneventful summer at the Sieglers'. Man Ray was not in the mood to venture forth into the New York gallery scene, except for one important call on an old mentor, Alfred Stieglitz, who customarily spent the summers relaxing at Lake George in the Adirondack Mountains of New York State. The two men had lunch together soon after Stieglitz's return to the city in

September. The 291 Gallery had closed in 1917, but the indomitable Stieglitz, now nearing seventy-seven, had moved on, arranging exhibitions at the Anderson and Intimate galleries during the twenties, then in 1929 establishing the American Place, a new gallery to showcase his favorite artists. Georgia O'Keeffe, Arthur Dove, Marsden Hartley, and John Marin numbered among Stieglitz's select group. Whether he asked Man Ray to participate is not known.

There was excitement in the air: the Museum of Modern Art had made plans to open a photography department. Man Ray, however, did not make any effort to reach another old friend, Alfred Barr, nor did he seek out Beaumont Newhall, the museum's librarian and the guiding spirit behind the collections of the new department. Rather, Man Ray persisted in turning his back on any professional involvement with the medium he continued to insist was not art.

It was time to take refuge in the home of sympathetic relatives, where everyone understood that Brother Man needed to take stock of his career and make some hard choices about the next move on the complicated chessboard of his life. Elsie and Sam were a two-career couple. She worked as an executive secretary in the city for a lawyer-accountant, and Sam, an accountant himself, occasionally helped Man Ray extricate himself from delicate tax matters. Although the Sieglers did not ask Man Ray to pay his way, he insisted upon it for the five weeks he lived with them, selling the Picasso *Minotauromachy* he had brought over on the boat to meet expenses.

Domestic by nature, Man Ray showed his nieces and sister the Continental way to make salads (which should properly be eaten after the entrée); proselytized for the Hay diet he still pursued assiduously, reminding them that starches and proteins must never be consumed at the same meal; and made coffee every morning the French way, never percolated, always the plunger method, pushing the grounds down through the boiling water, just so, to arrive at the cleanest, most powerful and authentic taste.

Man Ray was taking life one day at a time through the summer of 1940, certain that he did not want to stay in New York but with no specific notion of where to go. A compromise solution came along one night in mid-September at a party given in New York by Harry Kantor, ex-husband of Naomi's piano teacher, quasi-bohemian, and traveling necktie salesman. Kantor was preparing for his seasonal sales jaunt to the West Coast. Would Uncle Man like to accompany him, share the driving, and in the process take a free trip to L.A.? The possibilities were sweetened by a fervent plea from a young woman at the party, Elsa Miller, who overheard Kantor's offer and asked Man Ray if he would get in touch with an old and dear friend of hers who had left for the coast in April of the preceding year. Elsa and her friend, Juliet Browner, had taken dancing lessons together in the late thirties from Ray Piazza, who had studied with Martha Graham. Juliet had also been employed as a model during the W.P.A. years and had become part of the Eighth Street crowd. She had enjoyed a brief flirtation with a young artist who arrived in Hoboken as a stowaway from Rotterdam and worked as a housepainter before moving to New York—a fellow by the name of Willem de Kooning.

Elsa scribbled Juliet's name and address in Los Angeles on a scrap of paper and thrust it into Man Ray's hands, telling him that her dear friend was "desperate and hungry and her only job in Hollywood was looking after a friend's child and there was no money in that." Perhaps, Elsa suggested, Juliet could earn some cash modeling for Man Ray (she was, after all, a professional) to pay for a train ticket back East.

The prospect of a change of scene began to seem appealing, even tantalizing to Man Ray, and he readily accepted. On September 24, depositing a carefully plotted itinerary with Elsie, Man Ray took a quick trip to Brooklyn to say farewell to his parents. Then, he and Harry were off to Cleveland, the first stop on a journey that would take them through Detroit, Chicago, Indianapolis, Louisville, St. Louis, Memphis, New Orleans, Houston, Shreveport, and Dallas before their scheduled arrival in Hollywood on October 13. Man Ray told himself that the sojourn in California would be a "short rest." Little did he know that more than a decade would pass before he returned to his beloved Paris.

Despite the visual grandeur of the scenery during his American odyssey, Man Ray passed through it with indifference. Not once did he photograph the broad, unfamiliar landscape, although he made several promises to the family that he would send back "views" for the kids. He was too preoccupied, he wrote Elsie, with the need to "forget now and then what [he] had left behind." Chicago ignited a glimmer of interest, however, for Man Ray's work had been on exhibition at the Arts Club there in 1929, and

Moholy-Nagy's Institute of Design, founded in 1937 as the new Bauhaus, was in full gear. Man Ray paid a brief call on Moholy and met Katharine Kuh, the art critic, as well as the painter Emerson Woelffer, who was working at the institute. Passing through the Painted Desert on the last leg of the journey, Harry sitting beside him, Man Ray daydreamed as Route 66 unraveled into the distance. So lost was he in half-formed mental images of St. Germain-en-Laye, with its expanses of forests and noble châteaus, so wrapped up in his own private mirage, that he failed to notice his foot pressing the accelerator firmly to the floor. Lost in time, Man Ray thought back to the places he had been, for he had no secure idea of the places that lay before him.

The two arrived in downtown Los Angeles at nightfall. Hollywood appeared oppressive, brutal, yet fascinating, and little more than a frontier town: "No buildings seemed to be higher than two stories," Man Ray wrote, "the sky was visible everywhere, pierced occasionally by shafts from searchlights . . . heralding the presentation of a new film, or the opening of a supermarket." If Man Ray's visit was meant to be a forced vacation of sorts, it was bound to be different from anything he had experienced before. Settling in at the Lido Hotel on Yucca at Wilcox in Hollywood, he began to feel more relaxed and resigned to the open-endedness of his stay. He planned to look for a proper studio where he could work, and he asked Elsie to send him some painting supplies. Meanwhile, true to his promise to Elsa Miller, Man Ray picked up the telephone the morning after his arrival and called the number where Juliet Browner was staying, at her friend Georgia Anderson's home.

She was petite, birdlike, with a soft, unassuming voice, a self-deprecating manner, a winsome smile, and a gentle, lilting laugh. Her movements were graceful. She had a way of letting her delicate hands float this way and that, as if they had lives of their own, independent of her slender arms and wrists. Her hands fluttered in the air as she spoke, and she seemed unconscious of their movements. Her hair was brown, piled high in great curls; her eyes large, liquid, slightly slanted. With her lightly tanned skin, Juliet appeared almost Oriental. She had a dancer's or a model's body, firm and well conditioned, and she walked in that particular way dancers do, her feet turned out slightly.

Juliet Browner was a gentle young woman of twenty-eight when Man Ray at fifty first set eyes upon her that hot California autumn of 1940. Within hours, seduced by her exotic manner and ingenuous, unforced charm, he had made two sketches of her. Within days, they had dined together, danced the beguine at an all-night jazz club, gone rowing in the park, and shared deep confidences. The oldest of seven children—she had five brothers and one sister—Juliet had grown up in the Bronx, the daughter of a pharmacist. Her mother had often been ill and incapacitated during her adolescence, and she had taken on more than her share of a nurturing role long before she was ready, helping her father to raise the Browner brood. Man Ray told her of the adventures he'd been through, of his interrupted life, and he confessed to her his dream to begin anew, to throw himself completely into his first love, painting. Juliet was a welcome change—she was in and of the present time and place. Such freshness drew them together quickly. She, too, was adrift in a strange city and in search of a feeling of connectedness. Juliet came to Man Ray with an instinctive admiration for him. Whatever sense of autonomy she possessed was immediately invested in him. Whatever strength of will she may have built up, she immediately gave over to him. As a model, she was superb—pliant, agreeable, always available to conform to his wish.

The couple moved into a residential hotel in Hollywood, the Château des Fleurs, and the move triggered Man Ray's resolve to "stay here for some time," he wrote Elsie, without mentioning the motivation for his decision. The family did not need to know just yet that he had found his love, although Man Ray did, responsibly, write to Juliet's friend Elsa immediately so as to assuage her fears.

Renting separate rooms in the Château des Fleurs soon became a tiresome pretense. Early in the year, Man Ray and Juliet found a charming apartment at 1245 Vine Street in the heart of Hollywood, a deep U-shaped building with a long central courtyard graced with banana and palm trees and hibiscus bushes. Hummingbirds darted up and down the sun-drenched, ivy-covered walls. The flat the couple chose was farthest from the street, a duplex with huge arched windows looking out onto the courtyard and on a verdant garden in back. Man Ray photographed Juliet there on moving day, gracefully seated among their secondhand furnishings. The rent was just fifty dollars a month, including maid service, and quite a bargain considering the spaciousness of the place. With a simple curtain, Man Ray converted the dining room into a darkroom. That still left a den, kitchen, bedroom, and bath. The upstairs balcony brought back memories of the two-tiered rue

Campagne-Première studio. One of Man Ray's first decorative decisions was to drape the 1911 *Tapestry,* which had stayed with him all these years, over the railing, where it would be noticed by every visitor, a constant reminder of how he had begun.

Vine Street between La Mirada and Fountain was heavily traveled, but a visitor would never have known it from the depths of Man Ray and Juliet's long, cool space between two wings of the building. This womblike calm was enhanced by the fact that the apartment had windows on two sides only—the wall facing Fountain Street was solid brick. And the jungle-thick bushes that grew as high as the arched windows kept the interior of the place dim and the light pearly, perfect for painting.

The apartment was directly across the street from a twenty-four-hours-a-day, open-air market, where Juliet chose fresh fruits and vegetables. Man Ray would not eat preserved foods of any kind. The Hollywood Ranch Market also carried an inexpensive red wine, Branger's, which, at three bottles for a dollar, reminded Man Ray of the peasant vintage he had enjoyed so much in France. He delighted in telling guests that it was "as good as any French *vin ordinaire.*"

Man Ray placed a down payment on a 1941 Graham-Page sedan, metallic blue and streamlined "like a submarine." Indulging his love for fast cars—Picabia had introduced him to that pleasure—Man Ray delighted in knowing he could easily top one hundred miles per hour thanks to the sedan's all-American super-charged engine.

He was not secretive about his economic problems during the early Hollywood years. Man Ray's earnings for the first twelve months in America amounted to a mere four hundred dollars—but thank goodness the mid- to late-thirties had been flush times in Paris. His savings from fashion work carried him through a period when an income of two thousand dollars a year was considered respectable for an artist of renown in America. Man Ray's photographic work supplied the means that enabled him to turn his complete attention to painting. Julien and Joella Levy, early visitors to the Vine Street studio, received the brunt of that message. Man Ray told his old friends unequivocally that for the time being, he would refuse to take photographic portraits. "I tell you again and again," he said to them, "I am not a photographer. I am fautegrapher, I take a faute-graph," he stressed, playing upon the French pun, "a false line. My true line is the pencil and the brush."

Obsessed by the fear that he would never again see the paintings he'd left in Paris, Man Ray set out to reestablish himself as a painter. His solution to this problem was to begin by recreating the most prominent of the canvases, both by memory and with the aid of thumbnail photographs in his ever-present card file. The portrait of Sade emerged with a green background instead of a red one; *The Woman and Her Fish II* was more sinuous than the original, tinged with haunting shades of blue; *La fortune II* recapitulated Man Ray's favorite theme of chance played out upon a one-legged billiard table. He tried his hand at a duplicate of *Le beau temps,* and reached even further back, to *Promenade* and the *Revolving Doors* series of the early 1920s. It was almost as if Man Ray felt compelled to put the pieces of his fragmented past together, to rebuild the foundation, before he could extend himself into new territory. He had passed through the looking glass. Having lost his woman, home, work—even his beloved car—he labored at systematically replacing each of those elements, reconstructing the assemblage of his life. The few new works of Man Ray's early time in Hollywood reflected past concerns. He found driftwood along the beaches of Santa Monica, bringing back memories of forays to Biarritz, and crafted odd icons. He refashioned an old mask of papier-mâché and called it *Repainted Mask.*

In a radio talk Man Ray gave in Santa Barbara, "Art in Society," he alluded to the disorienting difficulties of *"le trouble moderne"*: "In the twentieth century, the artist is beleaguered. Society has imposed a general, social conscience upon him which causes his individual conscience to suffer. Instead of glorifying, idealizing, or simply transforming the subject in front of him, he feels he must reproduce it as faithfully as possible. . . ." Taking care to sound objective, Man Ray enunciated the theme most applicable to himself, for, "having suffered through not being appreciated, the artist becomes too self-conscious . . ." but, he concluded, in a burst of self-encouragement and idealism, if the artist can succeed in "banishing all ulterior motivations and can accept the unusual and the unknown," if he can "intensify his energies on purely individual effort, [he] may succeed in producing monumental and valuable work."

It was a lonely, solitary time, relieved only—Julien Levy and others noticed—by the reassuring presence of Juliet. Man Ray drew deeply upon resources of perseverance he had forgotten he possessed. "I am committed to my way, whether it turns out well or not," he declared. "One of the satisfactions of a genius is his will-power and obstinacy."

Man Ray sent for more and more paintings, photographs, and supplies left behind in New Jersey, asking for work that had been pulled out of storage and housed at Elsie's after the recent settlement with the Daniel Gallery. As a result, his first exhibition since returning to America, at the Frank Perls Gallery in February 1941, was something of a retrospective. It included several small paintings on cardboard from Ridgefield days, one of the stylish aluminum chess sets, a selection of rayographs, a first edition of *Les mains libres,* as well as the striking 1926 photograph of Kiki holding an African sculpture head, *Noire et blanche* (sometimes known as *Composition*). The show also featured a new, symbolic piece: Man Ray had taken two wooden mannequin figures, precursors of what he would name in later years "Mr. and Mrs. Woodman," and staged them in conflict on a chessboard grid. Despite (or because of) the eclecticism of the show, nothing sold. Unfortunately, it was the first of many Man Ray exhibitions in California yielding no commercial benefit.

One of the first shafts of light to break the gloom of Man Ray's adjustment to Hollywood came through Hazel Guggenheim McKinley, Peggy's younger sister, who was determined to establish a regular series of soirées at her place in Santa Monica. Hazel had taken a new couple under her wing, Gilbert and Margaret Neiman. He was a poet and translator of Federico Garcia Lorca's play *Blood Wedding,* she was a talented fabric artist who became known for her splashy tie-dye creations. Margaret served as Hazel's social secretary, seeking out new arrivals to the West Coast and inviting them to the McKinley parties. When Peggy Guggenheim finally returned by clipper to America in the summer of 1941, accompanied by Max Ernst, who had separated from Leonora Carrington, the couple made a quick trip to the Coast, and Peggy seriously considered opening a gallery in Los Angeles for her extensive collections. Man Ray and Ernst enjoyed a happy reunion; the two Surrealists had not seen each other since the outbreak of the war. George Biddle, Isamu Noguchi, and the Wadsworth Atheneum's Chick Austin were also guests at the McKinleys'.

It was one of Margaret Neiman's great social coups to introduce Man Ray and the writer Henry Miller. Although the two men had lived as Americans in Paris all during the 1930s, it took the upheaval of the war to bring them together at Hazel McKinley's place. Miller, lonely and poor, had moved in with the Neimans for two years in their home on Beverly Glen Road, where Man Ray and Juliet soon became frequent visitors. It was a movable feast, for Vine Street parties were equally memorable.

Man Ray and Henry Miller were kindred spirits. Born a year apart, both men had grown up in Brooklyn and had spurned college to work at a variety of odd jobs. Both were sons of tailors, had put in time at hard labor, and had sought creative release in Paris, only to be driven back to the States by the war. They shared an abiding love of language. Miller was disarmed and awed by Man Ray's "extraordinary memory. It was as if he never forgot anything, whether names, faces, titles of books, dates, events, meetings, or his disposition on a certain day in a certain place at a certain hour. One might call it a photographic memory." Miller was also taken by the atmosphere he found at Man Ray's place, such a refreshing change from the typical, showy Hollywood social scene. Man Ray knew very well how to have a good time—while he strummed the ukulele or guitar and Juliet played her violin, everyone would don bizarre, homemade masks and dance gaily until four or five o'clock in the morning. There was likewise, Miller found, a substantiality to Man Ray. He had the capacity to dominate a room, even if he chose merely to sit on a couch and interject piercing bons mots from time to time, his eyes shining beneath his pale brow and wavy hair, pitch black even now. Man Ray habitually shifted from his initial brusqueness to dry humor to unusual warmth. His quietly aggressive nature was put all the more in relief by Juliet's gentleness and unwavering support.

"California is a beautiful prison," Man Ray wrote his sister, "I like being here, but I cannot forget my previous life, and long for the day when I can return to New York and eventually to France." From the moment the United States entered the war, Man Ray felt anxious about ever being able to pick up threads abruptly cut by the conflict. And when German troops moved to occupy Vichy France, he seemed to retreat even further into a quasi-hermetic life. Man Ray concentrated on his variations upon the theme of paintings left behind, pulled together photographs of objects for a possible album, and toyed with the idea (which never came to fruition) of donning his portraiture hat once more, declaring his reentry into that long-abandoned profession. Halfhearted attempts to contact the movie studios and offers to help produce Defense Department films were to no avail. While he referred vaguely to wanting to "make connections for the future," Man Ray did not know what that future would hold, whether at any moment he might be able to pick up stakes and dart back to Paris. Clutching at this fantasy prohibited him from making firm commitments beyond the one he'd always had to his painting.

It was a tough path to stick to at a time when American Scene painting was the only style that seemed commercially acceptable. True seriousness in art was a goal that fairly guaranteed economic hardship. Man Ray was torn between seeking the limelight and shrinking from it. He was fast approaching the point where he knew that he would become more vulnerable to the exigencies of the marketplace, yet he was desperate to continue working on his own terms. And he was in the especially difficult position of not only being an artist in America at a juncture when that métier was hardly respected, but also being an exile in his own country. Man Ray may have referred to himself as a refugee, but his position was even more tenuous and emotionally problematic because he had begun as an expatriate and had had every intention of carrying out his entire life that way—whereas the Surrealists and others who found their way to New York City during the war were united in their separation from native lands.

The Chilean painter Matta Echaurren was one of the very first to reach these shores from Paris at the beginning of the crisis years; he came in the late fall of 1939 and was soon followed by the English designer Gordon Onslow-Ford; Yves Tanguy arrived in New York a few months later. Salvador Dalí, who had accompanied Man Ray to New York, settled in Pebble Beach for eight years. Eugène Berman also lived nearby, as did Man Ray's old friend from the Jockey Club, Hilaire Hiler. André Breton, Claude Lévi-Strauss, and Wifredo Lam were shipmates traveling together from Marseilles via Martinique to New York early in 1941. S. W. Hayter, the English artist who had been Man Ray's neighbor on the rue Campagne-Première, transported his renowned Atelier 17 to the New School during the war and continued to conduct his etching workshops there. There were also Jacques Lipchitz, Marc Chagall, Ossip Zadkine, Kurt Seligmann, Fernand Léger, and Piet Mondrian among the seemingly endless list of the uprooted and dispossessed.

The balance shifted radically, until there could be no shred of doubt, by mid-1942, that "the art center of the Western world," had moved from Paris to New York (or so Alfred Barr put it chauvinistically). James Thrall Soby, another partisan critic, stated the case for American prominence even more strongly in his preface to the *Artists in Exile* catalogue published in conjunction with the exhibition of the same name mounted at Pierre Matisse's gallery on West Fifty-seventh Street that June. The new influx of artists, he asserted, signaled nothing less than "the death of Paris." Now that a vacuum had been created there, it was up to New York to pick up the challenge and open itself to the fertilization of European art. The riches of three decades of progress in France were now available to a new generation of American artists. Surely, this was the beginning of an era. The "abstract expressionist" label had not yet been coined, and the collective term "New York School" was still a few years in the distance, but excitement was in the air.

Within the regrouped forces, however, there was constant tension, produced mainly by Breton's desire to preserve his leadership in America. That strain is almost palpably evident in the group photograph taken by George Platt Lynes, Man Ray's former colleague at *Harper's Bazaar,* on the occasion of the opening of the Pierre Matisse Gallery show. The artists assembled at nine o'clock sharp in the photographer's studio and began to mill around fitfully, trying to avoid speaking to one another. Lynes was having such trouble posing the group that he finally had to clap his hands like a schoolteacher demanding order in front of a classroom of recalcitrant students. He insisted that the men sit down in the very order they were standing at that moment. Thus, Breton found himself in the company of Mondrian, Ernst rubbing shoulders with Chagall—strange bedfellows, to be sure. In addition to their internecine struggles over how to reconstitute Surrealism on alien ground, there was the difficulty, many of the artists complained, of convening in the same kind of spontaneous manner so naturally allowed by Parisian café society. "The unconquerable American space," Kurt Seligmann pointed out, "has scattered the group of Europeans who were accustomed to meeting regularly" at the Café Flore. Fernand Léger tried unsuccessfully to create the semblance of a café scene at the Jumble Shop on Eighth Street, calling it "Le Jeumble." Others, such as Yves Tanguy and Kay Sage, found refuge in Connecticut or in the Hamptons—hospitable, isolated, countrified environments.

Marcel Duchamp was conspicuous by his absence from the notorious George Platt Lynes shot, as was his friend Man Ray. During the early years of the war, Duchamp had managed to hide with Mary Reynolds in Arcachon for a while; then he returned to Paris and obtained a permanent pass to travel back and forth into the free zone with false credentials that presented him as a cheese buyer. Duchamp had sailed from Lisbon two years after Man Ray left Europe, arriving in New York in June 1942, just in time to take a role in the founding of two important efforts that served to bring exiled Surrealists and native American talents together: *VVV* magazine and Peggy Guggenheim's Art of This Century Gallery.

The rivalries that fueled the creation of *VVV* magazine help to explain why Man Ray decided to keep his distance from the New York Surrealist battles. He had never been a real joiner, although his calming presence might have served as an example to the artist-warriors in New York.

Charles Henri Ford's journal, *View,* guest edited by Nicholas Calas, was already a forum for Surrealism when André Breton sufficiently overcame his mistrust of young American artists to ask David Hare to edit a rival magazine. It would present, in its first issue, the New York version of Breton's *Prolegomena to a Third Manifesto of Surrealism or Else.*

There was an ironic discrepancy between what twenty-five-year-old photographer-sculptor David Hare proclaimed to be the symbolic significance of the three V's in the title and what Breton saw as the didactic purpose of his essay within. According to Hare, the V's were "a vow—and energy—to return to a habitable and conceivable world, Victory over the forces of regression and death . . . and that double Victory, again over all that is opposed to the emancipation of the spirit . . . or again, the View around us, the eye turned towards the external world . . . towards [finally] a total view, VVV, which translates all the reactions of the eternal upon the actual. . . ."

With a cover by Max Ernst and behind-the-scenes editorial guidance by Marcel Duchamp, *VVV* enjoyed an impressive debut. Matta illustrated the manifesto by Breton, or "The Pope" (as he was often called, under the breath)—a declaration of independence for the benefit of American audiences. In his essay, Breton boldly declared his desire to maintain "integrity within this movement,"

243

and one of the first artists he castigated was "Avida Dollars," alias (anagramatically) Salvador Dalí, who, since his arrival in America, had become inexcusably mercenary. Seeing Dalí walking toward him once on the street, arms outstretched in a conciliatory gesture, Breton had pointedly crossed to the other side to avoid making any contact.

It was necessary, Breton went on, in the present upheaval, to remember to "declare against all conformism," and to build "a new myth" in temporary exile, until such time as all would be returned to their rightful homes. In *VVV*'s pages, William Carlos Williams joined Benjamin Péret; Leonora Carrington joined Valentine Penrose, Pavel Tchelitchew, and Arthur Cravan; Robert Motherwell joined André Masson. At least on paper, there was evidence that cross-cultural influence was briefly, momentarily possible. However, with production costs at eighteen hundred dollars an issue, the magazine was doomed to be short-lived, hampered by the classic Surrealist belief that commercial endeavors of any kind were anathema to its central doctrines. And, typically, the forces behind its inception—Ernst, Breton, and Duchamp— became bored with having to put out the quarterly magazine, which had originally been planned as a monthly. Editor Hare, meanwhile, was disenchanted with Breton's manipulative manner of working with people. While he had grown to admire the Surrealists' advocacy of freedom at all costs, Hare rejected their principled involvement with insanity as a prerequisite for creativity.

View, however, survived into the mid-1940s and came to represent a more mainstream Surrealist approach. Duchamp saw to it that the magazine published several provocative pieces by Man Ray, which tied in to his friend's more regular showings in New York during the middle years of the decade.

Duchamp also saw to it that Peggy Guggenheim was properly advised on the structure of her Art of This Century Gallery when it opened in the fall of 1942, signaling the beginning of the avant-garde New York art scene. Thanks to Duchamp's discriminating eye, as well as to the advice of Herbert Read, James Johnson Sweeney, Alfred Barr (who would lose his position at the Museum of Modern Art the following year), James Thrall Soby, Ernst, and Breton, Peggy Guggenheim created the first transatlantic exhibition space. William Baziotes, Mark Rothko, Clyfford Still, Robert Motherwell, and, of course, Jackson Pollock took their places on her walls beside the artists in exile. The convergences were obvious. The young New York–based artists, like the European elder statesmen, valued intellectual content and tangible energy on the surface of the canvas. Like the Surrealists, the young expressionists were absorbed by the process that gave shape to their ideas and were devoted to releasing unconscious impulses behind the work, attempting to represent an inner landscape.

Man Ray was far more at home in L. A. than he would ever have been in the thick of the struggles that riddled the Surrealist movement back East. As always, he remained steadfastly unengaged, which invariably meant more work time. He would rather spend a long evening stretching until daybreak in conversations with Juliet and close friends Margaret and Gilbert Neiman— during the course of which the foursome might indulge in an elaborate game of charades, or complex role playing, pretending they were in an asylum being cured of alcoholism, improvising poetry, or singing songs—than talk about Art with tiresome critics. A long afternoon with Juliet and a few close friends at a small jazz club listening to Benny Goodman, Jack Teagarden, or Sidney Bechet was infinitely preferable to wasting time at yet another gallery opening. Man Ray was easily bored by shop talk with fellow artists. His way of demonstrating dissatisfaction was to rise quietly from the living-room couch and walk silently out of the room until the conversation was more to his liking.

Man Ray was fond of remarking that "New York was always twenty years behind Paris in its appreciation of contemporary art, and California was twenty years behind New York. . . ." Cultural disjunction and the constant feeling of being out of the mainstream were an obvious component of life in Los Angeles. Within California in the forties, in the Bay Area of San Francisco, a core community of artists dedicated to color and lyricism was beginning to form. The presence of Clyfford Still, Mark Rothko, Richard Diebenkorn, and Robert Motherwell made the Bay Area in those days a kind of suburb of the New York School. Man Ray wanted no part of it. He refused to participate in the Los Angeles County Museum of Art's "Artists of Los Angeles and Vicinity" exhibitions. Despite the decade he spent in Los Angeles, he never developed a regionalist sensibility. He simply was not connected. He was a transplant.

MAN RAY AND JULIET PLAYING CHESS, HOLLYWOOD,
MID-1940S. *Private collection.*

M A R R I A G E S
A N D
M A N I F E S T O S

M A N R A Y worked very hard during the California years, living, as he often put it subsequently, within his own four walls, a world of his own making defined by an endlessly moving imagination. His painting was cerebral—(that is, not derived from the natural world); object-making was done for specific exhibitions; and rayographs were produced once again, this time easily distinguished from their predecessors by the way they were developed. In California, Man Ray had the time and the introspective turn of temperament to indulge his belief in the power of the written word. He now took a critical stand on issues that had preoccupied him for decades.

Three very different kinds of statements by Man Ray were made within the space of a few short months in 1943. The first, a reprise of that persistent theme, "Photography Is Not Art," appeared in the April–October *View,* having been solicited by the magazine's editor, Man Ray's friend, Charles Henri Ford. The piece continued in the December issue, with Man Ray's choices of "what [he] considers the ten best photographs [he] has produced until now." Man Ray dwelled upon the wholly "automatic" nature of the camera, an instrument that "waits for the human hand to catch up with it." Beneath a stern self-portrait boasting a half-goatee, covering the right half of his face only—a symbolic statement about the artist's divided self—Man Ray launched a diatribe against the photographer who continues to be obsessed with "how the thing is to be done, instead of what is to be done." He concludes with a prescient and ironic thought: "When photography will have lost that sourness [i.e., of new wine], and when it will age like Art or alcohol, only then will it become Art and not simply AN art as it is today."

To underscore the very nonartness of photography for an entirely different set of readers, Man Ray simultaneously published a how-to piece in the October 1943 issue of *Minicam Photography*, a magazine for amateur practitioners. Man Ray chose five photographs—including one of a dying leaf, its edges curled inward like the fingers of an arthritic hand, the very photograph he had cited in the *View* essay as one of his ten favorites—and accompanied them with captions explaining how he had managed to achieve his startling effects. The tone of the article surprises. It is warm and engaging, the master not hesitating to share his secrets with colleagues. "If you are using your camera purely as a recording instrument," Man Ray advises, "set it up first at the proper distance which, for portraits, should be not nearer than eight feet to avoid any distortion. Make all the adjustments necessary in advance, and then forget your instrument. Now give all your attention to your subject . . . do not hurry the subject or yourself, and push the release leisurely. . . ."

In another caption, for a sylvan snapshot of Juliet seen through branches, sylphlike and grinning, Man Ray reveals that he has achieved a startling effect simply by turning the image onto its side. In the caption for a dramatic portrait of a ravishing blonde, her head tilted upward, eyes shining, he divulges precisely how he took a brunette model and transformed her hair color through a step-by-step process, taking two exposures on one plate and cutting away the face from the hair, as if it were a mask, then synthesizing and reprinting the two images as one. This was easier said than done, but a simply posed, unthreatening challenge for the amateur photographer.

Finally, also in October, Man Ray gave a talk prior to a screening of his films at Barbara Cecil's American Contemporary Gallery, a popular gathering place on Hollywood Boulevard. "The world may be roughly divided into two parts," he began, "one part that moves and one part that does not move. . . . It is necessary that I call attention to this aspect of things, because we are looking at moving pictures in an art gallery primarily dedicated to the presentation of static works of art. . . . When art stands still, one must move about. When art moves, one may remain motionless." The talk was a study in equivocation, endorsing then demeaning silent versus sound films, expressing optimism for the future of film, then pessimism about its fate as "great art."

Man Ray's conflicted feelings about film were exacerbated because he lived in the center of Hollywood, where, after more than three years, he was still distant from the film industry and ambivalent about participating in it. He had been a loner as a filmmaker, a true *auteur.* The final result always had his inimitable stamp. His lunches with movie executives at palm-tree–lined, swank restaurants always ended poorly. Man Ray would never accept a role as only cameraman, or only editor. He would have to be involved in the entire concept or there could be no deal. He refused to recognize the committee system of "big" movie-making. As a filmmaker who had not picked up a movie camera in fifteen years, he struggled to rationalize his past accomplishments. He continued to dream of a day "when the production of film would be in the hands of one mastermind."

Man Ray's old friend from Dada days, the German filmmaker Hans Richter, was living in New York during the forties as supervisor of the Institute of Film Techniques at City College and asked him to contribute to an ambitious, multiscenarioed project, *Dreams That Money Can Buy.* Richter had noticed Man Ray's bizarre short narrative published in *View* (December 1944), a story called "Ruth, Roses, and Revolvers," and asked him to contribute it as a segment of the film, joining the ranks of Max Ernst, Fernand Léger, Marcel Duchamp, Alexander Calder, and Richter himself. Man Ray refused to tamper with the text. Rather, he sent it along unaltered to his friend, "insisting [the film] be realized by others."

"Ruth, Roses, and Revolvers" was not intended to be the basis for a screenplay, but it fit well into the mosaic of Surrealist imagery created by the other members of the disparate crew. "Desire," Ernst's "dream" starring himself and Julien Levy, grew out of the collage-imagery of the artist's celebrated book, *Une semaine de bonté* (A Week of Kindness); music by Paul Bowles added the mysterious atmosphere. Léger's dream-scenario was a love story between two dummies in a department store. Duchamp reprised and joined two favorite iconographies: his rotary disks last seen in *Anemic Cinema* and an animated version of the celebrated *Nude Descending a Staircase;* John Cage provided the music for the segment. Calder's "Ballet" and "Circus" featured his mobiles in action. And Richter's "Narcissus" told the story of a dream-salesman named Joe.

By stipulating that his contribution to the film be produced by other filmmakers while he resolutely kept his distance, Man Ray believed he was carrying "the idea of . . . projection . . . to a consistent end . . . so that I could get the same surprise out of it that any other spectator would have." A dream narrative following the free-associated actions of Man Ray and Juliet, "Ruth, Roses, and Revolvers," as it appeared in the magazine, and in its visualization on screen according to Richter's interpretation, centered upon a recurring theme in Man Ray's work, the intermingling of artist with audience, in much the same way that the Surrealists believed in the interpenetration of waking and dream life. At the end of the *View* story, Man Ray had even provided his address (albeit incorrectly), inviting readers to "consult" him at home "for further details." The story was a provocative calling card, another attempt to disturb and amuse through its blurring of artifice and reality.

The Pasadena Art Institute mounted Man Ray's first-ever retrospective show in the fall of 1944. Jarvis Barlow, the institute's director, was an inveterate Man Ray fan and regarded him as "an outstanding creative artist of our time." "The chronological list of paintings does not imply any fancied progress," Man Ray declared. "I do not believe in progress in art." Indeed, the well-chosen image for the cover of the exhibition catalogue was a pen-and-ink drawing from the fertile days of the 1930s, *Espoirs et illusions optiques* (Optical Hopes and Illusions). Cyclists on a race track in a cloudless Mediterranean setting spin in hot pursuit around an endless course. The wheels of their bicycles are skillfully transformed into eyeglasses through the magic of Man Ray's hand.

The paintings covered a thirty-year span, from the Ridgefield days (sent along by Elsie) through to the remade works of California. Man Ray also included photographs of paintings left behind when he had been forced to depart France so precipitately. Watercolors, drawings, rayographs, and photographic portraits made up a less significant part of the show, and for good reason: Man Ray was playing down these other facets of his voluminous

ABOVE: MAN RAY. *JULIET WITH NAVAJO HEADDRESS*, 1944. *The J. Paul Getty Museum.*

BELOW: MAN RAY. *JULIET*, 1940. PEN AND INK AND WATERCOLOR. *Collection Juliet Man Ray.*

output. Painting now stood first and foremost in his mind, and he did not want his audience to doubt that priority.

Man Ray's insistence on displaying "old things" (as he liked to call his youthful pastoral canvases) as well as reconstituted paintings continued in the new year with a show at Julien Levy's gallery in New York. The exhibition was an excuse for a quick springtime trip back east and a hastily arranged reunion with his parents. Man Ray dropped a card to Max and Minnie's on Prospect Place in Brooklyn only after he had, as he put it, "quite unexpectedly" arrived in the city. He did find the time for several chess games with Levy, as well as with Duchamp, who designed the cover for the catalogue. Man Ray also took his niece Naomi on an instructive field trip to the Metropolitan Museum of Art. In his opinion, looking at pictures would always be the best way to learn about art.

The Levy show featured many important paintings that seemed at times destined to be a permanent and all-too-familiar part of Man Ray's life. For years, he would continue to refuse to leave works on consignment at art galleries after his shows had come down, insisting they be returned to him as soon as the exhibition had ended. This was frustrating for gallery owners, who wondered whether Man Ray's professed love of selling his work was counterbalanced by an equally powerful desire to keep his hands on the all-precious "objects of his affection."

Man Ray's two weeks in New York provided him with the opportunity to reaffirm his enduring friendship with Duchamp. ("The most insignificant thing you do," Man Ray wrote of Duchamp soon after, "is a thousand times more interesting and fruitful than the best that can be said or done by your detractors.") The visit also reinforced his conviction, temporarily dimmed by time and distance, that this was not the city for him and never would be. He left New York drained and exhausted, with just enough energy remaining to make the stopover in Chicago once again to meet with Moholy-Nagy and lecture to students at the Institute of Design. Immediately upon his return to Hollywood, Man Ray came down with "a bad cold and a bad knee," both of which he unhesitatingly blamed upon the New York sojourn.

But good news arrived in the mail from Paris. Ré and Philippe Soupault had been to Man Ray's house in St. Germain-en-Laye and had made a thorough inspection. The walls and windows were intact, unblemished and unbroken, the Soupaults wrote. Though nearly empty, the building remained in sound condition. In the basement, the Soupaults discovered several pieces of furniture draped with sheets and unharmed. This fresh word from the old country, accompanied by the war's end that August, lifted a great weight from Man Ray's shoulders. The prospect of returning seemed closer to becoming a reality. The doors that had been shut now swung partially open with the knowledge that Man Ray had, at least, the opportunity to go back, should he decide to seize it.

Ady, the lover he had left behind in Paris, was now married, actively pursuing a career as a dancer in a Negro club on the Champs-Elysées. Although she wrote to Man Ray often, he did not respond. Ady was forced to garner news of him through Lefevre-Foinet, who was still keeping a watchful eye on the artist's possessions. Ady cherished the hope that Man Ray would come back to roost in his beloved Paris. From her letters, it is evident she did not know he had been with Juliet for five years.

Man Ray's friends in Paris continued to believe his sojourn in America could not possibly be anything but temporary. However, Man Ray remained inhibited by fears about the costs of relocating, by inertia, and, in an odd way, by Juliet's contentedness with their life in Hollywood. She was happy being with him and secure on native ground. She did not speak French, had never even been abroad, and feared the day Man Ray might decide to go back. Indeed, Man Ray knew all too well that he ran the risk of losing her if he made such a great leap. And he had also lately come to accept the physical reality that he was "not as strong and resistant as [he] was before the war, and while [he] had no ailment, [he] did get a very tired feeling now and then."

The spring and summer of 1946 were marked by a new surge of creative activity in an area that had always been of interest to Man Ray, the fabrication of chess sets. The regular, geometric pattern of the chessboard had been a key image in Man Ray's work since as far back as 1911, when he had made the *Tapestry*, as well as other compositions based upon a grid of squares. The famous *Lips* had begun as a similar grid upon a photograph of Kiki's mouth. "It helps you to understand the structure, to master a sense of order," he wrote at the time. "When the ancient masters composed a painting, they used to divide the surface into regular squares."

With the chess sets made during this period, Man Ray set out to build up a cottage industry of sorts, constructing a first group of thirty-six sets in wood and anodized aluminum and selling them as an edition, signed and numbered on the base of the white king. Unlike Yves Tanguy's rough-hewn approach to the project, chessmen cut from a broomstick, Man Ray's were cast firmly in the Deco mode, sleek and minimal. The bishops's mitre was reduced to a Brancusi-like curve with a V-incision at the top; the knight's steed evoked by a quarter-circle arc with an eye-hole drilled through it; the rook's castle a rectangle on end with a crisscross incision. "The art galleries have handled it for me," he told Elsie, "retailing for $60.00 and giving me $40. Of course, if produced in quantity, they will sell cheaper and many more people will buy." He had also managed to interest department stores on the West Coast in marketing the sets. By the fall, Man Ray had developed enough momentum to commission fifty more sets in aluminum. The endeavor gave him a much-needed lift, allowing him to mass-produce a product straddling art and design without compromising his principles about either.

And so, Man Ray was on an emotional upswing when his friend Max Ernst, having left Peggy Guggenheim, arrived back in L. A. that fall for a one-week visit, now accompanied by his latest love, the artist Dorothea Tanning. She was meeting Man Ray and Juliet for the first time. The two men had known each other from the Paris Dada group, to which Ernst had come via Cologne. He was a cosmopolitan man—a dramatic painter, quirky sculptor, film actor, gallery impresario, articulate theoretician, pamphleteer, and polemicist. All good Surrealists hid behind some form of persona, anthropomorphic or otherwise, and "Loplop, King of the Birds" was Ernst's most popular guise. With his shock of fair hair, ice-blue eyes, and predatory nose, Max Ernst did come across as a courtly bird of paradise.

Ernst and Man Ray shared a consuming interest in the interventionist way of making art. Through his "*frottage,*" Ernst drew out the essence of objects he wished to replicate by placing them beneath tracing paper, then rubbing the surface of the sheet with a broad edge of charcoal. And he delved into other, similar methods of disturbing surfaces—"*grattage*" (scraping), "*éclaboussage*" (splattering), "*coulage*" (pouring), and collage—all with the intention of reconstituting the expected, conventional picture plane. Ernst was one of the most dream-directed of all Surrealist painters. In Dorothea—whom he had first met in New York at the end of 1942 while she was guest-curating an exhibition for Peggy

Guggenheim's gallery—he had, at last, after Louise Straus, Marie-Berthe Aurenche, Leonora Carrington, and Peggy Guggenheim, found a woman to share his imaginative life. At twenty, Dorothea had escaped from Galesburg, Illinois, the small town where she was born and raised, and landed a job as a restaurant hostess in Chicago to pay her way through art school. After living and working in New York, she, too, needed a faraway place to paint, undisturbed and free. In February 1946, the two had settled in Sedona, Arizona, and, with her savings, bought a supply of lumber and two and a half acres of property, building what she delighted in calling an "improvisational house" with a shed about forty paces up the hill as Max's workplace.

Max and Dorothea came to Hollywood with the intention to marry, and they wanted Man Ray and Juliet to serve as their witnesses. One evening the four were having drinks in the studio on Vine Street, when Man Ray only half-jokingly said, "If Max and Dorothea can do it, maybe we should, too!" After all, Man Ray later wrote Elsie, "We have been together six years now, so it was not such a revolutionary step." On the afternoon of October 24, 1946, the foursome went quietly to justice of the peace Cecil D. Holland in Beverly Hills, hoping to avoid publicity and attention. But he recognized Max Ernst, and an annoying horde of photographers trailed the wedding party out into the street.

Man Ray and Juliet drove over to the gallery-home of Hollywood art dealer Earl Stendahl on Hillside Avenue, near Franklin and La Brea. They were warmly welcomed with free-flowing champagne. Conveniently enough, Walter and Louise Arensberg lived right next door, where there was more champagne awaiting. The next day, all four newlyweds were feted at dinner by producer-director and art collector Albert Lewin and his wife, Mildred. They were photographed by Florence Homolka, an occasional student of Man Ray, who went on to publish a collection of her own work. Man Ray photographed Dorothea, who made a beautiful painting of Juliet with a fantastic white headdress like a bridal veil; later, Max painted a large canvas called *Double Wedding in Beverly Hills*. There was also the usual dressing-up, Man Ray and Max donning gowns and tribal wigs and jewelry, Juliet pasting a tiny, black mustache to her pouting upper lip. It was a happy time.

With the war over and travel restrictions lifted, Man Ray daily felt the pressure to take a quick trip back to Paris and put his affairs in order. He wanted to decide what to do about the country house, assess the condition of his personal effects and artwork in storage and dispersed among friends' homes, and, most important, through quick sales, amass some much-needed capital. He had decided to put the idea of permanent relocation in abeyance for the time being, out of deference to Juliet.

The couple flew to Paris via New York and were there in time for Man Ray's fifty-seventh birthday. Once settled in the Hôtel l'Aiglon on the boulevard Raspail, Man Ray spent most of his days at Lefevre-Foinet's, sorting through his books, paintings, objects, negatives, photographs, and drawings, busily packing material into boxes for eventual shipment back to California.

He was able to sell the house in St. Germain-en-Laye to an English army major. There was a problem, however, in gaining permission to transfer the money into dollars, so Man Ray literally stuffed his pockets with francs for the trip home. The sale of five hundred copies of the Soby album of *Photographs 1920–1934* to an American bookseller in Paris conributed further to his liquidity.

Returning to New York, Man Ray and Juliet spent a few weeks at the Sieglers', a familiar and comforting resting place. Since her mid-teens, niece Naomi had dreamed of following in her uncle Man's footsteps and becoming a photographer. Now, poised on the brink of her senior year at Bennington, she decided to take a good stretch of time to apprentice with him in California. Her mother was all in favor of the move, but Papa Max objected, concerned about what Juliet might think about having Naomi living with her for such a long period. "Papa, I'm the boss!" son Man told him in no uncertain terms, and that settled that. Elsie gently questioned her new sister-in-law about brother Man's domineering nature. "She doesn't have to account for her existence," her husband said, simply, as if that were enough of an explanation.

The departure of the three westward travelers was delayed because Man Ray was spending most of his time listening to the World Series on the radio. Always a passionate sports fan (decidedly not a participant), he had arrived back in the States just at the peak of the baseball season and was unable to tear himself away. Each morning Naomi would awaken and ask Man Ray if today was the day they would be embarking on their trip. "Not yet," her uncle would mutter.

Finally, toward the middle of October, they were off. The

stopover in Chicago to change trains was an opportunity for a visit to Katharine Kuh at her gallery and a whirlwind tour of the Art Institute to view Seurat's *La grande jatte,* a favorite inspirational work for the Surrealists. "In spite of the huge white bathroom frame which threw its dimming colors out of key," Man Ray recalled of the painting, "its calm majesty was unperturbed."

Man Ray continued to teach by example, rather than by dictum. In his darkroom sessions with Naomi, he impressed upon her the importance of economy of movement and material. One could—and should—use any amount of paper necessary to make attempt after attempt but be most fastidious and careful with the more costly chemicals. The darkroom, he told her, was a place to make fearless tries at whatever images came to mind. There were no such words as "don't, can't, or shouldn't" in that shadowy and sacred place. It was the end result only that mattered.

He was an artist who worked with a minimal amount of agonizing and *sturm und drang.* As far as a constituency for his work was concerned, he told her repeatedly, "You don't need a huge audience. You really need only five or six people who care, and are there to encourage you." He advised his niece to "do her work by herself as much as possible, at home. You know, that is how I work."

"Don't worry about idealism and practicality," Man Ray told Naomi. "Try to get paid for what you do, and don't worry if you don't. Just keep on working. You'll make up for it in time."

Over the five months she lived and worked with her uncle Man, Naomi enjoyed repeated opportunities to see Man Ray break the artistic rules of the game with utter awareness of what he was doing, and always with directness. Technical excellence, as such, was never an overriding goal in Man Ray's mind. Rather, he was proud of the throwaway, almost callous attitude with which he viewed his equipment. ("They're all about the same, equally bad," he told Naomi when she asked him to recommend a good camera— whether it was Ciroflex, Argoflex, Kodak, or the one-lens reflex Korelle he used most often in the forties.) No matter what "instrument" he employed, Man Ray's desire came through—to make the thing in the world seem his own, to possess the object or person and by instinctive action bring it into his work. The stylistic twist always identified it as an effort only one artist could have achieved: himself.

MAN RAY. *NAOMI WITH FAN, HOLLYWOOD, 1947–48.*
Collection Naomi Savage.

P R A C T I C A L
D R E A M E R

AT THE VERY moment most of the Surrealists in exile returned to
Europe, a young man with plenty of time and money decided to
open a small art gallery in Beverly Hills. His name was William
Copley. He had been introduced to Surrealism by his wife's brother-
in-law, John Ployardt, an artist who worked for the Walt Disney
studios. Copley himself was the first to acknowledge that "no one in
his right mind would have considered trying to open a Surrealist
gallery in the California environment," but he and Ployardt were
undaunted in their enthusiasm. They had surveyed the competition
and found it unintimidating: the Los Angeles County Museum was
still predominantly interested in natural history, and it had been
one of several institutions in the area to turn down the Walter
Arensberg collection. Among the private dealers, there were Earl
Stendahl, who specialized in pre-Columbian art, Dazil Hatfield,
Frank Perls, and Paul Kantor. Otherwise, "the place was an
intellectual desert" in Copley's opinion.

In the fall of 1948, Ployardt brazenly quit his job with the
Disney studios and Copley sold the house where he, his wife, Doris,
and their two young children had been living and moved to Laurel
Canyon. He found a bungalow at 257 North Cañon Drive, a low-
slung, wood-frame building with a huge window in front surrounded by dense shrubs, and ivy, and put up a brass plaque

proclaiming the place as "Copley Galleries." Inside, he devoted four rooms, complete with fireplaces to accentuate the homey feeling, to exhibit space. The gallery was casually elegant and without pretensions. There were polished wood floors and off-white walls, freestanding pillars and latticework room dividers, intimate, indirect lighting, and cozy alcoves that set the paintings off to their best advantage.

The two entrepreneurs began recruiting a half dozen artists for their inaugural season. Man Ray was the first they approached, being closest at hand. When they called upon him one autumn morning, they were greeted by the hostility Man Ray customarily reserved for first meetings. He told them he was never free before eleven A.M. On their second visit, as was his way, Man Ray relaxed, realizing that Copley and Ployardt's intentions were serious. He agreed to show with the gallery on two conditions: first, that he be guaranteed 15 percent revenues. (Copley went on to set this as a policy for all six shows he mounted and as a result, by buying nearly a fifth of all the paintings in each show, built up one of the most comprehensive collections of Surrealist art in the world.) The second condition was standard with Man Ray. He insisted upon complete autonomy in choosing the work to be shown. He wanted to push his most recent creations, and, until the eleventh hour, Copley could not be certain that Man Ray was going to permit any photographs at all to be hung. In the end, the artist relented, hoping to make some sales.

The cantankerous but warm veteran artist and the bold, entrepreneurial scion of the Copley newspaper chain soon became fast friends, and they grew even closer when young Bill decided he, too, wanted to paint. He developed a colorful, comic-book style, with tricky imagery and bright, upbeat tones. Copley admired Man Ray's originality and was inspired by it in his own work. The two couples became frequent dinner companions, and Copley had no hesitation about picking up the tab at the end of a meal. It was enough of a treat for him to listen to Man Ray for an entire evening.

The gallery finally opened in October. Two shows had been scheduled to precede Man Ray's: Magritte and Matta. Only one Magritte painting was sold, for nine hundred dollars, although, as Copley recalled, "all Hollywood was in attendance, out of curiosity, and much whiskey was consumed."

The Man Ray opening, "To Be Continued Unnoticed," on

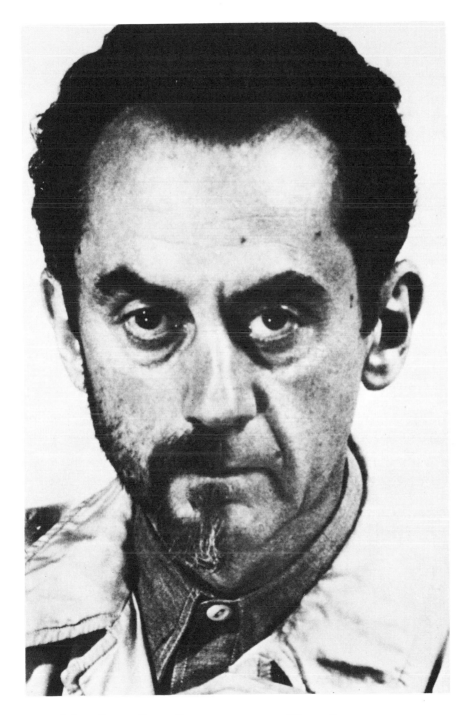

MAN RAY. *SELF PORTRAIT WITH HALF BEARD*, 1943.
Private collection, New York.

December 13, 1948, was a festive affair. The gallery was converted, for one night only, to "Café Man Ray," and the expensively produced invitation, featuring the portrait of the artist with his face half bearded and half clean-shaven, as seen in *View,* promised red wine, French bread, and American cocktails. The patio in front of the gallery was converted to a sidewalk café, with red-checkered tablecloths and candles on each table. Juliet, Doris Copley, and Françoise Stravinsky, the composer's daughter-in-law, who worked as the gallery's secretary, cooked up a batch of onion soup. Juliet wore glitter in her hair and drifted, wraithlike, through the crowd. Even the beret-clad artist—who usually receded into the background at such affairs—was in high spirits. Man Ray appeared poised, relaxed, and pleased with the way the work looked.

The Copley show was one of the most impressive displays of Man Ray's art. It was well chosen and intimate, encompassing paintings that went back to the Ridgefield years and a couple of canvases from the 1920s. *Place de la Concorde* was featured. One of a series of paintings Man Ray dashed off during the first three years he was in residence in Paris, it showed the landmark public square through the eyes of an enthralled tourist.

There were also a few spectacular surprises. The awesome *Lips* made another dramatic appearance, having been rescued from Nazi-occupied France by Mary Reynolds. She had managed to smuggle Man Ray's rolled-up canvas out of Spain in a secret walking trip over the Pyrenees in the summer of 1942. Arriving in New York, she transported *The Lips* and *Le beau temps* across the country and delivered them to Man Ray in his Vine Street digs. "Statuesque, unmelodramatic, New Hampshire–born, and nobody's fool," as Janet Flanner described her, Mary Reynolds, in taking responsibility for *The Lips,* provided one more dramatic chapter in the life of this great Surrealist icon. The painting caught Copley's eye, and he purchased it from the artist for two thousand dollars. *The Lips* stayed in Copley's personal collection for thirty years.

Cleaning out one of the closets in the gallery in preparation for the opening, Doris had dug up a tangled mass of coat hangers, and Man Ray, who never liked to waste found materials, constructed a mobile out of them, which hung prominently in the entranceway. There were several chess sets on view as well and a number of paintings repatriated from Paris, shipped back as a result of Man Ray's trip the previous summer.

A brand-new series of seventeen paintings called *Equations for Shakespeare* (later changed to *Shakespearian Equations*) was also included in the show. These were "translated" from the photographic series of *Mathematical Objects* done twelve years earlier in Paris. Man Ray was once again borrowing from himself and updating, revising, and transforming imagery. The paintings reflected a new surge of creative energy that had been occasioned by the promise of the show. Copley's dedication to perpetuating Surrealism no matter what the personal cost—and it was great, for everyone knew that the Copley Gallery would probably not last the winter—had been a powerful stimulant.

There was a dreamy quality to paintings such as *Macbeth*, *The Merry Wives of Windsor*, and *The Tempest*—to take just three examples of Man Ray's most vibrant work in the Shakespeare series. Although hurriedly produced and not painterly in style, they were intellectually compelling. Despite Man Ray's denial of any connection between the paintings and the plays themselves, one could not help but connect the *Wives* to the anthropomorphic group of four teardrop-crowned, shrouded shapes hovering in green space. The drama of *Macbeth*'s impending doom was suggested in the way the curtainlike borders of that canvas parted to reveal a gray sky. The turbulence of *The Tempest* and the play's complex intermingling of characters were implicit in the painting's gaudy red field and multifaceted, floating assemblage of planes. In the *Equations for Shakespeare*, Man Ray pillaged his past to high advantage.

The catalogue contained some of Man Ray's most powerful and straightfoward writing: "I simply try to be as free as possible," he declared, echoing Robert Motherwell's belief (even though Man Ray never approved of him) that the history of modern art was in fact synonymous with the history of modern freedom. "In my manner of working, in the choice of my subject, no one can dictate to me or guide me." Furthermore, the artist wrote, in words that placed him even more firmly in the modernist mode, "All opinion is transient and all work is permanent."

With no sales except to the producer Albert Lewin and to the gallery owner Bill Copley, who had offered a guarantee, the show closed on January 9, 1949.

Ambitious exhibitions by Joseph Cornell, Yves Tanguy, and Max Ernst followed. The Ernst show was a thirty-year retrospective, his first in America. A Dorothea Tanning show was planned, too, but because of the gallery's financial woes, it had to be done at

Barbara Cecil Byrnes's American Contemporary Gallery instead. And Copley had also very much wanted to do a Paul Delvaux exhibition. It never materialized because, Copley mourned, "It was time to listen to the lamentations of the bookkeeper. His evidence could not be refuted. What the venture had cost in terms of rent, maintenance, salary, printing, postage, packing, shipping, insurance, liquor, and money suddenly was staggering. . . . There was nowhere further to go."

These had been six heady and uplifting months for Man Ray. He relished the exposure, welcomed Copley's support and friendship, and especially enjoyed being able to connect him with Marcel Duchamp in New York. Man Ray's instructions for the meeting were explicit, and Copley followed them to the word, sending a telegram to Duchamp's apartment on West Fourteenth Street, then awaiting the penny postcard telling Copley and Ployardt to meet the mysterious Marcel in the lobby of the Biltmore Hotel at noon the following day. They found the shabby but dignified artist slouched on a sofa smoking his pipe, repaired to Luchow's for lunch, then were allowed back to the studio to view the lair of the "Grand Sorceror," as Copley called him. Man Ray was pleased with the report from Copley, who went on to become one of Duchamp's closest friends and—although the rest of the world did not know it until years later—the steadfast supporter of Duchamp's last and most utterly secret work.

The Copley Gallery was not the only attempt to put modern art before a broader audience that failed to take hold in Los Angeles during the 1940s. The Modern Institute of Art on Rodeo Drive in Beverly Hills lasted a scant fourteen months before it closed in the spring of 1949, despite several ambitious exhibitions made up of work drawn from the collections of such stellar members as Walter Arensberg, Averell Harriman, Vincent Price, and Edward G. Robinson. At the gala opening, which attracted thirteen thousand guests, Man Ray in a momentary fit of pique refused to pose for photographs in front of a Léger canvas. There was an ambiguous, longstanding feud between the two former friends, its roots now forgotten. But he had held high hopes for this endeavor, and when the institute and Copley's place shut their doors within months of each other, Man Ray was vastly disappointed, and he returned to his barely concealed opinion of Los Angeles.

Reaffirming his doctrine that there was "no progress in art," Man Ray directed his energies toward a series of still lifes. Naturalism was simply another rabbit to be pulled out of his inexhaustible top hat of genres. He redoubled his efforts at "getting [his] things back" from various warehouses, squirreling them away in the packed-to-the-rafters studio on Vine Street. He confided crankily to niece Naomi that he had "lost his enthusiasm for hero-worship" and was "no longer going to go out of [his] way" to seek subjects for his photographs. Any work of that kind was done on an ad hoc basis, if someone happened to be visiting and Man Ray took a liking to a nuance or shadow in his or her face.

It was also at about this time that Man Ray began to set down preliminary notes toward an autobiography, beginning with an account of the decades in Paris. The local scene held less and less promise, and he continued to flirt with the fantasy of returning to that magical city. Man Ray the writer took time in the gray light of evening at the small desk in the far corner of his living room to play back his memories. Such retrospective thinking was further inspired by word from George Heard Hamilton and Katherine Dreier that the Société Anonyme was planning a big show and the publication of a catalogue celebrating its three decades of life. Marcel Duchamp volunteered to compile brief critical profiles of the more than thirty major artists included. Man Ray was excited at the prospect of reaffirming his ties with the organization. After all, as late as 1945, he was still listed as vice president. "What good times we used to have," he told Miss Dreier, "and how glad we all will be when [the Société] is safely established with its catalogue."

Man Ray attended to filling out the detailed questionnaire Duchamp required for the massive catalogue. There it all was, in black and white, the chronology of an artist who listed his important personal influences as "Everybody": "Brooklyn, 1897–1913; Ridgefield, 1913–1916; New York City, 1916–1921. . . ." His group memberships Man Ray considered to have begun with the "Independents" of 1917, where he had his first intoxicating tastes of rejection by mainstream critics; "Dada" he entered as "1920–1924"; the Surrealists, "1924–1929," followed by the "Surindépendants," with an open-ended date, "193-."

When it came to setting down a "Personal Creed," Man Ray was straightforward: "To paint as much as possible unlike other painters," he wrote, "above all, to paint unlike myself—so that each succeeding work, or series of works, shall be entirely different from preceding works." Even after so many decades, Man Ray was still in thrall to his boyhood idols—Thoreau, the champion of individualism, and Whitman, who accepted self-contradiction as the artist's credo. And there was also the unmistakable agreement with Ezra Pound in Man Ray's endorsement of the need to move from one innovation to the next, the classic modernist compulsion to "make it new."

After such soul-searching, Man Ray was especially sensitive when Andrew Ritchie, director of Painting and Sculpture at New York's Museum of Modern Art, stopped by the studio with James Byrnes, the young curator of the Department of Contemporary Art at the Los Angeles County Museum of History, Science, and Art. Ritchie was seeking to borrow works for the Modern's forthcoming exhibition, planned for early 1951, "Abstract Painting and Sculpture in America." Ritchie's eye wandered over a good number of Man Ray's more recent paintings and alighted upon the celebrated *Rope Dancer* of 1916. This was the kind of work the museum desired for the show. "Dr. Ritchie," Man Ray snarled, suddenly lashing out at the unsuspecting fellow, voicing a lifelong grudge, "you join the host of critics and museum people who have me dead as an artist after 1919!" Ritchie was embarrassed and crestfallen. However, four years later, the monumental work was purchased by G. David Thompson of Pittsburgh and given to the Modern for its permanent collection.

Some of Man Ray's anger about the chronic problem of lack of recognition for his recent painting may have stemmed from the bitterness he felt toward his former friends Walter and Louise Arensberg. Their mansion on Hillside Avenue—"as far away from New York," Walter put it, "as we could get without crossing the ocean"—was jammed, floor-to-ceiling, living room, dining room, bedrooms, bathrooms, even closets, with paintings by Rousseau, Matisse, Picasso, Braque, Gris, Rouault, de Chirico, sculpture by Brancusi, and the major works (or, as their creator preferred to call them, "organic effusions") of Marcel Duchamp. In the words of James Thrall Soby, all this great art by the modern masters crowded "belligerently close together, but not fight[ing], broke all the rules of light, space and height." Yet, somehow, the special character of each painting pressed shoulder to shoulder with other paintings was revealed. Only one artist was conspicuous by his absence: aside from a single small assemblage, *Décollage,* the Arensbergs did not at that time (and never did, in all their years of collecting) own a work by Man Ray. In fact, the contentious and contrary Walter made it painfully clear that he did not consider Man Ray's painting to be of high enough quality.

That spring of 1949, Man Ray's standoffishness toward the Arensbergs (who, after all, had been supporters thirty-five years earlier in New York City) reached such a pitch that he was no longer on speaking terms with them. This unfortunate turn of events gave rise to awkwardness when Duchamp made a "visitation" to the Arensberg home for a week in May, stopping by between a Round Table Symposium on Modern Art at the San Francisco Museum of Art and a jaunt to Sedona to spend some time with Max Ernst and Dorothea Tanning.

During Duchamp's visit, scholar and critic Katharine Kuh, who was the curator of Modern Art at the Art Institute of Chicago, was also at the Arensbergs' daily, industriously cataloguing their vast collection (much of which had been acquired for them by Duchamp) in preparation for a major exhibition at the Art Institute

MAN RAY LOOKING AT *THE WOMAN AND HER FISH II,* 1941. *Private collection.*

that coming fall and winter. When Duchamp arrived, he walked through the entrance hall, past Brancusi's brass *Princess* and Joseph Stella's Futurist-inspired canvas, and into the living room and an adjoining garden room where most of his important life's work was displayed, including the three versions of *Nude Descending a Staircase*, the *Chess Players*, *The King and Queen Surrounded by Swift Nudes*, *The Bride*, and *Chocolate Grinder*. Kuh and the Arensbergs silently and apprehensively followed him from room to room as Marcel Duchamp, the man who insisted he had given up painting, but who had in fact for the past several years been secretly laboring on the monumental work of his life, coolly and quietly surveyed the "retrospective." At last, Duchamp pointed to *The King and Queen* and said to the three, "This one still holds up," declining to comment on anything else.

Scrupulous as always, unfailingly conscious of not offending his hosts, yet wanting to see Man Ray, Duchamp devised a simple ruse. In the afternoon, he would either announce that he was going for a walk or slip out unobtrusively. Man Ray, by prearranged agreement, would drive by in his midnight-blue Cord sedan and pick up his friend, accompanied occasionally by Mrs. Kuh. They might start by chatting over drinks with Juliet at Vine Street. Then Bill Copley and his wife would stop by and take everyone out to lunch or dinner. During these otherwise congenial times, Man Ray refused to talk about photography, and he was annoyed by Kuh's laudatory remarks about his work in the medium. It seemed to her as if one part of Man Ray was jealous of the other. He was unable to admit to the great talent he possessed and vehemently insisted upon the viability of his painting.

Man Ray enjoyed the admiration of a small cadre of supporters who consistently purchased paintings from him over the decades. Albert and Mildred Lewin were prominent in this group.

Albert ("Allie" to nearly all who knew him) Parsons Lewin was born in Brooklyn in 1894, the son of immigrant parents, and grew up in Newark, New Jersey. He attended New York University and Harvard, where he received a master's degree in English and was a member of the Poetry Society. From a young age, in fact, Lewin found "the poet's role" more suitable than any other. He was always writing, whether it was theater criticism for the *Jewish Tribune* during his graduate student days, script synopses for Sam Goldwyn, or screenplays, as personal assistant to Irving Thalberg at MGM, after brief apprenticeships with King Vidor and Victor Seastrom. Lewin stayed with Thalberg until 1936, when he moved to Paramount under the aegis of Adolph Zukor. After he finally retired and moved back to New York in the 1950s, Lewin wrote a strange, surreal literary novel called *The Unaltered Cat.*

A compact, dapper, and energetic man, Lewin was aggressive and opinionated in his visual style. He rose quickly to the peak of a profession he had turned to only when the cloistered scholarly life became boring. A string of successes as a writer, director, and producer enabled him to commission a house on the beach in Santa Monica designed by the Viennese architect Richard Neutra, a former Bauhaus member who was recognized as the preeminent modern architect living on the West Coast. The house's low-slung furniture, off-white walls, expanses of windows fronting the ocean, and endless daylight were a dramatic backdrop for Lewin's vast collection of modern, Surrealist, and primitive pre-Columbian art, as well as for his stimulating parties where artists and show-business people mingled, brought together by their host's desire to effect a union between art and film. And it was here, too, that Albert Lewin, an early and steadfast admirer of Man Ray, tried to introduce his friend to moviemaking colleagues and establish some connections that might lead to his employment in show business.

Lewin's years with Thalberg had helped him develop a flair for the pictorial beauty of cinema; like Man Ray, he had a natural affinity for detailed, opulent, and occasionally decadent imagery. Rich elegance had become Lewin's trademark. In the highly acclaimed *Moon and Sixpence,* which he directed, black and white audaciously shifts to color during the conclusion, as the artist destroys his works in a bonfire. For *The Picture of Dorian Gray,* Lewin doubled as author of the screenplay based upon the Oscar Wilde story, and as director. A décor of blacks and whites symbolizes the struggle of good and evil. The notorious full-length portrait resembles a grotesque Tchelitchew creation.

In his *Pandora and the Flying Dutchman,* an elaborate literary tale of perverse love starring Ava Gardner and James Mason, set in a de Chirico–like landscape, Lewin used a Man Ray painting and chess set as background props, and in 1950 he commissioned Man Ray to photograph the leading lady. This Man Ray accomplished with a telephoto lens set up across the room from the actress, to provide the grainy, sultry detail Lewin sought.

Lewin developed a broad and varied collection of work by Man

MAN RAY. *THE DYING LEAF*, 1942. CHOSEN BY MAN RAY
FOR AN ARTICLE IN *VIEW* MAGAZINE (APRIL–OCTOBER 1943)
AS ONE OF THE TEN BEST PHOTOGRAPHS OF HIS CAREER.
The J. Paul Getty Museum.

Ray over the years of their friendship. He purchased almost exclusively recent work, which endeared him all the more to the sensitive artist. On one wall in Lewin's white living room hung a unique wood-collage, *A la lumière lunaire,* a silver-dollar-sized orb of lightly stained wood set neatly into a darker-grained wooden rectangle, creating the effect alluded to in the title: a ghostly moon afloat in a night sky. Lewin also owned several paintings dating from the *Les mains libres* period of the late thirties, including *Le roman noir* and *Rose-verte.* And the producer's enthusiasm for the whimsically figurative canvases from Man Ray's return to cartoonish naturalism in the late 1940s was evident as well. In *Dance in the Subway,* animated figures reminiscent of those from Ridgefield days cavort in a dark grotto. In *Vase-figure,* a face melts into a vessel, and a vessel into a face. Albert Lewin's collection of Man Rays was chosen with a discriminating eye.

The other important Man Ray patron during the Hollywood years was Mary Stothardt, who also lived in a Bauhaus-style house in Santa Monica. An MGM actress and singer by profession, Mary was a creative and accomplished *collagiste* as well, with an intelligent appreciation for the avant garde. She had an affable nature and was charmed rather than put off by the way Man Ray could be "disagreeable with people who were stupid." Her stately home on La Mesa Drive was the scene of Sunday barbecues where one might mingle with Jean Renoir, Charlie Chaplin, Paulette Goddard, and Hedy Lamarr.

Mary's husband, Herbert, was a successful songwriter. After he died in 1947, she signed over his ASCAP royalty checks to Man Ray, in occasional exchange for paintings, her way of helping an artist who had come upon hard times and was too dignified to ask for support. Mary believed that Man Ray "was brilliant and very much ahead of his time." She was also aware that he was starving despite his brilliance, but that "if he was in trouble very few people would know it."

JULIET ON THE STEAMSHIP *DE GRASSE*, EN ROUTE
FROM NEW YORK TO LE HAVRE, MARCH 1951.
Photograph by Gloria de Herrera. Courtesy David de Herrera and James B. Byrnes.

FAREWELL
TO
TINSEL TOWN

WITH THE NEW year, 1950, Man Ray's hints about his intention to leave Hollywood became more frequent and overt. He wrote of the plan to his former lover, Ady Fidelin. Her husband, André, responded warmly by inviting Man Ray and Juliet to stay with them when they arrived in Paris: "Feel free to live here if you do not have enough money. There is enough space in the dining room for the two of you." André reassured Man Ray that his personal effects were still in the safe care of Lefevre-Foinet.

For a Father's Day present, in a rare display of thoughtfulness and, perhaps, residual regret—for Minnie had died five years before, but her intransigent older son had not come east for the funeral—Man Ray sent Max ten dollars, promising in a short accompanying note that he "hope[d] soon to see [him]," telling his father to buy "something to remember us by until we see each other again." By the fall of the year, newlywed niece Naomi was in Paris with her husband, and Man Ray made no attempt to conceal his yearning to be with them. "Perhaps I'll get over while you're still around," Man Ray told Naomi.

Man Ray's combination Christmas-season open house and yard sale left little to the imagination of anyone fortunate enough to attend. It was clear he was getting rid of excess baggage and trying to raise some cash. Stacks of *Les main libres,* the original Jeanne

Bucher hardcover edition of 1937, were on sale for twelve dollars a copy, and Ribemont-Dessaignes's ground-breaking 1924 *Peintres nouveaux* monograph on Man Ray could be had for a dollar. For the foresighted collector a number of exquisite, spiral-bound 1934 Soby collection catalogues published in Paris were also available for a pittance. Toward the end of the afternoon, several "objects of my affection," forlorn and suddenly encumbering, were unceremoniously thrust into people's hands.

"I am in a whirl now," Man Ray told Elsie, "my rent has been doubled, with the controls off." It was a radical leap, from fifty to one hundred dollars a month, made all the more painful for someone without a dependable income. "I can't take this town anymore," he confessed to pal Bill Copley soon after. And Copley, for his part, was also growing restless. His marriage to Doris had ended and he was living with his girlfriend, Gloria de Herrera, in an old converted firehouse, painting sporadically, and presiding over chess tournaments. Juliet, too, was lonely. Her husband was dissatisfied ("feeling like a black sheep," he complained) and living in the past, treading water most of the time.

Copley purchased a couple of paintings to bolster Man Ray's cash reserve, and the landlord wrote out a check on the spot for the artist's automobile. Elsie received word in early February 1951: "The die is cast," brother Man wrote, "we have reservations to sail for Paris on the 12th of March on the *De Grasse.*" On the eve of the long train trip to New York, Man Ray was still able to wax philosophical to Juliet, Bill Copley, and Gloria de Herrera. "The maturest people make mistakes," he said. "We all did in 1939. I think I can profit by them now."

During the decade he lived in Hollywood, Man Ray had indeed paid an immeasurable price for adhering to iconoclasm. But he remained stoic. "I do not despair," he wrote with particular pride, in "Photogenic Reflections," an article for *Berkeley* magazine, and his final, almost religious manifesto of the Hollywood decade. "Painting is directed by the heart through the eye. Photography is directed by the mind through the eye. But desire and love for the subject direct both mediums. One cannot replace the other. . . someday heart and mind will become one, that is, an all-embracing and economical medium will enable us to realize all our desires instantly."

And so, Man Ray left Hollywood, not in an anguish of

MAN RAY, JULIET, WILLIAM COPLEY, AND MARCEL
DUCHAMP ON BOARD THE *DE GRASSE*, NEW YORK,
MARCH 12, 1951. PHOTOGRAPH BY GLORIA DE HERRERA.
Courtesy David de Herrera and James B. Byrnes.

departure, but with much the same mixture of hope and anticipation that had taken him there. The wheel had come full circle.

For the time being at least, Man Ray put it all behind him. He
leaned against the railing on the deck of the steamship *De Grasse,* his
arm around the wasp-waist of his lovely, smiling wife who held her
hat firmly against the chill March wind, and traded off taking
snapshots with Bill Copley and Gloria de Herrera, his congenial
traveling companions. It was to be the final transatlantic crossing
for the ship, and Man Ray and his friends had managed to obtain
first-class accommodations.

A special visitor came by the ship to wish Man Ray a fond
adieu: Marcel Duchamp. The Frenchman had found a cosmopolitan and comfortable anonymity in New York City, and just before
leaving, Man Ray again flirted with the notion—no longer taken
seriously by sister Elsie, so often had it been broached—of taking up
his painting in New York. But France offered something America

could not: a reverence for the dedicated artist. And Man Ray wanted nothing more than to sink into the relaxed rhythm of rising at midday, sipping café-au-lait and munching on a baguette in bed or at a little bistro, thinking a good deal about painting or object-making, and, perhaps, engaging in serious industry for an hour or two between puffs on his pipe, all in an ambience not replicable in the United States.

The two friends repaired below deck for a private parting. In the seclusion of Man Ray's cabin, Duchamp presented him with a token of their friendship, the *Feuille de vigne femelle* (Female Fig Leaf) sculpture, one of a pair Duchamp had fabricated in galvanized plaster. He had kept the other for himself as an artist's proof. The *Feuille de vigne,* a cast of the female genitalia, was the first of a series of erotic objects Duchamp produced during the early 1950s. To Duchamp, eroticism was "a way to bring out in the daylight things that are constantly hidden . . . because of social rules. To be able to reveal them, and to place them at everyone's disposal." It was a concept Man Ray understood, and, even before Surrealism, had embraced in his photographic works. Perhaps that was why Duchamp authorized his friend Man Ray to make an edition of ten plaster casts of the *Feuille* in Paris later that same year.

The little sculpture (it stood a mere 3 $^9/_{16}$ x 5 $^1/_2$ x 4 $^{15}/_{16}$ inches) appeared to have been made from life. Not so; rather, it was cast from a painted leather-over-plaster relief of a headless nude torso Duchamp had fashioned a couple of years earlier. The torso was the first known study for his last major work, *Etant donnés: 1. La chute d'eau; 2. Le gaz d'éclairage* (Given: 1. The Waterfall; 2. The Illuminating Gas), begun in New York in 1946. It was widely rumored—and, of course, Duchamp did nothing to counter any talk—that he had virtually given up artistic activity of all kinds.

Was Duchamp handing Man Ray a signal, or "sign," as he considered his work, that there was some deeper activity in his life, beneath the negation of art? The *Feuille de vigne femelle* may have been an object-lesson or metaphor for the twenty-year construction of the *Given* or Duchamp's idiosyncratic, circumspect way of parting the curtain of eroticism for an instant and allowing the one person in the world who had ever witnessed Rrose Sélavy in the flesh to view the beginnings of his secret opus. Duchamp had declared that "modern beauty is bizarre because it is different from yesterday's." The *Given,* when it finally came together two decades later as a mixed-media assemblage, was a dramatic fleshing-out of themes first articulated on the theoretical ground of *The Large Glass*. Through a peephole in a massive wooden door installed in the Philadelphia Museum of Art (thanks to the generosity of William Copley's Cassandra Foundation) one person at a time was able to enjoy Duchamp's concoction of bricks, velvet, wood, and leather stretched over an armature of metal in the shape of the female body, holding a lantern in one hand, with a backdrop of a constantly flowing artificial waterfall.

Inspired as he always was by a tête-à-tête with Duchamp, no matter how brief, Man Ray put his time to good use on the nine-day crossing. Between rounds of chess with the insatiable Copley and ministering to the seasick Juliet—luckily the couple had laid in a good supply of Dramamine—Man Ray clacked away on his portable typewriter and knocked off a rough draft of the first four chapters of the memoirs he'd been working on since the late forties. He also composed yet another essay on a subject of perennial concern to him: the artist's function in society. Such speculations always arose at transitional junctures in his career. Once more, Man Ray adopted the mantle of objectivity, writing of "the artist" rather than overtly of himself, probing within, rethinking and rearticulating the sources of his motivations as an artist who had never wanted to make his living in any other way.

"The artist," Man Ray wrote, "is his own most severe judge . . . his mistakes cannot hurt any other member of society, and at the worst retard his own progress." It was a theme he had sounded often before, the notion of the artist's benign influence. "After all," he once remarked jokingly, "we're not exactly making guns to shoot, are we?"

Man Ray and Juliet arrived in Le Havre in the midst of a railroad strike. They took a bus to Paris and were met at the station by niece Naomi and her husband of six months, David Savage. There was a flurry of confusion when it appeared as if Juliet's precious violin, which she had played since childhood, had been lost, but Naomi retrieved it and, after depositing Man Ray and Juliet's possessions at the Hôtel Pont Royal on the rue du Bac, the two couples went off for a festive dinner at La Coupole.

Man Ray and David Savage took to each other immediately. The young man, an architect by training and an accomplished painter in his own right, had become an admirer of Man Ray's work while still an undergraduate at the University of Virginia in the early 1940s. There had been a decisive moment during a senior-year course on the history of art taught by John Canaday; slide after slide flashed by on the screen as the professor traced the course of Surrealist painting. Then, suddenly, far larger than life, the image of *The Lips* inspired David Savage to pursue painting. He, too, would make a living in another field, architecture, but he derived much of his courage to stick with painting and sculpture from Man Ray as a role model. The younger man noted the deliberate way in which the older man simply *chose* to be an artist, even during the economic pressures of the 1950s. "I already did that; I just don't want to do it anymore," Man Ray told David bluntly of his rejection of commercial photography.

The two strolled along the boulevards and dropped in on gallery openings. Through the ensuing decades, as Man Ray introduced David and Naomi to his surviving colleagues of earlier days—Brancusi, Ernst, Giacometti, Duchamp—David came to perceive Man Ray as "the single greatest risk-taker of all the artists [he] had ever learned about."

Man Ray spent the damp weeks of spring 1951 moving restlessly with Juliet from hotel to hotel, anxious to settle down, engaged in "the great hunt . . . for a studio, which [was]," as he told Elsie, "very difficult." He was constrained by tight finances, driven by the need for a certain kind of two-tiered space, as all his studios had been, and no longer interested in Montparnasse. The scene of action had shifted northward since the war, toward St. Germain des Prés. The Café Flore—square banquettes, brass railings, mirrored walls, marble tables, and elegant, silvery bowls of hard-boiled eggs—had taken center stage. There, "intellectuals, existential riffraff, and tourists," or so Man Ray grouped them, huddled in earnest conversation.

A few twisting streets away from the hubbub was the place St. Sulpice, an intimate square graced at its eastern side by the massive church of that name. It was just enough off the beaten path to appeal to Man Ray's isolationist tendencies, and close to his beloved Luxembourg Gardens. At the center of the square, the nineteenth-century Fontaine des Quatre Points Cardinaux sent forth rushes of spray lending constant mildness to the air. Bounded by trees and overshadowed by the church's massive bulk, the square remained cool during the heat of the summer. The Café de la Mairie on the square was reputed to have served as a model for the night spot in Djuna Barnes's roman à clef, *Nightwood*. The Church of St. Sulpice had challenged the talents of six architects during the 134 years it was under construction. Man Ray was intrigued by this fact and he grew to like the church's odd assortment of styles, ranging from Greco-Roman to Florentine and Romantic, and its Delacroix murals. The building's two dissimilar towers—the one on the right incomplete because, so the story went, the architect became despondent during reconstruction and committed suicide by jumping from it—added to its appeal.

Near the cobblestoned front of St. Sulpice, the rue Férou rose from the square and wended its way at a gradual incline toward the rue de Vaugirard where, beyond that broader street, a green sliver of grass promising the latticed gates of the Luxembourg Gardens could be seen. Halfway up the rue Férou, on the right, a sculptor's studio had been improvised by blocking off and roofing an alleyway between a thirty-foot-high seminary wall and a private house, and, in effect, forming a cube with reinforced glass panes at top and front, to allow in floods of light. The unheated raw space had an average temperature of forty-two degrees on winter mornings. Man Ray, undaunted, sensed inherent possibilities. However, "I was no celibate," Man Ray told an interviewer, recalling the first time the couple stepped inside for a closer look. "Juliet had to be consulted and I brought her around. . . . It depressed her." She saw the moisture seeping down the cement walls, felt the cavernous chill, and, he remembered, "was terrified." She cried, telling her husband, "It was absolutely like a garage," which, in fact, the place had been, in an earlier incarnation. How Juliet missed those sun-drenched days by the pool in Hollywood! She knew she would have to capitulate, for her husband's mind was made up and, once that happened, there was simply no room for discussion. By late June, they had moved in, and Man Ray spent the summer "putting everything [he] had into fixing it up," admitting to sister Elsie that for the time being life at 2 bis, rue Férou was "more like camping."

Man Ray's final studio—he would live there for his last twenty-five years—was the most homemade and improvised of all, stretching back to Ridgefield days and, even earlier, to the front room of his parents' brownstone in Brooklyn. The studio on the rue Férou was self-contained and firmly in the hermetic tradition of

Brancusi's dust-coated space on the impasse Ronsin; Giacometti's sparse nest on the rue Hippolyte-Maindron; Duchamp's cell above Walter Arensberg's apartment on West Sixty-seventh Street in New York; Balthus's large, quiet aerie tucked away in the shabby but genteel cour Rohan; and Kurt Schwitters's Merzbau lined with wooden stalactites in Hannover. For these modernists, a studio could never be merely the place where they worked. It was, rather, a dramatic and comprehensive setting, a necessary extension of their imaginations. Man Ray's studio was both a museum and a self-portrait. As the years passed and the accretion of objects and artworks grew unabated, Man Ray and his studio developed in tandem, as mirror images of each other. The rigors of order there became so powerful, one visitor recalled, that when Man Ray momentarily left the room and she picked up an object to examine it more closely, he noticed the change immediately upon reentering and replaced the item in its proper location. It was as if the artist held a template for the room permanently fixed in his brain. Despite the growing clutter, Man Ray was never able to bring himself to have someone come in to clean the place, he was so fearful of change.

To make the space manageable and accommodating to separate activities as well as a multiplicity of media, Man Ray divided it with partitions. Past the triple-locked front door, set about a foot into a cement wall flush with the street, all but obscuring the entrance for visitors approaching from downhill, a long and dim corridor extended straight to yet another door, beyond which the massive room suddenly appeared as if conjured. To the left, one wall extended upward ten feet. On one side of it, Man Ray built a partitioned series of shelves he named "the cemetery," which became the resting place for objects he created or collected. Here he also kept a display of primitive idols. On the other side was a rudimentary kitchen. At the end of the kitchen farthest from the entryway, Man Ray set up a pot-bellied, coal-burning stove, supplanted after two years by an American kerosene-burning one, direct from the Automatic Products Company of Milwaukee, Wisconsin. Elsie dutifully sent him replacement parts when requested.

At the rear of the space, Man Ray built a bathroom where, in consideration of his guests' comfort against the chill, he lined the toilet seat with cut-off woolen socks and covered the hot- and cold-water taps with half tennis balls. The bedroom was womblike, accommodating not much more than two bookshelves and a big bed, where he and Juliet often huddled together, devouring eggs, coffee, and toast on particularly chilly mornings. The darkroom, also along the rear of the studio, was closed off by burlap curtains and had no running water. A ladder climbed from the right side of the rear wall to a loft-platform set up expressly for painting. It was closest to the skylight and above the system of parachute-cloths Man Ray rigged up, to be raised and lowered with pulleys, spread like great wings over the main level. This lyrical touch had a protective purpose—for once, after a trip to England during the winter of 1954, Man Ray and Juliet returned to the studio to find it flooded. Chestnuts from a neighbor's tree had plummeted onto the skylight and cracked it, allowing rain to seep in.

Seen from the loft, gazing down, the main floor of the studio seemed to have been laid out according to a definite scheme. The basic activities of daily life had been placed secondary to the hunger for the right kind of light and the proper display and storage of works of art. Every shelf along the perimeters of the room could be concealed with a sliding panel or a burlap curtain hung on a wooden rod. On many of the shelves were arrayed tins and wooden cigar boxes of all sizes that Man Ray had saved. In these boxes were stored glass-plate negatives arranged by subject, index cards listing artworks, and postcards from friends around the globe.

There was a pack-rat dignity to Man Ray's studio, a democracy of arrangement reflecting his feeling that all his works sprang commonly from the excitement of making something—anything. Drawings were stacked cozily against the wall. On a workbench behind the comfortable sofa that bisected the living room was a favorite photograph of the double-eyed Marquise Casati, nestling against a spray-paint can, which, in turn, supported a documentary snapshot of Man Ray and Marcel Duchamp enjoying a private joke. Behind the phallic *Priapus* sculpture set on the floor near the entranceway stood a nondescript wooden file cabinet. In it, Man Ray preserved archival subject-files of copy prints; documentary photographs of works in booklet form by Picasso, Ernst, Dalí, and Le Douanier Rousseau; and photos arranged by topic ("En Plein Air," "Flowers and Trees," "People").

Artworks by other artists displayed in Man Ray's studio were difficult to find. The place was overwhelmingly devoted to himself, alone.

MAN RAY, PRINCETON, 1963. *Photograph by Naomi Savage.*

A T   H O M E
A B R O A D

TO SIMONE DE BEAUVOIR, Paris in the wake of World War II resembled "the moribund capital of a very small country. The Seine was flowing in its bed; the Madeleine, the Chambre des Députés were in their places, the Obelisk, too. One could easily have been led to believe," she wrote, "that the war had miraculously spared Paris. . . . But, actually, the once proud capital of the world had been destroyed. . . ." Exterior signs of continuity belied an instability beneath. France was literally on its knees, "the sick man of Europe," its political system in disarray. There had been no fewer than fourteen cabinets in office between 1947 and 1954. The recovery and rebirth of the state meant to follow liberation had not come about. Although Communism had increased the number of its followers (including, to Man Ray's chagrin and disapproval, Picasso and Louis Aragon), it had lost intellectual strength. Existentialism, the philosophy of extreme self-determination, had developed as a response to the postwar malaise and characterized this period of depletion in a convalescent culture.

Man Ray had always been impervious to the influence of prevailing movements. Those who encountered him in the cafés of the Quartier—or perhaps in one of his favorite restaurants, Chez Alexandre, on the rue des Canettes just by St. Sulpice—felt he was a man truly *en règle* (in tune) with his situation; *disponible,* as the French expression goes, pleasantly distanced, and nonjudgmental.

The Korean crisis in 1951, the Algerian war in 1954, and the Suez troubles in 1957 elicited the same response from Man Ray, a man living "within [his] own four walls," predominantly concerned about whether he could still obtain fuel for his stove during wartime. The prevailing view among the French people was that the mood in their country in the fifties seemed a rerun of what it had been in the thirties. Man Ray, however, was at home abroad—just as Duchamp was glad to be back in New York, had laid claim to it, in fact.

The old crowd had regrouped. Many of those who had weathered the war were still around. Man Ray and Juliet even ran into Kiki on the street in Montparnasse, her old stomping ground. It was an affectionate reunion for the former lovers, and a timely, final one, for she died in late 1951. Paul Eluard had been moving from place to place underground in Paris, continuing to write his hypnotic love lyrics under the pseudonyms of Jean du Haut, Maurice Jaubert, and Brun. He was a frequent visitor at 2 bis, rue Férou until his death in November of 1953. Despite the bond between the two, Man Ray refused to attend Eluard's funeral because of the poet's Communist affiliations. Max Ernst and Dorothea Tanning left Arizona for Paris in 1950 and found a minuscule flat, a former maid's quarters on the quai St. Michel. Picasso was reinterpreting his old paintings and entering a prolific period of drawing in his studio on the rue des Grands Augustins. Roland Penrose was now embarking upon the great work of his life, the biography of Picasso, and therefore spent a good deal of time in Paris with the master, as well as in Collioure and Antibes, once again a favorite southern spot for painters. Man Ray and Juliet saw Penrose and his wife Lee Miller and also crossed the Channel frequently to visit the Penroses and their young son, Antony, at Farley Farm in Sussex.

André Breton had been back since 1946, and he had opened a gallery, A l'Etoile Scellée, which met with little success. Duchamp had prophesied in the preface to the Société Anonyme Catalogue that "Movements begin as a group formation and end with the scattering of individuals." However, Breton was still capable of gathering artworks and mobilizing people (with the exception of Giacometti, who adamantly refused to rescind his rupture with the Surrealists of 1935), and his polemical writing was as dogmatic as ever. He even found the energy to bring two new journals to life, *Medium* and *Le surréalisme même*. There was no question that his movie-star magnetism worked on an ad hoc basis. He still attracted a crowd at his table at the Café Deux Magots. In 1952, Breton organized a major exhibition at the Saarbrucken Museum (which included the work of Man Ray), "Surrealist Painting in Europe," and wrote an overview essay for the catalogue. But very few of those represented in the exhibition were in ongoing contact with Breton.

Wifredo Lam, Tristan Tzara, André Cartier-Bresson, Dora Maar, Matta, Jacques Prévert, Cocteau, Michel and Louise Leiris, Léonor Fini, Raymond Queneau, and Roland Barthes also continued to populate the postwar landscape, and were occasionally joined by Duchamp on surprise visits from New York with his new American wife, Pierre Matisse's ex-wife Alexina, or Teeny, as she was known to all. The familiar, pale blue *pneumatique* message in Duchamp's unmistakable spidery scrawl would arrive summoning Man Ray and Juliet to dinner on the spur of the moment. These invitations were gleefully accepted. But, as he had always done, Man Ray chose most other social engagements with care. Within his nest, he was more and more approachable. It seemed appropriate to all who tracked him down at the rue Férou that Man Ray be surrounded—enveloped, even—by his work.

When Man Ray and Juliet did venture out on a Saturday night—he, fastidiously attired in American broadcloth shirts adorned with the trademark shoelace-string tie; she, in Dior dresses, with closely fitted bodices and padded shoulders—it would typically be across the river to the fashionable Sixteenth Arrondissement and the great palatial townhouse at 11, place des Etats-Unis, of Marie-Laure, Vicomtesse de Noailles, and her husband, Charles. *Samedi-soirs chez Marie Laure* were glittering affairs, where guests were constantly challenged by their hostess's imagination. Her *bals masqués* were legendary. She was known on occasion to require guests to dress as characters from literature. Man Ray and Bill Copley once appeared as Tweedle Dum and Tweedle Dee. On another occasion, Man Ray entered as Walt Whitman, complete with the long beard of the good gray poet he had admired since high-school days, while Juliet was a dark-braided Pocahontas.

Marie-Laure and Charles had been patrons of Man Ray during the late twenties, when their Château Saint-Bernard at Hyères was the setting for the film, *Les mystères du château de dés*. Hyères continued through the fifties and sixties to be the locale for the Noailleses' summer social activity. Marie-Laure was a passionate and unfailing patroness of the arts who came naturally to the avant garde. She had grown up in the family mansion as Marie-Laure Bischoffsheim. As a young girl, she met Jean Cocteau, who had made such an impression on her that she had no hesitation about drawing upon her inherited millions a decade later to finance his film *Blood of a Poet,* as well as Dalí and Luis Buñuel's *L'age d'or.* Her grandmother and namesake, Laure de Sade, was a relative of the marquis, patron saint of the Surrealists, and she also served as the thinly veiled model for Proust's imperious Duchesse de Guermantes.

Marie-Laure's paintings—evolving under the watchful eye and loving, if manic influence of "the Minotaure," the hulking Oscar Dominguez, her troubled lover—bore a resemblance to the dreamy interiors of Odilon Redon. Max Ernst, Man Ray, and the ever-elusive Balthus were also important *amis peintres,* who often found themselves mingling in the same *samedi-soir* company at Marie-Laure's.

Balthus's large portrait of Marie-Laure de Noailles, painted in 1936, reveals an eminently composed woman in a sensible black suit, who is seated in a straight-backed chair with her hands clasped in her lap, legs extended and crossed at the ankles. Her austere and somber countenance is a study in serene relaxation. The setting resembles a bare-walled, deserted schoolroom, bathed in pale orange light.

As a result of an automobile accident during the war, Marie-Laure lost some of the open good looks of her youth and self-consciously adapted a hairstyle that made her resemble Louis XIV (some friends said) to hide the injuries to her face. But she suffered no diminution of her interest in human beings. Late in life, replying to an anecdote about a young man who had turned to prostitution to make his living, despite numerous other talents, she said, "I myself have walked the streets. They are full of wonderful people."

Marie-Laure's Saturday soirées often followed the piano recitals of the young American composer Ned Rorem, her close friend for many years. And it was through Marie-Laure that Man Ray and Juliet met this strikingly handsome, fair-haired young man with deep-set, dark eyes and flawless skin. They became a casual threesome, dining together often in the Quartier. Between two and five in the afternoon, when Man Ray was most inclined to be working, Juliet frequently went out on excursions with Rorem.

Man Ray may have given up photography insofar as using it for making a living and may have denounced it as a medium for his art, but his undeniable visual instincts still led him to action when the material presented itself. His famous portrait of Ned Rorem was just such an instance. Man Ray had continually remarked upon the beauty of the composer's face and had insisted time and again, "Oh, Ned, I must take your picture." The young man finally replied in frustration and mock anger, "Well, Man, take it or shut up!" A few weeks shy of Rorem's thirtieth birthday, in the fall of 1953, the event at last took place. Man Ray had phoned Rorem just before he was due to stroll over to the studio and told him to wear something white, so he had borrowed a white raincoat and red scarf from his friend, the choreographer Jerome Robbins. In three quick snaps, it was over: "Face front. Face left. Face right," Man Ray told Rorem, shooting with his tripod-mounted, large-format camera.

Saturday afternoon, a couple of days later, Man Ray asked Rorem to stop by the studio to scratch into the negative of the full-front portrait the opening notes of "*Tout beau mon coeur,*" a Rorem song dedicated to the photographer and based upon a poem by Georges Hugnet, their mutual friend. In the finished photograph, unsmiling, Rorem glares straight ahead at the viewer, eyes so dark as to be impenetrable, hands crossed in front of his chest in a dramatically self-protective, almost vulnerable pose, while white notes extend in an undulating dance before him. The leftward-glancing pose is coquettish and coy; the rightward firm-jawed and secure. Ned Rorem was pleased: "I like these [pictures] better than those of Georgette Chadourne, or Cartier-Bresson," he wrote in his diary that evening, "who made me look like an oriental orphan. . . . Friday I'll be thirty," he added ruefully, "but the picture stays twenty-nine."

"I don't know what a good photograph is," Man Ray stated opaquely, in a rare interview he gave in the early 1950s, "unless it's one I like? . . . To make an 'authentic' photo, it is sufficient that man, the subject, and the camera meet, find themselves in the same place at the same moment. Simple passers-by." Ned Rorem's experience graphically contradicts Man Ray's aesthetics of seren-dipity. The Rorem portrait session was planned in advance. The photographer firmly dictated to his subject what sort of clothing to wear and followed up by asking Rorem to help him manipulate the negative in such a way that the final image embodied within it a permanent tracing of the composer's artistic identity.

"I was like a doctor," Man Ray recalled, two years after the Rorem portrait, looking back yet again upon the ways in which he was never able to resolve or accommodate to his complex of emotions about photography as art or livelihood, "but I handled people who were healthy." The physician finds himself ethically unable to turn his back on suffering. The photographer finds himself unable to avoid making a document when compelled by the strength of the situation.

There was another dimension to his talent from which, try as he might, Man Ray could never shake free. In the fall of 1957, James Thrall Soby, Man Ray's old friend and the publisher of his 1934 book of photographs, curated an exhibition of the work of Juan Gris for the Museum of Modern Art, and he wrote to Man Ray requesting his 1922 photographic portrait of Gris. Soby then went on to inquire whether Man Ray still had in his files "any other photographs of Gris, alone or with friends." Man Ray complied. His archives were exhaustively complete. But privately he complained to friends about the irony of the situation. When would the Museum of Modern Art find its way to accepting Man Ray as an artist worth representing in his own one-man show and stop looking to him merely as the historian of a "lost generation"?

Beaumont Newhall, in Paris on a collecting trip for the George Eastman House in Rochester, New York, where he was curator, gravitated toward Man Ray's documentary work. In addition to taking back with him a number of the photographer's street scenes, Newhall latched on to several dozen vintage Atgets that had languished in Man Ray's possession for three decades. "If you ever think of parting with these, please let me know," Newhall offered casually, as they sat on the couch in the studio over predinner drinks. Man Ray stepped away for a moment to confer privately with Juliet. "We do feel like parting with them. How much do you think you can pay?" the artist inquired. Newhall obtained the lot for $750. These were precarious economic times for Man Ray, who once again had no steady means of supporting himself.

"Painting was an adventure, in which some unknown force might suddenly change the whole aspect of things," Man Ray observed of his revitalized attitude toward his first love. During the Parisian homecoming years of the early to mid-1950s, painting

MAN RAY AND JULIET BY THE SEINE, LATE 1960S.
Private collection.

helped him "find a bit of [his] youth again." Poised before the easel, Man Ray would sense an almost erotic anticipation of "a certain anxiety. . . a sort of misgiving of the outcome of [his] enterprise." But he also recognized that intimation of self-doubt as a prerequisite for making art, and "once engaged in the act, all uncertainty disappeared, and [he] carried on with complete assurance." For Man Ray, the problem of painting was a noble one, to be resolved with pride by marshaling one's best efforts, never made light of or shrugged off, or (as in taking a photograph) viewed as "a matter of calculation," of sheer mechanics and little else.

Georges Ribemont-Dessaignes had been one of the first critics to evaluate Man Ray as a painter. His graceful monograph, written in 1924, was followed by a long silence that lasted until 1953, when Man Ray's friend Paul Wescher wrote an appreciative piece for the January *Magazine of Art*. Mary Stothardt Wescher had been Man Ray's patron during his last years in Hollywood. Her second husband was now a curator at the Los Angeles County Museum, and during a visit to Paris the previous year, accompanied by other dear friends from stateside, Mildred and Allie Lewin, Paul had conceived the idea for a long-overdue examination of the Man Ray oeuvre from the earliest days to the present.

Wescher's piece was the first attempt to track Man Ray's thematic concerns and stylistic development over the years. Wescher argued that the earliest canvases, in their preoccupation with dream-imagery, set the stage for Man Ray as a Surrealist. The critic's analysis of Cubist-inspired works from the Ridgefield, post–Armory Show phase was complimentary and lyrical. "If the world is going to tumble," Wescher wrote, "these works [*The Village, Backyard, Ramapo Hills*], exempt from the law of gravity, will still keep their balance. In their juggling with positive and negative, their firm and loose-knit structure, in the sensitivity of their colors, they already show so personal a note as to need no signature."

Wescher placed Man Ray on a par with Picabia and Duchamp as forerunners of Dada. No critic before that time had seen these three, together, as "medicine men or primitive witch doctors . . . exorcis[ing] the evil by the evil itself." To Wescher, Picabia, Duchamp, and Man Ray "conjured and sublimated the mechanical by giving to it poetic names and content."

Wescher pointed out that Man Ray had been able to achieve a synthesis of the concept of the readymade with the rigors of Cubism. And, ignoring Man Ray's own chronic compulsion to place a barrier between photography and painting, Wescher seized upon the rayograph as the new, mediating art form that brought the two together, making use of the best aspects of both. He also drew analogies between the *Shakespearean Equations* of the 1930s and 1940s and the rayographs, in the way they trod a thin borderline between representationalism and abstraction.

Wescher concluded his assessment of Man Ray with a reference to Apollinaire, the ideological precursor for so much that informed the work of Man Ray's generation. The mission of these last modernists was, as Apollinaire had put it, "to keep [their] work free from all perceptions which might become notions." Indeed, Man Ray's best paintings—and Wescher had managed to cull the wheat from the chaff, ending with an image of *The Lips* and a discussion of the Sadean *Aline et Valcour*—stressed above all else the central modernist preoccupation with the constancy of change. Ideas were plastic and malleable, meant to be manipulated by the artist, skillfully setting off resonances in the imagination of the viewer.

Man Ray's homecoming statement, *La rue Férou* (1952), takes its place among his most successful canvases. It is an intimate work, barely two feet by three feet, and mysteriously evocative. On a decidedly Utrilloesque street, a beret-clad man (perhaps the artist himself) pulls an antique cart that looks as if it had been borrowed from an Atget photograph. The shadows are long enough, extending from the west over the narrow pavement, to make one think it is the very end of the day, perhaps the end of an era. On the rickety cart is a wrapped bundle—the important early Dada assemblage, *Enigma of Isidore Ducasse* (1921), an unmistakable icon to those who know Man Ray's work. Just up the road on the right is the hidden entrance to his studio, where he pursued his livelihood like the tradesman in the painting.

The revivifying atmosphere of Paris, and Man Ray's compulsive urge to populate his studio, to surround himself with a universe of his own making where he would spend increasing amounts of time as the years went by, gave rise to a surge of object-making. Like an animal feathering his nest, the artist would typically spend several hours on weekend afternoons at flea markets scrounging for bits of flotsam and jetsam abandoned by others, which would be transformed by the force of his imagination.

Man Ray's objects played many roles in his life. They literally kept him company. He felt reassured by their silent presence as his witnesses. The artist's friend Patrick Waldberg, biographer of Max Ernst, likened them to the *churingas* of the Aborigines, ritualistic talismans with magical properties. To the French critic Brigitte Herman, the objects were "the nourishing substance of a personal mythology," a system never fully explained by the artist, a secret complex of signs.

Every completed object, even if it might then become lost, intentionally or accidentally, was photographed and would often resurface in a painting or a lithograph. Furthermore, many of the objects found their way into multiple editions in bronze or close replicas of the original materials, produced and signed under the artist's supervision. To meet economic necessities in later years, Man Ray had no qualms about seeing his original work multiplied many times over. He was unabashedly gleeful about the revenue-producing potential of such activity. The initiating impulse—the exciting, informing idea—was what mattered most.

Object-making had become legitimized as a form of sculpture in and of itself. To William Seitz, who in 1961 curated the Museum of Modern Art's important exhibition of assemblages, which included several works by Man Ray, assemblage was a three-dimensional descendant of collage. Because these synthesized works drew materials directly from the environment and lent themselves to "eccentric experimentation," their making seemed "especially suited to the American temperament."

Man Ray's objects from the 1950s celebrated the inventive use of *mains libres,* hands free to perform and construct as they pleased. *Miroir à mourir de rire* (Mirror to Die Laughing By, 1952), was reminiscent of Marcel Duchamp's rotary punning disks employed in the collaborative film of the early 1920s, *Anemic Cinéma.* The *Ombre de cuir* (Leather Shadow, 1953) was made of a *cuillère de bois sur cuir* (a wooden spoon on leather), mounted in such a way that the three-dimensional shadow picked up the outlines of the gently curved spoon.

Double entendre was always important to the inveterate Dadaist. The play of light and shadow, of concern to Man Ray as a photographer, was also evident in these objects. The spiral motif first developed in the early twenties was reprised in *En dernier ressort, tournez* (As a Last Resort, Turn, 1956). Here, a curve of metal resembling a watch spring was wound around a wooden knob, inviting the viewer to participate, but with what result, except bemusement? Spirals also found their way into the popular *Smoking Device* (1959), where a pipe rack served as the frame for a network of interlacing plastic tubing. Viewers were meant to blow smoke in one end and watch it perambulate in and out of the holes in the rack. Man Ray delighted in demonstrating this process to any and all comers. The marbles resting in the indentations for pipe bowls underscored the subversive nature of the thing, betraying conventional expectations about its normal use. *Ballet français* (1956) represented yet another skillful play upon language coupled with a visual pun. *Balai* is the French word for *broom,* and this simple object was merely a broom upended in a static dance leading nowhere. *Monument au peintre inconnu* (Tomb of the Unknown Painter, 1953) served a similar purpose. The croupier's stick replaced the broom; mounted upon a pedestal, fixed and inactive, it suggested that art was a harmless gamble, but very much a risk.

Over twenty-five years, the rue Férou studio became densely inhabited by these and scores of other concoctions. As new objects were born, reprising themes of the past needing to be expressed in different ways, others disappeared, were sold, or were given away to surprised and gratified visitors. The cast of characters was in constant flux; arrayed along the shelves of the studio was a city of unique beings.

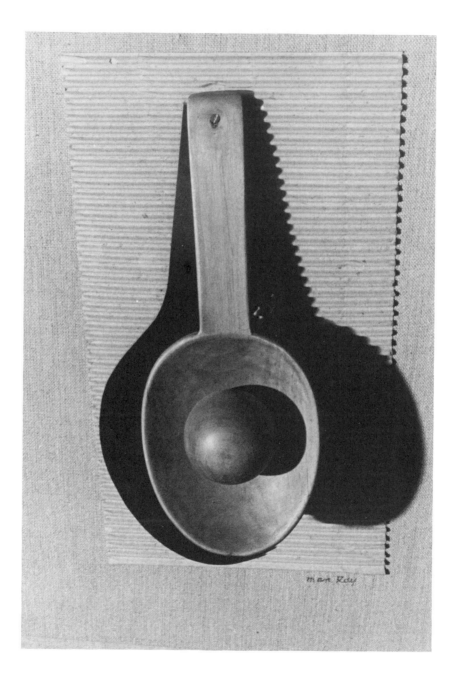

MAN RAY. *LEATHER SHADOW*, 1971. GALLERY IL FAUNO
EDITION OF 1953 ASSEMBLAGE.
Photograph by Ira Nowinski taken in la rue Férou studio, March 1983.

THE ARTS OF SURVIVAL

DESPITE THE surge in his productivity after returning to Paris, Man Ray continued to feel ambivalent about entrusting his career to any commercial dealer. Patrick Waldberg called Man Ray "a Captain Nemo of the imagination," a single-minded figure intent upon navigating his own way through (and, subversively, beneath) the choppy waters of the art world, stubbornly resisting leaving works on consignment with a gallery after a show had closed. "I have no official dealer. . . I am not a dealer's painter," he flatly told Elsie, although several business associates had trouble agreeing with the perception, among them Paul and Josephine Kantor.

Man Ray and Juliet had met and become friends with the Kantors in Hollywood, through the art dealer René Lefevre-Foinet. Josephine worked as the secretary and assistant to René, expatriate brother of Maurice Lefevre-Foinet, guardian of Man Ray's paintings in Paris. René's Sunday soirées, with steak and free-flowing liquor in his home on Silver Lake, in the hills above L.A., rivaled Mary Stothardt's Saturday parties.

Man Ray remained in touch with the Kantors, great admirers of his work, after his return to Paris. In May of 1952, the couple finally opened their long-dreamed-of art gallery at 9013 Beverly Boulevard, near Chasen's restaurant. Their first show was of the works of the local artist Ynez Johnston, their second of abstract paintings by the Bay Area's Richard Diebenkorn, who, along with Robert Motherwell, was a particular favorite of Josephine's. While Paul remained behind the scenes in the back room, keeping the books and building all the frames for the works exhibited, Josephine sat at the front desk and attended to what few patrons there were.

The third one-man show the Kantors mounted consisted of twenty-seven paintings and five drawings by Man Ray (and no photographs, of course), which were on view for one month, from March 23 to April 25, 1953. The works were taken out of storage from Brugger's Fine Arts Warehouse in Los Angeles where—for the time being—a large amount of Man Ray's work remained. Among the paintings displayed were his fine 1923 portrait of Kiki, done almost entirely with a palette knife (price: six hundred dollars), and a 1913 *Dual Portrait* of an anonymous sitter in oils for two hundred dollars. Despite the earnest efforts of the Kantors, nothing sold.

From his vantage point several thousand miles away, Man Ray was increasingly apprehensive, fearing once again that he was losing control of his inventory. He was piqued to discover that the Kantors had lent the portrait of Kiki out "on approval. I am furious," he told Elsie, "as I never agreed to any such procedure, and have ordered [them] to get it back at once." The artist seemed to have difficulty understanding the dealers' honest attempt to stir up interest in his work.

Several times during this anxious season, Man Ray hinted to Elsie that he would like to have her act as proprietor for any and all works in America not in private hands. By the summer of 1953, Man Ray finally managed to arrange for all work outstanding with the Kantor Gallery to be returned to Brugger's. By the following winter, after asking Elsie ingenuously if she would "still have some room for [him]," the artist had successfully gathered all unacquired works in the States into one locale: the basement of his sister's house in Jersey City. Man Ray trusted Elsie as he trusted no one else. He had come, over three decades, to cherish her sense of organization and responsibility. Elsie's allegiance to her brother and her practical ability to carry out his byzantine instructions were a source of pride and reassurance. He rarely let more than a letter or two go by without expressing his debt to her. He felt secure that his paintings and vintage rayographs still on the other side of the Atlantic were safe and sound in the family. "One cannot push the thing [selling works of art] like automobiles or toasters," big brother confided.

" . . . Let them come to you now. . . . You have to be careful with dealers," he wrote subsequently, talking as much to himself as to Elsie. "If you want to go into business for me, you are entitled to 30%." "[Do not] stick your neck out where I am concerned," he further cautioned her, "but wait patiently until people come to us and are really anxious to get something."

Another dealer, Jack Mayer, found his allegiances tested in a predicament similar to the Kantors', wanting to be supportive of Man Ray but unable to live up to the artist's terms. Mayer, an old friend of David Savage's from the days of his engagement to Naomi, had seen Man Ray's work in Elsie's home. A veteran observer of the art scene, Mayer firmly believed that Abstract Expressionism, then so much in vogue in New York, had roots in Surrealism, a mode that was out of favor, and he was especially excited about the clear fact that Man Ray was "derivative of no one." Mayer had little patience with the lack of historical memory evidenced by his colleagues in the New York City art world. Clement Greenberg, who said that he considered the American artist in Paris to be "out of sight, out of mind," asked Mayer point-blank why on earth he wanted to show Man Ray.

But Mayer went ahead and mounted two exhibitions at his Madison Avenue gallery in 1958 and 1959. Dore Ashton, reviewing the second show for the *Times*, found Man Ray to be exercising "the flexibility of his fancy." Although she described the works as "witty" and intriguing—especially the drawings from *Les mains libres*—ultimately, she wrote, "they have that distant quality [of being] no longer shocking but have entered docilely into history." Sales were lackluster, although one notable enthusiast at the drawings show, the collector Armand Erpf, purchased a sketch from *Les mains libres*. Jack Mayer's friendship with Man Ray was soon tested by another dealer, Jean Larcade of Paris, who offered to form a direct purchase relationship with the artist. After a forthright talk, Mayer reluctantly had to let Man Ray go. "I'm tied up with the gallery here," Man Ray told Elsie after the deal with Larcade was done, "and they know my stock and have a right to first choice according to our contract which is generous to me."

Man Ray found the traditional practice of prolonged consignment to be exploitative. In his view, dealers should own up to the courage of their convictions and purchase the paintings of the artists they believed in, after which they were free and clear to resell them at whatever the market prices would bear—such was the arrangement with Jean Larcade. Man Ray did not appreciate the idea of having his work languish in a netherworld, neither lent nor owned. He was always a fiercely proud person, and because of his pride, this conflict about how to release his works into the world was lifelong.

While he wanted his work to sell well, Man Ray often spoke with nostalgia about works sold and never seen again. Even during periods of economic hardship, he refused to peddle his wares. While he desired an audience, he shunned group shows with their opportunity for much-needed exposure because he no longer viewed himself "with" any other artist.

"It has been a hard winter," Man Ray wrote Elsie, as he emerged into the spring of 1954, "but Bill Copley has come to my rescue and bought another painting to celebrate his wedding and to express his gratitude! You see, he met Noma through us. He's been wonderful to us, and promises to see me through this year. . . ." If Man Ray had any consistent patrons during the lean times of the 1950s, they were Bill and Noma Copley, although their generous support was ad hoc and unofficial.

Bill's relationship with the lovely Gloria de Herrera, who had embarked for France with him, had lasted less than two years. When Noma Rathner came to Paris, Man Ray and Juliet introduced their friend from Hollywood to Copley one night at the studio. Oddly enough, the two had never met in California. They were married soon after; Man Ray was Copley's best man and also designed the wedding cake, an upside-down pie tin with frosting slathered all over it, comic precursor to Claes Oldenburg's plaster concoctions.

With regard to the art of Man Ray, Bill Copley had a simple philosophy—he purchased works at times when the cash would make the most vital difference to the artist's daily survival. Copley was blessed with the finances to satisfy his admiration for the elder statesmen of Dada and Surrealism as well as any other artists he admired.

It was clear that the Copleys needed a place to display their vast collections. They purchased a *maison bourgeoise* in Long Pont, a tiny village twenty-five miles south of Paris, on the road to Orléans, graced with a twelfth-century church and little else, not even a market. For food shopping or an occasional visit to the cinema, one needed to travel to the neighboring town of St. Geneviève du Bois. The property was surrounded by a stone wall. A winding driveway led past a carriage house to the long, narrow main building with small windows.

The Copleys' substantial domestic staff included a secretary to help Noma catalogue and maintain the art collection and also to keep the voluminous correspondence and records of the Copley Foundation, through which Bill and Noma made grants to struggling artists and musicians. At various times, Man Ray, Marcel Duchamp, Darius Milhaud, Julien Levy, and Roland Penrose served on the foundation's board of directors and gathered to make decisions about colleagues in need of support, including themselves. There was also a master chef to prepare food for the Copleys' renowned dinner parties and weekend get-togethers. Long Pont was an important social gathering place for Man Ray and Juliet throughout the decade, the perfect complement to Marie-Laure de Noailles's soirées in town. Noma was always willing to pick them up at the rue Férou studio if they were too tired to take the train. And Bill was ready to extend an evening's stay into a week's, if the rue Férou was too chilly in winter.

Around the long table in the Copley's spacious dining room, or outdoors on the lawn for luncheon when the weather was fine, one might on occasion meet Wifredo Lam, the Mattas, Marcel Duchamp and Teeny in from New York, René Magritte, Roland Penrose and Lee Miller, Max Ernst and Dorothea Tanning, Patrick Waldberg, and Henri Cartier-Bresson. The conversation was by turns serious and gossipy, homey and relaxed, depending upon the crowd. After dinner, some guests would gravitate to Bill's study for pipe-smoking and tête-à-têtes. Others would gather around the living-room fire for lengthy chess games, surrounded by the monumental paintings Bill favored and the fetishistic Joseph Cornell boxes and bizarre objects that inhabited the room's nooks and crannies. While at the dinner table Man Ray was the epitome of wit and charm, delighting the company with his jocular humor and acerbic observations, at chess he displayed his dogmatic side—the rules were paramount and had to be obeyed. Man Ray could not tolerate, for example, novice players who advanced their pawns and showed little tactical prowess. He grew livid and impatient when an opponent touched a piece preliminary to moving it and then removed his hand. Juliet, distracted, might drift silently off into a corner and start dancing, alone, as her husband became absorbed by the game.

The family of artists and writers gathered around the Copley hearth was comforting to Man Ray and helped make up for his continuing distance from his natural family in America. During his constant communication with Elsie, he always inquired after everyone. When nieces and nephews were born, he received photographs and was quick to comment upon resemblances. As Naomi progressed with her art, Man Ray preached his philosophy: "While some are satisfied with the effort to please," he wrote her once, early on, with deliberateness of expression, "there are others who wish to surprise. It is these that we must look to for the permanent pleasure that a work can give, irrespective of current standards of beauty." It was always more natural for Man Ray to communicate through issues of art rather than familial sentiment.

Since Minnie's death, Papa Max had been living alone in the Brooklyn apartment. Sisters Elsie and Do and Do's daughter Florence were concerned about Max's ability to carry on by himself. There was talk about moving him into a home for the aged, perhaps away from New York, and closer to Do and Florence and their families in the Philadelphia area. From great distance, Man Ray entered the deliberations: "He needs so little," the artist wrote, rare words about his father revealing intimations of some deeper identification. "He's very individual, you know, and it will always be hard for him to live with others." However, Max, nearing ninety, did at last consent to uproot himself from New York, settling into the Jewish Home for the Aged in Philadelphia.

In the winter and spring of 1956, Florence and Elsie came up with the idea of presenting a one-man show of Man Ray's works at the home where Max was living. Perhaps they saw it as a way to bring father and son closer together and to put a native son back on the map at the place of his birth. With great industry and enthusiasm, Florence enlisted the help of the Philadelphia Museum of Art, convincing the curators to assign several men to assist in hanging the show. Elsie drove down from Jersey City to Florence's house in Melrose Park with selections from her Man Ray collection.

Uncle Man, while flattered by all the attention, did establish some ground rules. He would be unable to send any newer works from his studio in Paris. He could not come over for the opening, despite sister Elsie's offer to advance him the plane fare. In fact, he regarded the show primarily as a way to interest the Philadelphia Museum of Art in mounting a retrospective of his work, an event which, like the hoped-for exhibition at the Museum of Modern Art, never took place in his lifetime. There was one final, incontrovertible rule: "Show NO photographs. Eliminate all Rayographs. I want to keep the two activities separate, otherwise there is confusion if not downright devaluation of the paintings."

Suddenly, within a matter of weeks, the grand scheme fell apart. First, the management of the home expanded their plans for the exhibit to include the works of other artists. This decision violated Man Ray's cardinal rule that at this stage in his career he would not show with anyone else. Papa Max began to decline. Seeming to know the end was near, much too weak and drowsy to play old peasant tunes, he handed his precious violin to Florence's elder daughter, Joan, at his bedside on their final Sunday visit. On the morning of March 10, 1956, Max Ray died quietly in his sleep.

"I feel as if a part of myself is gone," his son wrote, "in preparation for the time when I shall go, too. I have been thinking quite a lot lately," he told Elsie, "about how short our stay is in this world, even if we can near the hundred year mark." Making it clear to his sister (and, through her, to the rest of the family) that his bereavement was sincere, Man Ray nevertheless flatly stated that the show must be canceled. And he would not be present at his father's funeral. He was "afraid of getting into the rush and competition of New York," and had "just enough energy to carry on [his] work." Papa was laid to rest in Philadelphia in the same cemetery as his sister, Jenny Levinson—separated from Minnie as they had been their first night as newlyweds and from his younger son, Sam, both buried in Brooklyn.

Elsie's sudden death a year and a half later at the age of sixty was a complete shock. She collapsed of a massive brain hemorrhage at her office desk at eleven in the morning and suffered a second stroke at two in the afternoon. Man Ray's ally and helper, the link with his work in America, was gone. Yet even this wrenching event, which left him "in a daze . . . [unable to assess] the full force of [his] bereavement . . . ," could not draw Man Ray back. The whole family expected the tragedy would surely precipitate Man Ray's return, but again he demurred. There were shows to plan, collectors to meet, projects to complete. From time to time, over the decades, Elsie had broached the subject of a trip to Paris, curious to see her brother Man in his natural habitat. In each instance, he had managed to dissuade her from coming, just as he had succeeded in turning Do away from similar travel plans. Neither sister ever visited Paris. It was always more convenient and so much easier for Man Ray to remain an enigma to his family, to sit down at his typewriter and speak frankly and openly on paper of his fears and dreams. The legacy of Man Ray's collection in America now naturally passed to Naomi. She inherited the responsibility of keeping her uncle's affairs in order, and she performed the task with the same responsiveness as her mother.

For Man Ray, a Dadaist before the word was even coined, family was seductive and dangerously redolent of the past, subverting Dada's cult of individualism. Varying personae had become a way of life, and a means of denying the factual basis of his origins. Fabricating masks in various designs—some primitive, others wistful, even pastoral, like apparitions out of *A Midsummer Night's Dream*—was a consistent sidelight activity of the artist's long career.

During his sojourn among the Dadaists in the movement's heyday, Malcolm Cowley noted one governing principle, that "the only laws the artist should be allowed to observe were private ones, the laws of art." As the years passed, Man Ray heeded only the voice of his imagination. The pleadings of well-intentioned relatives that he return to America were echoed by a chorus of close friends, former lovers, trusted artists, and even his wife, Juliet. But other opinions, other principles, other rules, meant nothing to Man Ray unless they happened to conform to his point of view.

Dadaists made art out of studied outrageousness. The crowd Man Ray fell into through the good graces of Marcel Duchamp had pledged themselves to respect nothing; they prided themselves on the denial of hard work. They were not *ouvriers,* they said, but rather individuals who indulged in focused periods of intense concentration, at what Man Ray called "white heat."

The advent of acrylics in the late fifties allowed Man Ray to give form to this aesthetic of indolence. He invented *peintures naturelles* (natural paintings) by squeezing raw pigment directly from the tubes onto wood or cardboard, creating zigzag patterns of thick paint. Then, he carefully placed another panel upon the fresh surface and pressed them together, Rorschach-like. The final and most significant step was to sit upon this paint-sandwich, a gesture as much an expression of scorn directed at those who took "Art" too seriously as it was a Dada *acte gratuite.*

Toward the end of the decade, Man Ray was asked to show in two Dada exhibitions, one at the Stedelijk Museum in Amsterdam, the other at the Düsseldorf Kunsthalle. For the latter, "Dada, Dokumente einer Bewegung" (Dada, Documents of a Movement), set for the autumn of 1958, Man Ray specified a number of works for Naomi to send, including *The Rope Dancer, Suicide, Theatr* (one of his first collages, from newspaper), *Cutout,* and *Legend.* Man Ray also created a new object especially for the occasion, *Pain peint,* an actual loaf of French bread painted blue—the first of many that were eventually editioned.

In the months before the Düsseldorf show was due to open, Man Ray stayed with Bill and Noma Copley at their summer home in Ramatuelle, near Cannes—also, appropriately, near the birthplace of Louis-Auguste Cézanne, the painter's father—and labored for a week on an essay for the Kunsthalle exhibition catalogue. "I am supposed to be vacationing," he wrote Naomi, "but I have work to do." He called the written piece, "Dadamade." "Who made Dada?" he asked, "Nobody and everybody. I made Dada when I was a baby and I was roundly spanked by my mother...." The free-associative ruminations went along smoothly in Man Ray's neat longhand script until the final paragraph, when he tried to articulate his feelings about the contemporary revival of Dada in Europe. "Now you are trying to revive Dada. Who knows? Who cares? Why? Who doesn't care? But dada is dead. Or dada is still alive. We cannot revive anything that is dead/alive, just as we cannot revive anything that is alive/dead...." Man Ray played with the variables, back and forth, scribbling, then crossing out alternatives, in an attempt to resolve Dada's death or life. Finally, he settled for an equivocal conclusion: "Is dadadead? Is dadalive? Dada is. Dadaism."

Between bouts with the composition of this short essay, Man Ray took walks along the beach below the house with the composer Ben Lees, another friend of the Copleys, who lived in the carriage house at their Long Pont estate. Lees, also a camera buff, tried to convince Man Ray to take his apparatus along on their strolls, but the artist refused, carrying only a light meter as a way to test his eyes

against the readings he took, guessing at the setting, then confirm-
ing his guesses—which were, to Lees's astonishment and admiration, invariably correct. On one such leisurely promenade, Man
Ray recalled the exercises he used to posit for his occasional and
select photography students in California. A favorite was to tell
them they could only take two shots in the course of an entire
afternoon of fieldwork. This forced the students to hone their
perceptions and become more selective and less indiscriminate—in
short, to value the impact of a moment. "Take a $30 camera or a
$100 camera," Man Ray said to Ben Lees. "What's the difference?
In the early days in Greenwich Village, I began working with a
pinhole in a box, covered with a strip of black tape which I peeled off
and then replaced, and was able to make perfectly decent pictures.
When was the last time you used 1/500 of a second, anyway? Most of
those extra features are useless." Man Ray playfully shrugged off
any special skill, insisting that "ninety-nine percent of the credit
should go to Mr. Zeiss and Mr. Eastman and one percent to the man
who happens to stand behind the camera."

The summer of the following year, Man Ray received a
manifesto-letter from André Breton, asking if he would be willing to
participate in the "Exposition inteRnatiOnale du Surréalisme
(EROS)" cosponsored by Marcel Duchamp, to be held at the
Galerie Daniel Cordier in Paris, from December 15, 1959, through
February 1960. The invitation was most notable for its use of a
stylized phoenix on the letterhead, a symbolic attempt to show
Breton's continued fight for the movement's rebirth.

It seemed as if André Breton—who had so much personal
energy invested in Surrealism—was waging a one-man battle to
keep it going in a formalized way. To him, all other art movements
remained incidental, including those that were beginning to arise in
Surrealism's wake. Michel Tapiès and Jean Dubuffet were at the
forefront of the emotionally explosive Art Brut; COBRA and
Tachisme were still other spinoffs during the 1950s, characterized by
an automatism that was *"physique"* rather than *"psychique."* In
America, the New York School's debt to Surrealism had been
acknowledged by Leo Castelli in shows at Sidney Janis's gallery in
the early fifties, where the two styles were hung side by side.

"With respect to the situation in the plastic arts today. . . of
which," Breton parenthetically but indignantly noted in his letter,

MAN RAY AT PARIS ART OPENING, 1959.
Courtesy Noma Copley.

"the most noticeable are mere tributaries deriving from surrealist automatism, surrealism itself must reaffirm itself. . . especially in the realm of the EROTIC." The exhibition would stress works that "gravitated around the theme of fleshly temptation . . ." and would be structured in two sections: "Retrospective, made up of a collection of works by the most representative artists," the old school, and "works of the Present." Furthermore, remaining open even at this late date for new recruits, Breton "reserved the opinion to call upon a small number of artists who were not surrealists but whose work nevertheless fell under the rubric of the overall theme of the exhibition." Breton invoked the famous Surrealist exhibitions of Paris 1938, New York 1942, and Paris 1947, citing EROS as a continuation of that theme. And he never abandoned his enduring respect for "the trapper of sun, the celebrant of shadows . . . the prince of the shutter. . . my friend Man Ray."

"I was a Surrealist even before I became a photographer," Man Ray declared in an interview published soon after his postwar return to Paris, "and I flatter myself at having remained a Surrealist in the most profound sense of that word . . . in relation to its being a movement transcending all eras." These were the words of a survivor, an artist who lived deep enough into a new epoch to read his name among the list of immortals inscribed on the wall of a movie theater erected on the site where the old Montparnasse café, La Rotonde, had been torn down: Apollinaire, Aragon, Bourdelle, Cocteau, Anatole France, Hemingway, Man Ray.

For the EROS catalogue, as for the Dada show, Man Ray was moved to set down thoughts in commemoration of the theme. Although in his memoir, *Self Portrait,* published three years later, he disparagingly refers to this text, *"Inventaire d'une tête de femme"* (Erotic Aspects of a Woman's Face), as having been "dashed off. . . without changing a word," in fact several early drafts were composed in the labor to make it natural.

Man Ray's canvas of a nude was hung, to his great amusement, on the ceiling of the Daniel Cordier Gallery and was missed initially by many visitors to the EROS show. However, his essay was prominently featured in the catalogue. It was an erotic meditation on the faces of women he had known: Adon Lacroix, asleep (" . . . in repose, when the features, eyes, mouth, are not being used to express sex consciousness . . ."); his massive painting *The Lips,* based upon reminiscences of romance with Lee Miller (" . . . the two lips as a symbol of two bodies closely joined together. . ."); photographs and sketches featuring women with their necks arched back ("the ear. . . whether covered by hair or completely disengaged . . . furnishes a focal point . . ."); sensual interpretations of Juliet, her face modestly veiled (" . . . to reduce the inquisitiveness of males who are not their husbands . . ."); and lengthy *maquillage* sessions with Kiki before the lovers ventured out into Montparnasse nightlife (" . . . make up [has] been resorted to in all times and countries to enhance the beauty and attractiveness of women . . ."). "The face," Man Ray concluded, "is only the key to further mental exploration."

MAN RAY AT THE CAFÉ DE LA
MAIRIE, PLACE ST. SULPICE, CIRCA 1959.
Photograph by Naomi Savage.

S E L F
P O R T R A I T

EXCEPT FOR some business initiatives in New York, which laid the groundwork for a series of gallery shows still several years off, Man Ray's brief trip to the States during the winter of 1959 was an uneasy one. In a conciliatory gesture, Man Ray and Juliet spent Thanksgiving with Do, Florence, and their families. Late one night, sitting quietly in the living room while everyone else in the house was asleep, Man Ray selectively unburdened some thoughts to Florence. His instincts may have told him it was time to clear the air. Florence felt deep respect for Uncle Man's convictions; the unerringly consistent, almost religious strain in his character, evident since boyhood, had pointed in one direction only: to be an artist. But why, she asked fearfully and plaintively, did her uncle believe he had to "close the door" so definitively on nearly everyone in the family?

Man Ray made an attempt at an answer by recalling those who had passed on. "My mother," he said in measured tones, "was a very nice woman—but she wanted me to be like other people, and I couldn't. She knew how much I needed to be an artist. That disappointed her. My father was a sweet man, although ineffectual, and I loved my sisters and brother—but I had my own life to live, and no one was able to accept the consequences of that decision." Florence pushed on. In following that isolated path, he had become a stranger to her, a mystery. Who was Man Ray? Her uncle smiled and shrugged: "I am an enigma," he replied, ever the Dadaist, smugly pleased at that unhelpful definition. "Answers, if they are to be had, will be found in my paintings and drawings. That is where my fears and anxieties are spelled out. You must look at my work. There, you are free to discover whatever you like." Florence felt that comment effectively signaled the end of the conversation. She dared not go further.

How much simpler it was to be back within the comforting boundaries of the Sixth Arrondissement, where he promenaded languidly with Juliet on his arm and where he was known without explanation to one and all as "Monsieur Man Ray." No questions were asked; there was only subdued respect. How delightfully simple it was to don one's beret, proud symbol of the artist's calling, to tie a yellow shoelace around the collar of one's American-made shirt, to pluck a silver-handled walking stick from the assortment near the door, slip a fresh pack of Gauloises into one's coat pocket, and step out onto the sunny street at midday for the briefest of walks: left on rue Férou, past the intersection of the rue Canivet, then straight across the cobblestoned place St. Sulpice, to the rue des Canettes, where, a few paces from the corner on the left, Chez Alexandre and a delightful lunch awaited. It was a modest, intimate place, a menu posted in one of the panes of the white-curtained front window. Up a few steps, the door opened with the tinkling welcome of a little bell.

Man Ray and Juliet always chose the first table on the right, just beyond the small bar. Sitting with his back to the wall, Man Ray could survey the restaurant. At street level, there was a mere handful of tables; off to the rear, the kitchen was visible beyond a Dutch doorway, where dishes were handed through. Next to a steep stairway leading to another dining area upstairs was a sectioned rack mounted on the wall where in days past patrons' individual linen *serviettes* were reserved. And adorning the white walls was a valuable array of nineteenth-century paintings of Posillipo and scenes of the Bay of Naples.

A creature of habit, Man Ray would order lasagne or one of the house specialties, steak Tartare mixed at his table, and a glass of red wine. He never failed to relax in his favorite spot at Chez Alexandre, chatting and joking with the *propriétaire* and her husband. If a few visitors to town accompanied him, lunch could become a two- or

PHOTOGRAPH BY MAN RAY OF HIMSELF (*LEFT*),
DOROTHEA TANNING (HOLDING HER DOG, KATCHINA),
JULIET, MAX ERNST, AND FRIENDS AT HUISMES, CA. 1957.
Collection Dorothea Tanning.

LEE MILLER. MAN RAY AND JULIET AT FARLEY FARM,
1954. ROLAND PENROSE SECOND FROM RIGHT; ANTONY
PENROSE LEANING AGAINST WINDOW.
Copyright © 1988 Lee Miller Archives.

three-hour affair. Then, it was back to the studio for the customary afternoon work session.

Entering his eighth decade, Man Ray was at last enjoying wider acceptance by artists and critics of the younger generation. Like Duchamp in New York, he began to create a deliberate historical record for himself, allowing journalists greater access while continuing to maintain his distance from mainstream art critics. He was an expert at controlling interviews. In the eyes of one such visitor, Morris Gordon of *Infinity* magazine, Man Ray was a "fiery elf," a "five-foot-two-inch oak-stout and brisk-walking (like Harry Truman) modern Saint George battling the dragon, status quo."

Man Ray, the eternal rebel, told Gordon he would continue to fight the established order of things so long as he had "a single breath left in [his] body." Eyes flashing and voice rising, the artist rhetorically asked his interlocutor how any young photographer currently coming up through the ranks could manage to ignore tradition: "How is it possible," said Man Ray, sounding a theme that had obsessed him since his youth, "to replace the classics unless one knows intimately the thing he wishes to replace?"

At the time of their encounter, Man Ray was in the thick of a critical struggle with posterity. Looking back over his own career and offering advice to other artists, he was hurrying to complete the task before a history of his life he might not approve was created for him. "You cannot shut the door in the face of history, because history will kick it in violently. You must ride with the tide," he declared, "and—more than that—anticipate history. Run, not walk, to meet it." Since early 1961 Man Ray had been laboring a couple of pages a day on his memoirs, tentatively (and with good reason) titled *Self Portrait*.

In the winter of 1961, he threw himself with enthusiasm into the composition of his autobiography, borrowing John Rewald's vacant flat on rue Lepic in Montmartre, which, unlike the studio, was centrally heated, where he could concentrate away from the social distractions of the studio. He refrained from swimming and lounging in Cadaqués during the summer. To intimate friends, Man Ray referred to the work in progress as "ma légende."

Commissioned by Seymour Lawrence, director of Atlantic–Little, Brown in Boston and a great admirer of the artist's oeuvre, the autobiography took early shape as a dateless, quotationless, impressionistic and adamantly not dependable account. As for the order of names and incidents, Man Ray told Lawrence when he submitted the first of four chapters, "I have purposely avoided a too chronological, or simply logical order, always keeping in mind [the term] 'Self Portrait.'"

Man Ray's self-portrait in words was modeled after the approach he might have taken for a self-portrait painting. He depicted what he saw as he saw it, a fragment here, a detail there, always centered upon himself, rather than his broader context. This approach was in direct contrast to Lawrence's editorial urging for more facts and more background. "What taught you to idealize artists at such an early age?" the editor asked, in his first review of the manuscript. "What, in your family, bored or dissatisfied you? Were your special childhood gifts recognized?" No reply from the author.

Lawrence was likewise understandably curious about Alfred Stieglitz. Could Man Ray provide "some [more] tangible detail" about the master in his gallery, 291? "Someday," Man Ray agreed, sardonically, "if I write *his* autobiography." To Lawrence's observation that Man Ray's comments seemed ambiguous about the influences of Baudelaire and Poe on his early artistic development, the artist retorted, "The whole book [is] meant to be ambiguous for the average reader. This is my way," he insisted, "as in my painting." Man Ray shrugged off similar appeals by Seymour Lawrence for more information about Alanson Hartpence from the Ridgefield period; his first wife, Adon Lacroix; Marcel Duchamp; friend and colleague Samuel Halpert, who was sister Do's first serious suitor; and the rest of the fascinating cast of characters from pre–World War I Bohemian New York. "All this is a jigsaw puzzle to me now," wrote Man Ray. "If I painted it, I'd give all the elements the same helter-skelter importance." The book took shape rapidly. Man Ray completed the five-hundred-page draft within just twelve months.

Over long seafood lunches at the bistro La Mediterranée near the Odéon, where the two men delighted in numerous glasses of Blanc de Blancs, Seymour Lawrence and Man Ray engaged in a persistent but respectful tug-of-war. The editor continued to plead for orderly reminiscence, transitions that made logical sense, and a chronology the uninitiated reader could follow. The artist, meanwhile, countered that he was "allergic" to numbers and dates. Rather, he favored white spaces on the canvas to give the appearance of incompleteness and to remind the observer of the artifice. Man Ray suggested that altering the title so that the first word would be in all capital letters, *SELF Portrait,* might help to defuse some expected criticism from readers finding the main subject too much in the foreground, while the supporting cast hovered vaguely in the background. This idea was, however, rejected. "Inspiration, not information, is the general purpose of the book," Man Ray told Lawrence, with publication date less than six months away.

He was equally outspoken about the form of the memoir, insisting on large, clear type and generous blank stretches both within chapters and at the end of the book, to convey an intentional incompleteness and open-endedness, for he was still very much among the living. He had final say on every photograph included, viewing them as purely documentary, and therefore requesting they be surrounded by white margins rather than bled. Man Ray carefully composed the captions for the illustrations as well. Finally, he designed the dust jacket and chose its distinctive black-and-pale-gold motif.

Man Ray was devoting more time than ever before to promoting himself. He consented to appear in the rue Férou studio in a film produced for French television, also featuring Ernst, Tzara, and Giacometti. Several of his works were included in the "Art of Assemblage" exhibition at the Museum of Modern Art. In recognition of his achievement in photography, he received the Gold Medal at the 1961 Venice Biennale and the annual citation of the American Society of Magazine Photographers. The Bibliothèque Nationale in Paris mounted an exhibition of his color photographs, followed by a major show surveying his entire photographic oeuvre in the spring of 1962.

Man Ray muttered complaints about the "retrospective" mentality that seemed to pursue him doggedly no matter how many new works he produced, but he consented increasingly to such exhibits, and to being regarded as an iconic figure with historic value. More institutions from stateside—the University of California at Berkeley, the Cincinnati Art Center, the Walker Art Center in Minneapolis, the Dallas Institute of Fine Arts—approached Man Ray for shows. The demands on Man Ray and Juliet became so great that they were unable to take any much-needed vacations from Paris, what with the voluminous correspondence with museums and other institutions, preparing for a rayograph show in Stuttgart, and negotiating the rights for the French publication of *Self Portrait*. There were also shuttle trips to Switzerland attempting to gather back paintings dispersed by a neglectful dealer, unsatisfactory business arrangements to be resolved, restless movement from gallery to gallery still in search of the impossibly ideal arrangement, and the ongoing flow of visitors from abroad (including William Camfield, writing his exhaustive book on Picabia and seeking Man Ray's recollections).

Juliet's operation for cataracts in the spring of 1962, which kept her confined to bed for several weeks, and the onset of Man Ray's serious circulatory and degenerative joint problems that plagued him in old age added to the couple's problems during this frenetic time. Always a heavy smoker but never much of a drinker, Man Ray had enjoyed reasonably good health throughout his life, with the exception of his illness after Lee Miller left him, spells of exhaustion brought on by excessive party-going, and occasional fluctuations in weight.

Entering his seventies, Man Ray was forced to confront the fact that the unrelenting pressures of his imagination were at odds with the decline of his body. A painful attack of lumbago kept him from working on his book during one rough patch in the winter of 1961. In letters to Duchamp and other friends throughout the early and mid-sixties, he complained of "rheumatism . . . or something," pain in his hip so severe he had to retreat to bed for days on end. These symptomatic bouts with osteoarthritis became so incapacitating that Man Ray sought physiotherapy treatment in London, he said, for "a system of lessons for posture re-education . . . to take the kinks out of my spine and hips." Hunched against the cold in the damp and drafty studio, his shoulders ached so much from the bursitis brought on by half a century of easel painting that he would be unable to hold a pen or a brush for long periods.

Self Portrait was set for April 1, 1963, publication, and with that target date in mind, Man Ray planned a trip to New York City that would include several media appearances as well as the openings of two major shows of his work, one at the Princeton University Art Museum scheduled for March, and the other at Cordier-Ekstrom

Gallery in May. Man Ray was excited and optimistic about the forthcoming journey. His attitude toward the American art world had been mellowed by self-confidence, a natural consequence of increased recognition. And besides, the social scene had changed markedly. Many old friends now lived in New York or had returned to settle there since the end of the war: Albert and Millie Lewin, Julien Levy, the Duchamps, Bill and Noma Copley.

New York was no longer the cold and alienating place it used to be for Man Ray. There was no reason for him to make a pilgrimage to Brooklyn; all vestiges of the family threat were gone. He could plot his own way without being shadowed by ancestral ghosts.

The couple had met and become quite close with Roz Gersten, sent their way by the Copleys in 1955 when she was a novice buyer on her first trip abroad for Macy's. From the moment Man Ray told the impressionable young woman that "the ostrich egg was the most perfect shape in nature," and that "there was no progress in art any more than there was in making love, there are simply different ways of doing it," she formed an immediate attachment to him. She extended a carte blanche invitation to Man Ray and Juliet to stay with her any time they were in the city.

Roz had introduced Man Ray and Juliet to Leo Farland, an investment banker at Lazard Frères and an art collector who had lived in Paris after the war, and through Farland they met another businessman/art collector, the furrier Jacques Kaplan, who, much to Juliet's delight, traded extravagant wraps for paintings. Man Ray instantly reminded Kaplan of "the little French guy in Poitiers who goes to the café every afternoon to sip Dubonnet—with one difference: an extremely stylized self-image." Roberta Kimmel, a book designer for McGraw-Hill, was another new acquaintance. On the strength of her first encounter with Man Ray, she decided to become a collector of photographs and was soon acting as another of his unofficial agents, attempting unsuccessfully for more than a decade to interest a trade publisher in bringing out a book-length collection of rayographs, with critical commentary that included the early essays by Tzara and Ribemont-Dessaignes.

As they had on their previous trip, Man Ray and Juliet decided to stay on East Seventy-ninth Street with Leo Farland, a brilliant raconteur and bon vivant, who liked nothing better than to stay up until all hours trading stories. Once settled in with Farland, Man Ray plunged into the business of being an artist. One of his first appointments was with the new Director of Photography at the Museum of Modern Art. John Szarkowski had come to the job by way of the Walker Art Center in Minneapolis and the Albright Art School in Buffalo. The author of a well-received monograph on the architecture of Louis Sullivan and a photographer himself with several exhibitions to his name, Szarkowski had assumed the mantle when the previous head of the department, the venerable Edward Steichen, retired at the age of eighty-two. Man Ray was perturbed to note the narrow selection of his work represented on postcards published by the museum; for, after all, with James Thrall Soby's gift of more than 150 carefully selected vintage prints, the museum did own what was arguably the finest group of Man Ray photographs to be found anywhere. Why, Man Ray mused, had the Modern never taken it upon itself to show his work en masse?

During their brief conversation, the photographer presented the curator with some examples of his Polaroid color snapshots. The following fall, when Szarkowski reciprocated with a "court visit" to the rue Férou studio, he came away regretful that Man Ray seemed uncomfortable accepting his own undeniably great talent in the medium of photography. Man Ray still could not rest easy in the knowledge that his technical proficiency knew no contemporary equal. He did not like to hear himself revered as a graceful craftsman. These disparaging inclinations about his photographic expertise made it difficult for Szarkowski (and other curators and critics through the years) to evaluate or position Man Ray as seriously and precisely as he might have liked. For his 1973 book, *Looking at Photographs,* Szarkowski chose a rayograph to represent Man Ray as an artist with the propensities of a virtuosic juggler, "to whom art was a sublime kind of play."

There was proof positive that Man Ray's artwork had managed to survive the vicissitudes of critical and commercial attention in mid-March 1963, with the opening of the Zabriskie Gallery show, "The Forum Exhibition—1916," an imaginative attempt to recreate the event of forty-seven years past. Virginia Zabriskie was able to gather many works that had been part of the original exhibition as well as additional paintings by all the participants—Benton, Dove, Hartley, Marin, Maurer, Sheeler, and the rest—including three canvases by Man Ray. *Study for Black Widow, Grand Arrangement of*

Forms, and *Still Life* were all from his 1916–17 phase when, as he conceptualized it in his statement for the original exhibition catalogue, Man Ray was preoccupied with "linking [the] absolute qualities of painting" which so appealed to him, "color and texture of pigment . . . the possibilities of form, invention and organization, and . . . the flat plane on which these elements are brought to play. . . ." These well-articulated goals had not altered in the more than four decades since Man Ray's thoughts had been set down.

Several of the original Forum artists who were still living attended the opening reception, including Ben Benn, William Zorach, and Abraham Walkowitz. Man Ray was in rare and jovial form that evening, an event in himself. His comic timing was on the mark, blending Gallic humor with the native American sensibility he had never lost. These were not Man Ray's "recent pictures" on the wall, but he responded happily to the historic meaning of the occasion and to the show representing him exclusively as Man Ray, painter.

On March 14, a large and well-conceived one-man exhibition of paintings (fifty-two of them, spanning the years from the 1915 Ridgefield landscapes to 1950s *peintures naturelles*), drawings, watercolors, rayographs, chess sets, books, and ten *Objects of My Affection*—photographs were once again conspicuous by their absence—opened at the Princeton University Art Museum. Assembled by the Savages, Patrick Kelleher, director of the museum and its curator of Painting and Sculpture, and art historian Carl Belz, the exhibition had been in the works for several years.

In the spring of 1961, Belz, a graduate student in art history at the university, was casting about for an appropriate dissertation subject. Reading Robert Motherwell's *The Dada Painters and Poets* (1951), Belz was impressed by the fact that there was very little literature available about Man Ray, one of the movement's most central figures. He wrote to the artist in Paris asking if he would agree to become the subject of a full-length study. Man Ray agreed and referred Belz to Naomi and David, who, in turn, helped cover the expenses for a visit to Paris. Belz was at the studio two and three times a week for lengthy conversations with the artist. Man Ray was warm, witty, pleasant, and sweet; he responded gratefully to serious attention, especially from the younger generation. "I only know people now who have met me halfway," he told the young man. "That flatters me—people who visit me!" Photographing Belz while their interviews were in progress, Man Ray let fly a stream of remarks against photography, making certain his visitor understood that he had only done it to make a living.

The Princeton exhibition catalogue concluded with the memorable Man Ray aphorism, a self-portrait assessment in miniature: "The streets are full of admirable craftsmen, but so few practical dreamers."

With the publication of *Self Portrait* by Atlantic–Little, Brown in April 1963, Man Ray the author promptly took to the New York airwaves, interviewed on WRFM's "Casper Citron Show" by the noted art critic Irving Sandler, at that time writing for the *New York Post*. To the program's cosmopolitan listeners, most of whom were undoubtedly hearing him speak for the first time, Man Ray must have sounded like a New York neighbor; the radio microphone did not lie. "Work" was "woik," "certain" was "soitain," "heard" was "hoid." But overlaying the street-wise manner were the measured tones of a skilled talker who made conversation into an art. Many of Man Ray's replies were direct quotes from the *Self Portrait* text.

The two men began with a brief review of the Dada movement. There was no question in the artist's mind that the burgeoning Pop Art movement in England and America, and the Nouveaux Réalistes in France were both Dada outcroppings.

Sandler questioned him about Alfred Stieglitz and the 291 Gallery. "The Secessionist school was a vague forerunner of Dada," Man Ray admitted, reflecting about the impact of seeing "high art" and "perverse art" hanging side by side on those dun-colored walls so many years ago. And what of the notorious Armory Show? Man Ray was quick to take that up: "It convinced me I was on the right track," he said, "showing me the artist could do anything he pleased, not just to satisfy the public or the critics."

That night, following a book-signing reception at the Gotham Book Mart, Roz Gersten (now Jacobs) and her husband, Mel, threw a big party for Man Ray and Juliet to celebrate the new book. Paper dresses were all the rage, and Juliet, always fashionable, wore a silvery one. At two in the morning, Man Ray and Marcel Duchamp, co-conspirators once more, were busily cutting creatively placed designs in the dress, whittling it away with glee.

In an interview a few weeks later, Man Ray reminded Brian O'Doherty of the *Times* that he had "been through two wars, driven cars like a madman, and survived all [his] athletic friends . . . I'm trying to do a one-man job," Man Ray insisted, "something that leaves me free. It's the only thing that's left to us in present-day society."

The following month, as the conclusion to his successful stay in America, Man Ray's second one-man show of the spring season opened at the Cordier-Ekstrom Gallery, in the Parke Bernet Building at 980 Madison Avenue. Diagonally across Madison Avenue at that time was the picture-framing shop of Bob and Barbara Kulicke. During the preceding winter, the couple had been hard at work preparing Man Ray's paintings for the Princeton show, and the Savages and the Kulickes had hit upon the idea that Ekstrom, a gentlemanly connoisseur with a keen eye, a soft-sell philosophy, and an affinity for Duchamp's work, might be just the person to represent Man Ray. Duchamp seconded the idea in response to Man Ray's query about Ekstrom's credentials, reassuring him that "being associated with Cordier-Ekstrom here [in New York] would be very favorably looked-upon; and besides, his exhibitions are often very successful." Furthermore, Duchamp wrote, pressing gently but firmly, the gallery was well appointed and elegant, and Ekstrom had already taken the liberty of asking him to write a note for the exhibition catalogue.

Shortly after Man Ray and Juliet's arrival in New York, Naomi had given a luncheon in her home to introduce the artist and dealer, who took to each other instantly. Ekstrom sensed that Man Ray was an old master waiting to be acknowledged in the country of his origins. He appreciated Man Ray's paintings for the ideas they expressed, and he understood that their intellectual content took primacy. Man Ray delighted in Ekstrom's affinity for wordplay, laughing when the dealer pointed out wittily that the location of the Paris studio, "2 [deux] bis [rue] Férou," made a fine pun when spoken as German, "Du bist verrückt" (You are crazy). As their friendship developed over the next decade, Ekstrom presented two more Man Ray shows: "Objects of My Affection" in 1965, and a 1970 retrospective tribute, on the occasion of the artist's eightieth birthday.

The handsome catalogue for the 1963 Cordier-Ekstrom exhibition featured Duchamp's appreciative poem to Man Ray, "La Vie en Ose," ("The Life of Daring," and an untranslatable resonance with

Edith Piaf and "Rrose Sélavy"). Much like the Princeton exhibition earlier in the spring, the show took the long view, stretching back to pictures made in the aftermath of the Armory Show and through the Hollywood era and beyond. It did not, however, cover the twenties at all and intentionally made no attempt to touch upon Man Ray's work as a filmmaker or photographer. In a brief review in the June 1963 issue of *Art International* magazine, art historian William Rubin, chairman of the Department of Painting and Sculpture at the Museum of Modern Art, summed up the critical conflict about Man Ray, acknowledging he was "the best . . . [of] the native-born artists" to flower in the Dada movement. However, Rubin asserted that Man Ray had not been able to grow as a painter beyond the 1916–17 period, when he "became the master of his talents." He had nurtured an expertise in design at the cost of "any real sensibility to paint." He criticized Man Ray for "stylistic meanderings" and for "not progress[ing] from painting to painting"; yet, Rubin concluded, that "erratic" quality made the artist, "at his best, intellectually challenging."

Man Ray was disappointed that Rubin had not acknowledged his more recent paintings, but the review was nonetheless an affirmation of one of his guiding principles. There were no logical lines of progress and influence in art, Man Ray believed, only the individual imagination as a touchstone for inspiration.

MAN RAY. *PORTRAIT OF NED ROREM*, PARIS, OCTOBER 1953. THE COMPOSER ETCHED INTO THE NEGATIVE THE OPENING NOTES OF "TOUT BEAU MON COEUR," HIS SONG DEDICATED TO MAN RAY.
Collection Ned Rorem.

THE NEXT
WAVE

PARIS WAS gloomy, cold, and rainy, but blessedly familiar. Springtime had not quite yet arrived in late May of 1963, when Man Ray returned with Juliet, "a bit dazed" after the whirlwind goings on in New York. But he plunged into the business that awaited him, much of it concerned with the publication of *Self Portrait* in other languages and other countries. Word had spread of its anecdotal style and its collagelike depiction of an era. Man Ray also pressed on producing and marketing his work through editions. When his *Object to Be Destroyed* metronome was smashed by a group of young anarchists invading a 1957 gallery show in Paris, Man Ray vigorously refused to prosecute. He responded, instead, by authorizing the fabrication of a half dozen new assemblages, changing their name to *Indestructible Objects* "The work has already been done," Man Ray would say to purists who scorned mass production. He elaborated upon this dictum in a carefully formulated statement, "Originals Graphic Multiples":

> An original is a creation
> motivated by desire.
> Any reproduction of an original
> is motivated by necessity.
> The original is the result of
> an automatic mental process,

the reproduction, of a mechanical
process. In other words:
Inspiration then information;
each validates the other.
All other considerations are
beyond the scope of these
statements.
It is marvelous that we are
the only species that creates
gratuitous forms.
To create is divine, to reproduce
is human.

As far back as the thirties, Man Ray had acknowledged that a certain amount of contempt for the uniqueness of his materials was necessary for the artist wishing to express his ideas in their most vivid form. Technical excellence was equally necessary, but should never be so noticeable that it interfered with the expression of the impulse that had fueled the work. The ease with which Man Ray was able to embrace the full process of a work of art, from idea through execution and viewer response, made it easy for him to avail himself of the possibilities for formal editioning that were available in Paris in the 1960s. His lifelong experience with photography had served as a prelude; each print was a multiple, so to speak, of its template negative. Economic imperatives also helped to make editioning attractive. The time Man Ray devoted each day in the studio to painting could remain above the commercial struggle while replicas (as he most often called them) could be created and openly acknowledged as commodities. "I am swamped with work," he wrote Naomi, excitement evident in the accelerated, open flow of his rounded handwriting, "making replicas of my objects. A gallery is manufacturing limited editions in bronze, plastics, silver, gold, wood, lead, feathers, etc. . . . [The] reproductions of old works, lost or destroyed [are] very beautiful," he said with pride, "sometimes better than the originals!"

Man Ray was a purist only insofar as capturing the soul and spirit of an original, but not when it came to selling. His signature, scratched into the surface of a bronze base, or in pencil on a new impression, became ubiquitous with opportunity. There was aesthetic and economic comfort in dissemination.

Though Man Ray was in every respect a hands-on artist, he did not, of course, actually carry out the execution of editions himself. For the last fifteen years of his working life he had the assistance of a dedicated friend and colleague, a young teacher named Lucien Treillard. The two met in the early 1960s, when Treillard was seeking out works for reproduction in new media for the lithographer Georges Visat. One of the first projects the two men worked on together was an interpretation of Man Ray's early aerograph from New York days, *La volière*, transposed onto Plexiglas. Man Ray found this surface particularly exciting; transparent like glass, yet flexible and durable, ideal for adapting old imagery to new technologies. During the years to follow, he authorized the reproduction of paintings lost or destroyed onto the same material. Man Ray also saw his drawings from *Les mains libres* given new life as bronze statuettes. The transition from two dimensions to three made the re-creation more akin to reincarnation.

From the outset, Lucien Treillard and Man Ray were ideally suited as coworkers: the scholarly, articulate, and meticulous Frenchman, with his precise yet intensely warm manner, and the cantankerous older artist who spoke French just as well, but always with an endearing American accent. They soon arrived at a workable system. For reasons of efficiency first and the artist's eventual difficulty walking later, Man Ray saw no reason to go to Visat's studio or any other place where the actual editioning work was done. Rather, he entrusted Lucien with the supervision of contracted work. Man Ray was precise in his directions, and Lucien returned with proofs for his scrutiny and approval.

Over the years, their routine hardly varied. Lucien would teach his literature classes in the morning. Man Ray, for his part, was never up and about much before noon as he and Juliet woke late and sipped their coffee in bed. Virtually every day, when Lucien arrived at the rue Férou shortly after two o'clock, the men would set to work, while Juliet went to the market, returning at aperitif time.

The brilliant, visionary collector and dealer from Milan, Arturo Schwarz, who had been one of the first to publish Man Ray in multiples, also embarked upon a full program during the mid- to late-1960s, as Man Ray and Treillard were overseeing editioning closer to home. Through Galleria Schwarz, he supervised the replication of such important works as "*Elevage de poussière*," the mysterious photograph Man Ray had taken of Marcel Duchamp's *Large Glass; Sculpture by Itself*, first made in 1918; *Obstruction*, the interlocking pyramid of coat hangers suspended from the ceiling; *Emak Bakia,* a prop used in the film, the assemblage of cello neck and horsehair; *What We All Lack,* the graceful clay pipe and soap bubble; *Venus restaurée,* the torso in bondage; *A l'heure de l'Observatoire—Les amoureux,* a color serigraph so true to the painting that, the artist claimed with pride, "people think it's the original . . ."; and, not least, the *Cadeau* iron with fourteen tacks, which had made its appearance and disappearance at the Librairie Six exhibition welcoming Man Ray to Paris during the winter of 1921. Of this last important work, Man Ray told Naomi, "Schwarz of the Milan Gallery has made an edition of ten irons signed and numbered, and I'm not supposed to make any more for five years!" Man Ray set down casual instructions to anyone who might have been thinking of a convenient way to travel with such a cumbersome (and potentially dangerous) device. One had merely to remove the tacks temporarily and paste them on at one's convenience with strong glue. First, however, "it is necessary to draw a pencil line down the middle, right angle to the base, as a guide, and dip the head of the tack in some glue on a piece of paper—let dry for a couple of days. To facilitate the handling," the artist noted, "place the iron upside down between two piles of books."

In the age of mechanical reproduction, as the German philosopher Walter Benjamin called it, the so-called unique work of art cried out for generations of itself to be born and reborn in a variety of permanent media, from metal to lithography. If the consumer in the rapidly expanding art market, which became more omnivorous with every new gallery opening, every new collector who appeared on the scene, could find reasonably priced versions of otherwise unattainable goods, so much the better.

Over the next ten years, Georges Visat and Arturo Schwarz were joined by other enterprising dealers in producing Man Ray editions: Marcel Zerbib and Jean Petithory in France and Giorgio Marconi and Luciano Anselmino in Italy. At times, with his advancing years, the artist let material slip through his fingers that was never meant to, diluting the quality of the effort. Man Ray could easily become enthralled because someone new had recognized him and was coming to see him, and, in the process, forget to preserve his right of approval. He was an innocent in many ways, and he knew it, complaining to close friends that he really was not meant to be a businessman and did not possess the sophistication to engage in protracted bargaining.

▪   ▪   ▪

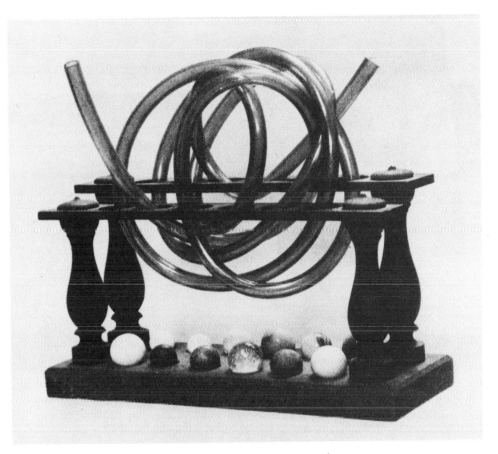

MAN RAY. *SMOKING DEVICE*, 1959. ASSEMBLAGE.
Collection Mr. and Mrs. Melvin Jacobs.

Man Ray enjoyed his position as "the Dada of us all" (to invoke William Copley's phrase of homage and humor), a bridge between the past and the future, during the anything-goes epoch of the sixties. "Nothing can be done whether you call it new, whether it appears new," Man Ray told the English art journalist John Jones, during a wide-ranging interview in Paris in October 1965, "unless something went before it."

Indeed, the emerging French artists of the early sixties looked to Man Ray and his generation with renewed respect. The most concrete manifestation of this regard was Nouveau Réalisme, a group convened by the noted critic Pierre Restany. On October 27, 1960, Martial Raysse, Camille Bryen, Niki de Saint-Phalle, Jean Tinguely, Yves Klein, Raymond Hains, Daniel Spoerri, and several other artists in Paris signed a manifesto (such a declarative act in itself was expressive of a bygone time) pledging themselves and their work, in a "Neo-Dada" spirit, to "*nouvelles approches perceptives du réel*" (new perceptual approaches to what is real).

As in the 1920s and 1930s, the object once again achieved primacy. Daniel Spoerri, for example, took dishes with half-eaten food on them, an ashtray with a cigar stub, and a glass or two, glued them all to a tray, and named the work *Marcel Duchamp's Breakfast*. Yves Klein discovered an unusually powerful, deep blue pigment and made casts of his torso drenched with this evocative color. He mounted sponges on slender stems instead of platforms and glorified them as mundane sculptures. Jean Tinguely became well known for his self-destructive objects, including the giant infernal machine he built in the Sculpture Garden of the Museum of Modern Art where, Rube Goldberg–like, it proceeded to clank and crank and unwind itself to death before a stunned crowd.

The Nouveaux Réalistes, like the Dadaists before them, as the critic and curator Jean-Hubert Martin has noted, "took pieces of reality and included them in their work." They were continental Europe's more erudite answer to Pop Art (or, as Man Ray enjoyed calling it, "pup" art, capitalizing upon the comic-book style as a plaything of the young), which sprang up in England and then emigrated to America but never reached France. Where Pop Art was forthright, simplistic, and strong, Nouveau Réalisme was sophisticated. It was intellectually grounded in the use of what the practitioners called *objets-témoins* (objects as witnesses), found objects, like readymades, which were interfered with, consciously deployed, and then given an overlay of color. In one of Yves Klein's most dramatic works, he applied paint to a woman's naked body and then had her imprint herself onto a vast sheet of paper, so that her shape became both instrument of and an implement in the work.

Man Ray watched this fanfare from the sidelines with bemusement and, for the most part, tolerance. "They're nice, the youngsters," he remarked to Jean-Hubert Martin, who visited him while planning for an exhibition at the Musée Nationale de l'Art Moderne. "Naturally, they're doing things we did forty years before." It was typical of Man Ray simultaneously to accept and be skeptical of the next wave. He accepted the Nouveaux Réalistes because he knew their work could not have taken place without his trailblazing. He was skeptical because the young people, in a hyped-up marketplace, were making so much more money than he ever dreamed of in his early days.

But whether he was *engagé* or dispassionate (or both, true to the vicissitudes of his personality), Man Ray was a living presence in the revolution of Paris in the 1960s, putting artists in their thirties in touch with an era as old as their grandparents.

Members of the new generation of French artists were not the only ones to be affected by Man Ray's legacy. The publication of *Self Portrait* created a stir in America as well, and a small but steady parade of visitors from the States began to appear on the master's doorstep.

In the autumn of 1965, twenty-three-year-old poet Ron Padgett, a New Yorker by way of Oklahoma, arrived in Paris for a year's stay on a Fulbright grant. Already a Man Ray aficionado, having practically memorized the autobiography, Padgett was one of a number of writers who were especially sympathetic to Man Ray's respect for the written word. One evening within a few short weeks of his arrival in the City of Light, Padgett and his wife were dining at Aux Charpentiers, a charming restaurant in the heart of the Sixth Arrondissement, or Man Ray territory, when he looked up from his meal only to see the man himself eating alone at a table across the room. His heart pounding, Padgett scribbled a note and handed it to an obliging waiter. Man Ray opened the folded paper, read the kind words, and nodded in Padgett's direction. A few minutes later, he got up, walked slowly over to Padgett, and thanked him briefly, apologizing that he could not stay to chat.

Four or five months went by before the poet overcame his shyness and decided to pay a call at the legendary studio. Padgett's friend, Ted Berrigan, another poet of the New York school, sent him a few copies of the literary magazine *C*, which they were both editing at the time, and Padgett took these along as an offering. It was late morning. He rang the doorbell next to the unmarked door set into the massive wall on the gently sloping street. No response. Padgett rang again. The sound of shuffling feet. The door yanked open, and an angry, sleepy-eyed, and unshaven Man Ray appeared. "Whaddaya want?" he bellowed. "Just to give you this," Padgett managed to say, trembling, as he thrust the magazines into Man Ray's hands. The door slammed as quickly as it had opened and Padgett beat a hasty retreat, dejected.

The third approach was magical. In June of 1966, aware that Man Ray's first major retrospective in America was planned for October at the Los Angeles County Museum of Art, editor (and fellow-poet) John Ashbery assigned Padgett to write a piece on the artist for the November issue of *ARTNews*. Padgett then enlisted the help of his friend Jacqueline Monnier, who, in addition to being a fine artist in her own right, was in a way a member of the "extended family," as Henri Matisse's granddaughter and Marcel Duchamp's stepdaughter through his marriage to her mother, Alexina Sattler. Jackie Monnier took Padgett to the studio, made brief introductions, and departed, leaving the two very much alone, for Juliet did not arrive on the scene until somewhat later.

Man Ray did not remember Padgett in the slightest from their previous encounters, much to the young man's relief. At the outset, the suspicious subject warned his interviewer that he would benefit only from "an hour of [his] time." However, once it became clear that Padgett was a poet, not a critic, and that he had read *Self Portrait*, Man Ray's entire demeanor was transformed. "You read my book, eh?" Man Ray said with a warm smile. "What did you think of it?"

Three hours later, Padgett was still there, having been treated to a grand tour of the studio. Man Ray pointed out every artwork visible on the crowded shelves, recalling to Padgett's astonishment the virtual month, day, and year of their creation. Furthermore, Man Ray revealed that he had a cabinet full of notes for hundreds more works he would most likely never get to achieve: "Sometimes, I don't even make notes. . . . There's enough pleasure in simply *imagining* the works!"

The artist was voluble, spontaneous, and reminiscent that day. The impending retrospective and the presence of a much younger man turned his thoughts to the past, and to the active days of his own youth, the brawls along the boulevards: "Ah, fistfights," Man Ray said, as he sat on the couch gazing upward, midafternoon light filtering down from the skylight, diffused through the parachute cloth canopy. "Aragon got into some fights, he was tough. But Benjamin Peret was a physical coward—Me, I'm a coward, too; oh, I was in some good ones. You know, you and the other fellow throw your arms around each other and fall on the floor so you can't hit each other. Now you take René Char," Man Ray went on, extending his catalogue of belligerent poets, "He was a great big fellow, and boy, could he punch. He was terribly strong and always good to have on your side."

Juliet returned from her afternoon out and greeted Padgett cordially, but she remained silent as the two men concluded their visit. Man Ray expressed anxiety about the Los Angeles show. He was ambivalent about such a vast undertaking that involved proving himself at this late time in his life, and was hesitant about returning to California after so long. As always, Man Ray was also apprehensive about letting so much work out of the studio. Padgett asked him what would be in the show. Glancing upward again, lifting his arms in a gesture of abandonment, Man Ray answered, "Everything! It all goes!"

On the way out, a grateful Man Ray insisted that Padgett take home first-edition copies of the 1937 classic *Les mains libres*, and a 1948 publication from the Copley Gallery in Hollywood, *Alphabet for Adults*, fanciful cartoons based upon the letters of the alphabet. Padgett was ecstatic when he emerged onto the dusky street, reflecting, however, that Man Ray's work—so noticeably and insistently nondevelopmental—"paid the price of no apotheosis."

Back in America by the following autumn, Padgett sent Man Ray a copy of his published piece, "Artist Accompanies Himself with His Rays." "It's the best thing ever written about me," came the reply.

Within the month following Ron Padgett's visit, Man Ray crated most of the works in his studio for shipment to the Los Angeles County Museum of Art for the retrospective exhibition, set to open on October 27, 1966. He wrote gleefully, if sarcastically, to Naomi in Princeton, from amid a sea of customs forms, "Here are the insurance values [for the artworks]. . . . Having just filled in 12 pages for the Museum with similar evaluations for my things being sent from the studio in Paris, I had no idea I was so rich! nearly half a millionaire! Just about approaches the price of one Van Gogh portrait recently sold."

Nearly two and one-half years in the planning, this first full-scale retrospective came in the artist's seventy-sixth year. It was the brainchild of Jules Langsner, a dynamic, energetic art critic and freelance curator hired by the museum as guest director for the project. Man Ray was standoffish when Langsner, a scholar of his career and an admirer for more than two decades, first proposed the idea in the spring of 1964. He had mixed memories of a decade of doldrums in Los Angeles when the numerous shows mounted there during the 1940s had felt like "sowing in the desert." Langsner envisioned the retrospective as Man Ray's triumphant return to the town that had failed to accept him when he was in its midst.

As time passed, and the two conferred in Paris about the content of the exhibit, Man Ray's sentiments shifted. Langsner discovered his job was all the more difficult because Man Ray was a surprisingly international artist, whose works were scattered all over Europe and America: "It's not possible," he admitted to James Elliott, chief curator at the museum, "to go to places like the Virgin Islands, Toledo, Minneapolis, Brussels, Stuttgart, etc." in search of Man Ray's prodigious output. In the course of putting the show together, Langsner came to rely heavily upon Man Ray's friends and acquaintances, and upon the works housed in the artist's own collection. There were many more personal than institutional lenders to the exhibition. The list in the front of the catalogue read like a family of true believers, a cadre who stood by Man Ray: Leo Farland, Roz and Mel Jacobs, Jacques Kaplan, Harold and Virginia Knapik, Millie and Al Lewin, Roland and Lee Penrose (now Sir Roland and Lady Lee), Frida and Hans Richter, Naomi and David Savage (and Naomi's father, Sam), Mary and Paul Wescher.

With the opening date drawing close, Man Ray became more committed to the idea of a full-scale survey of his life's work, but there would be no photographs. Nothing Langsner or anyone else said would sway the artist from this decision. And he insisted upon having the final cut: "As in all previous shows," Man Ray wrote Langsner, "I shall make the final decision, if there is a choice to be made." Furthermore, he was completely involved with the design of the catalogue, now shaping up to be a glossy, 150-page perfect-bound book with the artist's signature boldly inscribed in gold on the cover. Although the typography for the rest of the book was to be done in eight-point type, Man Ray instructed Langsner to tell the printer, Bruder Hartmann in Berlin, that the statement, "I Have Never Painted a Recent Picture," should be set in 16-point-size type. He reversed the earlier implications of this declaration and complained that requests to show his *newer* work tiresomely overlooked what had come *before*.

Man Ray made some last protestations in the autumn weeks before he and Juliet set out—he was feeling weak in the legs; he abhorred crowds; there were too many ancillary events scheduled around the show—but the couple traveled to Los Angeles without incident.

The Lytton Gallery of the museum was spectacularly arrayed. Once more, as it had in the Museum of Modern Art show three decades before, *The Lips* loomed large over an archway, dominating the scene. The three hundred works included paintings, collages, sculpture, more than thirty objects (among them a sizable number of editioned ones), drawings, rayographs, chess sets, and first editions of books. The catalogue provided a sympathetic and well-conceived framework for the art, with essays by Man Ray about himself; by Man Ray's friends—Eluard, Duchamp, Breton, Tzara, Richter—about their friend; and by two affectionate critics, Jules Langsner and Carl Belz.

During the festive week of the opening, Langsner arranged two lectures for Man Ray, one in a theater at the museum before a glittering crowd of donors and collectors, another outdoors at nearby Chouinard Art Institute before an enthusiastic gathering of students.

Introduced by Langsner at the museum event as comparable in his multifaceted identity to "Isis, the goddess of the ten thousand names," Man Ray was measured, ponderous, and uncomfortable under the spotlight. Admitting that he had never addressed an audience as large as this one—but also reassuring himself out loud that "we need words; they're very important"—Man Ray launched into his major theme, a justification for what never failed to weigh upon his mind, the relationship between photography and the serious artistic pursuits of his life over more than half a century. And he managed to do it without mentioning the word *photography*, referring instead to "some means of social contact by which [he] could live, earning enough to be able to go on doing what [he liked] to do." He spoke of this unnamed pursuit as a "hobby," as "doing something else," which then permitted him to withdraw from public view and hide within the real work, the painting.

Man Ray sounded defensive that night, falling back upon

allusions to nameless and confused critics who undervalued him for not nestling in a convenient pigeonhole. He managed to perk up during the question-and-answer period and swing with the mood of the moment, finding some spontaneity. "If I were a teacher and you were my class," he told the amused audience, "I would give marks for the most intelligent questions—not for their answers." A question came in response: "When you began to paint," someone called out to Man Ray, "did you have any idea of the talent you had?" "That's a very intelligent question," Man Ray shot back, then fell silent. As it dawned upon the audience that the Dada of them all was not about to reply further, laughter began and swelled, and Man Ray joined in the mirth, chuckling to himself. He had seized control of the moment and made it his, the way he knew best, through understated humor, his saving grace.

Four days later, at two-thirty, outdoors under the trees on a sunny afternoon, Man Ray was markedly more at ease at the Chouinard Art Institute. The artist was in sprightly form, and, knowing he was with a group of current and would-be artists, his remarks assumed a paternal, tolerant tone. These were people on the verge of their careers facing a man who had never wanted to be anything other than what he had become.

His mood was honest and playful as he delineated the painter as "one of the most selfish persons in society," a person who must consider himself above all others. He cautioned the students to avoid becoming too familiar with the paint medium; a little "contempt" for it was healthy—it would preserve them from hubris.

Studiously unprepared (or was he? It was always so hard to tell), Man Ray confessed that not having developed a consistent style had caused him grief among dealers: "You keep changing. We can't handle you," they would say. Man Ray took solace in this tradition of rejection to which he obviously belonged, represented by Manet, Delacroix, and Cézanne, three of his enduring idols.

But he was far from lugubrious or maudlin about his lot in life. In an era of "happenings," he himself was a happening, and the students sensed it. His verbal discourse, like a stream-of-consciousness, existential text, seemed to create itself. The speech appeared spontaneous, in much the same way that Man Ray's most successful objects looked like they had been literally thrown together, but upon careful examination exhibited an eerie deliberateness of composition.

"I've been talking," he concluded, laughingly, "to convince

myself of the value of my ideas." No matter how generally he might have been speaking or how democratic the environment appeared to be, "Tomorrow I shall say the opposite of what I say now. I want to be contradictory and irrational," Man Ray declared, sounding very much like the Walt Whitman of "Song of Myself" he had read and idolized in high-school days.

It was as if Man Ray had prophesied the critical response to the Los Angeles retrospective. Less than a week later, Philip Leider's review appeared in the *New York Times*. Under the headline, "Man Ray, Wandering Knight," the artist was summarily dismissed as a "failure," someone who returned to the U.S. from Europe in 1940, went straight to Hollywood, and disappeared. To the author of the piece, this was a sin of the highest degree, distinctly un-American. "Nothing, perhaps," Leider observed, "tells so much of the pervasiveness of his Europeanization than the fact that he could remain in America for the entire decade of the birth, maturation, and flowering of the Abstract Expressionist movement without seeming to have any grasp of its significance." Carl Belz, on the other hand, writing in the December 1966 issue of *Artforum,* found something inherently American—or, "at least, non-European—in Man Ray's ambivalence, as if Art were something foreign and unattainable, but which should nevertheless be brought down to earth." To Belz, sympathetic to Man Ray's work and thought in view of their long association, "it [was] the message rather than the medium" that interested the artist most.

Man Ray, meanwhile, was back on the rue Férou, permitting the L.A. letdown to filter in gradually. To his great chagrin, only two of the works in the show were sold to collectors. The museum did not deem it necessary to purchase any works of importance from the exhibition, which did not travel because too many of the lenders were unwilling to prolong their loans, or so the museum administration told him.

Then, nearly a year later, Man Ray received the tragic news that his outspoken partisan and friend Jules Langsner had died of a heart attack at the age of fifty-six. It was a sudden blow. Man Ray lost a loved and respected ally, a man who had performed a yeomanlike service for an artist he believed was long overdue for recognition.

MARCEL DUCHAMP AND MAN RAY AT THE
HOME OF NAOMI AND DAVID SAVAGE, PRINCETON, N.J.,
MARCH 1963.
Photograph by Naomi Savage.

DEATH OF A
VIEUX
COPAIN

AS GERTRUDE STEIN might have put it, the flowers of friend-ship were quickly fading. By this time, Man Ray was relatively alone. Eluard, Matisse, Léger, Derain, and Picabia were long gone. Brancusi died in 1957; Oscar Dominguez, tragically, by his own hand the same year. The ranks of the old guard had thinned, and Man Ray fought back with a quality of mind that especially endeared him to Juliet: a tough, witty humor. His ripostes were especially in evidence the memorable night of October 1, 1968. Three couples reveled in one another's company—the Man Rays; the critic Robert Lebel and his wife, Nina; and Marcel and Teeny Duchamp, all assembled at Duchamp's flat, 5, rue Parmentier, in the suburb of Neuilly. It had been a typically active summer for Duchamp at Cadaqués, where, on July 28, he had celebrated his eightieth birthday. However, he had overextended himself and now suffered from a lingering virus. Stock-still and pale in his armchair, Duchamp traded sarcastic quips about his health with Man Ray. To the ever observant Lebel, the two *vieux copains* seemed to be "joyously macabre" that night, playing upon the art of survival, resisting the passage of time by enumerating how much there was yet to be done.

After a few snifters of brandy, Man Ray was able to persuade Duchamp to smile more broadly. The salutary effects of laughter seemed to be lifting his friend's low spirits. Then, suddenly, Man Ray remarked, as much in truth as jest, "No, Marcel, you are sad, you've been that way forever, for as long as I've known you, because you've always been the 'sad young man in a train.'" In a flash was revealed the depth of Man Ray's knowledge of his friend. The fleeting reference was to Duchamp's December 1911 painting, a self-portrait with pipe completed at the Neuilly studio more than a half century in the past, its slivered, fragmented kineticism an undeniable precursor of the notorious *Nude*.

Toward midnight, Duchamp rose, deliberately, laboriously, and walked his old friends to the elevator; he remained there staring into their eyes for an uncommonly long time, his face more pale and his eyes more liquid than usual. His smile was unusually restrained, and he breathed with difficulty, the pulse beat in the prominent vein on the right side of his brow evident through his translucent skin. Duchamp's radiance seemed especially bright at that instant, sending out powerful and silent messages. Lebel was overcome by uncertainty and foreboding.

It was a cold night, icy underfoot, and Man Ray walked with difficulty. His stick beat a determined path, but he stumbled and slipped as he tried to enter the car, and Lebel lunged to prevent a nasty fall. Man Ray recovered himself. Unhurt, he laughed heartily and said, "You thought I'd dropped dead!"

All the way to rue Férou, the four sang and laughed, repeating the phrase—"drop dead"—like the punchline to an irresistible joke. An hour later, in the earliest morning hours, the phone rang in the Lebels' apartment. It was Teeny: "Marcel," she told the stunned Robert, "has just dropped dead." A stroke had come suddenly.

Duchamp was cremated and his ashes buried at the family plot in the Cimetière Monumental at Rouen. At his request, the gravestone bore an ironic inscription: *"D'ailleurs c'est toujours les autres qui meurent"* (Besides, it's always the others who die).

Like *The Large Glass,* his monumental work, Duchamp left his friendship with Man Ray unfinished. Man Ray did not—perhaps could not—speak at length about the impact of such an absence, conversations never completed, thoughts now never to be shared, but to his close friends, the plain shock of the event was clear. Duchamp and Man Ray were complementary conspirators, "alter egos," as Bill Copley, who knew them both intimately, described it. They never tried to impress each other. Pleasantries, gossip about other artists assiduously devoid of rancor—such was the predominant substance of their discourse in later years. They gained support simply through the magic of their mutual presence. Duchamp's spontaneity was a perfect foil for Man Ray's manic intensity.

Janet Flanner understood one of the most important connectives joining Duchamp and Man Ray: the game of chess, "a form of conversation," she wrote in a "Letter from Paris" soon after Duchamp's death, "in which one's character emerged as one exposed oneself to the opponent, the conversation being rather like an argument—except that in chess the argument reaches a decision." Duchamp and Man Ray had been chess companions since Pepper Pot Café days in Greenwich Village, never having a care for the imbalance in their skills, Man Ray the perpetual initiate against Duchamp the veteran champion.

Across the chessboard as across the tennis court, Man Ray and Marcel Duchamp were *en face,* squared off, opposed, but, in Duchamp's usage, fully reconciled. Their art had the same apposite nature, like the squares of the game board. Duchamp's work was studiously sequential, an interlocking series of conundrums, segues, mind-twisting cross-references, and erotic footnotes. Man Ray's oeuvre was a meandering and cluttered landscape. Yet both men depended upon irony, played with all the stops removed, and, in any case, would have strenuously discouraged comparisons.

Where in his art Duchamp was a private man, in his chess he was very much a public one. Since 1923, when he purportedly if apocryphally gave up art for chess, Duchamp had spent considerable energy gently but aggressively persuading other artists to design chess sets—at first for aesthetic delectation, but in the later years of his life, tirelessly, for sheer fund-raising purposes, for the benefit of the American Chess Foundation. Proceeds from sales of donated chess sets were used to send American players to foreign tournaments and to advance the cause of chess in general. *"Je suis dans le* 'chess business' *maintenant,"* Duchamp wrote to Man Ray in June 1961, *"missionaire en quête de l'argent pour les échecs"* (a missionary in search of funds to support chess matches). Through his easy charm and the emotional debt owed him by so many artists, Duchamp was able to extract virtuosic and unusual chess sets as contributions to the Chess Foundation from Max Ernst, Alexander Calder, Salvador Dalí (the design of his pieces based upon fingers and parts of hands), Arman Fernandez, and, of course, Man Ray, whose set was dubbed "The Knights of the Square Table." Duchamp was ecstatic in his praise for Man Ray's set, on view for a time at Parke Bernet. Flattered, Man Ray went on to design a silver trophy for the Chess Foundation as well: "It was a satisfaction," he wrote to Naomi, "akin to Degas' when his work began to sell; he felt like the horse who had won the sweepstakes."

Both men proceeded through their careers with greater reverence for the person that lay behind the work than for the work itself: ". . . man as man, brain as brain, if you like," Duchamp told Pierre Cabanne in his most comprehensive, extended interview, "interests me more than what he makes, because I've noticed that most artists only repeat themselves." Anyone who faced Marcel Duchamp across a chessboard, who looked into that craggy face wreathed in cigar smoke and felt the depth of Duchamp's silence and the power in those heavy-lidded eyes, supremely relaxed yet alive and aware—needed no convincing that a master was at work, without a paintbrush.

"For Duchamp," Octavio Paz has written, "there is no art in itself; art is not a thing, but a medium." Duchamp's work aggregates to a metawork, one referred to as a "whole body" he always dreamed of seeing united. Hence, the appropriateness of the Arensberg room at the Philadelphia Museum of Art, where forty-three creations in all, installed under Duchamp's direct supervision in 1950, can be viewed and reviewed textually, one chapter reading naturally into the next. Like Man Ray, Duchamp was a consummately literary artist—both men revered the poet as the ultimate imaginer. Duchamp often credited Raymond Roussel's poetic novel, *Impressions d'Afrique* (1910), with having left its mark upon him from an early age; it was no secret that as a beginning painter he had been more influenced by writers than by other painters.

"He was twenty-nine years old [in 1915] and wore a halo," his friend the collector and dealer Henri-Pierre Roché recalled years later of Duchamp's arrival in New York. "He was creating his own legend. . . . At that time Duchamp's reputation in New York as a Frenchman was equalled only by Napoleon and Sarah Bernhardt." And what always remained astonishing about Duchamp as a

LOURIE SAVAGE, JULIET MAN RAY, DAVID SAVAGE,
MARCEL DUCHAMP, MAN RAY, AND TEENY DUCHAMP,
PRINCETON, MARCH 1963.
Photograph by Naomi Savage.

celebrity was that he did not promote himself. He simply glided along, doing his work, making money when he needed it through various humble jobs. People gravitated to Duchamp and became addicted to his presence. Men were attracted to his refinement and his impeccable politeness. Women found him alluring. He was simply one of the kindest people anyone had ever known, completely lacking in malice or rancor.

But Duchamp was constantly on the move in the last decade of his life, mirroring Man Ray's restlessness in his shuttling between his adopted home in New York and his French home in Paris. In 1955, Duchamp had become a naturalized United States citizen. Soon after, with conscious gestures to posterity, he started to codify the major editions of his work: the hand-assembled valises, the collected critical writings edited by Michel Sanouillet and Robert Lebel, the catalogues raisonnés, the plaster castings from life. Duchamp spoke at symposia around the world, laying down his aesthetic principles for ever larger audiences. His travels took him to America's West Coast, South, and Midwest. His first major retrospective was mounted in the fall of 1962, curated by Walter Hopps at the Pasadena Art Museum. A second retrospective came four years later at the Tate Gallery in London.

While in the last five years of his life Marcel Duchamp was involved in a series of major efforts to lend coherence to his life's work, another, concurrent project was moving forward behind the scenes, in his secret studio, apartment 403, at 80 East Eleventh Street in New York. Here, in the fall of 1966, twenty years after Duchamp had started it, *Given: 1. The Waterfall, 2. The Illuminating Gas* came to completion.

Duchamp spent much of the following year writing notes and taking photographs for his elaborate instructions on how to dismantle and reassemble the *Given*. It was not until early summer 1968, just before he left New York for Spain—eagerly anticipating aperitifs outside the Café Meliton in the Cadaqués town square— that he summoned Bill Copley to the studio to show him the finished *Given,* and to tell his old friend that he wished to see this opus join the rest of the family of works in the Arensberg room at the Philadelphia Museum. Through the resources of his Cassandra Foundation, Copley was able to fulfill Duchamp's request.

How appropriate that the *Given* can only be seen by one person at a time, looking through peepholes at eye level in a massive wooden door set into a wall of bricks. Just inside the door, once the viewer's eyes are focused, he sees another wall of bricks that has been "broken" through. Beyond that wall, in a bed of branches and twigs, lies the nude female torso. Beyond her stretches an artificial landscape, a lake and wooded hillside, with the illusion of water falling. Try as we might, twist and turn as we will, we cannot get beyond the boundaries of this fixed image. Duchamp is in control. Is it the final *Bride* lying there, offering herself to us, given false yet verisimilitudinous flesh?

No one felt the anguish of Marcel Duchamp's departure more than Man Ray. Six years later, he finally found sparse and poignant words to express his loss. "October first," he wrote, "Marcel, toward midnight, gently closed his eyes. He had a little smile on his lips. His heart obeyed him and stopped. (Like his work, formerly.) Ah yes! it's tragic, like the end of a chess game. I can't tell you any more about it."

William S. Rubin's ambitious exhibition, "Dada, Surrealism, and Their Heritage," originated at the Museum of Modern Art in March, then traveled to the Los Angeles County Museum of Art, and finally to the Art Institute of Chicago, closing in December 1968. Very much of the moment, it opened just prior to the spring student uprisings in Paris (*les événements de mai*) and closed just after Duchamp's death. The show was the first attempt to substantiate the impact of Dada and Surrealist art on the upheaval of society and the varied new movements of the 1960s.

It was Rubin's view that since the 1950s there had been no true Dada or Surrealist art. Rather, these philosophies had been completely assimilated into all contemporary art. Man Ray, represented generously in the exhibition, would have agreed with Rubin that the art of the present day was greatly derivative of the old wave. The new built upon and incorporated the old.

The public was becoming more educated and sophisticated through exposure to instructive exhibitions and was at last coming to understand, in critic Harold Rosenberg's opinion, that "ignorance in the face of the artist's will was acceptable." Collectors began to believe in the importance of Man Ray's legacy. One such American, who soon joined the ranks of Roz Jacobs, Bill Copley, and Lucien Treillard as Man Ray's spiritual sons and daughters, was Arnold Crane, an attorney and photographer from Chicago.

The odor of tear gas, a residue of the May 1968 rioting, still hung heavy in the air when Crane arrived at Man Ray's doorstep, camera and tape recorder in hand, having walked the two and a half miles from les Invalides. Crane's original intent was to photograph and interview Man Ray as part of a book on great living photographers, and he did so. But conversations over the course of the next few months turned toward more businesslike matters, as Crane began gradually to purchase a stunning group of photographic works direct from the studio.

Arnold Crane was an inquisitive fellow, and Man Ray found his persistent interest appealing. The young man refused to be put off by Man Ray's disclaimers about photography. Their meetings were further helped along by their shared passion for fast cars— Man Ray was thrilled to measure his new Porsche 911-T against Crane's Ferrari. And Juliet, who seemed to feel more at ease with Crane than she did with others who knocked on the door of 2 bis, rue Férou, never left her husband's side during the visit. Between the two of them, Crane and Juliet were able to steer Man Ray off the track of his usual gripes. Once he had finished running through the list of his standard complaints, Man Ray succumbed willingly to Juliet's praise: "You are going to get the Nobel Prize," she whispered proudly to her husband. At one point in the conversation, as Man Ray reminisced about his unacknowledged early avant-garde works from the New York period, she interjected, "Well, now he is the father of all that," referring to the modern movement.

Over the course of several visits, Man Ray was unusually candid with Arnold Crane. He still did not feel Americans understood his work and probed for a reason. Perhaps they had a culturally inherent antipathy toward revolt of any kind. And he was forthcoming about some of the secrets of his techniques—from portraiture and rayography to solarization and clichés-verre. In all artistic situations, what preoccupied him the most, Man Ray told Arnold Crane, was the search for an interesting line, something "with an edge to it," fabricated through the use of light and chemicals instead of pigments and oil. The motivation that drove him to define a "fine-neutral zone" in solarizing a portrait was the same impulse pushing him when he executed the virtuosic drawings for *Les main libres* or the delicate filaments in the gelatin-coated glass plate of the cliché-verre. Portrait photographs, too, always began with the clearest lens possible, but in the darkroom, he would "throw the lens out of focus," manipulating features to make the image move from direct document of nature to translation.

Arnold Crane's collection of Man Ray's work grew to over 170 items: vintage rayographs, photographs from virtually every epoch of the artist's career, including a wide range of portraits, fascinating color-process experimental proofs dating from the early 1930s, clichés-verre, photo-collages, and books and ephemera from New York Dada days. At the heart of the Crane collection were most of the works exhibited in Man Ray's 1962 Bibliothèque Nationale show, "Man Ray, l'oeuvre photographique." Although a major photographic exhibition planned by Crane for spring 1970 in Chicago never materialized, the Milwaukee Art Center did present a show three years later spotlighting the entire group.

"To know Man is to love him," Crane reverently wrote. "He was the break away, the artist who did the New every day of his life . . . one of the cornerstones of all that has happened in art the past number of years." In his striking, high-contrast portrait photographs of the artist, Crane, like many other younger visitors, demonstrated his conviction that he was in the presence of a living legend. He photographed a dignified Man Ray, like a statue, cane in right hand, umbrella in left, wearing a fedora hat, dark suit, sweater, and string tie, his hair brushed forward Caesar-like. He caught him unsmiling, with a piercing, scowling stare, the solemnness so pronounced that the lines at the corners of Man Ray's mouth seemed etched. Crane also captured Man Ray in the studio, head slightly inclined, nattily attired, conspicuously showing off a shiny new pair of loafers, an unlit, expensive cigar in his hand. In another exposure, Man Ray held a giant, square magnifying glass in front of his face, distorting his features, once again for a split-second the *farceur* playing a visual joke upon the world.

Another spiritual son who entered Man Ray's sphere of influence at this time and stayed loyally associated with him for the last seven years of his life was Timothy Baum, a poet, writer, art collector, private dealer, and fiercely (if the occasion required it, even pugilistically) dedicated scholar of Dada who, in the summer of 1969, was engaged in the conclusion of an effort to track down the one hundred people in the world he most wanted to meet. Man Ray was among them.

During the preceding spring, Baum had mounted a show at the Noah Goldowsky Gallery in New York called "Dada, 291—1924" (a reference to the short-lived avant-garde gallery and the terminal date of the Dada movement). Philippe Soupault had sent a special, handwritten letter from Paris for the occasion, recalling how his colleagues were looked upon as "*aliénés*" by critics, journalists, academicians, pedagogues, "*les snobs,*" and the like, because "*Dada voulait faire table rasé*" (Dada wanted to make a clean slate). Its goal had been nothing less than to "change life itself."

In his brief introductory essay to the exhibition catalogue, Baum mounted a spirited and knowledgeable defense of Dada, as "never an underground movement whispered from one cellar or street corner to another." Rather, Baum advised his audience, Dada was "an inherent part of the contemporary culture right from its earliest days . . . well-attended by the choicest of gentlemen and critics."

Already a close friend of Richard Huelsenbeck, another Dada survivor and cofounder of the movement, Timothy Baum came to Man Ray well versed in its history and with a sense of Dada's current popularity. The two took to each other immediately. The hardworking artist made it clear that the basic values of his childhood in lower-middle-class Brooklyn still held sway— although, at the same time, he obstinately refused to talk about "family, religion, or sentimental topics" of any kind. Even the most fleeting references to ethnicity were shrugged off with the comment, "I am a Dadaist." Man Ray appeared to be democratically trusting and respectful of people who came to call, consumed by a naïve but not unnatural desire for attention and flattery. At times, therefore, because of his well-meaning nature, he was too easily exploited, especially by dealers eager to use Man Ray's name to their advantage.

Baum found a devoted husband who would not dream of dalliances behind Juliet's back; a man possessed with "an endless fountain of good humor, like a latter-day Mark Twain," despite the discomfort of his physical afflictions; an elderly man who still tried to walk around the city he loved, even if it meant using two canes, and who knew Paris backward and forward, down to the condition of the cobblestones.

In Baum's view, Man Ray did not simply take photographs— he created them. He did not use photography in the reductive sense;

rather, the medium took on new life in his hands, adding deeper character to his subjects' features. He did not have to think about employing the medium, because he himself *was* the medium. He was supremely "agile at making the most of very little." The rayograph was perhaps the pinnacle of Man Ray's photographic achievement, approaching automatic poetry in its unexpectedness and spontaneity.

Man Ray, photographer, was supposedly in retirement, yet Baum was present on occasions when an attractive woman might be visiting the studio for drinks and, in the wink of an eye, Man Ray would set to work, despite himself, effortlessly persuading her to relax, distracting her attention by talking smoothly about, say, the Calvados they were sipping (or, perhaps, it was the beloved decanter of Armagnac bottled in the year of his birth). Then, subtly, he would ask her to incline her head this way or that, all the while moving the floodlights into position, conjuring up a small camera as if from thin air, snapping the shutter as easily as breathing, and, in Baum's words, "integrating the photograph into the moment at hand."

Early in 1970, Arne Ekstrom put on a show at his New York gallery that paid serious tribute to Man Ray. Ekstrom was one of those old friends who never gave up trying to help Man Ray achieve respectability as a painter. The windowlike cover of the lavishly produced catalogue revealed a tipped-in color plate of the *Rope Dancer* and was scored four times down its outer edges with vertical lines to commemorate the artist's four-score years. Ekstrom sought to gather a strong selection of paintings, among them *Ramapo*, a Ridgefield study in light and shadow; the abstract, rarely seen *Symphony* of 1916, its cracked surface a symptom of Man Ray's hurried application of fresh layers of paint before the underpainting had a chance to dry; the monumental and foreboding wartime canvas, *Le beau temps;* the garishly red *Tempest,* part of the Shakespearean series done in Hollywood—Ekstrom kept this one for his personal collection; and, finally, the haunting *La rue Férou,* lent for the occasion by Sam Siegler.

Ekstrom's heart was in the right place. The exhibition was intimate and well focused, a noble attempt to infuse a checkerboard sixty-year career with coherence. Predictably, hardly anything was for sale, making the show seem hermetic and self-contained, like

Man Ray's little world in the Sixth Arrondissement. Any coherence the exhibition achieved remained undetected by the critics who bothered to come. *New York Magazine* decided, in frighteningly familiar language, that ". . . things didn't really add up," predicting further that "Man Ray [would] undoubtedly go down in history as a clever, mildly outrageous artist who never quite found himself."

In a conversation with Sanche de Gramont in Vence the following summer, Man Ray poignantly revealed his awareness that time was running out: "My mind races," he said. "Manet died with a brush tied to his arthritic fingers. It's a lifelong habit. I have to invent." For the aging artist, work was a hedge against mortality—each new creation a victory over the inevitability of death yet another day.

Time was also running out for members of Man Ray's family eager to visit with him even after decades of estrangement. Loving sister Do never did get to see the studio on rue Férou. For his part, on occasional forays to New York, it was difficult for brother Man to arrange side trips to Elkins Park or even to phone his sister. Over the years, Man Ray and Do found it simpler to exchange brief cards and letters, most often around the time of each other's birthday. She would send packages of clothes in August, and he fell into the habit of sending "stray checks" or "little paintings" as close to December as he could.

A dutiful uncle, Man Ray reported on his discovery of a street in the Sixteenth Arrondissement immortalizing Florence Blumenthal, an American philanthropist who had lived in Paris during the 1920s and 1930s. Surely his niece would be thrilled to hear she had such an illustrious precursor with the same name. Man Ray thanked Do for always having been such "a patient darling" with him, warning her at the same time not to give any interviews or information about him to anyone, especially the press.

Niece Helen Faden, brother Sam's daughter, heard the same words of caution when she finally succeeded, over her uncle's protestations, in entering the studio early in 1971. "Promise me you'll never give any family history to the newspapers," Man Ray cautioned the niece he had not laid eyes on since his departure for Paris fifty years before. At the center of a space that looked to her rather like a garage, she saw an old man, his back now curved from scoliosis (hunched over, the way her poor father had been), dressed in a beret, a loosely fitting blouse decorated with a shoestring tie, and a shawl wrapped around his waist.

It was chilly in the room. Helen had expected grander, more prepossessing quarters. At first, Man Ray was polite but distant, shaking her hand in formal greeting, gesturing to the couch, asking Helen to please sit down. She had brought family pictures along— of her father (Sam and Man had once been so close); and her mother, the beautiful, dark-haired Lena; and of an intense, slight boy on the brink of manhood, dressed in his new bar mitzvah suit, wearing the traditional skullcap and sacred tallith. It was Emmanuel. Man Ray seized the photograph and suddenly put his arm around Helen, pressing her to him. "Ah, this is so nostalgic!" the old man sighed, warming to the moment. He wanted to keep this picture. He did not say why. In exchange, Man Ray gave Helen a photo of Kiki, symbol of another past life. The visit stretched on for a long time. And when Helen finally left, her uncle Man kissed her.

MAN RAY. *LA RUE FÉROU*, 1952. OIL. *Private collection.*

THE LIGHT
AND THE
DARK

MAN RAY was entering his eighties. European museum curators realized time was running out for them, as well. In November 1971, a monumental retrospective of 278 works was launched at the Boymans–van Beuningen Museum in Rotterdam, eleven rooms full of every conceivable species of Man Ray creation. Most exciting to the artist, the plan was to tour the show to the Musée Nationale de l'Art Moderne in Paris, then to the Louisiana Museum in Humlebaek, Denmark, and finally, in triumph, across the seas to the Philadelphia Museum of Art. With the tantalizing prospect once again of a big show in his hometown, Man Ray asked Naomi to begin helping him "recuperate" (*sic*) all works belonging to him so that the exhibition would be the broadest and most representative ever. His anticipation was short-lived. The Philadelphia Museum decided it did not have the funds to bring Man Ray's show to America.

"My hands are full with Europe," Man Ray was forced to rationalize, once more rebuffed. Turning his back on America, he warmly welcomed Jean-Hubert Martin, the young curator from the Musée Nationale de l'Art Moderne who would be managing the Paris show. It was a pleasure to plan for the opening with such an intelligent and imaginative fellow, one who had tracked the course of Man Ray's career with dedication. Man Ray made no attempt to conceal his delight at having been approached by the museum. It felt good not to have to fight for the privilege of showing there, but, rather, to be recognized as a national treasure.

Coming to the rue Férou for the first time, Martin had assumed Man Ray would be dogmatic about his instructions for the show. But the artist was flexible and gave the curator complete freedom in the installation, making it clear that he very much wanted to be understood by his audience. To assist that public comprehension, Martin came up with a creative solution to the perennial problem of showing Man Ray's objects. Fearful of imprisoning them in enclosed vitrines, which would effectively destroy their impact, rendering them passive and unnecessarily sacred, Martin thought to put them on high, wide tables, exposed, safely just out of reach but more visible without intervening glass.

The show was an overnight success when it opened in early January 1972, and its massive catalogue sold out immediately. The stress of preparation during the harsh winter season put the artist in bed for two weeks the following month with a bronchial infection, but not before he had summoned up the energy to sound off one more time in defense of eclecticism. "I have no style," Man Ray told the assembled press at the opening, smoking a big cigar, sporting a *chemise de cowboy*, staring at them with big eyes through thick glasses, looking very much the wise old owl, "I am afraid of being bored. . . . Serious," he mused, "Now that's a word I crossed out of my vocabulary. . . ." Man Ray even found time to show off his newest creations at a parallel exhibition in his favorite bookstore, La Hune, next door to the Café Flore on the boulevard St. Germain. They were pen-and-ink drawings called "*anatoms,*" half men, half beasts, which would, the artist noted, probably only prove to be of interest to the sole people left in the world still harboring a fascination with anatomy, "sportsmen, doctors, and lovers."

Anatoms were soon followed in Man Ray's parade of late-life inventions by *Les voies lactées* (Milky Ways), which he whimsically said were "discovered while drinking buttermilk." This suite of eleven photographs published in ten proofs under the Atelier Man Ray imprint once again elicited a response of "How did he do it?" among intrigued viewers. The images looked like curdled tributaries, parallel dark rivulets leading nowhere, or mysterious cross-sections of a blanched tree trunk.

In June 1974, as Man Ray was perfecting his "Milky Way"

technique and preparing for yet another major exhibition, this one
to be held at the New York Cultural Center on Columbus Circle, he
received word from family in Philadelphia that news articles had
begun to appear reporting he had died in Paris a few months earlier.
The "out of sight, out of mind" specter haunting him since the war
had reached its fullest implications. "The sad news of my demise is
exaggerated," Man Ray told Naomi, invoking the words of Mark
Twain. On the contrary, he was proud to report, he was working
harder than ever with the devoted, skillful Lucien Treillard,
managing a veritable cadre of gallery owners and craftsmen.

Man Ray was now more capable than ever before of influencing the shape of his bigger shows. Mario Amaya, the new, young
director of the New York Cultural Center, met Man Ray at a time
when the artist was feeling particularly rejected—"snubbed," he
told Naomi—by America. But when Amaya came up with the idea
of a huge show in New York, with Roland Penrose as co-organizer,
Man Ray concurred, knowing from a pragmatic standpoint this
would be the first of its kind in the city. However, he refused to lend
anything from the studio and insisted that Amaya instead seek out
private collectors throughout the States who owned Man Rays.
Amaya, also a Brooklynite, described Man Ray as "testy, crusty,
wasp-tongued," speaking "in short sentences and usually incorporating some outrageous pun delivered with a faint Brooklyn
accent."

The conflicting responses to Man Ray's New York show, when
it opened in spring 1974, demonstrated that, along with the aging
artist himself, critical confusion was very much alive. John Russell
and Hilton Kramer, writing for the *New York Times* within three
weeks of one another, exemplified the contrary perceptions of Man
Ray. Russell, newly arrived at his post from the *Times* of London,
pointed out that most followers of modern art would be hard-
pressed to say who Man Ray was, where he was at any given time,
what he did, or when he did it, and noted further that Man Ray was
largely responsible for this difficulty because he was "so adept at
covering his tracks and generally throwing an admirer off the
scent." Russell nonetheless recognized Man Ray as the premier
portrait photographer of the century, even though it was evident
that a great many photographs had been held back from this and
other exhibitions. Russell also defined him as a nonpareil "poetical
tease, all-purpose allusionist and commentator on the day's preoc-

cupations." In short, he was "one of the most remarkable Americans of his generation."

To Hilton Kramer, Man Ray's early canvases, admired by so many and a source of pride to the artist as well, were little more than "accomplished rehearsals of Post-Impressionist modalities," content to assert the "standard theme" of figures in a landscape "without significant modifications." Kramer believed that Man Ray had to be evaluated through the lens of Duchamp. The author of an unsigned article in *ARTnews* agreed that "Duchamp does more than cast a shadow on his friend's work; he totally eclipses it."

Eight months before Man Ray's death, Harold Rosenberg joined the fray, writing of him as an "American vanguardist," grouping him in the same august company as Joseph Stella, Charles Demuth, Marsden Hartley, and Stuart Davis. It was a very important identification. Although he always resented his native land, insisting that his work remained critically misunderstood there (and in large measure he was correct), and although Man Ray's bearing and orientation were perhaps more cosmopolitan than local, a profusion of elements in his work and personality struck an inescapably American chord.

Man Ray had long had a succinct response for his various critics, positive and negative: "All opinion is transient," he wrote, "and all work is permanent." He well knew that the history of art is predicated upon exhibitions, major commissions, and monographs. When the artist does not gain the right kind of attention from these expected modes but seeks, instead, to hew his own path through the decades, he runs the risk of falling outside the purview of history as it is being composed. The critic and the art historian become "uncomfortable," to use Serge Bramly's apt term, in his 1980 memoir *Bon Soir, Man Ray,* when they cannot classify an artist. They become frustrated when there is no clear track of development in an artist's career.

The irony of this continuing historical dilemma in Man Ray's life was compounded by a sudden, accelerated interest in photography among art galleries in the mid-seventies. By late 1977, the market for contemporary photographs had come completely alive. The collector Jacob Deschin was not alone in his view that photography was "the new art form." He predicted that "photographers [would] now have more money than they've ever had before." Escalating prices had made graphics and paintings out of reach, and photographs now became a nonelitist way into the art market for beginners. The pursuit was all the more exciting because so many of the modern masters who had put the art on the map were still flourishing. However, Man Ray continued to place prohibitions on the exhibition of his photographic works, and he turned down documentary and fashion assignments from most of the major feature magazines. Forward-looking American dealers—Harry Lunn, Lee Witkin, Joyce Schwartz, Janet Lehr, and Tennyson Schad—began to purchase vintage photographs even as Man Ray continued to insist he no longer had old works available for sale. Museum curators pleaded with Man Ray to no avail for an opportunity to buy more photographs. At the end of his life, Man Ray paradoxically succeeded in avoiding financial success through the sale of his photographs in a revitalized market.

The New York Cultural Center retrospective traveled to London and a triumphant opening in the spring of 1975 at the Institute for Contemporary Art on the Mall near Buckingham Palace. Founder-director Sir Roland Penrose had wanted so much to present this show by his friend Man Ray, and one to follow by Max Ernst, before he retired from the chairmanship. Man Ray and Juliet flew over from Paris for the occasion.

It was an evening replete with nostalgia. Surrounded by milling crowds of visitors, the artist sat in a wheelchair, immobile, white-haired, dressed in a dark suit and string tie, a wan smile on his lips. Those who wanted to speak with Man Ray had to crouch down, as if kneeling before him. And there was Lee Miller, known now as Lady Lee, sharing confidences with her old teacher and lover, looking deep into his eyes with the intent, blue stare she had never lost.

The passage of time and the onslaught of depression, drugs, and drink had taken a ruthless toll on Lee. An underlying boredom had set in after the end of her glory days as a war correspondent for *Vogue,* but she and Roland had fought loneliness by establishing a lively domestic scene at Farley Farm. The couple specialized in bringing groups of people together and creating excitement from their personal chemistries. In the kitchen of the main house, Lee entertained a flow of weekend guests who would sip endless cups of tea, read the newspapers, and listen to her declaim about the state of the world. She labored and performed with her back to her visitors, her close-cropped hair covered with an ever present scarf, concocting complex gourmet meals at a six-burner stove and occasionally putting her guests to work, too, even if just to peel potatoes, or the beloved Macintosh apples she missed so dearly, imported from her native upstate New York by American friends. Lee's library of more than two thousand cookbooks and her apprenticeship and friendship with James Beard, combined with her sure genius, made dinner at Farley Farm a transcendent experience.

Man Ray and Juliet had been treated to Lee and Roland's hospitality often during the fifties and sixties. The visits never failed to inspire Man Ray, and he would invariably assemble snapshot-adorned scrapbook-letters upon his return to Paris, then send them along to the Penroses, especially to little Tony's delight. But those days were now lost to memory. Lee would soon discover she had terminal cancer, just as Tony's wife, Suzanna, became pregnant with Lee's first grandchild.

After a brief stay in London, Man Ray and Juliet flew back to Paris for a rest, then, in July, they were off to Rome for the opening of the third stop of the exhibition, at the Palazzo delle Esposizioni. Dealer-friend Luciano Anselmino sent a private jet for their trip and put them up for a month in a villa at Fregene, twenty minutes outside the city, by the sea, where Juliet could swim to her heart's content. Man Ray had to be satisfied by fine cigars and quiet conversations with visiting friends. He wore sunglasses that clipped over his prescription lenses, so he could flip them up, visorlike, at will, the better to gaze out over the water.

"I made some new drawings," he wrote Naomi, "where the trembling lines are considered very sensitive." The tenuous shapes and shadows were not deliberate, but the consequence of painful arthritis that prevented him from holding the pencil firmly. But he kept at it, in the summer sun.

Shadows now populated Man Ray's works, reminders of the past, intimations of a dwindling future, as he became increasingly obsessed with chiaroscuro. In his last drawings, shadows cling tenaciously to sparse, twiglike shapes, thinly sketched and ephemeral as if depicting a soul reluctant to leave the stubborn body. And in his last *déchirages,* collages made from torn paper, black crosses cut through pristine white backdrops like images of angry death attempting to prevail over resistant life. Until the end, Man Ray struggled with light and dark, returning to the most fundamental

MAX ERNST, M. JEAN, ROZ JACOBS, MAN RAY,
DOROTHEA TANNING, AND JULIET MAN RAY CELEBRATING
SURPRISE BIRTHDAY FOR JULIET AT LA MÉDITERRANÉE
RESTAURANT, PARIS, APRIL 1971.
Collection Mr. and Mrs. Melvin Jacobs.

materials and away from the convenience of photography. In his last letter to Naomi, Man Ray once more shrugged off the camera and its uses, referring casually to "photo... You see, I am even impatient with spelling out the word. . . . You cannot apply the same standards to photography as to the other graphic works."

Day in, day out, the bells of the Mairie on place St. Sulpice struck the hours in high tones, against the deeper song of cathedral bells across the way, as the fountain continued its endlessly rushing murmur. Man Ray and Juliet tried to follow a consistent routine. On the infrequent days when they did not share luncheon at Chez Alexandre, under the solicitous care of M and Mme Mimola, there was always La Méditerranée, over near the Odéon, La Coupole, or Brasserie Lipp and Café Flore on boulevard St. Germain. It was difficult for Man Ray to go much farther afield: "These cobble-stones were made for horses, not for men," he complained to Juliet as he felt hard surfaces under the thin soles of his shoes. Man Ray built up an astonishing collection of walking sticks and canes—his favorite had a handle shaped like a dog's head—which he kept in the rue Férou vestibule for ready access. Over time, their decorative function had become far less important than their physical one. Man Ray often needed to use two canes and, one in each hand, he would hobble across the cobblestones of the place St. Sulpice. His calves and lower legs ached from shortage of blood, and he would have to pause every few steps.

Dressed most frequently all in black, his back bent, the glint in his eye still apparent as he peered up over the top of his glasses, the thread of a smile still on his lips, Man Ray leaned on his wife's arm with ever greater weight. A pleasure jaunt had become an ordeal, but, ever the proud jokester, he lightly cautioned sympathetic passersby that appearances were deceiving: although it looked as if she were propping him up, Juliet was in fact leaning on *his* arm, he would say with a smile. When others tried to help him, to grasp his elbow as a curbside neared, he reacted vehemently. "I can help myself!" was his response. Toward the very end, Man Ray found he needed to take a taxi just to cover the hundred yards from his studio to the Mimolas' restaurant on rue des Canettes.

One day, proceeding slowly forward, the couple encountered Max Ernst and Dorothea Tanning walking on the square, similarly linked. "It seems all the Surrealists' legs are giving out at the same time," Man Ray observed to his old friend. Ernst died on April 1,

1976, in his flat on the rue de Lille, after nearly a year in bed following a massive stroke. "Something has gone wrong," Dorothea wrote in her journal, once the interminable vigil by her husband's side had come to an end, "There is no light in the studio, nothing moves and the colored jokes are stale."

To make circumstances more convenient for themselves, Man Ray and Juliet set up housekeeping in a two-room, centrally heated apartment on the rue de la Chaise, just across the boundary in the Seventh Arrondissement, perpendicular to the rue de Varenne and a few minutes' walk from the studio. It was sparsely furnished and modern, yet Man Ray managed to impose his stylistic stamp. In one corner of the main room, he set up a huge, unprimed stretched canvas, six feet by four. "I've hauled it around from one place to the other for the past fifteen years," he told a visitor, "and the more I look at it, the more finished it seems." In another corner, a *porte-bouteille* bore a striking resemblance to Duchamp's readymade bottle rack. Juliet had found it discarded in the street. Upon its prongs were hung "Mr. and Mrs. Woodman," Man Ray's whimsical assemblage of miniature dummies posed for anatomical study. The rack was crowned by a bust of the Marquis de Sade editioned from Man Ray's notable *Imaginary Portrait*. The rue de la Chaise flat was a welcome concession to Juliet, a cozy defense against the long winter chill, a place to answer letters and receive visitors without having to huddle shivering, dressed in overcoats, around a kerosene stove.

But even in the dead of winter a daily visit to the rue Férou studio was obligatory. During the spring and summer months of 1976 Man Ray insisted upon being there, although he was now almost always in bed in the back room, behind burlap curtains, under layers of blankets, his feet propped up with telephone books to aid the circulation. The geography of Man Ray's outer world had contracted severely, but the inner landscape of his mind was boundless as ever. Dressed "at home" in flannel shirts and cashmere towels wrapped around his waist, sometimes wearing gloves against morning chill (or to model examples of his handmade rings), Man Ray could lie for hours staring into space, or watching color television not for its content but, rather, to manipulate the colors, which intrigued him; playing "Scrambled Word Games" in the *International Herald Tribune,* or chess with himself; smoking a pipe, a sketchbook on his lap, just in case a new idea came along, not

ABOVE: LA RUE FÉROU STUDIO, MARCH 1983. WORKS BY
MAN RAY INCLUDE DANGER/DANCER, 1920; LE BEAU
TEMPS, 1939; LE VIOLON D'INGRES, 1924, AND THE LIPS,
1932–34. *Photograph by Ira Nowinski.*

LEFT: LA RUE FÉROU STUDIO, MARCH 1983. WORKS BY
MAN RAY INCLUDE REPRODUCTION OF LA RUE FÉROU,
1952; AND LE MANCHE DANS LA MANCHE, 1967 EDITION FOR
MARCEL ZERBIB. PHOTOGRAPH OF JULIET'S SISTER,
SELMA, IS BY NAOMI SAVAGE.
Photograph by Ira Nowinski.

idle, always thinking, he assured everyone. Women friends were especially welcome to come behind the curtain into the intimate half darkness, sit on the edge of the bed, and listen to Man Ray talk. His conversation was a strange mélange of reminiscence and projection, of humility and wit, humor and sarcasm—but lucid, always incisive, in the perfectly precise French vocabulary he'd acquired.

On August 27, 1976, Man Ray celebrated his eighty-sixth birthday, a double commemoration, for he had received the Order of Artistic Merit from the French government that week. Juliet arranged an intimate party with two other couples. She served smoked salmon and for dessert a chocolate cake in the shape of a heart. Always fond of dressing up, Man Ray, in an ebullient mood that night, donned a curly blond wig for the occasion.

In the fall, weakening, Man Ray could not bear to limit the parade of visitors distracting him from his thoughts of infirmity. Roz Jacobs spent an afternoon with her old friend. Looking up at her, reading to Roz from a *New Yorker* profile of Gandhi, Man Ray was amused to discover than in advanced age the great man slept with fifteen-year-old girls next to him, to prove he could maintain the discipline of celibacy. Man Ray rose laboriously from bed and guided Roz to a secret shelf to show her his collection of matchboxes containing coins from the different countries in Europe where he had traveled: England, Germany, Italy, the Netherlands. He showed her the one-thousand-dollar bill he had saved as a souvenir, payment for a painting sold long ago. There were bureau drawers stuffed with cash. Man Ray was in a disparaging mood, playing upon the irony of the situation: "When Julie and I were hungry, this money wasn't here. It's all come too late," he told her, softly. "I don't know what to do with this now. I've forgotten how to spend it."

Late October, David and Naomi phoned, as they had been doing more frequently, to ask how Man was faring. David was on the line first. The two men chatted about family affairs. How were the children, Lourie (who carried resonances of Minnie Ray's maiden name) and Michael, Man Ray wanted to know. Naomi spoke with her dear uncle. The gruff warmth was there, but beneath it she heard the rumble of phlegm and congestion in the lungs: "Listen," Man Ray said, "it's old age. There's nothing you can do about it." That was the last time she heard his voice.

■ ■ ■

Even as he grew weaker with each passing day, every movement cause for pain, Man Ray requested that Lucien Treillard
continue to come to the studio for their afternoon work sessions.
These had of late become little more than discussions about plans
for projects to be initiated and books to be written. Man Ray
directed Lucien to "get his house in order," arranging files in the
studio, repairing the roof, and generally refining details in the
complex environment. Piles of papers, sketches, schematic drawings, and so on were strewn about Man Ray's coverlet and arranged
on the makeshift writing table he had built, which could swing out
over his lap with the touch of a finger as he lay in bed. His voice low,
Man Ray looked up when Juliet slipped out for her customary
afternoon walk, "Now don't you go too far," he would caution her;
while to his young friend Lucien, he would turn and say, "Don't
worry. There's still plenty of work to do."

In mid-November, complaining of shortness of breath and
feeling feeble, Man Ray was secretly taken to a small, private
clinique in the suburbs, where Lucien and Juliet hoped to avoid the
attention of the press. There he shared a room with a teenage boy
and the two amused themselves by counting their pulses along with
the attending nurse. An X ray revealed large, dark patches in Man
Ray's lungs, filled with fluid.

After three days in the hospital, Man Ray told Lucien he
wanted to go home. It was clear the end was coming. Lucien phoned
Juliet from the artist's bedside and told her to prepare for his arrival.
He drove Man Ray back to the rue Férou, laid him gently in bed
behind the curtain, and left.

The next day, November 18, when Juliet awoke, her husband
was struggling for breath. She held him and comforted him as best
she could. In the late morning, Man Ray died in the studio where he
had spent the last quarter century of his life.

It was predawn in New York. Desperate to make contact with
someone, Juliet called Naomi and David in Princeton. There was
no answer. Later she found out they had been on holiday in Puerto
Rico. Juliet then tried to reach Timothy Baum. His number was
unlisted. By the third call, she found and awoke Roberta Kimmel.
Juliet sounded calm. She was not crying, and in fact she later told
friends she couldn't cry for a year after Man Ray died, so deep was
her grief. Roberta asked if she should catch a plane that day and
come to the funeral. Juliet said no, it would be small and private,

according to Man's wishes. He did not believe in rituals. No ceremony was planned. Roberta understood. Instead, she sent calla lilies, flowers usually displayed at weddings in France. Man Ray had loved them and photographed them often in their white, arched glory.

Roberta Kimmel had only just seen Man Ray in Paris a month earlier. After her visit to the studio, he had summoned the strength to walk her out to the street. Leaning on two canes, standing on the sloping sidewalk, he had watched fixedly as she departed down the hill toward St. Sulpice and lunch. "*Bon appétit!*" he shouted after her. Now, remembering clearly Juliet's fear that Man Ray might be forgotten after his death—even though he often remarked that posterity had no meaning for him, that he hoped someday to be unknown and anonymous, and found comfort in the thought—Roberta deliberated a long time that morning with her husband, Richard Cohn, about the appropriate course of action to take with her news. Finally, she called the *New York Times.*

The next morning, a photograph of Man Ray, unsmiling as usual, graced the *Times'* front page. He would surely have been pleased at being described as a "painter and photographer," with painter noted first. He would have been pleased at having virtually monopolized the obituary page, with three well-known icons of his long career—*MCMXIV, Cadeau,* and *Violon d'Ingres*—making a fine triptych. He might have been less pleased at the descriptions of "Mr. Ray," as "elfin" and "impish." However, Alden Whitman's respectful and thorough homage did succeed in summarizing the high points of Man Ray's career, emphasizing his innovative, inventive, and experimental nature, and stressing with finality that Man Ray did not—would not—belong to any stylistic movement or school of thought, remaining the resolute outsider who lived long enough to see his notions become absorbed into the mainstream of modern art.

To the right of the page, there was a modest death notice (listed alphabetically, as Man Ray would have wanted, and always insisted upon, under *M,* not *R*), sent by Timothy Baum, in loving tribute—and in memory of the late-August birthday they shared—to the original founding member of "The International Virgo Dada Club."

▪ ▪ ▪

There was an intimate group in attendance at Man Ray's funeral in the Cimetière du Montparnasse. Lucien was there, of course, and Gertrude Neher (Man Ray and Juliet's constant friend from the American embassy), as well as old pals Peter Lyon, Marcel Zerbib, and Jack Mayer. Afterward, all walked slowly down to Chez Alexandre for lunch. It seemed the only place to go.

Juliet was resolutely quiet and dry-eyed that day. Man Ray, who always made the decisions, had never gotten around to telling her what sort of adornment, if any, he wanted on his grave. His widow left it unmarked for the time being. There had barely been enough room in the Seventh Division of the cemetery, bounded by the avenue de l'Ouest and the allée des Sergeants de la Rochelle, hemmed in between the far more elaborate plots of the Familles de Pascal et Alexandre—a sepulcher adorned with a stained-glass window and a wrought-iron Christ in final agony—and the Famille Lagriffoul's massive, gray marble tombstone. Fields of marble stretched out on all sides, a city of marble. Man Ray, in death, stood out, covered merely by raw, untended earth. Had not his idol, the Marquis de Sade—baptized, it so happened, at the Church of St. Sulpice—written in his last will and testament that he wanted to be thus unceremoniously buried in a ditch? Once he was covered over, Sade told his survivors, they should scatter acorns upon the site, so that it would soon become green again. Bushes and grass would obliterate all traces of him from the face of the earth, "as I trust the memory of me shall fade out from the minds of all men," Sade wrote, except for "those few who in their goodness have loved me until the last and of whom I carry away a sweet remembrance with me to the grave."

Eventually, a plain, plywood, shield-shaped sign affixed to a weathered stake was placed into the ground, white lettering proclaiming simply, ambiguously, "Man Ray—86 ans—1976." Every few months, a faithful artist friend came by to touch up the lettering with her nail polish. Occasionally, visitors picking their way among the tombstones placed a scattering of wildflowers upon the patchy moss.

MAN RAY'S GRAVE AT THE
CIMETIÈRE DU MONTPARNASSE,
NOVEMBER 1984.
Photograph by Neil Baldwin.

P O S T S C R I P T

NEARLY A DECADE later, on a chilly afternoon toward the end of March during one of my Paris sojourns, Juliet Man Ray and I were sitting in the living room of her comfortable new flat overlooking the Jardin de Luxembourg on the rue d'Assas. It had rained all week. From our vantage point on the third floor, through wide windows, the trees lining the periphery of the park still stood fuzzy gray, just barely beginning to bud. Groundkeepers methodically raked the flower beds, occasionally looking upward as clouds drifted across the slate-blue sky. Crowds of schoolchildren headed home with faint bursts of laughter. It was a drowsy time, after lunch, and we spent the hour chatting in a desultory way. Juliet was curled up on the sofa underneath a huge blue-and-white Man Ray painting, *Piscinema,* of 1951, actually an upside-down Rorschach-like relief portrait of herself and her husband. Suddenly, she peered across the room at me through her thick glasses and said, "Shall we visit Man's grave?"

We set off arm in arm through the narrow streets that flowed like tributaries to the broad and teeming boulevard Montparnasse. Juliet had to walk slowly; her eyes had been bad for years—and her back was bothering her, because of the humidity. She was wrapped in a bulky sweater, a scarf tied around her curly hair and, stepping carefully and delicately along the pavement, she seemed almost catlike, hardly speaking except to point out a familiar building (Modigliani's studio, the Académie Julian, Lefevre-Foinet's shop, Ezra Pound's apartment). She would nudge me in the right direction with the slightest pressure of her hand on my elbow. We shared this silence as we had a multitude of others over the past few years. Now, my long labor nearly ended, I had come to know and be comforted by her silences, no longer as impenetrable as I once believed them to be.

We stopped at a florist's shop on the boulevard. Juliet selected a pot of miniature geraniums. The woman behind the counter asked us if we were on our way to the cemetery. Yes, I replied. She offered her trowel to help us plant the flowers. I thanked her, promising to return it.

A guard watched us through the massive iron gates of the Cimetière du Montparnasse; he bowed slightly from the waist, and Juliet, who loved the courtliness of men, acknowledged his politeness with a little murmur of delight. It was difficult to find the grave, even with the landmark she had long ago picked—two stone lions indicating the approach to the Seventh Division was near, way over on the right-hand side of the grounds. Juliet fidgeted nervously on the paved path while I scrambled among the tombstones looking for a telltale gap in the marble. Suddenly, like an afterthought, there was the humble wooden marker. I beckoned Juliet over. She sat down unceremoniously on a polished marble slab nearby and pulled a pack of Gitanes from the pocket of her cardigan, tearing it open, lighting up, and taking a deep, deep draw, chuckling with relief.

I stood there, looking at her, then down at the ground covering Man Ray. It was hard and scrabbly with bits of hardy grass, littered with the dried remains of forgotten bouquets. Silence again, except for the harsh wind. I raised my collar and gripped the front of my jacket, wavering, not quite certain what to do next. "Well, dear, don't you want to ask him any questions?" Juliet said to me. "Now is your chance." I shook my head and knelt down to plant the geraniums—as I did so, feeling the movement was a gesture of homage. I dug a hole quickly, tugged the plant from the pot, and placed it in the earth, patting the soil in place. Bright red blooms touched the wooden sign. I stood up again, noticing the dark, damp patches on each of my knees, brushing bits of dirt from my trousers.

"I'm seriously thinking of putting a headstone there," she said between puffs on her second cigarette, "a version of Man's sculpture, *L'oeuf plat.* I've been considering doing that for a while ..." I knew Juliet was ambivalent about marking the grave and that she probably feared violating Man's wishes. But the tenth anniversary of his death was approaching in November. It seemed the right time to do something, and I said so. She did not reply, merely smiled, and I saw for an instant the smile that graced old photographs from Hollywood days—Juliet drenched in sunlight, her head tilted back, teeth gleaming, her long, thin fingers holding the brim of a straw hat; Juliet in the backyard among a surreal assortment of debris, reading a book as if the world were passing her by and she did not care; Juliet looking up with admiration at her expressionless husband (why did he never smile when his picture was taken?).

We walked back to her place in silence, by the same route we had come. A mother passed by, pushing one child in a stroller, another strapped to her back. My mind flashed to my own children at home in New York. Juliet said, as if hearing my thoughts, "How are your children?" She often asked after them. I wondered why she never had children of her own—but dared not inquire.

This scenario had been played out before countless times in my relationship with Juliet. Often finding myself (as biographer, after all) on the verge of formally interviewing her about Man Ray and their life together, I refrained, as if she were signaling me that it would be fruitless. I was able to count on the fingers of one hand, not much further, the fragmentary, unsolicited statements she had made about him directly to me. The very first time we spoke, I had phoned her from London two years earlier, unable to get across to Paris that trip, still wanting to make contact. She had been cordial and distant. I later realized it was shyness. She had simply reminded me, as if I didn't know full well, that I "couldn't write that book without [her], you know."

I finally did meet Juliet the following summer at Naomi and David Savage's house in Princeton. When I arrived, heart pounding, Juliet was sitting by the pool, her hair wet, having just emerged from a long swim. I was impressed first by how thin and fragile she seemed in the simple, flowered shift she was wearing, and by the theatricality of the heart-shaped sunglasses pushed up onto her forehead to make room for a second pair of tinted prescription glasses. She did not offer very much that day, beyond casual comments about how "Man and I knew so-and-so quite well," or,

"Yes, we used to spend a lot of time with so-and-so and his wife." For most of our time together, I was trying to impress her with my background and experience—my suitability to write the book. She was not visibly moved, and spoke only when spoken to. But she did comment that Man Ray was "always an American," no matter where he lived and no matter how antagonistic he might have been toward his native land. "You must come to see me in Paris," she insisted, as an excuse for not saying more. "That's where I am most comfortable." It was offered like a challenge, as if to say, If you are really serious about Man Ray, you need to prove it.

Once in Paris, I soon discovered what she meant. Juliet Man Ray was a beloved figure in the Sixth and Seventh Arrondissements. One trip to the Café Flore was especially telling. She wore an exquisitely cut, dyed-green mink coat that afternoon and, as we entered arm in arm, the white-jacketed waiter kissed her hand and led us to the booth where she and her husband used to sit. At the center of the table was a silver bowl of peeled eggs. As I had a hot chocolate and Juliet sipped tea, several people came over to pay their respects to "Madame Man Ray." She took all the attention with grace; moreover, she expected it, for this was the limelight formerly occupied by her husband and now she represented him. Some observers suggested that Juliet even tried to imitate Man Ray. I did not agree. Rather, she was gathering what was her due. And why not? She had lived in Man Ray's shadow, albeit a loving one, for three decades. She had sacrificed her own needs and seen to his every desire so that he could work with the freedom required for his art. As we sat in the Flore, Juliet questioned me closely about the people I had seen that day: who had I interviewed, and what had they said to me? She was protecting Man Ray even now, and I tried to reassure her that no harsh words had been spoken, that my purpose remained objective in the pursuit of truth, that she need not fear my obstinacy—I was merely there to write the book that needed to be written.

Another day, we went out to lunch at Chez Alexandre, sitting, of course, at the booth just to the right of the entrance, Man Ray's traditional place next to the bar. We were joined by Lou Mollgaard, a young woman who had just finished writing a biography of Kiki. The two of us, enthusiastic authors, were comparing notes throughout the meal, engaged in animated conversation, trying to draw Juliet in. She was content to sit quietly next to me, apparently attentive, but saying nothing as Lou and I had a grand time regaling each other with stories about our respective subjects, agreeing that we had reached the point now where we were actually having dreams about them; surely that meant we were completely immersed in the work!

At one juncture in our conversation I asked Lou how old she was. A casual and harmless remark, I thought. The next evening, I was strolling through the Luxembourg Gardens with Juliet on her daily constitutional from the apartment to the studio, when she suddenly stopped in her tracks in the middle of a gravel path and said, "Neil, that really was quite improper of you, to inquire of Lou's age!" "When did I do that?" I asked, astonished by her acute recall. "Why, yesterday at lunch, darling, don't you remember?" I realized then that while Juliet at times gave the impression she was drifting away from the situation at hand, in fact she was very much present, very much a *presence* in the fullest sense of the word. Perhaps that was what comforted Man Ray during his long interior sessions, just the thought that she was there with him, no more or less

Our early sessions in the rue Férou studio were tense. Letting me in by opening three archaic, clinking locks, Juliet took her place on the couch and lit a cigarette, allowing me to roam and explore, but always tracking me with her eyes and ears, periodically asking, with more than a hint of suspicion in her voice, what I was doing, what I was touching. I kept telling myself that she had every right to be so vigilant, considering some of the scandalous things that had happened in the late 1970s after Man Ray died and the place was infiltrated by merchants and charlatans in search of a quick dollar. Like Man Ray, she knew the location and identity of every object in the studio and its sacredness to the place where it belonged. Even as I leafed reverently through photo albums, boxes of postcards, portfolios of prints, and folders filled to bursting with correspondence, all organized and arranged alphabetically, Juliet seemed to know what I was looking at. She was as familiar with this material— the flotsam and jetsam of Man Ray's life—as he himself had been. And she did not want anything displaced. She was adamant on this matter, her lips pursed, her feet planted firmly on the ground. The studio was a temple. To alter its makeup was to meddle with the memory of Man Ray. So be it.

Seasons passed. Juliet and I next caught up with each other at her suite in the Westbury Hotel, when she was in New York for a show of Man Ray's works at the Zabriskie Gallery. I found her surrounded by vases of flowers, the room in disarray, breakfast dishes still on the table though it was nearly lunchtime. She was in a gloomy and disoriented mood, besieged by the telephone (she preferred making calls to receiving them, and she was usually at it by early morning), unable to sort out legitimate visitors from opportunists. We watched television—or, more accurately, looked at it and listened to it—and chatted superficially while I waited for an appropriate moment to begin our interview, until it became clear there would not be one. The time was just not right. Her thoughts were on the exhibition. The Man Ray business was growing, and Juliet was responsible for attending to it.

There had been the usual last-minute customs technicalities to deal with, which had left her drained. The opening itself was a madhouse of bodies pressing together, a din of conversation mixed with a cloud of smoke. The works, *Objects of My Affection,* delicate and subtle, were further diminished by the mob. Juliet made an entrance about an hour into the evening, wearing a floor-length gown with a Man Ray eye motif, mingled and shook hands for a while, then retired to a back room, where she sat and received visitors. I shook her hand but felt distinctly extraneous that night.

Undaunted, I followed her to Hollywood the next summer, where she was staying with old friends for several weeks. I would conduct my usual grueling gamut of interviews with artists, dealers, and collectors who had known Man Ray and Juliet, then drive over to see her around five o'clock, and we would take a swim together. She was relaxed and open, chatting easily with me between strokes and glides across the pool shaded by huge trees. She remembered Hollywood days with clear happiness, how she and Man Ray would go to hear jazz late at night, driving along beneath the palm trees. And there were the parties in Malibu and up in the hills! And the time she jumped into someone's swimming pool with all her clothes on, and the times when she would think nothing of taking all her clothes off and doing the same. She had not wanted to leave Hollywood, pastel dreamland of tanned bodies and cool waters, pungent air and summer lawns and tall drinks and casual talk—dreaded moving halfway across the world to a gray city where she did not speak the language and knew no one, where the seasons were so unpredictable.

It grew late, the balmy heat lifted, and the moment came when

I would gently tell Juliet I had to be getting back to my hotel. I'd been out on the road all day; my throat was sore from asking questions of people, my hand tired from taking notes. She grew sad, even panicked; Juliet hated to be alone. The very thought of someone departing threw her into tremulous despair. I felt a twinge of regret as I kissed her on both cheeks, promised to phone her first thing the next morning, eased my car down the driveway, and looked back at her forlorn, slight figure in the shadows.

ACKNOWLEDGMENTS

T H E B I O G R A P H E R ' S particular compulsion is toward the impossible goal of completeness—the desire to read every letter, view every work, find the spirit of every place, talk with every friend and acquaintance of the artist, and thus come to know him exhaustively. As my writing progressed over the past five years and I delved ever deeper, more hidden passages opened up: Man Ray's life turned out to be a palimpsest, layer upon layer of secrets. A stray reference in a handwritten note led me to a person I had never heard of; an unexpected conversation in a café led me to a collector with a cache of unknown photographs; a caption in an auction catalogue, oddly enough, led me to the correct address of one of the artist's friends in Montmartre. Late-night telephone calls turned into marathons of reminiscence by long-silent aficionados, who asked after one another through me. The trail became splintered with sidelines and shortcuts.

I came to depend more frequently upon the support of Man Ray's widow, Juliet Man Ray. From her very first reply to my speculative introductory query—how she viewed the proposal that I, or anyone, would want to write a biography of her husband—Juliet was obliging, cooperative, tough at times, but always fair. She made letters and manuscripts freely available, set up interviews on the spot with the aid of her densely packed Rolodex, and was always thinking about new connections she wanted me to make. Juliet and I both knew that Man Ray would have at best grudgingly sanctioned an effort such as mine. Had he not approached his own history as a massive *tabula rasa*? Still, she understood and accepted my clear need to write the book. I thank her for that quiet laissez-faire spirit.

I also thank Mme Man Ray's administrative assistant, Jerome Gold. He was responsible for making me feel at home on my first and subsequent visits to Paris, seeing to it that my hotel room was well situated, my research needs were met, my detailed schedule of meetings came together as planned—and that I did not lose my way in expensive restaurants. He has done much to set Man Ray's affairs in order.

Naomi Savage, the artistically gifted niece of Man Ray who learned the craft of photography side by side with her loving uncle, has selflessly given me countless hours of her good-humored and energetic support. We sat together in her Princeton studio on many a Saturday afternoon, drinking coffee, as she thought back over the decades of her close relationship with Man Ray and shared her valuable insights about him as a complex artist and personality. Naomi offered me complete access to the fascinating correspondence spanning more than thirty years, between her mother, Elsie Ray Siegler, and Man Ray, a body of writing that helps support one of the core themes of this book. She also opened up her complete collection of Man Ray's works to my examination, and skillfully reproduced many of the photographs included here. Naomi's husband, David, joined our conversation sessions on several occasions, giving his own trenchant insights into Man Ray as a modernist force. I am grateful to the Savages for their very early encouragement and faithful hospitality, carrying me through dark and difficult spots in the making of this biography.

I would also like to thank Man Ray's surviving sister, Do Ray Goodbread, and her daughter, another niece of the artist, Florence Blumenthal, for their responsiveness and hospitality during the several visits I made to their home. Do's memories of childhood, growing up in Brooklyn in the earliest years of this century, were priceless and clear as if they had happened yesterday. I appreciated the notes of encouragement and vignettes about the past she offered along the way.

I must also make mention here of two Man Ray authorities and collectors, in New York and Paris, who provided necessary check-points when I felt I was straying too far afield: Timothy Baum and Lucien Treillard. Timothy is the most passionate defender of Man Ray on either continent who, as a practitioner himself, gave me a rare sense of Dada in the 1980s. His assortment of works by Man Ray is unique and special. And his willingness to talk about the artist is boundless. My intensive encounters with Lucien Treillard in his spacious and quiet apartment on the rue de Rome always took place on rainy days, somehow adding to the seriousness of the occasions. We spoke in French; this was Lucien's way, I think, of testing the strength of my commitment, and I welcomed it. His take on the artist is pure and intellectual, grounded in a broad awareness of cosmopolitan culture, and his knowledge of Man Ray's context in the span of modern painting is without parallel.

Because I have written other books, I have acknowledged this fact of life before, but it bears repeating. The act of composition—as Gertrude Stein aptly called our craft—must be solitary: one faces the keyboard, or the white space of the page, alone, in the most extreme form of necessary isolation. Yet other hours and days of constant interchanges and encounters with people help sustain the writer during these requisite points of solitude. Because I set out to make the biography a fundamentally anecdotal work, I decided to harvest the impressions of a multitude, with no specific notions of how large the Man Ray crowd might become. I was surprised by two things: first of all, while it is true—because of his occupation as a photographer and the social milieus he inhabited—that Man Ray knew many people, relatively few actually knew him well enough to talk at length about him. And second, I was gratified beyond my expectations by the willingness of those who did love and respect Man Ray—or even envied, devalued, or criticized him—to spend time face to face with me, and let me push them to deeper levels of remembrance. I also thank others named below for favors that are less easily quantified but equally valuable and varied, including permission for access to hidden papers, assistance with arcane points of art history, memories of nearly forgotten epochs and cultural moments, warm drinks on cold nights, tolerant guidance, and honesty even when the truth suddenly seemed painful: Berenice Abbott, Bettina Bergery, Margaret Neiman Byers and Dene Byers, Jim and Barbara Byrnes, Noma Copley, William

Copley, Alexina Duchamp, Arne Ekstrom and Parmenia Migel Ekstrom, Helen Ray Faden, Mike Frankel, Brendan Gill, Jacqueline Goddard, the late Maurice Grosser, Wesley and Carolyn Halpert, David Hare, the late Stanley William and Desirée Hayter, Sheila Hicks, Joanne Kitchener Horton, Mel and Roz Jacobs, Marcel Jean, Paul Kantor, Jacques Kaplan, the late André Kertész (and his assistant, Martha Acs), Roberta Kimmel Cohn, Katharine Kuh, Ben Lees, Genevieve LeGoff, M. Ray and Stella Levinson, Peter Lyon, Michael and Elsa Combe Martin, Jean-Hubert Martin and Carolyn Breakspear, Pierre Matisse, Gertrude Neher, Dorothy Norman, Hank O'Neal, Ron Padgett, Omar S. Pound, Ned Rorem, Joan Simon, the late Doris Copley Starrels, John Tancock, Dorothea Tanning, Virgil Thomson, Louise Varèse, the late Arthur Wallach and Gertrude Wallach, June Wayne, Monroe Wheeler, Emerson and Dina Woelffer, and Virginia Zabriskie.

Also: Perry Miller Adato, Charles B. Amirkhanian, Yves Arman, the late Mario Amaya, Lady Ashton, Pierre Assouline, Paul Avrich, John F. Baker, Halee and David Baldwin, the late Margaret Scolari Barr, Linda Bassett, Joella Bayer, Hanina Bellegarde, Carl Belz, Fabienne Benedict, Avis Berman, Robert Blake, Patricia Bosworth, Jeffery Briggs, Robert Burge, Edward Burns, Charles Byron, Claudia Carr, Mary Ann Caws, Brian and Bridget Coffey, Malcolm Cowley, Nancy Crampton, Arnold Crane, Robert Creeley, Carol Donley, M et Mme Dumas and the staff of the Hôtel Bonaparte in Paris, Ulla Dydo, Arnold Eagle, Kip Eggert, Susan Ehrlich, Mary Fanette, Evelyn Farland, Leslie Fiedler, M. F. K. Fisher, Peggy Fox, Pedro Friedeberg, Donald Gallup, Deborah Geltman, Ilse Getz, Annette Giacometti, Ira Glackens, Sam and Selma Goldwitz, Phyllis Gordan, Virginia Green, Murray Grigor, Andy Grundberg, Philip Hamburger, Susan Harder, Rose Hass, Deborah Hatch, Selda Held, James and Margaret Hogan, Alex Hollender, Chandler Hovey III, Jim Hughes, Pontus Hulten, the late Alexander Iolas, Brooks Jackson, Miani Johnson, Alan Kennedy, Susan Kismaric, Billy Kluver and Julie Martin, Lee Kolker, Linda Konheim Kramer, Rudolph Kuenzli, Kay Kuhn, Barbara Kulicke, William H. Lane, George Lang, Eyre de Lanux, Susan Larson, J. Laughlin, Mary Jane Laurent, Ursula Richter Lawder, Seymour Lawrence, Barbara Lekatsas, Calman A. Levin, Paul Levitt, Jean Levy, David S. Logan, James Lord, Sue Davidson Lowe, J. Russell Lynes, Hazel

G. McKinley, Giorgio Marconi, Nikki Marquardt, Malitte Matta, Jack P. Mayer, Urban Meininger, John Melin, Mary Lynn Melton, Douglas Messerli, Corinna Metcalf, Jeanne Miles, Laurence Miller, Steven Mohn, Lou Mollgaard, Jacqueline Monnier, Josephine Kantor Morris, Susan Morris, Natalia Danesi Murray, Francis Naumann, Beaumont Newhall, Gerald Nordland, Bob Noto, Ira Nowinski, Brian O'Doherty, Maureen Owen, the late Roland Penrose, Antony Penrose, Philippe Perebinossoff and Carol Ames, Irving Petlin, Sandra Phillips, Tanya Plutzik, Dennis Powers, Jarold Ramsey, Ariel Reiss, Suzanne Ribemont-Dessaignes, Krishna Riboud, Pat Rickey, Linda Roberts, Allison Rose, Mala Rubinstein, John Russell, Michael Savage, Tennyson Schad, Perdita Schaffner, Muriel Streeter Schwartz, Mutzie and Harold Schwarz, Robert Shapazian, Elizabeth Shaw, Rita Silverstein, Suzanne Slesin, Sid Solomon, Welton Smith, Michael Stauffer, Jacqueline Stuart, Peter Swales, Dorothy Tananbaum, C. F. Terrell, Patricia Van Ingen, Helen Bachofen Von Echt, John C. Waddell, Alan Warren, Leslie Warren, Brooke Wentz, Galen Williams, Bernice Yazbek, and Jerome Zerbe.

For scholarly assistance, archival information, access to institutionally restricted materials, reproductions of artworks, responses to historical queries and points of information, and all other support lending this biography a dimension of critical authority, I am grateful to the following: Jonas Mekas, director, Nadia Shtendera, librarian, and the staff of Anthology Film Archives; Bill McNaught, Catherine Keen (for exemplary and thorough research over the past several years), and the Archives of American Art, Smithsonian Institution, staffs in New York City and Washington, D.C.; Susan Glover Godlewski, head of Reader Services, Art Institute of Chicago; Christa Sammons, acting curator, and David Schoonover, former curator of American Literature, Beinecke Rare Book and Manuscript Library, Yale University; Charlotte Wiethoff and Talitha Schoon, curators, Department of Modern Art, Museum Boymans–van Beuningen, Rotterdam, the Netherlands; Robert J. Bertholf, curator, Poetry/Rare Books Collection, University Libraries, State University of New York at Buffalo; Philip Block and Lee Sievan, International Center for Photography; Dan Younger and Stan Trecker, Boston Photographic Resource Center; the staff of the Brooklyn Historical Society Library; Charlotta

Kotik, curator of Prints and Drawings, and Liz Reynolds, Registrar's Office, the Brooklyn Museum; Nanette Maciejunes, registrar, and Susan Visser, former registrar, the Columbus Museum of Art; Cindy Cathcart, librarian, and Diana Edkins, permissions editor, Condé Nast Publications, Inc.; Susan Damsky, assistant curator, Santa Barbara Art Museum; Merry Foresta, associate curator, Department of Twentieth Century Art, National Museum of American Art, Washington, D.C.; Judi Freeman, associate curator, Department of Twentieth Century Art, and Peggy Olson, Audiovisual Department, Los Angeles County Museum of Art; Peter Galassi, curator, Department of Photography, and Janis Ekdahl, assistant director of the Library, Museum of Modern Art; Leonard Gold, chief, Jewish Division, New York Public Library; Sonja Bay, librarian, Solomon R. Guggenheim Museum; Carlton Lake, executive curator, and Cathy Henderson, research librarian, The Harry Ransom Humanities Research Center, University of Texas at Austin; Betty Karow, librarian, Milwaukee Art Museum; Peggy Lewis, New Jersey Historical Commission; Joyce Pelerano Ludmer, head, and Ray Reiss, Special Collections, Art Library, University of California/Los Angeles; Keith McKinney, chief, Periodicals Section, New York Public Library; Evan Maurer, director, University of Michigan Museum of Art; Gordon Stone, former librarian, Costume Reference Library, Metropolitan Museum of Art; Stephen R. Miller, research assistant, Rose Art Museum, Brandeis University; Weston Naef, curator of photographs, Gordon Baldwin, study room supervisor, and Julia Smith, registrar's office, the J. Paul Getty Museum; Thomas Dunnings, manuscripts curator, New-York Historical Society; Joan Pedzich, archivist, George Eastman House/International Center for Photography; Miriam Phelps, librarian, *Publishers Weekly;* Marge Kline, Department of Twentieth Century Art, and Ann Percy, curator of drawings, Philadelphia Museum of Art; Rodney Phillips, associate director for Public Services, and Lola Szladits, curator, the Berg Collection, New York Public Library; Caroline Pincus, library assistant, Emma Goldman Papers, Institute for the Study of Social Change, University of California/Berkeley; Charles Green, keeper of the Rare Books Reading Room, Princeton University Library; Michele Richet, conservatrix of the Musée Picasso; Andrea Sheen and Yuin Chin, News Archives Services, NBC, Inc.; Helen Stark, librarian, *The New Yorker;* John Szarkowski, director, Department of Photography, Museum of Modern Art; Robert Rainwater, The Miriam and Ira D. Wallach Librarian of Art, Prints and Photographs, and Roberta Waddell, Curator of Prints, New York Public Library.

I also thank Jessica Copen and Thomas O'Sullivan for typing a lengthy and convoluted manuscript with dedication and skill, on very short notice.

The relationship between an author and his editor is complex and often fraught with difficulty. Each needs the other, in what is essentially an intellectual tug-of-war. In my case, these stimulating contraries were predicated upon mutual respect. I thank Nancy Novogrod, executive editor at Clarkson N. Potter, Inc., for the gentle courage of her convictions and occasional suspensions of disbelief allowing her to accompany me on this journey from beginning to end. Our editorial conferences more often than not turned into philosophical dialogues between kindred spirits. I delighted in watching her natural enthusiasm grow, even as she maintained a watchful eye and wielded a professionally judicious pencil.

Carol Southern, editorial director at Clarkson N. Potter, gave rigorous support to the project from its inception. Shirley Wohl, editor, took on this book in its final year and was an enthusiastic, empathetic advocate. Jonathan Fox, assistant editor, was a conscientious, dependable helper at every step of the way. Gael Towey, creative director, brought sensitivity and a refined sensibility to the difficult task of determining the special style of this book. I would also like to thank the other in house staff for their meticulous work. An author could not ask for a more responsive publisher to bring his work to fruition.

My agent, Timothy Schaffner, assumed a role in the making of this book going far beyond that of a business associate. He was always available for impromptu *crises de conscience*—a sympathetic listener to the tribulations of an author vacillating between distress and elation. He was a unique source of unmediated acceptance, a consistent partner, and, finally, a friend.

Writing a book virtually eliminates the concept of "leisure" from one's life, especially when the author also has a full-time job during the day. And so, I have saved my expression of gratitude to my wife, Roberta, and my children, Nicholas and Allegra, for last. I long ago stopped counting how many weeknights, Saturdays, Sundays, and vacations were given up to the insatiable demands of Man Ray. There is no logical way of explaining the necessities embodied in this book except to say that it cried out to be written despite the knowledge of the impact it would have on our lives. My wife understands to an extent, because she, too, is a writer who has gone the hazardous route of producing a book half a dozen times. Perhaps when my children are old enough to read it, they, too, will accept what is here, and the irrepressible energies behind it.

All who helped in the ways I have enumerated, and more, remain blameless for any errors, infelicities, or misstatements that may have found their way into final form, despite the best of intentions. That responsibility is mine alone to carry.

—N.B.

Grateful acknowledgment is given for permission to use material from the following sources:

All quotations, both published and unpublished written matter by Man Ray, © Man Ray Trust/ADAGP-Paris, ARS-USA. All rights reserved. Used by permission of Man Ray Trust.

Alfred Stieglitz Archive, excerpts from "Impressions of 291," by Man Ray, edited by Alfred Stieglitz. All rights reserved. Used by permission of the Collection of American Literature, The Beinecke Rare Book and Manuscript Library, Yale University.

Société Anonyme Archive, letter, Man Ray to Tristan Tzara re: "N.Y. Dada," 1916 n.d.; letters, Man Ray to K. Dreier, 2/20/21, 9/24/28, 1/25/49; questionnaire, Man Ray to Duchamp, 1/49; letters, Dreier to Man Ray, 1/19/21, 3/16/21. All rights reserved. Used by permission of the Collection of American Literature, The Beinecke Rare Book and Manuscript Library, Yale University.

Gertrude Stein Collection, letter, Man Ray to Stein, 8/23/25; letter, Stein to Man Ray, 2/12/30. All rights reserved. Used by permission of the Collection of American Literature, The Beinecke Rare Book and Manuscript Library, Yale University.

Man Ray, lecture, Los Angeles County Museum of Art, 10/27/66, © 1966 by Museum Associates, Los Angeles County Museum of Art. All rights reserved. Used by permission of the Los Angeles County Museum of Art.

Excerpts from Jules Langsner Papers, The Archives of American Art, Smithsonian Institution. All rights reserved. Gift of the Art Library, University of California, Los Angeles.

Excerpts from Charles Daniel Papers, The Archives of American Art, Smithsonian Institution. All rights reserved.

Excerpts from interview of Man Ray, conducted by Irving Sandler, 4/1/63, The Archives of American Art, Smithsonian Institution. All rights reserved.

Two manuscript essays by Man Ray at Harry Ransom Humanities Research Center. All rights reserved. Used by permission of Harry Ransom Humanities Research Center, University of Texas, Austin.

Excerpt from letter by Ezra Pound, © 1988 by the Trustees of the Ezra Pound Literary Property Trust. All rights reserved. Used by permission of New Directions Publishing Corp., agents.

Photographs by Man Ray of The Others Group and *Others* magazine. All rights reserved. Reproduced by permission of The Poetry/Rare Books Collection, University Libraries, State University of New York, Buffalo.

Jazz by Man Ray. Reproduced by permission of Columbus Museum of Art, Ohio: Gift of Ferdinand Howald.

Woman Asleep by Man Ray, 1913. Oil on canvas. 12 × 16 inches. Reproduced by permission of Collection of Whitney Museum of American Art. Purchase 33.30.

A l'heure de l'Observatoire—Les Amoureux by Man Ray. Reproduced by permission of Niarchos, Ltd: Private collection

Large Glass by Duchamp. Reproduced by permission of Philadelphia Museum of Art: Bequest of Katherine S. Dreier.

AD MCMXIV by Man Ray. Reproduced by permission of Philadelphia Museum of Art: A. E. Gallatin Collection.

Photograph by Man Ray of a Cheruit dress, which originally appeared in *Vogue,* 5/15/25, © 1925, 1953 by The Condé Nast Publications, Inc. Reproduced by permission of *Vogue.*

Photographs by Lee Miller, © 1988 by Lee Miller Archive. All rights reserved. Reproduced by permission of the photographer.

Photograph by Man Ray of Louise Boulanger and the Schiaparelli gowns, which originally appeared in *Harper's Bazaar,* 3/36, © 1936 by The Hearst Corporation. Reproduced courtesy of *Harper's Bazaar.*

Self Portrait by Man Ray, © 1963 by Atlantic-Little, Brown. Reprinted 1979 by McGraw-Hill. Excerpts reprinted with the kind permission of Atlantic-Little, Brown.

N O T E S

Notes to quoted material are partial citations. For full citations to works referenced, see the annotated Bibliography. Unless otherwise indicated below, all translations from the French are by the author.

Introduction

Page xi   "A camera alone ... of the photograph." Man Ray letter to Jules Langsner, October 2, 1966, Collection Archives of American Art.

     xi   "second violin ... first violin." MR interview with Colette Roberts, n.d., Collection Archives of American Art.

     xi   "his passport ... perilous boundaries." Hilton Kramer, "Man Ray, Faithful Disciple," *New York Times,* January 12, 1975.

     xi   *trucages.* Marcel Jean interview with the author, March 27, 1986.

     xi   "It has never ... realize them." MR in Julien Levy exhibition catalogue, April 1945.

     xii   the highest price ... the ultimate irony. *New York Times,* November 6, 1979.

1: Emmanuel in Brooklyn

   1–3   Manya sewed ... a hard worker. Anecdotal information about MR's parents in Russia and emigration to America. Florence Blumenthal and Do Ray Goodbread, interviews with the author, May 14, 1984, and September 22, 1984, and Florence Blumenthal, *End of a Story* (unpublished memoir).

4   A graphic drawing . . . to copy it. MR, *Self Portrait,* Atlantic–Little, Brown, Boston, 1963, p. 4.

4   "Daughter, have you . . . could be killed!" Do Ray Goodbread interview with the author, June 4, 1984.

4   "strange people that . . . were very colorful." Arturo Schwarz, *Man Ray,* p. 72.

5   It was an . . . functions effortlessly. Description of object in collection of Florence Blumenthal.

5   When the show . . . came through. Ira Glackens, *William Glackens and the Eight,* p. 89.

5   more vilifyingly known . . . "outlaw salon." Charles Daniel papers, Collection Archives of American Art, Smithsonian Institution, p. 54.

6   "world of saloons . . . in a restaurant." Glackens, op. cit., p. 76.

6   The Radnitskys . . . $32.50 clear. Samuel Ray, *Man Proposes.* Unpublished memoir, ca. 1933, p. 1.

6–7   But life . . . Radnitskys make music. Do Ray Goodbread interview with the author, May 14, 1984.

7   All the other . . . already made up. Do Ray Goodbread, ibid.

8   Most mornings . . . " . . . duties to society." MR, *Self Portrait,* p. 10.

8   lush trees . . . "ER." Description of early paintings in collection of Florence Blumenthal.

8–9   Sister Dora . . . "Because of the *art.*" Do Ray Goodbread interviews.

9   "It would be . . . by all nations." MR interview with Arnold Crane, January 1970, Collection Archives of American Art.

10   Telling sister Dora . . . " . . . violent imagery." Do Ray Goodbread interviews.

10   Oils and Portraits . . . were on display. Brooklyn Institute of Arts and Sciences, *Annual Reports,* 1905–1912, and *Accession Records,* 1905–1912.

11   His first client . . . woman's fair skin. Do Ray Goodbread interviews.

2: First Mentors

13   "The eyebrows were . . . quick and hesitating." Djuna Barnes, *Interviews,* p. 215.

14   Stieglitz thought . . . "a place of contact." Dorothy Norman interview with the author, January 8, 1984.

14   How much is the picture . . . to change hands. Maurice Grosser, interview with the author, January 10, 1984.

14   At the same . . . advice on life. Djuna Barnes, op. cit., p. 216.

15   "a glorified fire-escape . . . genuine stimulus." Stieglitz cited in Dorothy Norman, *An American Seer,* p. 108.

15   "Picasso . . . big men's work." Dorothy Norman, ibid., p. 110.

16   "There is no . . . die for it." Waldo Frank et al., *America and Alfred Stieglitz,* p. 70.

16   His *Tapestry* . . . "Man Ray, 1911." Collection Juliet Man Ray.

16–17   Emmanuel had passed . . . legally altered. Do Ray Goodbread and Florence Blumenthal interviews.

17 the Ferrer Modern School . . . and aesthetic topics. *Modern School Magazine,* Spring 1913.

17 her shared belief . . . " . . . enemy of education." Schwarz, op. cit., p. 16.

17 "What is the . . . investigation and criticism." *Modern School Magazine,* Spring 1913, p. 20.

17 "seethed with animation . . . denied a hearing." Paul Avrich, *The Modern School Movement,* p. 118.

18 "a woman of remarkable . . . a very great woman." Paul Avrich, ibid., p. 148.

20 "never . . . criticized adversely." MR, *Self Portrait,* p. 23.

20 "If a man . . . command them." Robert Henri, *The Art Spirit,* p. 53.

20 "Art appears . . . of his growth." Ibid., p. 67.

20 "Art is art . . . piece of furniture." Ibid., p. 157.

20 "The one great . . . of value pass." Robert Henri, letter to Manuel Komroff, winter 1913–14, in *Modern School Magazine,* July 1914, p. 6.

21 "construct . . . by colored surfaces." John Elderfield, *Matisse,* p. 42.

21–22 Over the course . . . *Crime and Punishment.* Do Ray Goodbread interviews.

23 "He discards rhyme" . . . "rhapsody of joy!" *Modern School Magazine,* Spring 1913, p. 7.

24 "obscure geometry." Weston Naef. *The Painterly Photograph,* p. 7.

24 "a machine . . . the human spirit." Paul Rosenfeld, *Port of New York,* p. 245.

24 "to shove the nozzle . . . by fire escapes." Ibid., p. 238.

24 "Photography is . . . the material truth." Marius de Zayas, "Photography Is Not Art," *Camera Work,* no. 41, January 1913.

25 "was bound to . . . a great light." Sue Davidson Lowe, *Stieglitz,* p. 167.

3: Breaking Away

29 "the storm broke . . . they came." Walt Kuhn, in de Zayas (ed. Francis Naumann), "How, When and Why," pp. 106–107.

29 "Actors, musicians . . . in the pandemonium." Kuhn, ibid.

29 "pathological museum" . . . simply "fatuous." *New York World,* February 17, 1913.

29–30 "wire fence" . . . " . . . chains of naturalism." *New York Times,* Marcel Duchamp obituary, October 2, 1968.

30 "mind in a turmoil . . . ready to break through." MR, *Self Portrait,* p. 44.

31 "My dear Sam . . . without any goal." MR letter to Samuel Ray, n.d.

31 "cut [himself] off . . ." MR, *Self Portrait,* p. 45.

31–32 "There is no . . . from the sensate world." Albert Gleizes and Jean Metzinger, "On Cubism," 1912, pp. 6–13.

32 "While there is . . . room for more." MR letter to Samuel Ray, n.d.

32 "peculiarities." Alfred Kreymborg, *Troubadour,* p. 199.

33 "unless you're . . . Ezra Pound." Ibid.

33 "Get in touch . . . New Jersey." Ibid., pp. 204–205.

34 "The days are . . . Fatigued." *Modern School Magazine,* Autumn, 1913, pp. 20–21.

35–36 "Oh talk about . . . purr, purr, purr." MR, *Diaries,* Collection Helen Ray Faden, n.d.

36 He wrote a " . . . some of the Futurists." Alfred Kreymborg, "Man Ray and Adon Lacroix, Economists," *New York Morning Telegraph,* March 14, 1915.

37 "She began removing . . . and Baudelaire." MR, *Self Portrait,* p. 43.

37 "to be drunken . . . high places." Guillaume Apollinaire, *Alcools,* p. xi.

38 *"la rencontre fortuite . . . d'un parapluie."* Lautréamont, *Les chants de Maldoror,* VI, 3, i. Oster edition, p. 234.

38 "If I say no . . . to lose Man." Do Ray Goodbread interviews.

39 "O love bruised hands . . . Contains itself." Man Ray, *Adonisms,* 1914.

39 "Were I a painter. . . I love you!" Ibid.

40 "concreted . . . love, life, and art." Alfred Kreymborg, op. cit.

40 "with fish glue . . . house with bricks." MR, *Self Portrait,* p. 49.

4: Enter Marcel Duchamp

45 "Several small houses . . . Knows nothing about." MR, "Three Dimensions," *Others,* December 1915, vol. i, no. 6.

46 "called the strokes . . . same word: yes." MR, *Self Portrait,* p. 59.

46 "elegance in its . . . truly supreme ease." André Breton, in Robert Motherwell, *Dada Painters and Poets,* p. 209.

48 "Art, for Duchamp . . . message between conspirators." Octavio Paz, *Alternating Current,* p. 83.

49 "a little watercolor . . . over my bed." Charles Daniel papers, Archives of American Art, p. 51.

49 "would give him . . . collector-dealer." Alfred Stieglitz, editor, "What is 291?" *Camera Work,* 1914–15, no. 47, p. 286.

49 "strength and rich . . . analytical mind." Charles Daniel papers, op. cit., pp. 30–31.

50 "a mere instrument . . . of the mind." George Heard Hamilton, ed., Catalogue of the Société Anonyme.

50 "We cannot come . . . " MR letter to Samuel Ray, November 4, 1915.

50 "organized . . . scope and patronage." *New York Times,* November 14, 1915.

50 "decided after all . . . comfortable nullity therein." MR to John Weichsel, Collection Archives of American Art, November 3, 1915.

50 "puttering around one morning." MR, *Self Portrait,* p. 60.

50–51 "juxtaposing mechanical elements . . . *Uniforms and Liveries.*" Marcel Duchamp, *Notes for a Lecture,* Collection Philadelphia Museum of Art, November 24, 1964.

51 Like Baudelaire's *flâneur . . .* yet remain apart. See Moira Roth, "Marcel Duchamp in America," 1977.

52 "he who looks . . . a closed window." *Opus,* special issue, 1974, p. 37.

52 "the patience and . . . reweaving its web." MR, *Self Portrait,* p. 69.

52 "detached from aesthetic preoccupations." Lucy Lippard, *Dadas on Art,* p. 139.

52 "When one goes . . . think about it." Pierre Cabanne, *Dialogues with Duchamp,* trans. Ron Padgett, p. 29.

53 Virtually every night . . . anyone was listening. See Francis Naumann, "Walter Conrad Arensberg," *Philadelphia Museum of Art Bulletin.*

53 The drinking often . . . he called them. Louise Varèse interview with the author, December 29, 1983.

5 : The Artist as Tightrope Walker

55-56 At the beginning . . . making imagination concrete. See Francis Naumann, "Man Ray, Early Paintings 1913-1916."

56 "on a single plane . . . other popular subjects." Man Ray, in ex. cat., courtesy Virginia Zabriskie.

58 "go out and buy . . . colors and canvas." MR interview with Arturo Schwarz, *Arts Magazine,* 51.9, May 1977.

58 "a very mechanical . . . more Toulouse-Lautrec." Ibid.

59 "various pieces . . . color to another." Ibid.

59 "too decorative . . . a musical comedy." Ibid.

59 "so that [he'd] . . . knowledge of color." Ibid.

59 "with precision, yet lavishly." Ibid.

60 "While these works . . . equally important." MR, *Self Portrait,* p. 68.

61 Adon went on . . . " . . . as the gesture." Adon Lacroix, in Arturo Schwarz, *60 ans de libertés,* 1971, pp. 84-85.

61 "humor was . . . communication of all." Naomi Savage interview with the author, December 7, 1983.

62 The earliest versions . . . needlelike etching tool. See Marilyn Symmes, *Contemporary Cliché-Verre Prints,* 1981, for a thorough description of this process.

62 "formed a centre . . . music and poetry." Hans Richter, *Dada,* 1965, p. 16.

63 The origins of . . . *of the sacred cow.* Marcel Jean, *The History of Surrealist Painting,* 1967, p. 92.

63 "Order = disorder . . . to the past." Hans Richter, op. cit., p. 34.

63 "The bladder of . . . Cru cru cru." Ibid., p. 20.

63 "you should put out . . . face of the moon." Tristan Tzara, *Evening,* trans. Charles Simic and Michael Benedikt, in Paul Aster, ed., *The Random House Book of Twentieth Century French Poetry,* 1982, p. 165.

63 "gadji beri bimba . . . berida bimbala." Richter, op. cit., p. 42.

63 "a living force . . . antipoetically." René Lacôte and Georges Haldas, *Tristan Tzara,* 1952, p. 19.

64 "out and out anarchist." Arturo Schwarz, *Man Ray,* p. 49.

64 "a very radical . . . exploiters of workers." Ibid.
65 "Whether Mr. Mutt . . . for that object." Lucy Lippard, op. cit., p. 143.

6: Man Ray, Professional Photographer

67 "Paris in New York . . . to uninterrupted conversation." Louise Varèse, *A Looking-Glass Diary,* 1972, p. 127.
67 *"J'ai horreur de . . . m'embête."* Ibid., p. 132.
68 "I didn't want to . . . doing abstract painting." Jean-Hubert Martin, ed., *Man Ray Photographs,* 1982, p. 35.
68 "thin, interesting . . . a dazed camera." Hank O'Neal, *Berenice Abbott,* 1982, pp. 8–9.
68 "toot around . . . have fun." Berenice Abbott interview with the author, March 9, 1984.
68 "a quiet sort, very gentle." Ibid.
68–69 Berenice's roommate . . . black Djuna wore. Douglas Messerli, editor, *Smoke and Other Stories* by Djuna Barnes, 1982, p. 8.
69 "Mage" Levinson . . . " . . . that's good." M. Ray Levinson interview with the author, July 5, 1984.
69 "A florid gentleman . . . not very talkative." MR, *Self Portrait,* p. 103.
70 "grew in his . . . mull it over." Charles Daniel papers, op. cit., p. 8.
71–72 "While the bride . . . *Domaine de Duchamp."* MR, *Opus,* op. cit., p. 31.
72 "an effect of . . . obtained with paint." Marcel Duchamp, *Notes for a Lecture,* op. cit., p. 13.
72 "picture taken from an airplane." Jean-Hubert Martin, op. cit., p. 16.
72 *Elevage de poussière . . .* " . . . old boy!" MR, *Opus,* op. cit., p. 31.
72 "a Mona Lisa . . . time and space?" Moira Roth, op. cit., p. 94.
73 While Duchamp insisted . . . " . . . every other movement." Francis Naumann, "The New York Dada Movement," 1980, p. 146.
73 The magazine synthesized . . . *Her Pubic Hair.* Robert Motherwell, op. cit., pp. 214–18.
73 "definitely *not* a Dadaist." Dorothy Norman, interview with the author, January 8, 1984.
73 "There was only . . . in the desert." MR, *Self Portrait,* p. 101.
73–74 he reported to . . . " . . . remain a secret." MR letter to Tristan Tzara, Société Anonyme Archives, Beinecke Library, Yale University, n.d.
74 "Absolutely! . . . on their own." MR interview with Arturo Schwarz, op. cit., p. 121.
74 Perhaps Francis Picabia . . . by his absence. Robert Motherwell, op. cit., p. 21.
74 "belonging to no . . . spirit in art." Société Anonyme Catalogue Raisonné, 1984, p. 1.
75 "Traditions are . . . not to follow." Ex. cat., Collection Brooklyn Museum, November 1926–January 1927.
75 "heralding a new . . . from the past." Katherine Dreier, "The Société Anonyme," 1920.

75 "gladly bring any... with the artist." Yale Catalogue Raisonné, op. cit., p. 751.

76 "I hope you can... take the pictures." Katherine Dreier, letter to Man Ray, Société Anonyme Archives, Yale University Library, March 16, 1921.

76 *Lampshade,* one of... in his autobiography. MR, *Self Portrait,* p. 96.

77 "I was wondering... out of tin?" Société Anonyme Archives.

77 "still in the experimental... a bit exaggerated." MR letter to Katherine Dreier, February 20, 1921, Société Anonyme Archives, Yale University Library.

78 Man Ray, appropriately enough... "... a few serious words." Arturo Schwarz, "Interview with Man Ray," op. cit., p. 121.

78 "I wish that man... reading by laughing." Francis Naumann, "The New York Dada Movement," op. cit.

79 It only remained... she whispered. Do Ray Goodbread and Florence Blumenthal interviews.

7: To Paris

81 "father, mother... and ideals." Marguerite Bonnet, ed., *Lautréamont,* 1969, p. 236.

81 "I have arranged... where Tzara lives." Marcel Duchamp letter to MR, 1921, n.d., Lake Collection, Humanities Research Center, University of Texas at Austin.

81 In subsequent years... "... Man Ray." Timothy Baum interview with the author, August 3, 1984.

82 "almost was not born at all." Janus, *Man Ray,* 1979, p. 212. Made as part of an autobiographical statement for an exhibition at the Institute of Contemporary Art, London, 1959.

82 "a new-born baby." MR letters to Ferdinand Howald (Howald Correspondence, Collection Archives of American Art) and Samuel Ray, July 1921.

82 "a certain rhythm... to be enough." John Russell, *The Meanings of Modern Art,* 1981, p. 158.

82 "just a bit lonesome." MR postcard to Samuel Ray, July 21, 1921.

82 *"Je te remercie... je te dois beaucoup."* MR in *Opus,* op. cit.

83 "New York Chaos." Timothy Baum interview with the author, August 3, 1984.

83 "It's as difficult... as Brooklyn." MR letter to Samuel Ray, July 28, 1921.

83 "Everything is gay... than I expected." MR letter to Samuel Ray, August 22, 1921.

83 "a real American... nothing but champagne." MR letter to Samuel Ray, August 22, 1921.

84 *"l'époque floue...* the new movement." William S. Rubin, *Dada, Surrealism and Their Heritage,* 1968, p. 61.

84 "critics, journalists... in question." Philippe Soupault, in Ex. cat., Noah Goldowsky Gallery exhibition, May–June 1969.

84 who could remain . . . Breton *and* Tzara. David Savage interview with the author, May 24, 1984.

84–86 "I am not producing . . . in me for that." MR letter to Ferdinand Howald, August 18, 1921.

86 "make [his] first . . . to begin with!" MR letter to Ferdinand Howald, October 1921.

86–87 "the sartorial genius . . ." . . . even his hats. Janet Flanner, *Paris Was Yesterday*, 1972, p. 154.

87 "the privilege of the elite." Paul Poiret, *King of Fashion*, 1931, p. vii.

88 "ghastly . . . hangout for pederasts." Kay Boyle and Robert McAlmon, *Being Geniuses Together*, 1970, p. 30.

88 *"le quartier de loftingues."* Marcel Jean, op. cit., p. 160.

88 "had a reputation . . . doubtful connections." Roland Penrose, *Man Ray*, 1975, p. 82.

88 "He lived in . . . all his developing." Gertrude Stein, *The Autobiography of Alice B. Toklas*, 1960, p. 197.

89 "rather like . . . a big mouth." Kay Boyle and Robert McAlmon, op. cit., p. 255.

89 *"La lumière ressemble . . ."* . . . breast-fed). Ex. cat., Arensberg Collection, Philadelphia Museum of Art.

90 "a strange, voluble . . . some conservative bank." MR, *Self Portrait*, p. 115.

90 "I picked up . . . object in France." Ibid.

90 "I need more . . . a plastic poem." Arturo Schwarz, *Man Ray*, op. cit., p. 158.

91 "designed to amuse . . . works of art." William Seitz, *The Art of Assemblage*, 1961, p. 48.

91 "Truth in making . . . making by joy." Donis A. Dondis, *A Primer of Visual Literacy*, 1984, p. 143.

92 When seated on . . . as a "gift." Margit Chanin interview with the author, February 7, 1984.

92 "dumb, beautiful ministers." Lewis Hyde, *The Gift*, 1983, p. 173.

92 "But you'll ruin . . . tacks on there!" Naomi Savage interview with the author, December 7, 1983.

93 "the arrangement of . . . state of beauty." Fernand Léger, *Functions of Painting*, 1973, p. 52. Trans. Alexandra Anderson.

93 "Let us refresh . . . the flat-iron." Alfred Barr, *Fantastic Art, Dada, Surrealism*, 1936, p. 94.

93 "my exhibition . . . of its vitality." MR letter to Ferdinand Howald, dated February 3, 1921, actually 1922.

8: Painting with Light

95 *"J'ai fait revenir. . . ."* . . . a bit on it). Marcel Duchamp letter to Man Ray, 1922, n.d., Lake Collection, Humanities Research Center, University of Texas at Austin.

95–96 "Take a good look . . . a little publicity." Janus, *Man Ray*, op. cit., p. 194.

96 "mechanically placed . . . to the light." MR, *Self Portrait,* p. 129.

96 "photogenic drawings" . . . " . . . the artist's pencil." Beaumont Newhall, *The History of Photography,* 1980, p. 45.

96 Man Ray was . . . the status quo. Andy Grundberg interview with the author, July 2, 1984.

97 punctuated the plane. See Roland Barthes, *Camera Lucida,* 1981, p. 106 ff, for an extended discussion of this issue.

97 Once the exposed . . . as a "mistake." Naomi Savage, replication of rayograph technique in the darkroom for the author, May 24, 1984.

97 "objects were consumed . . . fixed by light." Janus, op. cit., p. 213.

97-98 "Is it a spiral . . . disturb the stars." Tristan Tzara, "When Things Dream," in Janus, ibid., p. 184. Tzara's complete tribute may be found in the preface to *Les champs délicieux,* written August 1922 and published in December 1922 in an edition of forty copies.

98 "Following him . . . hidden cellars." Robert Desnos in Janus, ibid., p. 215.

98 "The great responsibility. . . ." Moholy-Nagy, *Photography in a Flash,* in Richard Kostelanetz, ed., 1970, p. 54. The essay was originally published in London in 1936.

98 "all hand-produced . . . place of pigment." "Otto Stelzer, in postscript to Moholy's essay, "Painting Photography Film," 1967.

98-99 "made [his] first . . . [Man Ray's] Rayographs." Letter to Beaumont Newhall, in Moholy-Nagy, ed. Kostelanetz, op. cit., p. 57.

99 "Man Ray and I . . . with an aura." Laszlo Moholy-Nagy, *Vision in Motion,* 1947, pp. 187, 197.

99 Finally, in Chicago . . . "Very much." Katharine Kuh interview with the author, January 23, 1984. Moholy died on November 24, 1946.

99 *"Je suis enchanté . . ." . . .* you've dropped painting). Marcel Duchamp letter to MR, 1922, n.d., Lake Collection, HRC/Austin, Texas.

99 "You may regret . . . and never exhibit." MR letter to Ferdinand Howald, April 5, 1922.

99 "The dealer cannot . . . his work often." Letter from Ferdinand Howald to MR, May 16, 1922.

100 He hoped it would matter. . . . MR letter to Ferdinand Howald, May 28, 1922.

100 none other than . . . " . . . painting free again." *Vanity Fair,* November 1922, "A New Method of Realizing the Artistic Possibilities of Photography. Experiments in Abstract Form, Made Without a Camera Lens, by Man Ray, the American Painter." The term "rayograph" was used in the accompanying text.

100 "looks like photography . . . without a camera." MR letter to Ferdinand Howald, May 28, 1922.

100 "that certain pages . . . justly offend readers." Sylvia Beach, *Shakespeare & Company,* 1959, pp. 73-74.

101 "move all she liked . . . a snap shot." Gertrude Stein, *The Autobiography of Alice B. Toklas,* op. cit., p. 197.

101 "was as quick . . . or the lights." Sir Roland Penrose, in *Newsweek* interview by Daphne Davis, April 19, 1982.

101   "This method . . . recreate unaffectedness!" MR to Daniel Masclet, in Arturo Schwarz, *Man Ray,* op. cit., pp. 284–85.

101   "give the impression . . . an easy sitting.' " Ibid.

101–102   "ravishing, divine" . . . " . . . not a cocktail." Ibid.

102   "an old shoe." MR, *Self Portrait,* p. 174.

102   "Mr. Zeiss? . . . pushes the button." Pierre Bourgeade, *Bonsoir, Man Ray,* 1972, p. 84.

102   "great portrait . . . great mythologists." Roland Barthes, op. cit., p. 34.

102   "to produce an . . . communion with the sitter." Nadar, 1856, in Beaumont Newhall, op. cit., p. 66.

102–103   He seemed . . . invariably right. Jacqueline Goddard interview with the author, January 26, 1985.

103   "she ordered dozens . . . more exclusive circles." Jean-Hubert Martin, op. cit., p. 210.

103   "a swell place." MR postcard to parents, July 1922.

9: Love Affair with the Female Form

106   Yes, he was . . . " . . . to take pictures." Kiki, *Souvenirs,* 1929, p. 169.

107   "Kiki Man Ray." Joella Bayer interview with the author, February 13, 1984.

108   "Viens par ici . . . t'amuserai bien!" Alain Jouffroy, *La vie réinventée,* 1982, p. 182.

108   "She was incorruptible . . . fun of it." MR, *Self Portrait,* p. 150.

108   "Life is *au fond . . .* so *diabolique."* Djuna Barnes, *Interviews,* op. cit., p. 299.

108   "bedside dictionary." Malcolm Cowley, letter to the author, January 23, 1984.

108   "a nasty cold." MR letter to "My dear folks," October 28, 1922.

108–109   The great author . . . folded hands. George D. Painter, *Marcel Proust,* 1959, p. 363.

109   "been in bed . . . back to bed." MR letter to Ferdinand Howald, November 28, 1922.

109   "to do grotesque . . . as a kid." Author unknown, "Over the River" August 1924.

110   Ingres's *Baigneuse de Valpinçon.* Also known as *La grande baigneuse,* 1808.

110   "from the classicism . . . measurable, in itself." See de Zayas's notes to an exhibition at the Arden Gallery, New York, April–May 1919.

110–111   Jean-Auguste-Dominique Ingres . . . humble upbringings. James Thrall Soby, "The Case of Ingres," in *Modern Art and the New Past,* 1957, pp. 14–20.

111   "Having brought . . . of incompletion." Anne d'Harnoncourt and Kynaston McShine, *Marcel Duchamp,* 1973, pp. 192–93.

111   "I wasn't bothered . . ." . . . roulette gambling. Pierre Cabanne, op. cit., p. 67.

III   in an apartment . . . a mattress spring. Maurice Grosser interview with the author, January 21, 1984.

114   "yet she was . . . arrived from America." Peggy Guggenheim, *Out of This Century,* 1980, p. 24.

114   "a great figure. . . ."Hugh Edwards, ed. Art Institute of Chicago, *Surrealism and Its Affinities,* 1956, p. 6.

114   In letters home. . . . MR letter to Elsie Ray, October 4, 1924.

114   In the fall of 1923 . . . and wrote poetry. Joella Bayer interview with the author, February 13, 1984.

114–115   It was at one such . . . with clouds afloat. Ibid., and letter from Joella Bayer to the author, February 22, 1984.

115   "leading a rather . . . Why not?" Berenice Abbott interview with the author, March 10, 1984.

115   The studio . . . " . . . in those days." Ibid.

116   "There was a sudden . . . in each print." Berenice Abbott, *The World of Atget,* 1964, p. viii.

116   "a primitive." Berenice Abbott interview, op. cit.

116   "complained that . . . *vite, enfin.'* "Julien Levy, *Memoir of an Art Gallery,* 1977, p. 91.

116   DOCUMENTS POUR ARTISTES . . . " . . . remote, appealing." Berenice Abbott, *The World of Atget,* op. cit.

116   "use" Man Ray. Berenice Abbott interview, op. cit.

116   "became unwitting competitors." Jean-Hubert Martin, op. cit., p. 212.

117   "as people, not still-lifes." Berenice Abbott interview, op. cit.

118   "they had really . . . in the lottery." Brassaï, *Photographs,* 1968, p. 11.

118   two large mushrooms . . . and a visitor. Eyre de Lanux interview with the author, August 3, 1984.

118   "printed memory." Hilton Kramer, *Brancusi,* 1979, n.p.

10: From Dada to Surrealism

121   "one knows what . . . state of dreaming." William S. Rubin, op. cit., pp. 63–64.

122   Man Ray believed . . . were short ones. Alain Jouffroy, op. cit., p. 156.

123   "All the films . . . happens in life." Man Ray, *"Tous les films,"* in *Etudes cinématographiques,* Paris, Spring 1965, pp. 38–39, 43–46.

123   "hampered by Sonia Delaunay's . . ." . . . or torn open. Georges Hugnet, in Hans Richter, op. cit., p. 190; and William Camfield, *Francis Picabia,* 1979, p. 200.

123   "the true Dadas . . . from Dada." Robert Motherwell, op. cit., p. 246.

123   "Pure psychic automatism . . . play of thought." William S. Rubin, op. cit., p. 65.

124   "I am working for *Vogue.*" MR letter to Elsie, October 4, 1924.

124   "figures prominently . . . in the mode." *Vanity Fair,* December 1, 1925.

124   "what with abstract . . . a material form." MR letter to Katherine

Dreier, September 24, 1928, Société Anonyme Archives, Yale University Library.

125 In the presence... "...different languages." MR letter to Gertrude Stein, August 23, 1925, Yale University Library. This incident was also related to the author by Pierre Matisse in an interview on February 6, 1984.

125 "men... to cretins." Alain Jouffroy, op. cit., p. 369.

125 "although he does not... leadership from him." Robert Motherwell, op. cit., p. ccvi.

125 "nothing more than... dead leaves." Alain Jouffroy, op. cit., p. 108.

126 "The medium... only the *idea*." Arturo Schwarz, *Man Ray*, p. 164.

126 "the beauty of... man and the machine." Yvonne Brunhammer, 1925, pp. 173, 180.

126 "This is Sunday... have to write." MR letter to Elsie, December 13, 1925.

126–127 "leading a double... had ended tragically?" MR, *Self Portrait*, p. 134.

128 By adding simple... archways subtly shaded. *Vogue,* May 15, 1925, p. 90, and January–March 1926.

129 "busy as a cockroach." MR letter to Elsie, May 9, 1926.

129 One local newspaper... Brancusi's sculptures. Yvonne Brunhammer, 1925, op. cit., p. 88.

11: Cinematic Adventures

131 At a time when... one hundred dollars a month. Maurice Grosser interview with the author, March 29, 1984.

131 "have some money... happens here." MR letter to Elsie, March 18, 1926.

131 it all went straight to Elsie.... MR letter to Elsie, April 19, 1926.

132 His explicit requests... model-companion Kiki. MR letters to Elsie, May 9, 1926; December 13, 1925; July 29, 1926.

132 He even constructed... from one plate. Naomi Savage interview with the author, May 25, 1984.

132 "in the nature... other photographic commitments." MR, *Self Portrait,* p. 269.

133 all were printed... home front. Jean-Hubert Martin, op. cit., p. 183ff.

134 To Man Ray... "... remained a fragment." Carl Belz, "A Man Ray Retrospective," 1966, p. 45, quoted from his interview with Man Ray.

134–135 On March 7... at the same time. Do Ray Goodbread interview with the author, September 22, 1984.

135 Readers of the... "Give Us A Rest." Flyer for the film in Yale University Library Collections.

135 Aside from... with polite interest. Florence Blumenthal interview with the author, September 22, 1984.

136 critic Gilbert Seldes... "... or subsequent hundred." George Pratt, *Spellbound in Silence,* 1973, p. 500.

136   "to [have the spectator] . . . merely a spectator." Carl Belz, op. cit., p. 45.

137   "It's a lot . . . destiny of things." Pierre Cabanne, op. cit., p. 75.

137   "the whole body. . . stay together." Ibid., p. 74.

138   "looking more . . . tired actor." Berenice Abbott in Beaumont Newhall, op. cit., p. 237.

138   "For twenty years . . . art of photography." Berenice Abbott, *The World of Atget,* op. cit., p. xii.

138   "with the most . . . a spiritual emotion." Hank O'Neal, *Berenice Abbott,* op. cit., p. 12.

138   "For years I knew. . . unconceived France." Kay Boyle, *Being Geniuses Together,* op. cit., p. 267.

139   "whatever his initiation . . . open as eternity." See also *transition,* no. 15, February 1929, p. 266; and Ex. cat., Arts Club of Chicago, February 1929.

139   As the years . . . even getting out of bed. Juliet Man Ray interview with the author, August 30, 1984.

140   The film was . . . by extension, to the film. Inez Hedges, "Constellated Visions," *Dada/Surrealism,* no. 15, 1986, pp. 99–109.

140   "the very embodiment . . . simple like love." Marie-Claire Dumas, *Robert Desnos,* p. 387.

143   A columnist in . . . " . . . evolving arbitrarily." Author unknown, *Variétés,* December 15, 1928, p. 455.

143   Another writer . . . " . . . and unraveled." Jean Prévost, *Nouvelle Revue Française,* December 1928, p. 748.

144   "Man Ray derives . . . reproduction of 'nature.'" Robert Desnos, "The Work of Man Ray," *transition,* no. 15, February 1929, p. 265.

144   "more and more . . . shadow and light." Frank Crowninshield, Foreword, *Pictorial Photography in America,* 1929, n.p.

145   "getting very homesick . . . perpetuated, it seems!" MR letter to Elsie, July 20, 1928.

12: Atelier Man Ray

147   *"The doorbell . . . of a cricket."* Lucie Porquerol, "Man Ray," *Adam Magazine,* June 15, 1931.

147   "with the look of an orphan." Jacqueline Goddard interview with the author, January 26, 1985.

148   "the gaze of . . . in his mouth." Bettina Bergery interview with the author, November 21, 1984.

148   "came upon a . . . quiet street." MR, *Self Portrait,* p. 292.

149   Kiki often ended . . . her fellow-models. Jacqueline Goddard interview with the author.

149   "a drinker. . . to hallucinations." MR, *Self Portrait,* p. 155.

149   "an Era that is over." Hugh Ford, *Published in Paris,* 1975, p. 148.

150   ("He has an . . . way with him"). Ibid., p. 144.

150   "Kiki! Kiki! . . . or Montaigne." *This Quarter,* v.1, 1930.

150   "When you knocked . . . could come in." Kay Boyle, op. cit., p. 290.

151–152 "I wonder if . . . exact sound simultaneously." Arturo Schwarz, *Man Ray*, p. 303.

152 "Something is going . . . mourn over it." Janus, *Man Ray*, p. 218.

152 Man Ray pleaded . . . a broad audience. André Breton letter to Man Ray, April 16, 1930, Lake Collection, HRC/Austin. (May not be quoted directly by stipulation of Breton estate.)

152 "the greatest step . . . last ten years." George Antheil letter to MR, n.d.

152 Four years later . . . encouragement and pleading. George Antheil letter to MR, April 25, 1933.

153 "Brandt is quite . . . etc.—E.P." Ezra Pound note to MR, n.d. © 1988 by the Trustees of the Ezra Pound Literary Property Trust; used by permission of New Directions Publishing Corp., agents.

153 "Man Ray . . . learn,' he said." Avis Berman interview with Bill Brandt, *ARTNews*, March 1982, p. 95.

153 "signs and shop . . . archaic corners." Ibid.

155 "Photography can never . . . to be itself." Berenice Abbott, "It Has to Walk Alone," *Infinity Magazine*, 1951.

155 "atmosphere was the . . . and yet strange." Bill Brandt, Introduction, n.p. *Camera in London*, Focal Press, 1948.

155 "her pale hair . . . is Man Ray.'" Antony Penrose, *The Lives of Lee Miller*, 1985, p. 125.

155 "not dry . . . soft, silky skin." Mario Amaya, *My Man Ray*, 1975, n.p.

155–156 "What's your name? . . . So am I." Ibid.

156 "revulsion against classical . . . of doing photography." Ibid.

156 "greeted by a vision . . . they had come." Madge Garland (Lady Ashton) letter to the author, June 14, 1984.

157 "extremely beautiful and . . . decor by herself." George Antheil letter to MR, May 3, 1930.

157 In a much . . . diplomat-husband, Gaston. Bettina Bergery interview with the author, November 21, 1984.

157 "wasn't as big . . . fixed and washed." Mario Amaya, op. cit.

157 Whether it was the . . . executed by her. Roland Penrose, in *Atelier Man Ray*, p. 56.

158 Lee Miller took . . . " . . . called 'Solarization.'" Mario Amaya, op. cit.

158 "The tricks . . . of tomorrow." MR, *Self Portrait*, p. 220.

158 "This process was . . . them at will." *New York Sun*, March 27, 1935.

159 Man Ray would . . . the paper coating. For description of solarization process, see Schwarz, *Man Ray*, p. 282; and Beaumont Newhall, op. cit.

160–161 In an odd . . . " . . . Mr. Man Ray." Gertrude Stein, *The Yale Edition*, 1954, p. 244.

162 "getting known and . . . could pay something." MR, *Self Portrait*, p. 183.

162 "My dear . . . Gertrude Stein." Letter to MR, February 12, 1930, Gertrude Stein collection, Yale University Library.

NOTES

163 Man Ray was "acerbic" ... " ... simple portraiture." Perry Miller Adato interview with the author, December 28, 1983.
164 "the photographer...a painter." S. W. Hayter interview with the author, November 23, 1984.

13: The Lovers

165 she had been "dressed . . . shorts and blouse." MR, *Self Portrait*, p. 95.
166 "sort of Marco Polo." Ibid. p. 191.
166 "I've got some . . . this afternoon." William Seabrook letter to MR, ca. summer 1930.
166–167 "I have tried . . . of losing you." MR letter to Lee Miller, in Antony Penrose, op. cit., manuscript courtesy of AP, p. 16–17.
169 "Accounts never balance . . . pays enough." Ibid., p. 20.
167–170 The night Lee left . . . gun was loaded. Jacqueline Goddard, interview with the author, January 26, 1985.
170 "lost about fifteen . . . Dr. Hay diet." MR letter to Elsie, December 24, 1932.
170 "you could never. . . you ate meat." Mario Amaya, op. cit.
170 His complaints of . . . clear of him. Monroe Wheeler interview with the author, March 23, 1984.
170 "representing the Man Ray school of photography." MR letter to Elsie, December 24, 1932.
171 "in time to . . . private channels." Ibid.
172 "high and exacting . . . Surrealist activity." MR, *Self Portrait*, p. 249.
174 "painting was . . . of his solution." Peter Gay, *Art and Act*, 1976, p. 226.
174 "Your mouth becomes . . . you and me." Arturo Schwarz, *Man Ray*, p. 61.
174 "Every stroke . . . and interest." MR, *Self Portrait*, p. 255.

14: Middle Life

177 During the 1990s . . . her quiet way. Linda Roberts interview with the author, July 29, 1984.
178 As the private . . . house in order. Samuel Ray, *Man Proposes*, unpublished memoir, 1933; Helen Ray Faden interview with the author.
178–179 "I'm getting quite . . . my new process." MR letter to Elsie, September 4, 1931.
179 It was a Sunday . . . " . . . LOVE MAN." Samuel Ray, op. cit., pp. 7–9.
179 "I don't watch . . . hairs yet." MR letter to Elsie, August 31, 1934.
180 "Tell her. . . I come over." Ibid.
180 Man Ray remained . . . the Surrealists. James Thrall Soby audiotaped interview with Stephen R. Miller, August 16, 1972, in New Canaan, Connecticut. Courtesy Stephen R. Miller.

181   "Nothing can destroy. . . by burning it." MR, *Self Portrait,* p. 229.

181   "one of his consolations." Ibid., p. 241.

181   "clumsily, like a student . . . on his knees." Ibid., p. 225.

181–182   "From the first . . . images are presented." James Thrall Soby, *Photographs by Man Ray,* 1934, p. v.

182–183   "Dans la chambre . . . immediate likeness." Ibid., pp. 42, 25.

183   "You people this . . . supreme silence." Ibid., p. 84.

183   "an extremely adroit . . . second-rate academician." *The New Yorker,* September 29, 1934.

184   "Many American citizens . . . the bourgeois." Letter from Janet Flanner to MR, dated "Sunday" [October 1934].

184   "insolent, serious . . . face the world." James Thrall Soby, op. cit., p. 56.

185   "preoccupation with . . . it permanent." MR, *Self Portrait,* p. 239.

186   "an absolutely delightful little house." Letter from Marcel Duchamp to MR, August 21, 1933. Lake Collection, HRC/Austin.

186   Eluard and Duchamp. . . double issue (no. 3–4). Paul Eluard, *Lettres,* 1984, p. 457 note to letter of September 3, 1933.

187   "if it is practiced . . . give us documents." Beaumont Newhall, op. cit., p. 235.

187   "Documentary. . . not a negation." Roy Stryker in Newhall, ibid., p. 245.

187   James Thrall Soby. . . " . . . documents too!" James Thrall Soby, "Notes on Documentary Photography," 1940, p. 73; and Beaumont Newhall interview with the author, September 12, 1984. Article reprint courtesy Beaumont Newhall.

188   "the art director of the century." Nancy Hall-Duncan, *The History of Fashion Photography,* p. 68.

189   "The disease of . . . by surprise." George Tourdjman, *Alexey Brodovitch,* p. 118.

189   "breaking the stranglehold . . ." Phyllis Lee Levin, *The Wheels of Fashion,* 1965, p. 175.

189   "Astonish me!" George Tourdjman, op. cit., p. 121.

189   "never went to the dress houses." MR letter to Elsie, April 15, 1935.

192–193   For a succession . . . Man Ray fashion layout. *Harper's Bazaar,* January–March, 1936; January–March 1937.

193   And there was no . . . pink velvet heel. Julian Robinson, *Fashion in the 'Thirties,* 1978, p. 29.

193–194   "hate photography. . . of my output." MR letter to Elsie, April 15, 1936.

195   the artist must . . . instructively cured. Arturo Schwarz, *Man Ray,* p. 132.

15: Surrealism Across the Seas

197–198   "I think we can say. . . the littérateurs." David Gascoyne letter to MR, May 7, 1935.

198 "determined to free . . . was born again." Roland Penrose, *Scrap Book*, 1981, p. 27.

199 "set more tongues . . . bewildered London." Cited in Marcel Jean, op. cit., p. 271.

200 "public course . . . his blackboard." Russell Lynes, *Good Old Modern*, 1973, p. 144.

200 "I regret more than . . . rank and file." Letter from Alfred Barr to MR, August 6, 1936.

200 He was pleased . . . " . . . the outcome." Margaret Scolari Barr, "Our Campaigns," 1987, p. 45.

201 at the time . . . nos. 8–10. Giacometti–Man Ray correspondence, 1931–32, in Lake Collection, HRC/Austin.

201 "He told me" . . . she said. Jean-Hubert Martin, *Meret Oppenheim*, 1984, p. 17.

202 "This teacup and . . . fortuitous juxtaposition." Josephine Withers, "The Fur-Lined Tea-Cup," 1977, p. 88.

202 "after a winter . . . of clarifying storms." Herbert Read, *The Philosophy of Modern Art*, 1982, p. 105.

203 "retired to their . . . perhaps lovemaking." MR, *Self Portrait*, p. 227.

204 "the most talked . . . clamlike silence." MR interview, *New York Herald*, n.d.

204 "You aren't . . . this winter." *Harper's Bazaar*, November 1936.

205 "appalling task . . . over that!" Monroe Wheeler interview with the author, March 23, 1984.

205 One enthralled art . . . 8 East Fifty-seventh Street. Letter from Helena Rubinstein Titus to MR, February 1, 1937.

205–206 James Thurber . . . " . . . welcome to." "Talk of the Town," *The New Yorker*, December 12, 1936, p. 34.

206 "the conventions . . . spectacle of madness." Alfred Barr, op. cit.; and Russell Lynes, op. cit., pp. 125, 145.

207 "the man with . . . profound ideal." Arturo Schwarz, *60 ans de libertés*. p. 92.

207 "nine-tenths mechanics." MR, *Self Portrait*, p. 222.

207 "Photography is not . . ." . . . not trickery. John Pultz and Catherine B. Scallen, *Cubism and American Photography*, 1981, p. 19.

208 "poor stepchild." Jean Sagne, *Delacroix*, 1982, p. 13.

208 ("I have long . . . sweet to try . . ."). Letter from Margaret Barr to MR, May 25, 1937.

208 An elaborate *bal masqué* . . . over his chest. Alexandre Iolas interview with the author, March 31, 1984.

209 Roland Penrose . . . " . . . cup of gold." Roland Penrose, op. cit., pp. 104, 117.

209 Back at . . . Adon Lacroix. MR letter to Elsie, September 30, 1937.

209 "In these drawings . . . dreaming." Arturo Schwarz, *Man Ray*, p. 62.

209 "They are the . . . as painting." MR letter to Henry McBride, January 30, 1937, Collection Archives of American Art.

211 "The poet . . . by others." Paul Eluard, *La vie immédiate*, 1971, p. 11.

211 "waking dreams . . . on the mouth." Ibid.
211–212 "a man who . . . desire, not need." Paul Eluard, Preface to exhibition catalogue for Valentine Gallery show of Man Ray drawings, New York City, December 1936.
212 The popular . . . had been raised. Arturo Schwarz, *Man Ray*, pp. 60, 67, 85.
212 "we do not . . . his primitive instincts." Paul Eluard, *Uninterrupted Poetry*, 1977, pp. 12, 14.
213 "spent twenty-seven . . . for his beliefs." Arturo Schwarz, *Man Ray*, p. 186.
213 "This was . . . a church." Ibid., p. 322.
215 Man Ray managed . . . in Jersey City. Bill for services from Samuel Sootin to MR, December 6, 1938.

16: Escape to America

217 "Don't worry . . . Germany and Italy." MR letters to Elsie, April 6, October 12, and December 16, 1938.
218 It surfaced briefly . . . " . . . come to visit us." Jimmy Ernst, *A Not-So-Still-Life*, 1984, pp. 112–13.
219 "I'm going tomorrow . . . portrait maker *extraordinaire*." André Kertész interview with the author, June 1, 1984.
220 "a nation of . . . *de la guerre*." Alfred Cobban, *A History of Modern France*, 1965, p. 155.
220 "I wasn't getting . . . politically minded." MR, *Self Portrait*, pp. 284–85.
220 Antiwar feelings . . . Radnitsky past. Naomi Savage interview with the author, April 13, 1985.
221 "We loathed . . . modern warfare." Robert Motherwell, op. cit., p. 279.
221 "using all techniques . . . each other's throats." MR, *Self Portrait*, p. 297.
222 "gone seriously back to painting." MR letter to Elsie, January 10, 1939.
222 "Everyone is doing . . . really get serious." MR letters to Elsie, January 24 and May 19, 1939.
222 "no sign that France was at war." MR, *Self Portrait*, p. 296.
223 "The great highway . . . met my eyes." Joel Colton, *Léon Blum*, 1966, p. 354.
224 "exodus from Paris . . . character." MR, *Self Portrait*, p. 300.
224 despite his declaration . . . he had come. Ibid., p. 308.
224 "in such a climate . . . friends had disappeared." Ibid., p. 316.
227 Thomson had always . . . "cubist quilt." Virgil Thomson interview with the author, January 12, 1984.
227–228 Neither Thomson nor Man Ray . . . two men through. Ibid.

228 "a madhouse . . . over Europe." MR letter to Elsie, July 26, 1940.

229 He did not . . . such occasion. Virgil Thomson interview.

17: Beautiful Prison

231 Sister Elsie . . . Jersey City. Naomi Savage interview with the author, April 13, 1985.

231 "overcome . . . intense depression." MR, *Self Portrait,* p. 323.

232 More than one . . . " . . . Man Ray." Irving Petlin interview with the author, January 24, 1984.

233 Domestic by nature . . . authentic taste. Naomi Savage interview with the author, May 13, 1985.

233-234 A compromise solution . . . train ticket back East. Elsa Combe Martin interview with the author, April 23, 1984; and letter to the author, April 17, 1985.

234 "short rest." MR, *Self Portrait,* p. 327.

234 "forget now . . . left behind." MR letter to Elsie, written in St. Louis, n.d.

235 Man Ray paid . . . the institute. Emerson Woelffer interview with the author, August 21, 1985.

236 Man Ray did . . . assuage her fears. Elsa Combe Martin letter to the author, op. cit.

237 The Hollywood Ranch Market . . . " . . . *vin ordinaire.*" Letter from Josephine Morris to the author, June 22, 1985.

237 Man Ray placed . . . supercharged engine. MR letter to Elsie, January 30, 1941.

237 Julien and Joella . . . " . . . and the brush." Julien Levy, op. cit., p. 256.

238 In a radio talk . . . " . . . valuable work." "Santa Barbara Radio Talk," December 10, 1940, in Pierre Bourgeade, *Bonsoir, Man Ray,* 1972, pp. 127ff.

238-239 "I am committed . . . and obstinacy." MR letter to Elsie, May 18, 1941.

240 "extraordinary memory . . . photographic memory." Arturo Schwarz, *Man Ray,* p. 323.

240 Miller was also taken . . . unusual warmth. Margaret Neiman Byers interview with the author, August 7, 1984.

242 "the art center of the Western world." Peggy Guggenheim, op. cit., p. xvi.

242 Within the regrouped . . . to be sure. Pierre Matisse interview with the author, February 9, 1984.

242 "The unconquerable American . . . " . . . Café Flore. Marcel Jean, op. cit., p. 328.

242 Fernand Léger . . . "Le Jeumble." Margaret Scolari Barr, op. cit., p. 60.

243 "a vow. . . the actual." *VVV,* I. 1., June 1942, masthead page.

244 in the present upheaval . . . "a new myth." Ibid., pp. 18–26.

244 However, with production . . . for creativity. David Hare interview with the author, May 15, 1984.

245 Man Ray was . . . to his liking. Margaret Neiman Byers interview with the author, August 22, 1985; and M. F. K. Fisher interview with the author, November 10, 1985.

245 "New York was . . . New York." MR, *Self Portrait,* p. 335.

18: Marriages and Manifestos

248–249 "The world may. . . great art." Frank Stauffacher, *Art in Cinema,* 1947, pp. 25–26.

249 "insisting . . . by others." Program for *Dreams That Money Can Buy,* 1947, Collection Philadelphia Museum of Art, n.p.

250 "the idea of. . . spectator would have." Ibid.

250 "consult . . . for further details." *View.* IV. 4, December 1944.

250 "an outstanding . . . progress in art." Jarvis Barlow and MR, introductory statements, Pasadena Art Institute Ex. Cat., September 1944, n.p.

252 For years, he would . . . "objects of his affection." Paul Kantor interview with the author, August 21, 1985.

252 ("The most insignificant thing . . . by our detractors.") *View,* I. 1, 1945.

252 "a bad cold and a bad knee." MR letter to Elsie, June 13, 1945.

252–253 But good news . . . sheets and unharmed. Letter from Ré and Philippe Soupault to MR, August 28, 1945.

253 Ady, the lover. . . but temporary. Letters from Ady Fidelin to MR, April 17 and December 5, 1945.

253 "not as strong . . . now and then." MR letter to Elsie, May 13, 1946.

253 "It helps you . . . regular squares." Arturo Schwarz, *Man Ray,* p. 80.

254 "The art galleries . . . people will buy." MR letter to Elsie, August 29, 1946.

255 In February 1946 . . . his wife, Mildred. Dorothea Tanning interview with the author, February 9, 1984.

255 Conveniently enough . . . champagne awaiting. UCLA Oral History Project interview with Alfred Stendahl, p. 103.

255 *Double Wedding in Beverly Hills.* MR, *Self Portrait,* p. 362.

256 "Papa, I'm the boss! . . . for her existence." Naomi Savage interview with the author, April 13, 1985.

256 The departure of. . . uncle would mutter. Ibid.

257 "In spite of. . . was unperturbed." MR, *Self Portrait,* p. 368.

257 He was an artist . . . " . . . for it in time. MR letters to Naomi Savage, July 16, 1943, and March 16, 1949.

257 ("They're all about . . ." . . . often in the forties.) MR letter to Naomi Savage, January 22, 1947.

19: Practical Dreamer

259 "no one in . . . an intellectual desert." William Copley, *Portrait of the Artist as a Young Dealer,* 1979, pp. 6-7.

260 "all Hollywood was . . . whiskey was consumed." William Copley interview with the author, December 5, 1983.

262 Juliet wore glitter . . . the work looked. Doris Copley Starrels interview with the author, August 19, 1985.

262 There were also . . . great Surrealist icon. Janet Flanner, "The Escape of Mrs. Jeffries," 1943.

263 "I simply try . . . work is permanent." Arturo Schwarz, *60 ans de libertés,* 1971, pp. 50-54.

264 "It was time . . . further to go." William Copley, op. cit., pp. 32, 35.

264 "Grand Sorceror." Ibid., pp. 12, 13.

265 "getting [his] things back." MR letter to Elsie, February 17, 1949.

265 "What good times . . . with its catalogue." MR letter to Katherine Dreier, January 25, 1949, Société Anonyme Archives, Yale University Library.

265-266 "Everybody . . . from preceding works." Société Anonyme Questionnaire, Yale University Library.

266 Man Ray was . . . embarrassed and crestfallen. Letter from James Byrnes to the author, April 16, 1984. On the occasion of the museum's grand reopening in 1984, *The Rope Dancer* was taken out of storage, cleaned, and hung prominently in the second-floor galleries.

266 "as far away . . . crossing the ocean." James Thrall Soby, "Marcel Duchamp in the Arensberg Collection," 1945, p. 11.

267 Only one artist . . . high enough quality. Personal communication, Francis Naumann to the author, October 13, 1985.

267-268 During Duchamp's visit . . . on anything else. Katharine Kuh, "Walter Arensberg and Marcel Duchamp," 1970, p. 36.

268 In the afternoon . . . of his painting. Katharine Kuh interview with the author, January 23, 1984.

269 The house's low-slung . . . in show business. Noma Copley interview with the author, July 14, 1985.

269 This Man Ray . . . detail Lewin sought. Paul Kantor interview with the author, August 21, 1985.

271 On one wall . . . into a face. Sotheby Parke Bernet, "The Albert Lewin Collection," 1968. Courtesy James Byrnes.

271 "disagreeable with people . . . would know it." Mary Wescher taped interview with James Byrnes, ca. 1975, listened to by the author, August 20, 1985.

20: Farewell to Tinsel Town

273 "Feel free to . . ." . . . of Lefevre-Foinet. Letter from Ady's husband, André, to MR, January 31, 1950.

273   Minnie had died five years before. Minnie Ray died on July 4, 1945, at the age of 76.

273   "hope[d] soon to. . . each other again." MR letter to Max Ray, June 1950.

273   "Perhaps I'll get. . . still around." MR letter to Naomi Savage, November 20, 1950.

273–274   Man Ray's combination . . . into people's hands. Gerald Nordland interview with the author, February 16, 1985.

274   "I am in . . . the controls off." MR letter to Elsie, February 16, 1951.

274   "I can't take this town anymore." William Copley interview with the author, December 5, 1983.

274   "feeling like a black sheep." MR, *Self Portrait,* p. 370.

274   The die is . . . by them now. MR letter to Elsie, February 3, 1951.

274   During the decade . . . " . . . our desires instantly." MR, "Photogenic Reflections," 1950, p. 1.

276   a way to . . . at everyone's disposal. Pierre Cabanne, op. cit., p. 88.

276   "modern beauty is . . . from yesterday's." Octavio Paz, op. cit., p. 100.

277   Man Ray put his . . . function in society. Juliet Man Ray interview with the author, November 23, 1984; William Copley interview with the author, December 5, 1983.

277   "The artist . . . are we?" Naomi Savage interview with the author, December 7, 1983.

277   Man Ray and . . . at La Coupole. MR letter to Elsie, April 1, 1951.

277–278   Man Ray and . . . " . . . ever learned about." David Savage interviews with the author, May 25, 1984; November 23, 1985.

278   "the great hunt . . . very difficult." MR letter to Elsie, April 1, 1951.

278   "intellectuals, existential riffraff, and tourists." MR, *Self Portrait,* p. 379.

279   The Café de . . . roman à clef, *Nightwood.* Ned Rorem interview with the author, November 3, 1984.

279   "I was no . . . like a garage." *Architectural Digest,* 1982, p. 185.

279   "putting everything he . . . more like camping." MR letter to Elsie, August 5, 1951.

280   Despite the growing . . . fearful of change. Doris Copley Starrels interview with the author, August 19, 1985.

21: At Home Abroad

283   "the moribund capital . . . had been destroyed." Simone de Beauvoir, *The Mandarins,* 1960, p. 167.

283   "the sick man of Europe." Alfred Cobban, op. cit., p. 214.

284   Man Ray, however, . . . in fact. Jacqueline Monnier interview with the author, November 22, 1984.

284   "Movements begin as . . . scattering of individuals." Marcel Jean, op. cit., p. 344.

285   Her *bals masqués* . . . characters from literature. Roland Penrose, *Scrap Book,* 1981, p. 230.

286 Balthus's large portrait . . . pale orange light. Sabine Rewald, *Balthus,* 1984, p. 76.

286 As a result . . . to her face. Jack Mayer interview with the author, January 13, 1986.

286 "I myself have . . . of wonderful people." Philip Core, *The Original Eye,* 1984, p. 137.

287 "Oh, Ned, I must . . ." . . . firm-jawed and secure. Ned Rorem interview with the author, November 3, 1984.

287 "I like these . . . stays twenty-nine." Ned Rorem, *The Paris and New York Diaries,* 1983, p. 113.

287 "I don't know . . . Simple passers-by." Arturo Schwarz, *Man Ray,* p. 231.

288 "I was like . . . who were healthy." MR interview at Institute for Cassette Studies, Berkeley, California. Recorded 1956. Collection Juliet Man Ray.

288 In the fall . . . were exhaustively complete. Letter to MR from James Thrall Soby, November 11, 1957.

288 Beaumont Newhall . . . lot for $750. Beaumont Newhall interview with the author, September 12, 1984.

288–290 "Painting was an . . . matter of calculation." MR, *Self Portrait,* pp. 384, 385.

290–291 Wescher's piece was . . . of the viewer. Paul Wescher, "Man Ray as Painter," 1953, pp. 32, 37.

292 The artist's friend . . . with magical properties. Patrick Waldberg, "Les objets de Man Ray," 1968, p. 77.

292 To the French critic . . . complex of signs. Jean Hubert Martin, ed., *Objets de mon affection,* 1983, p. 8.

292 To William Seitz . . . " . . . the American temperament." William Seitz, *The Art of Assemblage,* 1961, p. 264.

22: The Arts of Survival

295 Patrick Waldberg . . . " . . . of the imagination." Patrick Waldberg, op. cit., n.p.

295–296 Man Ray and . . . patrons there were. Josephine Morris interview with the author, May 19, 1985, and letter to the author, June 22, 1985. Paul Kantor interviews with the author, May 20, 1985, and August 21, 1985.

296 He was piqued . . . "still have some room for [him]." MR letter to Elsie, October 30, 1953.

296 "One cannot push . . . or toasters." MR letter to Elsie, August 21, 1954.

297 "let them come . . . to 30%." MR letter to Elsie, May 15, 1956.

297 "[Do not] . . . to get something." MR letter to Elsie, October 4, 1956.

297 A veteran observer . . . show Man Ray. Jack Mayer interview with the author, January 10, 1986.

297 Dore Ashton, reviewing . . . " . . . docilely into history." *New York Times,* November 26, 1959, courtesy Jack Mayer.

297 After a forthright . . . Man Ray go. Jack Mayer interview with the author, January 10, 1986.

297 "I'm tied up with . . . generous to me." MR letter to Elsie, October 5, 1959.

298 "It has been . . . through this year." MR letter to Elsie, May 18, 1954.

298 When Noma Rathner . . . plaster concoctions. Noma Copley interview with the author, January 9, 1984.

298–300 They purchased a . . . absorbed by the game. Ben Lees interview with the author, February 3, 1984; Corinna Lothar Metcalf interview with the author, January 1, 1986.

300 "While some are . . . standards of beauty." MR letter to Elsie, August 6, 1953.

300 "He needs so . . . live with others." MR letter to Elsie, August 6, 1953.

300 In the winter . . . Man Ray collection. Letter from Florence Trichon Blumenthal to MR, February 9, 1956.

300–301 Uncle Man . . . " . . . of the paintings." MR letter to Florence, February 17, 1956.

301 "I feel as if . . . carry on [his] work." MR letter to Elsie, March 26, 1956.

301 "in a daze . . . of [his] bereavement." MR letters to Sam Siegler, November 15, 1957, and January 21, 1958.

302 During his sojourn . . . " . . . laws of art." Malcolm Cowley, *Exile's Return,* 1985, p. 151.

302 "white heat." "The Good Old Dada Days," *Time,* June 28, 1954, p. 74.

303 In the months . . . " . . . Dadaism." Manuscript in Lake Collection, HRC/Austin. Dated "Ramatuelle (VAR) 8-7-58."

303 "I am supposed . . . work to do." MR letter to Naomi, July 15, 1958.

303–304 Between bouts with . . . " . . . behind the camera." Ben Lees interview with the author, February 3, 1984.

304–306 "With respect to . . . of the exhibition." Letter from André Breton to MR, summer 1959, n.d.

306 "the trapper of the sun . . . friend Man Ray." Holograph poem sent to Juliet and Man Ray by André Breton, April 13, 1956, inscribed *"Avec tous mes affections pour vous deux"* (With all my love for both of you).

306 "I was a . . . transcending all eras." MR interview in *L'age du cinéma,* Paris, August–November 1951, p. 25.

306 Although in his . . . " . . . changing a word." MR, *Self Portrait,* p. 389.

306–307 It was an erotic . . . " . . . further mental exploration." Manuscript in Lake Collection, HRC/Austin. Original title, "The Visage of a Woman Seen Through an Erotic Eye," changed by MR to "Faces and Races."

23: Self Portrait

309–310 Man Ray selectively . . . not go further. Florence Blumenthal interview with the author, September 22, 1984.

312   "fiery elf... to meet it." Morris Gordon, "Man Ray, the Fiery Elf," 1962, pp. 27-29.

312   "ma légende." Lucien Treillard interview with the author, November 22, 1984.

313   "I have purposely... 'Self Portrait.'"MR letter to Seymour Lawrence, n.d. (ca. May–June 1961).

313   "What taught you... helter-skelter importance." Ibid.

313-314   Over long seafood lunches... numbers and dates. Seymour Lawrence interview with the author, April 19, 1984.

314   "Inspiration, not information..."... six months away. MR letter to Seymour Lawrence, November 26, 1962.

315   In letters to... days on end. MR letter to Marcel Duchamp, September 5, 1964.

315   These symptomatic bouts... for long periods. MR letter to Naomi Savage, May 8, 1968. Clinical analysis of Man Ray's condition, David S. Baldwin, M.D., personal communication, March 2, 1986.

316   The couple had met... in the city. Roz Jacobs interviews with the author, February 22, 1984, and March 1, 1986.

316   "the little French guy... stylized self-image." Jacques Kaplan interview with the author, March 5, 1984.

316   Roberta Kimmel... Ribemont-Dessaignes. Roberta Kimmel Cohn interview with the author, March 7, 1984.

317   During their brief... might have liked. John Szarkowski interview with the author, May 31, 1984.

317   "to whom... kind of play." John Szarkowski, *Looking at Photographs,* 1973, p. 82.

318   "linking [the] absolute... brought to play...." MR "Statement," 1916.

318   Man Ray was... had never lost. Virginia Zabriskie interview with the author, February 15, 1984.

318-319   Belz was impressed... make a living. Carl Belz interview with the author, April 28, 1985.

319   Man Ray the author... "... or the critics." Irving Sandler interview with Man Ray, April 1, 1963. Tape recording in Collection Archives of American Art, Smithsonian Institution, courtesy Catherine Keen.

319   That night... away with glee. Roz Jacobs interview with the author March 1, 1986.

319-320   "been through two... present-day society." Brian O'Doherty, "Light on an Individual: Man Ray," *New York Times,* May 6, 1963.

320   During the preceding... represent Man Ray. Naomi and David Savage interview with the author, February 29, 1984. Barbara Kulicke interview with the author, February 16, 1984.

320   "being associated with..."... the exhibition catalogue. Letter from Marcel Duchamp to MR, December 21, 1962.

320   Ekstrom sensed that... (You are crazy). Arne Ekstrom interviews with the author, January 10, 1984, and June 4, 1985; and letter to the author, March 10, 1987.

321   "the best... [of]... intellectually challenging." William Rubin, "Man Ray," *Art International Magazine,* June 1963.

24: The Next Wave

323 "a bit dazed." MR letter to Naomi Savage, May 26, 1963.

323–324 "An original . . . is human." MR, *Objets de mon affection,* p. 158.

324 As far back . . . fueled the work. See John Tancock, untitled essay, Ex. cat. Zabriskie Gallery show, "Objects of My Affection," January–February 1985, n.p.

324 "I am swamped . . . better than the originals!" MR letter to Naomi Savage, December 4, 1967.

325 The two met . . . at aperitif time. Lucien Treillard interviews with the author, November 22, 1984, and March 25, 1986.

326 "people think it's the original." MR letter to Naomi Savage, December 18, 1965.

326 "Schwarz of the . . . for five years!" MR letter to Naomi Savage, April 28, 1965.

326 "it is necessary. . . piles of books." Ibid.

328 "Nothing can be . . . unless something went before it." MR interview with John Jones, October 15, 1965, Collection Archives of American Art.

328 "took pieces of. . . in their work." Jean-Hubert Martin interview with the author, March 26, 1986.

329 "They're nice . . . forty years before." Ibid.

329–331 In the autumn . . . came the reply. Ron Padgett interview with the author, December 15, 1983; Padgett, "Man to Man," 1982, p. 15; Padgett, "Artist Accompanies Himself with His Rays," 1966; Padgett, unpublished journal entries.

331 "Here are the . . . portrait recently sold." MR letter to Naomi Savage, July 12, 1966.

332 It was the . . . in its midst. Letter from Jules Langsner to MR, March 1964, n.d. MR letter to Jules Langsner, April 4, 1964, Collection Archives of American Art, Gift of the Art Library, University of California, Los Angeles.

332 "it's not possible . . . Stuttgart, etc." Letter from Jules Langsner to James Elliott, June 15, 1965, Collection Archives of American Art.

332 "As in all . . . choice to be made." MR letter to Jules Langsner, March 21, 1966.

333–334 Introduced by Langsner. . . his saving grace. Tape recording of MR lecture at the LACMA, October 27, 1966. Collection Los Angeles County Museum of Art. © 1966 by Museum Associates, Los Angeles County Museum of Art. Reprinted by permission.

334–335 Four days later. . . high-school days. Tape recording of MR lecture at Chouinard Art Institute, October 31, 1966. Collection Emerson Woelffer.

335 Under the headline . . . " . . . of its significance." Philip Leider, "Man Ray, Wandering Knight," *New York Times,* November 6, 1966.

335 Carl Belz, on the other hand . . . interested the artist most. Carl Belz, "A Man Ray Retrospective in L.A.," *Artforum,* December 1966, pp. 23–24.

25: Death of a *Vieux Copain*

337-338   His ripostes were . . . others who die). Robert Lebel, "Dernière soirée avec M.D.," 1985, pp. 132 ff.

338-339   "alter egos." William Copley interview with the author, December 5, 1983.

339   They never tried . . . manic intensity. David Savage interview with the author, April 13, 1984.

339   "a form of . . . reaches a decision." Janet Flanner, "Letter from Paris," *The New Yorker,* November 2, 1968, pp. 170–71.

339   *"Je suis dans . . ."* support chess matches). Letter from Marcel Duchamp to MR, June 1961.

340   "It was a . . . won the sweepstakes." MR letter to Naomi Savage, September 20, 1961.

340   "man as man . . . only repeat themselves." Pierre Cabanne, op. cit., p. 98.

340   "For Duchamp . . . but a medium" Octavio Paz, op. cit., p. 175.

340   metawork . . . "whole body." Pierre Cabanne, op. cit., p. 74.

340   "He was twenty-nine . . . and Sarah Bernhardt." Moira Roth, op. cit., p. 92.

343   "October first . . . more about it." MR "Bilingual Biography," 1974 addendum to 1945 article, p. 31.

343   "ignorance in the . . . will was acceptable." Harold Rosenberg, "MOMA Dada," *The New Yorker,* May 18, 1968.

344-345   The odor of tear gas . . . nature to translation. Arnold Crane interviews with Man Ray, June 12, 1968; October 1968; January 1970, Collection Archives of American Art.

345   "To know Man . . . number of years." Arnold Crane, "Photo Graphics," 1973, n.p.

345   In his striking . . . upon the world. Arnold Crane photographs of Man Ray, Collection Archives of American Art.

345-346   Another spiritual son . . . condition of the cobblestones. Timothy Baum interviews with the author, November 1, 1984, and February 15, 1986.

346   *"aliénés"* . . . "change life itself." Philippe Soupault, "Dada 291—1924," May–June 1969, n.p.

346   "never an underground . . . gentlemen and critics." Timothy Baum, "Homage and Introduction," October–November 1971, n.p.

346-347   In Baum's view . . . " . . . moment at hand." Timothy Baum interview with the author, February 15, 1986.

347   The windowlike cover . . . four-score years. Arne Ekstrom interview with the author, January 10, 1984.

348   "things didn't really . . . quite found himself." [No byline] *New York Magazine,* February 2, 1970, p. 57.

348   In a conversation . . . " . . . have to invent." Sanche de Gramont, "Remember Dada—Man Ray at 80," *New York Times Magazine,* September 6, 1970.

348 Over the years . . . as he could. MR letters to Do Ray Goodbread, October 22, 1965; February 19, 1968; November 19, 1971.

348 A dutiful uncle . . . especially the press. MR letter to Do Ray Goodbread, February 11, 1974. Interview with the author, June 7, 1986.

348-349 Niece Helen Faden . . . Man kissed her. Helen Ray Faden interview with the author, May 30, 1984.

26: The Light and the Dark

351 "recuperate." MR letter to Naomi Savage, November 10, 1971.

351 "My hands are full with Europe." MR letter to Naomi Savage, November 10, 1971.

352 Coming to the . . . without intervening glass. Jean-Hubert Martin interviews with the author, December 17, 1984, and March 26, 1986.

352 "I have no style . . . sportsmen, doctors, and lovers." "Paris Honors Man Ray with Art Display," *New York Times,* January 1, 1972.

352 "discovered while drinking buttermilk." MR letter to Naomi Savage, June 18, 1974.

353 "The sad news . . . exaggerated." MR letter to Naomi Savage, June 18, 1974.

353 "snubbed." MR letter to Naomi Savage, July 30, 1974.

353 "testy . . . Brooklyn accent." Mario Amaya, "Man Ray," 1977, n.p.

353-354 "so adept at . . . of his generation." John Russell, "The Whole Man Ray at Cultural Center," *New York Times,* June 20, 1974, p. 20.

354 "accomplished rehearsals . . . without significant modifications." Hilton Kramer, "Man Ray: Faithful Disciple," *New York Times,* June 12, 1974.

354 "Duchamp does more . . . totally eclipses it." [No byline] *ARTNews,* April 1975.

354 "American vanguardist." Harold Rosenberg, "American Drawing and the Academy of the Erased De Kooning," *The New Yorker,* March 22, 1976.

354 Man Ray had . . . " . . . work is permanent." Man Ray, *To Be Continued Unnoticed,* Copley Galleries, 1948.

354 "the new art form . . . ever had before." Jacob Deschin, "The Print Prospectors," Spring 1976, p. 67.

355 The pursuit was . . . a revitalized market. Assessment of photography market in the 1970s, Laurence Miller interview with the author, May 24, 1984.

355-356 a lively domestic scene . . . a transcendent experience. Anecdotes about weekends at Farley Farm, Joanne Kitchener Horton interview with the author, February 10, 1984.

356 "I made some new . . . considered very sensitive." MR letter to Naomi Savage, July 24, 1975.

358 "photo . . . other graphic works." MR letter to Naomi Savage, March 9, 1976.

358 "These cobblestones . . . not for men." Juliet Man Ray interview with the author, November 23, 1984.

358 "I can help myself!" Dene Byers interview with the author, August 22, 1985.

358 "It seems all . . . the same time." Jack Mayer interview with the author, January 10, 1986.

359 "Something has gone . . . colored jokes are stale." Dorothea Tanning, in Alain Jouffroy, ed., *XXe Siècle,* Paris, 1977, p. 15.

359 "I've hauled it . . . finished it seems," Mario Amaya, op. cit.

362 On August 27, 1976 . . . for the occasion. Mary Jane Laurent interview with the author, March 24, 1986; letter to the author, July 31, 1986.

362 Roz Jacobs spent . . . " . . . to spend it." Roz Jacobs interview with the author, March 1, 1986.

362 Late October. . . heard his voice. Naomi Savage interview with the author, June 20, 1906.

362-363 Even as he grew. . . " . . . work to do." Lucien Treillard interview with the author, March 25, 1986.

363 In mid-November. . . the attending nurse. Mary Jane Laurent, interview with the author, March 24, 1986.

363 It was predawn . . . in Puerto Rico. Naomi and David Savage interview with the author, June 28, 1986.

363-364 By the third call . . . *New York Times.* Roberta Kimmel Cohn interview with the author, March 7, 1984.

364 The next morning . . . of modern art. Alden Whitman, "Man Ray is Dead in Paris at 86," November 19, 1976, p. 24.

BIBLIOGRAPHY

Abbott, Berenice. *The World of Atget.* New York: Horizon Press, 1964.
———. *Photographs.* New York: Horizon Press, 1970.
———. *New York in the Thirties.* Text by Elizabeth McCausland. (Formerly titled *Changing New York.*) New York: Dover Publications, 1973.
Adato, Perry Miller. *Gertrude Stein: When This You See, Remember Me.* New York: *Filmmakers Newsletter,* March 1972.
Ades, Dawn. *Photomontage.* New York: Pantheon Books, 1976.
Alexandrian, Sarane. *Man Ray.* Chicago: J. Philip O'Hara, Inc., 1973.
Amaya, Mario. "My Man Ray, an Interview with Lee Miller." *Art in America,* May-June, 1975.
———. "Man Ray, 1890-1976." *ARTnews,* May-June, 1977.
Apollinaire, Guillaume. *Alcools.* Translated by Anne Hyde Greet. Berkeley: University of California Press, 1965.
———. *Les peintres cubistes.* Paris: Collection Savoir, Herrmann, 1980.
Apter, Eleanor S. *Art for a New Era. The Société Anonyme, 1920-1950.* Exhibition catalogue, Yale University Art Gallery, New Haven. April 25-August 31, 1984.
Arman, Yves. *Marcel Duchamp joue et gagne.* Paris: Galerie Yves Arman; Galerie Beaubourg; Galerie Bonnier, 1984.
Audoin, Philippe. *Breton.* Paris: Gallimard, 1970.
Auster, Paul, ed. *The Random House Book of Twentieth Century French Poetry.* New York: Random House, 1982.
Avrich, Paul. *The Modern School Movement: Anarchy and Education in the United States.* Princeton: Princeton University Press, 1980.

Azéma, Jean-Paul. *De Munich à la Liberation, 1938–1944.* Paris: Editions du Seuil, 1979.

Bann, Stephen. *The Tradition of Constructivism.* New York: Viking Press, 1974.

Barnes, Djuna. *Smoke and Other Early Stories.* Edited by Douglas Messerli. College Park, Maryland: Sun & Moon Press, 1982.

———. *Interviews.* Edited by Alyce Barry. Foreword and Commentary by Douglas Messerli. Washington, D.C.: Sun & Moon Press, 1985.

Barr, Alfred H., Jr. *Fantastic Art Dada Surrealism.* New York: Museum of Modern Art, 1936.

———. *Picasso, Fifty Years of His Art.* New York: Museum of Modern Art/Simon & Schuster, 1946.

Barr, Margaret Scolari. "Our Campaigns." *New Criterion,* Summer 1987.

Barthes, Roland. *Camera Lucida. Reflections on Photography.* Edited by Richard Howard. New York: Hill & Wang, 1981.

Beach, Sylvia. *Shakespeare & Company.* New York: Harcourt, Brace and World, 1959.

Beaton, Cecil, and Gail Buckland. *The Magic Image.* Boston: Little, Brown and Co., 1975.

Beauvoir, Simone de. *The Mandarins.* Translated by Leonard M. Friedman. New York: Meridian Books, 1960.

Bedouin, Jean-Louis. *André Breton.* Paris: Pierre Seghers, 1965.

Belz, Carl. "A Man Ray Retrospective in L.A.," review in *Artforum,* vol. 4, December 1966.

Benjamin, Walter. *Illuminations.* Edited by Hannah Arendt. New York: Schocken Books, 1969.

Berger, John. "The Uses of Photography." *New Society,* London, October 13, 1966.

Berger, Pierre. *Robert Desnos.* Paris: Seghers, 1966.

Berman, Avis. "Bill Brandt, Through a Camera Darkly," *ARTNews,* 81.3, March, 1982.

Billy, André. *Apollinaire.* Paris: Seghers, 1965.

Bird, William. "Man Ray Turns New Trick in Photography." New York *Sun,* March 27, 1935 [article about solarization].

Black, Bernard Gallery. *Samuel Halpert, 1884–1930, a Pioneer of Modern Art in America.* Exhibition catalogue, January 7–25, 1969.

Blumenthal, Florence. *End of a Story.* Unpublished memoir.

Bohn, Willard. "Marius de Zayas and Visual Poetry: Mental Reactions," *Arts Magazine,* vol. 55, no. 10, June 1981.

Bony, Anne. *Les années cinquante.* Paris: Editions du Regard, 1982.

Bourgeade, Pierre. *Bonsoir, Man Ray.* Paris: Belfond, 1972.

Bramley, Serge. *Man Ray.* Paris: Gallimard, 1980.

Brandt, Bill. Marlborough Gallery press release, March 1976. Museum of Modern Art Artists File.

———. "The Man in the Mirror." *Newsweek,* October 5, 1981.

———. *Portraits.* Introduction by Alan Ross. Austin: University of Texas Press, 1982.

Brassaï. *Photographs.* Introduction by Lawrence Durrell. New York: Museum of Modern Art, 1968.

———. *The Artists of My Life.* Translated by Richard Miller. New York: Viking Studio Books, 1982.

Breton, André. "Surrealism Yesterday, Today, and Tomorrow." *This Quarter,* vol. 1, September 1932 [Surrealist number].

———. *Dictionnaire abrégé du surréalisme.* Paris: Galerie Beaux Arts, 1938.

———. "Prolegomena to a Third Manifesto of Surrealism or Else." *VVV,* no.1, June 1942.

———. "Lighthouse of the Bride," *View,* vol.1, March 1945 [Marcel Duchamp number].

———. *Le surréalisme et la peinture.* New York: Brentano's 1945 [reprint of 1928 edition].

———. *Poèmes.* Paris: Gallimard, 1967

———. *Manifestes du surréalisme.* Paris: NRF/Gallimard, 1967.

Brooklyn Institute of Arts and Sciences. Annual Reports, 1905-1912. Brooklyn Museum. Accession Records, 1905-1912.

Brown, Milton. *American Painting from the Armory Show to the Great Depression.* Princeton: Princeton University Press, 1955.

Browning, Arthur. "Portrait of a Distortionist" [on André Kertész]. *Minicam Monthly,* II. 2, August 1939.

Brunhammer, Yvonne. *1925.* Paris: Les Presses de la Connaissance, 1977.

Buckland, Gail. *Fox Talbot and the Invention of Photography.* London: Scolar Press, 1980.

Budnik, Dan. "A Point Vue: Photographs by André Kertész." *Infinity,* XIV. 3, March 1965.

Burns, Edward, ed. *Staying on Alone: The Letters of Alice B. Toklas.* New York: Liveright, 1973.

Cabanne, Pierre. *Dialogues with Marcel Duchamp.* Translated by Ron Padgett. New York: Viking Press, 1971.

Camfield, William. *Francis Picabia, His Art, Life and Times.* Princeton: Princeton University Press, 1979.

Cassidy, Victor. "Laszlo Moholy-Nagy, Adventurer in Light." *The New Criterion,* IV. 9, May 1986.

Caws, Mary Ann. *The Inner Theatre of Modern French Poetry.* Princeton: Princeton University Press, 1972.

———. *The Surrealist Voice of Robert Desnos.* Amerst: University of Massachusetts Press, 1977.

———. *A Metapoetics of the Passage: Architextures in Surrealism and After.* Hanover, N.H.: University Press of New England, 1981.

———. *The Eye in the Text: Essays on Perception, Mannerist to Modern.* Princeton: Princeton University Press, 1981.

Clark, Kenneth. *Leonardo Da Vinci.* Harmondsworth, Middlesex: Penguin Books, 1981.

Coates, Robert M. "Abstraction in America, 1912-present." *The New Yorker,* February 3, 1951.

Cobban, Alfred. *A History of Modern France, 1871–1962.* Harmondsworth, Middlesex: Penguin Books, 1965.

Coe, Robert. "The Intellectual Odyssey of Peter Swales." *Rolling Stone,* September 27, 1984.

Coffey, Brian. *Dice Thrown Never Will Annul Chance.* Translation of *Un coup de dés,* by Stéphane Mallarmé. Dublin: The Dolmen Press, 1965.

Colton, Joel. *Léon Blum: Humanist in Politics.* New York: Alfred A. Knopf, 1966.

Comstock, Helen. "Samuel Halpert, Post-Impressionist." *International Studio,* LXXV, no. 300, April 1922.

Connolly, Cyril. *Balthus.* Exhibition catalogue, The Lefevre Gallery, London, January 1952.

Conte, Arthur. *Le premier janvier, 1940.* Paris: Librarie Plon, 1977.

Copley, William. *CPLY: Reflections on a Past Life.* Exhibition catalogue, Institute for Arts, Rice University Museum, September 7–November 11, 1979.

Copley, The William N. Collection. Exhibition catalogue, auction at Sotheby Parke Bernet, November 5–6, 1979, New York City.

Core, Philip. *The Original Eye: Arbiters of Twentieth Century Taste.* London: John Calmann and Cooper Ltd., 1984.

Cowley, Malcolm. *Exile's Return.* New York: Viking Penguin, 1985.

Crane, Arnold. *Interviews with Man Ray.* Collection Archives of American Art. June 12, 1968; October 1968; January 1970.

———. *Photo Graphics.* Exhibition catalogue, Milwaukee Art Center, February 10–March 11, 1973.

Crespelle, Jean-Paul. *Montparnasse vivant.* Paris: Hachette, 1962.

———. *Picasso and His Women.* New York: Coward-McCann, 1969.

Dada Art, a Collection. The property of a Swiss private collector, formerly the collection of Arturo Schwarz, Milan. Exhibition catalogue, Sotheby's London, December 4, 1985.

Dada/Surrealism, no.10/11, 1982. Edited by Rudolph Kuenzli and Mary Ann Caws.

———. no.12, 1983. Edited by Kuenzli and Caws.

Daix, Pierre. *Picasso.* London: Thames and Hudson, 1965.

Davidson, Abraham A. *Early American Modernist Painting.* New York: Harper and Row, 1981.

Davis, Douglas. "Man Ray's Happy Accidents." *Newsweek,* April 19, 1982.

Deschin, Jacob. "The Print Prospectors." *35-mm Photography,* Spring 1976.

Desnos, Robert. "L'étoile de mer. Poème, tel que l'a vu Man Ray." Holograph scenario for the film with music, 1927–28. Museum of Modern Art Library.

———. *Photographic Compositions* [on Man Ray]. Exhibition catalogue, Arts Club of Chicago, February 1929.

———. "The Work of Man Ray." *transition,* no. 15, February 1929.

D'Harnoncourt, Anne, and Kynaston McShine, editors. *Marcel Duchamp.* Philadelphia and New York: Philadelphia Museum of Art and Museum of Modern Art, 1973.

Diehl, Gaston. *Max Ernst.* Naefels, Switzerland: Bonfini Press, 1975.

Dondis, Donis A. *A Primer of Visual Literacy.* Cambridge, Massachusetts: MIT Press, 1984.

Doty, Robert. *Photo-Secession, Stieglitz and the Fine Art Movement in Photography.* New York: Dover Publications, 1978.

Dreier, Katherine S. *The Société Anonyme, Its Why and Wherefore,* 1920.

———. Brooklyn Museum Catalogue of An International Exhibition of Modern Art Assembled by the Société Anonyme. November 19, 1926–January 1, 1927.

Drinnon, Richard. *Rebel in Paradise: A Biography of Emma Goldman.* Chicago: University of Chicago Press, 1961.

Dryansky, G.Y. "Historic Houses: The Man Ray Studio." *Architectural Digest,* November 1982. Photographs by Pascal Hinous.

Duchamp, Marcel. Notes for a Lecture at the St. Louis Museum of Art. Unpublished manuscript, collection Philadelphia Museum of Art, November 24, 1964.

Duchamp et après. Special issue of *Opus International Magazine,* No. 49, March 1974. Edited by Georges Fall.

Dumas, Marie-Claire. *Robert Desnos, ou l'exploration des limites.* Paris: Librarie Klincksieck, 1980.

Duncan, Isadora. *My Life.* New York: Liveright, 1927 and 1955.

Eddy, Arthur Jerome. *Cubism and Post-Impressionism.* Chicago: A.C. McClurg & Co., 1914.

Edelson, Michael. "The Diary of André Kertész." *Camera 35,* October 1975.

Edwards, Hugh, ed. *Surrealism and Its Affinities: The Mary Reynolds Collection.* Chicago: Art Institute of Chicago, 1956.

Ehrenzweig, Anton. *The Hidden Order of Art.* Berkeley: The University of California Press, 1971.

Ehrlich, Susan. "Los Angeles Painters of the 1940's." *Journal: Southern California Art Magazine,* no. 28. vol. 3, no. 8, October 1980.

Elderfield, John. *Matisse in the Collection of the Museum of Modern Art.* New York: Museum of Modern Art, 1978.

Eliot, T.S. *Selected Prose,* ed. Frank Kermode. New York: Harcourt Brace Jovanovich, 1975.

Eluard, Paul. *La vie immédiate.* Paris: Gallimard, 1971.

———. *Uninterrupted Poetry.* Translated by Lloyd Alexander. Westport, Conn.: Greenwood Press, 1977.

———. *Eluard et ses amis peintres.* Exhibition catalogue, MNAM/Centre Georges Pompidou, Paris 1982.

———. *Lettres à Gala, 1924–1948.* Paris: Gallimard, 1984.

Ernst, Jimmy. *A Not-So-Still-Life.* New York: St. Martin's/Marek, 1984.

Ernst, Max. *The Hundred Headless Woman.* Translated by Dorothea Tanning. Foreword by André Breton. New York: George Braziller, 1981.

Filler, Martin. "Monsieur Moderne, Robert Mallet-Stevens." *House and Garden,* April 1975.

Flanner, Janet. "The Escape of Mrs. Jeffries." *The New Yorker,* May 22, 29, and June 3, 1943 [story of Mary Reynolds].

———. "Letter from Paris." *The New Yorker,* November 2, 1968.

———. *Paris Was Yesterday.* New York: Viking Press, 1972.

Ford, Hugh. *Published in Paris.* New York: Macmillan & Co., 1975.

Fowlie, Wallace. *Age of Surrealism.* New York: Swallow Press and William Morrow, 1950.

———. *Lautréamont.* New York: Twayne & Co., 1973.

Fraigneau, André. *Cocteau.* London: Vista Books, 1961.

Frank, Waldo et al. *America and Alfred Stieglitz: A Collective Portrait.* Millerton, N.Y.: Aperture, Inc., 1979.

Frascina, Francis. *Modern Art and Modernism: A Critical Anthology.* New York: Harper and Row, 1982.

Frazer, Sir James George. *The New Golden Bough.* New York: Doubleday & Co., 1961.

Freedberg, S.J. "On Art History." *The New Criterion,* September 1985.

Freud, Sigmund. *The Interpretation of Dreams.* New York: Avon Books, 1969.

Freund, Gisele. *Photography and Society.* Boston: David R. Godine, 1980.

Gablik, Suzi. *Progress in Art.* New York: Rizzoli, 1976.

———. *Has Modernism Failed?* New York: Thames and Hudson, 1984.

Galassi, Peter. *Before Photography: Painting and the Invention of Photography.* New York: The Museum of Modern Art, 1981.

Gallop, Jane. *Intersections: A Reading of Sade.* Lincoln: University of Nebraska Press, 1981.

Gascoyne, David. *A Short Survey of Surrealism.* London: Cobden-Sanderson, 1935.

Gay, Peter. *Art and Act: On Causes in History.* New York: Harper & Row, 1976.

Geist, Sidney. *Brancusi: The Kiss.* New York: Harper & Row, 1978.

———. *Brancusi: A Study of the Sculpture.* New York: Hacker Art Books, 1983.

Geldzahler, Henry. *Jean Arp.* Exhibition catalogue, Museum of Modern Art, 1972.

Gernsheim, Helmut and Alison. *Alvin Langdon Coburn, Photographer.* New York: Dover Publications, 1978.

Gide, André. *Pretexts.* Edited by Justin O'Brien. New York: Meridian Books, 1959.

Giedion, Siegfried. *Mechanization Takes Command.* New York: Norton Library, 1969.

Glackens, Ira. *William Glackens and the Eight.* New York: Horizon Press, 1957.

Glueck, Grace. "Revisiting the Battleground of American Modernism." [on The Eight and the Armory Show]. *New York Times,* June 17, 1984.

Goldberg, Vicky. *Photography in Print: Writings from 1816 to the Present.* New York: Simon and Schuster, 1981.

Goodwin, George. "Los Angeles Art Community: A Group Portrait." Alfred Stendahl interview. UCLA Oral History Program. A project funded by the National Endowment for the Humanities, 1977.

Gordon, Morris. "Man Ray, the Fiery Elf." *Infinity,* November 1962, XI. 9.

Gramont, Sanche de. "Remember Dada, Man Ray at Eighty." *New York Times Magazine,* September 6, 1970.

Green, Jonathan, ed. *Camera Work: A Critical Anthology.* Millerton, N.Y.: Aperture, Inc., 1973.

Greene, Nathanael. *From Versailles to Vichy: The Third French Republic 1919–1940.* Wesleyan, Conn.: Wesleyan University Press, 1970.

Guggenheim, Peggy. *Out of This Century: Confessions of an Art Addict.* New York: Doubleday & Co., 1980.

Guilbaut, Serge. *How New York Stole the Idea of Modern Art.* Translated by Arthur Goldhammer. Chicago: University of Chicago Press, 1983.

Hall-Duncan, Nancy. *The History of Fashion Photography.* New York: International Museum of Photography/Alpine Book Company, 1979.

Hamilton, George Heard. *In Memory of Katherine S. Dreier (1877–1952), Her Own Collection of Modern Art.* Exhibition catalogue. Yale University Art Gallery, December 15, 1952–February 1, 1953.

Hare, David, ed. *VVV,* no.1, June 1942. Editorial statement.

Hartley, Anthony. *The Penguin Book of French Verse: The Twentieth Century.* Harmondsworth, Middlesex: Penguin Books, 1967.

Haworth-Booth, Mark. *Bill Brandt, Behind the Camera, Photographs, 1928–1983.* Essay by David Mellor. New York: Aperture, Inc., 1985.

Hayter, Stanley William. *New Ways of Gravure.* New York: Watson-Guptill, 1981.

Henri, Robert. *The Art Spirit.* New York: Harper & Row, 1984.

Herbert, Robert L., ed. *Modern Artists on Art: Ten Unabridged Essays.* Englewood Cliffs, N.J.: Prentice-Hall, Inc., 1964.

———. et al., eds. *The Société Anonyme and the Dreier Bequest at Yale University: A Catalogue Raisonné.* New Haven: Yale University Press, 1984.

Herrera, Hayden. *Frida: A Biography of Frida Kahlo.* New York: Harper & Row, 1983.

Higham, Charles. *The Art of the American Film.* Garden City, N.Y.: Doubleday & Co., 1973.

Homolka, Florence. *Focus on Art.* New York: Ivan Obolensky, Inc., 1962.

Honour, Hugh. *Romanticism.* New York: Harper & Row, 1979.

Huelsenbeck, Richard. *Memoirs of a Dada Drummer.* Edited by Hans Kleinschmidt. New York: Viking Press, 1969.

Humphreys, Richard, ed. *Pound's Artists: Ezra Pound and the Visual Arts in London, Paris, and Italy.* London: Tate Gallery, 1985.

Hyde, Lewis. *The Gift: Imagination and the Erotic Life of Property.* New York: Vintage Books, 1983.

Janus. *Man Ray, the Photographic Image.* Woodbury, N.Y.: Barron's Publications, 1979.

———. *Man Ray.* The Great Photographers Series. London: Collins, 1984.

Januszczak, Waldemar. "A Surrealist's Last Dreams" [on Roland Penrose]. *The Guardian,* London, May 8, 1984.

Jean, Marcel. *The History of Surrealist Painting.* New York: Grove Press, 1967.

Josephson, Matthew. *Life Among the Surrealists.* New York: Holt, Rinehart and Winston, 1962.

Jouffroy, Alain. *A l'improviste.* Exhibition catalogue for Meret Oppenheim exhibition at Galerie Suzanne Visat, February 1973.

———. *La vie réinventée. L'explosion des années 20 à Paris.* Paris: Laffont, 1982.

Kandinsky, Wassily, and Franz Marc, eds. *The Blaue Reiter Almanac.* New York: The Viking Press, 1974.

Kelder, Diane, ed. *Stuart Davis*. New York: Praeger, 1971.

Kern, Stephen. *The Culture of Time and Space, 1880–1918*. Cambridge, Mass.: Harvard University Press, 1983.

Kertész, André. *Of New York*. Edited by Nicholas Ducrot. New York: Alfred A. Knopf, 1976.

———. *Photographs*. Preface by Carole Kismaric. Millerton, New York: Aperture, 1977.

Kiki (Alice Prin). *Souvenirs*. Paris: Black Manikin Press, 1929.

Komroff, Manuel. "Our Art Class." *Modern School Magazine*, July 1914.

Kouidis, Virginia M. *Mina Loy: American Modernist Poet*. Baton Rouge: Louisiana State University Press, 1980.

Kovacs, Steven. "Man Ray as Filmmaker," *Artforum*, XI. 3, November 1972.

Kramer, Hilton. "Man Ray, Faithful Disciple," *New York Times*, January 12, 1975.

———. ed. *Brancusi: The Sculptor as Photographer*. Lyme, Conn.: Callaway Editions, 1979.

———. "Art Since the War: Who Will Write Its History?" *The New Criterion*, Summer 1985.

Krauss, Rosalind, and Jane Livingston. *L'Amour Fou: Photography and Surrealism*. Exhibition catalogue for Corcoran Gallery show, September–November 1985, New York: Abbeville Press, 1985.

Kreymborg, Alfred. "Man Ray and Adon Lacroix, Economists." *New York Morning Telegraph*, March 14, 1915.

———. *Troubadour*. New York: Boni and Liveright, 1925.

Kuh, Katharine. *Art Has Many Faces*. New York: Harper & Brothers, 1951.

———. "Walter Arensberg and Marcel Duchamp." *Saturday Review*, September 5, 1970.

Kuhn, Walt. "The Story of the Armory Show." *Arts Magazine*, vol. 58, no. 10, Summer 1984.

Lacôte, René, and Georges Haldas. *Tristan Tzara*. Paris: Pierre Seghers, 1960.

Lacroix, Adon. *A Book of Divers Writings*. Designed and published in Ridgefield, N.J., by Man Ray, January 1915.

———. "Intimacy," [poem]. *Others*, I. 6, December 1915.

———. "Visual Words, Sounds Seen, Thoughts Felt, Feelings Thought." *TNT*, 1919.

Langer, Suzanne K. *Feeling and Form*. New York: Scribner's, 1953.

Larmour, Peter J. *The French Radical Party in the 1930s*. Stanford: Stanford University Press, 1964.

Lautréamont. *Oeuvres complètes*. Edited by Marguerite Bonnet. Paris: Garnier-Flammarion, 1969.

———. *Oeuvres complètes*. Edited by Marcel Jean and Arpad Mezei. Paris: Eric Losfeld, 1971.

———. *Les chants de Maldoror*. Edited by Daniel Oster. Paris: Presses de la Renaissance, L'Univers des Livres, 1977.

Lebel, Robert. *Marcel Duchamp*. Translated by George Heard Hamilton. New York: Grove Press, 1959.

———. *Marcel Duchamp*. Paris: Editions Pierre Belfond, 1985.

Léger, Fernand. *Functions of Painting.* Translated by Alexandra Anderson. Edited and introduced by Edward F. Fry. New York: Viking Press, 1973.

Legrand, Francine-Claire. *Painters of the Mind's Eye: Belgian Symbolists and Surrealists.* Exhibition catalogue, New York Cultural Center, January–May, 1974.

Leider, Philip. "Man Ray, Wandering Knight." *New York Times,* November 6, 1966.

Lekatsas, Barbara. *The Avant-Garde Book: An Exhibition.* Hofstra University Library, New York, 1985.

Levin, Phyllis Lee. *The Wheels of Fashion.* New York: Doubleday, 1965.

Levy, Julien. *Surrealism.* New York: Black Sun Press, 1936.

———. *Memoir of an Art Gallery.* New York: G.P. Putnam's, 1977.

Lippard, Lucy, ed. *Dadas on Art.* Englewood Cliffs, N.J.: Prentice-Hall and Co., 1971.

Lord, James. *Giacometti: A Biography.* New York: Farrar, Straus & Giroux, 1985.

Lowe, Sue Davidson. *Stieglitz: A Memoir/Biography.* New York: Farrar, Straus & Giroux, 1983.

Loy, Mina. *The Last Lunar Baedeker.* Edited by Roger Conover. Highlands, N.C.: The Jargon Society, 1982.

Lynes, Russell. *Good Old Modern: An Intimate Portrait of the Museum of Modern Art.* New York: Atheneum, 1973.

Lyon, Ninette. "Man Ray: A Second Fame, Good Food." *Vogue,* February 1965.

McAlmon, Robert, and Kay Boyle. *Being Geniuses Together, 1920 1940.* London: Michael Joseph, 1970.

McClinton, Katherine Morrison. *Art Deco: A Guide for Collectors.* New York: Clarkson N. Potter, 1986.

Maillard, Robert, ed. *Vingt-cinq ans d'art en France, 1960–1985.* Paris: Larousse/Jacques Legrand, 1986.

Mallarmé, Stéphane. *Un coup de dés jamais n'abolira le hasard.* Paris: Editions Baudoin, 1979.

Marquis, Alice. *Marcel Duchamp: Eros, c'est la vie.* Foreword by Beatrice Wood. New York: Whitson Publishing Co., 1981.

Marrus, Michael R., and Robert O. Paxton. *Vichy France and the Jews.* New York: Schocken Books, 1983.

Martin, Jean Hubert, ed. *Man Ray Photographs.* London: Thames & Hudson, 1982.

———. *Meret Oppenheim.* Bern: Kunsthalle, exhibition catalogue (Sept.–Oct. 1984.

Maritain, Jacques. *Creative Intuition in Art and Poetry.* Cleveland, Ohio: Meridian Books, 1961.

Matthews, J. H. *Surrealism and Film.* Ann Arbor: University of Michigan Press, 1967.

Mayer, Ralph. *The Artist's Handbook of Materials and Techniques.* New York: Viking Press, 1981.

Mellow, James R. "The Last of the Red Hot Dadas." *New York Times,* February 1, 1970.

Michel, Henri. *Pétain, Laval, Darlan: Trois politiques?* Paris: Flammarion, 1972.

Miller, Stephen R. "The Surrealist Imagery of Kay Sage." *Art International,* XXVI.4, Sept.–Oct. 1983.

Moholy-Nagy, Laszlo. "Photography in a Flash." In *Moholy-Nagy,* edited by Richard Kostelanetz. New York: Prager, 1970.

——. Letter to Beaumont Newhall. In *Moholy-Nagy,* ibid.

——. *Vision in Motion.* Chicago: Paul Theobald and Co., 1947.

——. *Painting Photography Film.* Cambridge, Mass.: MIT Press, 1967.

Morton, Brian N. *Americans in Paris: An Anecdotal Street Guide.* Ann Arbor: The Olivia and Hill Press, 1984.

Motherwell, Robert, ed. *The Dada Painters and Poets: An Anthology.* New York: Wittenborn, Schultz, Inc., 1951.

Moure, Nancy Dustin Wall. *Painting and Sculpture in Los Angeles, 1900–1945.* Los Angeles: L.A. County Museum of Art, 1980.

Mumford, Lewis. "The Art Galleries." *The New Yorker,* September 29, 1934.

Myers, John Bernard. *Tracking the Marvelous: A Life in the New York Art World.* New York: Random House, 1983.

Nadeau, Maurice. *The History of Surrealism.* New York: Macmillan, 1965.

Naef, Weston. *The Painterly Photograph.* New York: Museum of Modern Art, 1973.

Nash, J.M. *Cubism, Futurism and Constructivism.* London: Thames & Hudson, 1974.

Naumann, Francis. "The New York Dada Movement, Better Late Than Never." *Arts Magazine,* 54.6, February 1980.

——. "Man Ray, Early Paintings 1913–1916, Theory and Practice in the Art of Two Dimensions." *Artforum,* May 1982.

——. *Walter Conrad Arensberg, Poet, Patron and Participant in the New York Avant-Garde, 1915–1920.* Philadelphia: Museum of Art Bulletin, Spring 1980.

——. *The William and Mary Sisler Collection.* New York: Museum of Modern Art, 1984.

——. *Man Ray and the Ferrer Center: Art and Anarchy in the Pre-Dada Period.* Unpub. diss. CUNY Graduate Center, 1985.

Newhall, Beaumont, ed. *Photography: Essays and Images.* New York: Museum of Modern Art, 1980.

——. *The History of Photography, 1839 to the Present,* revised and enlarged edition. New York: Museum of Modern Art, 1982.

Nin, Anaïs. *The Diary of Anaïs Nin.* New York: Harvest Books/Harcourt Brace & World, 1966.

Norman, Dorothy, *Alfred Stieglitz, An American Seer.* Millerton, N.Y.: Aperture, 1973.

Nowinski, Ira. *Objects Studio of Man Ray.* Portfolio ms., March 1983.

O'Doherty, Brian. "Light on an Individual: Man Ray." *New York Times,* May 1963.

——. "Man Ray, The Forgotten Prophet." *New York Times,* May 6, 1963.

O'Neal, Hank. *Berenice Abbott, American Photographer.* New York: McGraw-Hill, 1982.

Orr-Cahall, Christina, ed. *The Art of California: Selected Works from the Collection of the Oakland Museum.* Oakland: 1984.

Ortega y Gasset, José. *The Dehumanization of Art.* Princeton: Princeton University Press, 1968.

Osten, José, and Philippe Thomas. *Le Musée de l'Homme.* Rennes: Ouest France, 1982.

Overy, Paul. *De Stijl.* London: Studio Vista/Dutton, 1969.

Padgett, Ron. "Man to Man." *Camera Arts,* July–August 1982.

———. "Artist Accompanies Himself with His Rays." *ARTNews,* November 1966.

Page, Suzanne, and Beatrice Parent, eds. *Meret Oppenheim.* Paris: ARC Musée d'Art Moderne de la Ville de Paris, Exhibition catalogue, October–December 1984.

Painter, George D. *Marcel Proust.* New York: Random House, 1959.

Papageorge, Tod. "Amazing Grace" [review of Atget photographs, ed. Hambourg]. *Times Literary Supplement,* April 6, 1984.

Paz, Octavio. *Alternating Current.* New York: Viking Press, 1973.

———. *Marcel Duchamp.* New York: Viking/Richard Seaver Books, 1978.

Penrose, Roland. *Man Ray.* Boston: New York Graphic Society, 1975.

———. *Picasso, His Life and Work.* London: Granada Publishers, 1981.

———. *Scrap Book, 1900–1981.* New York: Rizzoli, 1981.

Penrose, Antony. *The Lives of Lee Miller.* New York: Holt, Rinehart and Winston, 1985.

Pepper, Curtis Bill. "The Indomitable de Kooning." *New York Times Magazine,* November 20, 1983.

Perl, Jed. *Man Ray.* Millerton, N.Y.: Aperture, 1979.

———. "Academic Surrealism." *The New Criterion,* November 1985.

Perlman, Bennard. "Prophet of the New" [Robert Henri]. *ARTNews,* 83.6, Summer 1984.

Picon, Gaeton. *Ingres.* Geneva: Skira Publishing Company, 1980.

Pincus-Witten, Robert. "Man Ray: The Homonymic Pun and American Vernacular." *Artforum,* XIII.8, April 1975.

Plazy, Gilles. *Dorothea Tanning.* New York: Filipacci Books, 1976.

Poggioli, Renato. *The Theory of the Avant-Garde.* Cambridge, Mass.: Harvard University Press, 1968.

Poiret, Paul. *King of Fashion.* Philadelphia: Lippincott, 1931.

Pool, Phoebe. *Impressionism.* London: Thames & Hudson, 1967.

Pratt, George C. *Spellbound in Darkness.* Greenwich, Conn.: New York Graphic Society, 1973.

Pultz, John, and Catherine B. Scallen. *Cubism and American Photography.* Williamstown, Mass.: Clark Art Institute, 1981.

Quinn, Joan. "Recollections: Life With Man Ray," an interview with Juliet Man Ray. *Interview,* May 1984.

Randal, Jonathan. "Man Ray, a Show at 82." *Washington Post,* February 26, 1972.

Ray, Samuel. *Man Proposes.* Unpublished memoir, ca. 1933.

Read, Herbert. *The Philosophy of Modern Art.* London: Faber & Faber, 1982.

"Review of Man Ray Retrospective at New York City Cultural Center." *ARTnews,* April 1975.

Rewald, John. *The History of Impressionism.* New York: Museum of Modern Art, 1973.

Rewald, Sabine. *Balthus.* New York: Metropolitan Museum of Art/Harry N. Abrams, 1984.

Reynolds, Graham. *Atelier 17: 1927 Paris—New York 1950*. Paris: Galerie de Seine, 1981, exhibition catalogue of show by William S. Hayter.

Ribemont-Dessaignes, Georges. *Dada 2. Nouvelles, articles, théâtre, chroniques littéraires 1919–1929*. Paris: Editions Champ Libre, 1978.

———. *Man Ray*. Paris: Gallimard, 1924.

Richter, Hans. *Dada: Art & Anti-Art*. New York: Harry N. Abrams, 1965.

Reif, Rita. "Marcel Duchamp: Where Art Has Lost, Chess Is the Winner." *New York Times,* May 22, 1968.

Richardson, Diana Edkins, ed. *Vanity Fair: Photographs of an Age.* Introduction by John Russell. New York: Clarkson N. Potter, 1982.

Ritchie, Andrew Carnduff. *Abstract Painting and Sculpture in America*. New York: Museum of Modern Art, 1951.

Robinson, Julian. *Fashion in the 'Thirties*. London: Oresko Books, 1978.

Rorem, Ned. *The Paris and New York Diairies, 1951–1961*. San Francisco: North Point Books, 1983.

Rose, Barbara. "Kinetic Solutions to Pictorial Problems: The Films of Man Ray and Moholy-Nagy." *Artforum,* X. 1, September 1971.

———. *American Art Since 1900, a Critical History*. London: Thames & Hudson, 1967.

Rosenberg, Bernard, and Harry Silverstein. *The Real Tinsel*. New York: Macmillan & Co., 1970.

Rosenberg, Harold. "MOMA Dada." *The New Yorker,* May 18, 1968.

———. *The Anxious Object: Art Today and Its Audience*. New York: Collier Books, 1973.

———. "American Drawing and the Academy of the Erased de Kooning." *The New Yorker,* March 22, 1976.

Rosenblum, Robert. *Cubism and Twentieth-Century Art*. New York: Harry N. Abrams, 1976.

Rosenfeld, Paul. *Port of New York*. Urbana: University of Illinois Press, 1976.

Roth, Moira. "Marcel Duchamp in America: A Self Ready-Made." *Arts Magazine,* 51.9, May 1977.

Rothenberg, Jerome, and George Quasha, eds. *America a Prophecy*. New York: Vintage Books, 1974.

Roussel, Raymond. *How I Wrote Certain of My Books*. Translated by Trevor Winkfield. New York: SUN Press, 1977.

Rubin, William S. *Dada, Surrealism and Their Heritage*. New York: Museum of Modern Art, 1968; 1977.

———. *Dada and Surrealist Art*. New York: Harry N. Abrams, 1968.

———. ed. *"Primitivism" in 20th Century Art, Affinity of the Tribal and the Modern*. New York: Museum of Modern Art, 1984.

Russell, John. *The Meanings of Modern Art*. New York: MOMA/Harper & Row, 1981.

———. "Galleries are the Seedbeds of Tomorrow's Art." *New York Times,* January 23, 1984.

———. "At Yale, One Publication Inspires Two Fresh Shows" [Société Anonyme exhibitions]. *New York Times,* May 27, 1984.

Sade, Marquis de. *Aline et Valcour*. Paris: Editions 10/18, 1971.

———. *Justine, Philosophy in the Bedroom, and Other Writings*. Translated by Richard Seaver and Austryn Wainhouse. New York: Grove Press, 1966.

Sagne, Jean. *Delacroix et la photographie*. Paris: Editions Herscher, 1982.

Sanouillet, Michel. *Dada à Paris*. Paris: Jean-Jacques Pauvert, 1965.

Sartre, Jean-Paul. *Literature and Existentialism*. Secaucus, N.J.: Citadel Press, 1980.

Sayag, Alain, ed. *Atelier Man Ray, Abbott-Boiffard-Brandt-Miller, 1920–1935*. Paris: Philippe Sers, 1982.

Schad, Tennyson. "Shooting from the Hip" [collecting photographs], in *How to Make Your Money Make Money*, edited by Arthur Levitt. Homewood, Ill.: Dow Jones-Irwin, 1981.

Schjeldahl, Peter. "The Anti-Master Now" [de Kooning]. *Vanity Fair,* January 1984.

Schwartz, Constance H. *The Shock of Modernism in America: The Eight and the Artists of the Armory Show*. Exhibition catalogue, April–July 1984, Nassau County Museum of Fine Arts.

Schwarz, Arturo. Man Ray, *60 ans de libertés*. Paris: Eric Losfeld, 1971.

———. *Man Ray: The Rigor of Imagination*. New York: Rizzoli, 1977.

———. "This Is Not for America, An Interview with Man Ray," *Arts Magazine*, 51.9, May 1977.

———. *Man Ray, Carte Varie e Variabili*. Milan. Gruppo Editoriale Fabbri, 1983.

Schwarz, Heinrich. *Art and Photography*. Chicago: University of Chicago Press, 1987.

Seitz, William C. *The Art of Assemblage*. New York: Museum of Modern Art, 1961.

Selz, Peter. *Alberto Giacometti*. New York: Museum of Modern Art, 1965.

Shahn, Ben. *The Shape of Content*. New York: Vintage Books, 1957.

Shattuck, Roger. *The Banquet Years: The Origins of the Avant-Garde in France, 1885 to World War I*. New York: Vintage Books, 1968.

Shroder, Maurice Z. *Poètes français du dix-neuvieme siècle*. Cambridge, Mass.: Integral Editions, Inc., 1964.

Soby, James Thrall. *Photographs by Man Ray*. New York: Dover Publications, 1979, reprint of 1934 album.

———. "Notes on Documentary Photography." *US Camera*, November 1940.

———. "Marcel Duchamp in the Arensberg Collection." *View,* V. 1, March 1945.

———. *Modern Art and the New Past*. Introduction by Paul J. Sachs. Norman: University of Oklahoma Press, 1957.

———. Audiotape interview with Stephen R. Miller, August 16, 1972 in New Canaan, Connecticut.

Sontag, Susan. *On Photography*. New York: Farrar, Straus & Giroux, 1977.

Soupault, Philippe, and Timothy Baum. "Dada 291—1924." Retrospective exhibition at Noah Goldowsky Gallery. New York, May–June 1969.

Stauffacher, Frank, ed. *Art in Cinema*. San Francisco: Museum of Art, 1947. Contains text of Man Ray address at American Contemporary Gallery in Hollywood, October 15, 1943.

Stein, Gertrude. *The Yale Edition of the Unpublished Writings*. New York: Books for Libraries Press, 1954.

————. *The Autobiography of Alice B. Toklas.* New York: Vintage Books, 1960.

Stéphane, Bernard. *Dictionnaire des noms de rues.* Paris: Editions Menges, 1986.

Stock, Noel. *The Life of Ezra Pound.* San Francisco: North Point Press, 1982.

Symmes, Marilyn F. *Contemporary Cliché-verre Prints.* Detroit: Institute of the Arts, 1981.

Szarkowski, John. *Looking at Photographs.* New York: Museum of Modern Art, 1973.

————. *Mirrors and Windows, American Photography Since 1960.* New York: Museum of Modern Art, 1978.

Tabart, Murielle and Isabelle Monod-Fontaine. *Brancusi photographe.* Paris: MNAM/CNAC/Pompidou, 1977.

Tashjian, Dickran. *William Carlos Williams and the American Scene, 1920–1940.* New York: Whitney Museum, 1978.

Thomson, David. *Europe Since Napoleon.* London: Penguin Books, 1967.

Thomson, Virgil. *Virgil Thomson.* New York: Knopf, 1967.

Thornton, Nicole. *Poiret.* London: Rizzoli, 1979.

Thurber, James and Charles Cooke. "The Fantastics" [review of Dada/Surrealism show at the Museum of Modern Art]. *The New Yorker,* December 12, 1936.

Toklas, Alice B. *What Is Remembered.* San Francisco: North Point Press, 1985.

Tomkins, Calvin. "Profile of Robert Rauschenberg." *The New Yorker,* February 29, 1954.

Tourdjman, George, ed. *Alexey Brodovitch.* Exhibition catalogue, Paris: Ministère de la Culture, Grand-Palais, October–November 1982.

Travis, David, ed. *Photographs from the Julien Levy Collection Starting With Atget.* Exhibition catalogue, Chicago: Art Institute of Chicago, December 1967–February 1977.

Vaizey, Marina. "The Muses Flee Hitler." *Art and Artists,* London, no. 211, April 1984.

Varèse, Louise. *Varèse: A Looking-Glass Diary. Volume I, 1883–1928.* New York: W. W. Norton & Co., 1972.

Varnedoe, Kirk. "On the Claims and Critics of the 'Primitivism' Show." *Art in America,* 73.5, May 1985.

Vollard, Ambroise. *Cézanne.* Translated by Harold L. Van Doren. New York: Dover Press, 1984.

Waldberg, Patrick. "Les objets de Man Ray," *XXe Siècle,* no. 31, December 1968.

Weaver, Mike. *William Carlos Williams: The American Background.* Cambridge, England: Cambridge University Press, 1977.

Welcker, Carola Giedion. *Constantin Brancusi.* New York: George Braziller, 1959.

Wescher, Paul. "The 'Idea' in Giuseppe Arcimboldo's Art." *The Magazine of Art,* XLIII.1, January 1950.

————. "Man Ray as Painter." *The Magazine of Art,* XLVI.1, January 1953.

Weston, Edward. *On Photography.* Edited and with an introduction by Peter C. Bunnell. Salt Lake City: Peregrine Smith Books, 1983.

Wheeler, Monroe. *Twentieth Century Portraits.* Exhibition catalogue, New York: Museum of Modern Art, 1942.

Whelan, Richard. *Double Take: A Comparative Look at Photographs.* New York: Clarkson N. Potter, 1981.

White, Mimi. "Two French Dada Films: *Entr'acte* and *Emak Bakia.*" *Dada/Surrealism,* no. 13, 1984.

White, Palmer. *Poiret.* New York: Clarkson N. Potter, 1973.

Whitman, Alden. "Man Ray Is Dead in Paris at 86. Dadaist Painter and Photographer" [obituary]. *New York Times,* November 19, 1976.

Wickes, George. *Lawrence Durrell and Henry Miller: A Private Correspondence.* New York: Dutton, 1964.

Williams, William Carlos. *Autobiography.* New York: New Directions, 1967.

Wilson, Edmund. *Axel's Castle.* New York: Scribner's, 1931.

Wilson, Simon. *Pop.* London: Thames & Hudson, 1974.

———. *What is Pre-Raphaelitism?* London: The Tate Gallery, 1984.

Wind, Edgar. *Art and Anarchy.* New York: Vintage Books, 1969.

Withers, Josephine. "The Fur-Lined Teacup and the Anonymous Meret Oppenheim." *Arts Magazine,* November 1977.

Wolff, Adolf. Poems, "Essay," "The Art Exhibit"; Essay, "The Modern School." *Modern School Magazine,* Spring 1913.

———. "Prison Weeds" [poem]. *Others,* I. 5, November 1915.

Wollen, Peter. *Signs and Meaning in the Cinema.* Bloomington: Indiana University Press, 1969.

Wollheim, Richard. *Art and Its Objects.* New York: Harper and Row, 1968.

Woody, Jack. *George Platt Lynes, Photographs 1931 1955.* Pasadena: Twelvetrees Press, 1981.

Worden, Helen. "Surrealist Prophet Man Ray Is in Town." *New York Times,* November 1936.

Wyman, David S. *The Abandonment of the Jews: America and the Holocaust, 1941–1945.* New York: Pantheon Books, 1984.

Zayas, Marius de. "Photography Is Not Art." *Camera Work,* no. 41, January 1913.

———. "The Evolution of French Art." In exhibition catalogue, The Arden Gallery, April–May 1919.

———. Edited by Francis Naumann. "How, When and Why Modern Art Came to New York." *Arts Magazine,* 54.8, April 1980.

Zwingle Erla. "A Life of Her Own" [Berenice Abbott]. *American Photographer,* XVI. 4, April 1986.

By Man Ray

(Listed in chronological order)

A Study in Nudes [painting]. *Modern School Magazine,* Spring 1913.

Untitled drawing. *Modern School Magazine,* Autumn 1913.

"Travail," [poem]. *Modern School Magazine,* Autumn 1913.

Cover drawing. *Mother Earth Magazine,* IX.6, August 1914.

Cover drawing. *Mother Earth Magazine,* IX.7, September 1914.

Adonisms, Some Poems [self-published]. Ridgefield, New Jersey, 1914.

"Impressions of '291'." *Camera Work,* no. 47, January 1915.

"Three Dimensions" [poem]. *Others,* I.6, December 1915.

Statement. Catalogue to The Forum Exhibition of Modern American Painters, March 13–25, 1916, Anderson Galleries, New York.

Revolving Doors [text]. *TNT,* March 1919.

Seguidilla [airbrush painting]. *Broom,* I.1, November 1921.

Statement. Librairie Six exhibition, December 3–31, 1921, Paris.

"Rayographs, A New Method of Realizing the Artistic Possibilities of Photography." *Vanity Fair,* November 1922.

Rose Sel A Vie [rayograph]. *The Little Review,* X.2, Autumn 1924.

Four rayographs. *The Little Review,* X.4, Autumn–Winter 1924–25.

The Rope-Dancer [drawing], and *Construction* [watercolor]. *The Little Review,* XI.1, Spring 1925.

Revolving Doors, 1916–1917, dix planches. Paris: Editions Surréalistes, 1926.

Statement in program for American premiere of *Emak Bakia,* March 6, 1927, at The Guild Theater, New York City.

Two stills from *L'étoile de mer; Paris Machine Shop* [photograph]. *Transition* no. 13, Summer 1928.

Cover rayograph; eight photographic studies [rayographs]; and portraits of Eluard and Desnos. *Transition,* no.15, February 1929.

Object of Destruction [drawing and text]. *This Quarter Magazine,* V. 1, September 1932, Surrealism number.

Portrait of Wallis Simpson [photograph]. *Philadelphia Bulletin,* November 1, 1936.

La photographie n'est pas l'art [twelve photographs with text by André Breton]. Paris: GLM, 1937.

Les mains libres [drawings by Man Ray with poems by Paul Eluard]. Paris: Aux Editions Jeanne Bucher, November 1937.

"Photography Is Not Art, Part I" [essay]. *View,* III.1, April–October 1943.

Cover. *View,* June 1943.

Folio, text, and photographs. *Minicam Photography,* October 1943.

"Ruth, Roses and Revolvers" [story]. *View,* IV.4, December 1944.

"Bilingual Biography" [memoir]. *View,* V. 1, March 1945, Marcel Duchamp number.

Questionnaire. Société Anonyme catalogue, edited by George Heard Hamilton, 1950. Responses in ms., Beinecke Library, Yale University.

"Photogenic Reflections" [essay]. *Berkeley, a Journal of Modern Culture,* February 1950.

"Cinémage" [essay]. *L'age du cinéma,* Paris, August–November 1951.

Self Portrait. Boston: Atlantic–Little, Brown, 1963.

"Then and Now" [symposium]. The *Paris Review,* no. 33, 1965.

Statements. Exhibition catalogue for Man Ray retrospective at the Lytton Gallery, Los Angeles County Museum of Art, October 1966.

Works 1914–1973. Exhibition catalogue, edited by Maurizio Fagiolo, Il Collezione d'Arte Contemporanea, Rome, October 24–December 8, 1973.

Photographs. Exhibition catalogue, Gallery Alexander Iolas, New York, May 1974.

Self Portrait. New York: McGraw-Hill, 1979; reprint of Atlantic–Little, Brown 1963 edition.

I 50 volti di Juliet [photographs]. Milan: Gabriele Mazzotta, editore, 1981.

Photographs [portfolio]. Introductory essay by Romeo Martinez, Milan: Electa Editrice, 1982.

Publications and Transformations. Exhibition catalogue, Zabriskie Gallery, New York, February 10–March 13, 1982.

Man Ray et ses amis. Exhibition catalogue, Galerie Marion Meyer, Paris, February 23–April 3, 1982.

Objets de mon affection. Preface by Jean-Hubert Martin. Paris: Philippe Sers Editeur, 1983.

Objects of My Affection. Exhibition catalogue, Zabriskie Gallery, New York, January 1985. Essays by Rosalind Krauss and John Tancock.

Man Ray disegni. Exhibition catalogue, Museo Regionale di Palazzo Bellomo, Siracusa, Italy, June 29–July 28, 1985.

Selections from the Collection of Dennis Powers. Exhibition catalogue, Light Gallery, New York, October 1–November 15, 1985.

Autoportrait. Paris: Laffont/Seghers, 1986. Reprint-translation of 1963/1979 American editions of *Self Portrait.*

INDEX